D1594737

HEART-PINE RUSSIA

JANE T. COSTLOW

HEART-PINE RUSSIA

Walking and Writing
the Nineteenth-Century Forest

CORNELL UNIVERSITY PRESS   ITHACA AND LONDON

Publication of this book was made possible, in part, by the generous support of Bates College.

Frontispiece: Oleg Vasil'ev, *Self-Portrait from the Back* (1971). Reproduced with permission of the Tretyakov Gallery, Moscow.

Copyright © 2013 by Cornell University

All rights reserved. Except for brief quotations in a review, this book, or parts thereof, must not be reproduced in any form without permission in writing from the publisher. For information, address Cornell University Press, Sage House, 512 East State Street, Ithaca, New York 14850.

First published 2013 by Cornell University Press

Printed in the United States of America

Library of Congress Cataloging-in-Publication Data

Costlow, Jane T. (Jane Tussey), 1955–
    Heart-pine Russia : walking and writing the nineteenth-century forest / Jane T. Costlow.
        p. cm.
    Includes bibliographical references and index.
    ISBN 978-0-8014-5059-4 (cloth : alk. paper)
    1. Russian literature—19th century—History and criticism.
2. Forests in literature.   3. Forests and forestry—Social aspects—Russia—History—19th century.   4. National characteristics, Russian—History—19th century.   5. Russia—Civilization—1801–1917. I. Title.
    PG3015.5.F67C67 2013
    891.709'36—dc23   2012019022

Excerpts from Dostoevsky, Fyodor, *A Writer's Diary*, vol. 1, translated by Kenneth Lantz, copyright Northwestern University Press, 1994, are published with the permission of Northwestern University Press and Quartet Books, London.

Cornell University Press strives to use environmentally responsible suppliers and materials to the fullest extent possible in the publishing of its books. Such materials include vegetable-based, low-VOC inks and acid-free papers that are recycled, totally chlorine-free, or partly composed of nonwood fibers. For further information, visit our website at www.cornellpress.cornell.edu.

Cloth printing   10   9   8   7   6   5   4   3   2   1

For Iosif, Rosa, Marina, and Natasha—
my guides to the "real" Russia

Contents

Acknowledgments

ONE OF THE GREAT PLEASURES of this project has been its interdisciplinary nature: I simply could not have conceived it—much less completed it—without the generosity and goodwill of colleagues, friends, and family. Carl Straub, Jill Reich, and Don Harward all contributed to this project through their strong administrative and intellectual support for interdisciplinary studies at Bates. My life in Environmental Studies began when Carl Straub realized I taught a course called "The Countryside in Russian Literature" and has led now to my permanent position in ES; it is a delight to work at a place where ecologists, chemists, and economists are curious about Russian novels and the history of human cultures of nature. At the very beginning of the process I was awarded a Phillips Grant for sabbatical research, and named to an endowed chair funded by the Christian A. Johnson Endeavor Foundation, in specific support of in-terdisciplinary scholarship. Numerous grants from the Bates College Faculty Support Fund—in an earlier iteration called the Schmutz Fund—have made it possible for me to travel repeatedly to Russia and to visit not just libraries but woodlands near Orel, Petersburg, and Nizhnii Novgorod. Colleagues in numerous locations have been sources of inspiration, information, and generous inquiry. Tom Newlin, Tom Hodge, Amy Nelson, Douglas Weiner, Stephen Brain, Rachel May, Jim Parakilas, and Chris Ely all helped to shape this project both in conversation and through the creative scope of their own considerations of Russian culture and the natural world. Masha Litovskaya and Elena Trubina provided an early opportunity to share my "forest work" at a conference on Gender Conflict and Its Representation in Culture in Ekaterinburg; Arja Rosenholm's energetic enabling of scholarly conversation has similarly strengthened and supported this project, as has her own scholarly work on the natures of Russian Nature. The third chapter of this book is a substantially rewritten and much expanded treatment of issues I first broached in a 2003 article in *Russian Review*; I am grateful to anonymous readers and colleagues who responded to that piece. My Environmental Studies colleagues at Bates have been sources of support and counsel; in particular, Holly Ewing has loved talking with me about everything from peat bogs to the structure of arguments. Margaret Ewing's enthusiasm about Dmitrii Kaigorodov was a source of delight and confirmation of the ways in which one's scholarly work may resonate in unexpected quarters. Dinesh and Leah have put up with a project that consumed so much of their mother's attention as they went from being schoolkids to the wonderful young adults they now are; my husband, David, is to be eternally thanked for his humor and patience, and also for his historian's insistence that I get my chronologies straight.

This project has also been sustained by friendships and scholarly support in Russia: the staff of the library at the Forest Technical Academy in St. Petersburg were extraordinarily generous and helpful with Kaigorodov materials; Professor Grigorii Red'ko at the Academy expressed strong confirmation of the project's linking of literary and scientific responses to the nineteenth-century forest. Librarians at the Bunin Library in Orel were also enormously helpful: in particular I express a debt of gratitude to the staff of their *kraevedcheskii*, or local history, section, and to Iulia Viacheslavovna Zhukova, who helped secure several of the Orel images in these pages. The staff of the Turgenev Museum gave me tea and *priannik* when I first stumbled into Orel from Moscow as a graduate student in the mid-1980s. Their hospitality proved to be representative of this small city: students and colleagues at the Pedagogical University have opened their doors to group after group of students from Bates; Natalya and Nikolai Vyshegorodskikh helped us learn more about the ecology of Polesye. Their own work as teachers and environmental activists suggests the ways in which Orel citizens' desire to protect their "native nature" continues. Elena Ashikhmina—whose acquaintance I made only near the completion of this project—was immediately generous with stories and photographs, for which I am enormously grateful.

Finally, my greatest debt goes to colleagues who have become friends— almost family—in Orel: to Iosif and Rosa Kesel'man, who have offered me a true *nochleg*—not just a place to lie down, but a place to take comfort and find the best sort of conversation, roaming from local history to jam making and old Russian films. Marina Shimchenok has been the impresario of many of my forays into the Russian countryside: she first took me and students out to Polesye, and once she realized I was game, we continued to Bolkhov, Kursk, Optina Pustyn, and numerous sites memorialized in Turgenev's fiction. To read Turgenev well it helps to see his landscapes: Spasskoe-Lutovinovo, certainly, with its graceful lindens and elegantly restored enfilade of rooms, but also the fields and woods running off into the distance beyond the pond. Finally, Natasha Zakharova has been a tireless guide to the flora and fauna of Orlovshchina: we have weathered rain, mud, and mosquitoes in forays along the Orlik and to Polesye, and it is thanks to her tracking abilities that this book has wonderful images of the early twentieth-century linden alley at the center of the city. This book would not exist without the conversations I have had with these friends in Orel. On my first trip to Orel with students, in 1988, a group of Russians in the Moscow train station looked shocked that I was taking young Americans out into the hinterlands. My image of the countryside from urban conversations had been shaped mostly by tales of drunkenness and poverty. How different the reality proved to be. It has been a privilege and delight to share the city with generations of Bates students, who have (almost) always fallen in love with it. I dedicate this book to Rosa, Iosif, Marina, and Natasha—who have in their own way introduced me to the "real" Russia.

Note to the Reader

ALL TRANSLATIONS, unless otherwise indicated, are my own. In citing family names that are likely to be well known to nonspecialist readers, I have chosen the most commonly used form (Dostoevsky rather than Dostoevskii, Tchaikovsky rather than Chaikovskii). The Library of Congress transliteration system is used in reference notes to Russian sources.

HEART-PINE RUSSIA

Introduction

One day a man departed home
with walking stick and sack
for distant parts
for distant parts
he left and didn't look back.

. . . . .

And one fine morning at the dawn
he entered a dark wood
and from that day
and from that day
it seems he's gone for good.

—Daniil Kharms

AT SOME POINT during a late April night in 1973, inhabitants of the central neighborhood of Orel, had they happened to look out their apartment windows, would have seen a startling and to many a saddening spectacle. Since the nineteenth century this bluff above the river Oka had been home to a boulevard of linden trees that formed the southwestern edge of the city's municipal park. Literary associations run deep in Orel, shaping its sense of identity and place; Nikolai Leskov, one of the city's literary sons, exclaimed that "more than any other Russian city, Orel has nourished with its gentle waters more Russian *literateurs* and offered them up to the motherland's benefit."[1] Local legend has it that Ivan Turgenev had been wheeled in a pram along the park's pathways as an infant; the high crowns of linden, maple, and chestnut had sheltered his afternoon naps, filtering the light that would awaken him. The park that made an outdoor cradle for the future lyricist of Russian nature was established in 1822 by order of the provincial governor. By 1971 the park and the alley of lindens were part of the well-established landscape of this city of 300,000. Despite the ravages of civil war and German occupation, the park and its lindens had survived. And now, in the dark of an April night, they were to be cut down in order to expand the city's public square. The marble Lenin on his pedestal in front of the Regional Party headquarters would henceforth look out on an expanded realm; he would have a clear line of sight for the drama theater,

Linden alley, central Orel, early twentieth century. Postcard from the private collection of L. Tuchnin, reproduced with his permission.

soon to be constructed in high modernist style and named for Turgenev. The infant writer's cradle grounds would at least in part be destroyed, replaced by ceremonial space more befitting the modern Soviet state. The lindens—part of what one local resident described as the park's delightful "mysteriousness"—would have to go.[2]

I first heard the story of Orel's trees not in any public venue but in the cramped and cozy kitchen of a colleague who teaches English at the local university. His wife, Rosa, as fine a storyteller as she is a cook, regaled me with stories of her childhood in Ukraine and their married life first in Siberia and then in Orel; she also first told me of the linden alley and the city park. Her version of this story, though, was not simply about destruction and loss. The lindens, she told me, had not gone down without a protest: Leonid Afonin, a local literary scholar affiliated both with the Pedagogical Institute and the local Turgenev museum, had written an impassioned letter of protest (never published) to *Izvestiia*. His rash if courageous actions had had no effect on the local government's actions; they did, however, have significant impact on his own life, leading to "difficulties" at work, compromised health, and an early death. People sat through the night by the lindens, Rosa told me; they couldn't bear the thought of losing them—the trees were associated with Turgenev, part of the memory of him in this city. At dawn the bulldozers came and wrenched

Linden alley, central Orel, May 1959. Photograph from the personal archive of Elena Ashikhmina, who kindly made it available to the author and granted permission to reproduce it here.

them out. Her story emphasized protest and defiance, in the Soviet Union of the early 1970s, in defense of a cluster of trees. This was surely a story to ponder, its intertwining of politics, place, and personality gripping and suggestive. What were the truths this story had to tell? Why had Soviet citizens been willing to protest in defense of trees, at a time when other forms of protest—for human rights—met with severe punishment? Who had been involved? How many people had known about it? Would they tell me their own version of the story?[3]

As it happens, Rosa's version was at least in part mistaken: on subsequent trips to Orel I spent time in the local library, reading back issues of *Orlovskaia pravda*, and more important, interviewing a number of local residents who remembered that night and were willing to share their memories with me.[4] As best I have been able to piece the story together, Rosa's original tale conflated two separate instances of urban renewal: the first (targeting the avenue of lindens in front of the regional party building) was carried out quickly, and without protest.[5] The second was in fact averted: an oak planted in 1861, situated in the path of a proposed street-widening project, was saved by concerted actions of a group of local citizens, inspired in part by their memory of the lindens they hadn't been able to save. The lindens themselves had been planted in the early twentieth century: postcards from a local historian's collection show trees just taller than a man: in one photograph a child in a sailor's cap stands pointing at an older boy seated on a park bench; in another, two girls with Edwardian sleeves and boaters walk away from us, the boundary of the linden boulevard and the city park marked by the suddenly much taller, older trees in the middle distance.[6] In a postcard from the 1930s the trees are at least forty feet tall; there is a tramline running by one end, a bust of Lenin, a poster for a film called *A Mistake at the Beach*. By the 1960s, city planners were laying out a newly reconstructed central square, one that would be "accessible and convenient for large scale events, civic, political and cultural activity."[7] Both the diagram and the maquette of their design show an open square, the lindens gone. Such planning no doubt happened among elite circles, approved by the Regional Party Committee, without public discussion.[8] These were years of urban renewal in U.S. cities as well; Soviet planners might legitimately have pointed to the trade-offs of modernization and postwar reconstruction.[9] They closed neighboring Lenin Street to traffic, made it a pedestrian thoroughfare and rerouted motorized vehicles elsewhere. Lenin Street, however, despite the fact that Ivan Bunin had worked there in the offices of *Orlovskii vestnik* when the street was Bolkhovskaia Ulitsa, had none of the associations of the lindens and the city park. The mythologies of meaning and sensibility accompanying those trees gave their loss special force, as did the exchange of a culturally evocative *place* for space made for, and appropriated by, official ideology.[10]

Within the puzzle of fact, memory, and misremembering that emerged from my conversations with Orel residents, there was a tissue of affection and strong symbolic meaning that hardly decreased with the story's challenged accuracy—in fact, the storytelling connected to this place seemed proof of just how important it was, how much *story* was essential to holding on to something that had been physically lost. Locals had indeed cared deeply about these trees, which they associated with their city's cultural inheritance; there had been acts of speech and protest; at least one of the trees they had fought for still stood; and the city park itself still gave them pathways for strolling and benches on which to watch the afternoon sun. Even if some of the trees were gone, their meanings, and the stories about them, remained. Those stories were constitutive of identity and place. Rosa's story was a good story, with its own truths, a story I wanted to better understand. The deeper truth—what Russians know as *istina* rather than *pravda*—is that individuals living in Soviet Orel treasured these trees at least in part because of cultural associations that extended back well before the Revolution. Exploring the contours of such association—just what trees and forests *mean* within Russian culture—is in large part what this book is about.

This book takes as its central focus the cultural resonance of the forest in nineteenth-century Russia—the forest of European Russia rather than Siberia, which has its own web of imaginative significance.[11] One of my contentions is that the meanings that accrue to trees, woods, forests—as to any natural species or habitat—are opaque to us unless understood in cultural context. The contemporary American eco-philosopher Thomas Berry has contended that in order to address contemporary environmental crises we must go "beyond" our cultural coding, since "our cultural traditions are a major source of our difficulty."[12] It is surely debatable whether humans—as meaning-making, social animals—can in fact go "beyond" culture; the twentieth century's violent exercises in repudiating tradition have left Russians disinclined to be swayed by such rhetoric. Our task, as I see it, should be to revisit cultural contexts with new eyes, to understand aspects of a tradition we may not yet have examined seriously, and in doing so gain insight into *human* nature—since without such understandings our environmental crises will perennially frustrate our fine intentions. By "cultural context" I mean a dense tissue of stories, images, and metaphors, a thick braid of meanings that emerge over time as authors and artists explore the emotional resonance and cultural significance of place. Russian critics who of late have studied their culture's traditions of imagining the natural world tend to speak of a "feeling for nature"—*chuvstvo prirody*. The term asks us to think about sensibility and the senses, about feeling—both tactile and inward—that precedes and accompanies *thinking* about landscape. Barry Lopez speaks of ways in which cultures have "conversations with the land." As with any cultural process, the conversation is both with the land and with previous conversants: our sense of a place's meaning emerges both from engagement with the place itself and with the cultural traditions already alive there. The lindens of Orel's city park are both specific trees within a given place, and evocations of the place's history. They are bound up both with the particular light, water, and soil of the hillside above the Oka where they were planted, and with those authors who have written about them or simply sat beneath them. They are bound up with a whole way of thinking about trees and nature and culture. That manner of understanding the relationship between "nature" (linden trees) and "culture" (Turgenev, or Pushkin, or poetry per se) exists like distillate within the fluid realities of Russian life. Thinking about stories such as Rosa's—or, as I will suggest below, about the nineteenth-century stories and paintings that still animate Russian culture and Russians' sense of self—makes it possible to separate out a bit of that suspended matter, to see the nature of the normally invisible medium in which we live.[13]

If this is true in a general sense of all cultures, it seems particularly germane to Russia. Cultural historians have long observed the importance of landscape in the dynamics of Russian history, with the forest playing a particular role in its narratives and icons of identity. Over a generation ago James Billington launched his pathbreaking essay in cultural history by observing the enormous significance of the forest for Russian culture. The geographer R. A. French noted in 1983 that while the "image of the Russian environment in the West European mind is not infrequently that of the steppes," it is relatively recently—within the last three centuries—that Russians moved south and east from their primary sylvan settlements: "For over 1300 years, ever since the beginnings of east Slav settlement, the forest has been the home of the Russians; even today the natural zones of *tayga* and mixed forest take up over half the enormous area of the USSR."[14] Scholars have cited the role of the forest as one aspect of the "megatext" of Russia's landscape, "foundational for understanding Russian culture"; they have mused on the "protectively sealed space of Russia's mythical northern forests," existing in complex tension with the space of freedom and movement embodied in the country's southern and eastern steppes. For the symbolist Dmitrii Merezhkovsky *both* forest and steppe expressed an "elemental nomadic expansiveness" in the wandering Russian soul, apparent in the "poetry of elemental spaciousness" of Pushkin, Lermontov, and Kol'tsov.[15] As Robin Milner-Gulland so wonderfully reminds us, traditional Russian villages were *made of* the forest in which they stood: "There is something ineffably moving in the prospect of the traditional Russian village . . . formed almost entirely out of the forest all around it, ready (since wood is so transitory) to return to the forest as soon as humans no longer maintain it."[16] When the twentieth-century writer Andrei Platonov describes these villages he describes dwellings returning to earth, with some of the beauty—but also the pathos—of human creations that are dwarfed and undermined by the forces of nature: "The wooden roof [of the peasant *izba*] had rotted and was covered with ancient moss, the lowest logs were now buried in the earth, as if returning back into the depth of their birthplace, and from these logs, from the very lowest body of the hut, were growing two new weak branches which would turn into mighty oaks and one day eat in their roots the dust of this exhausted dwelling that had been used up by the wind, the rains and the human race." Little if anything of Soviet heroism remains in this passage: humans and their dwelling return to the humility of humus. The forest remains.[17]

A relatively quick survey of post-Soviet popular culture suggests that the forest continues to be a wellspring for Russian explorations of identity, at numerous scales and with varied intentions—political, spiritual, and environmental. Nikita Mikhalkov's 1999 blockbuster, *The Barber of Siberia*, opens with a panoramic shot of gorgeous northern forest, emblematic of eternal and elemental Russia, vulnerable to American greed. Artists on street corners throughout Russia entice passersby with inexpensive canvases of forest landscapes, selling images of a natural world that seems miraculously to have escaped the twentieth century. The popular writer Vladimir Megre, author of a series of books called the *Ringing Cedars*, spins tales of hidden springs and untouched forests in which urbanized Russians can find new-age renewal; his website presents his meeting with the muse of this rebirth as a real event that took place in the forests of west Siberia, and calls for an early twenty-first-century "back to the woods" movement. Calls for defense of local woodlands quote nineteenth-century poets, and a newspaper image in 2000 asks lawmakers to obey a higher ecological good; the collage of prerevolutionary images places lawmakers in a grove of oak trees, melding Ilya Repin's legislative body with Ivan Shishkin's woodland. Images and stories like these tap legacies of canonic culture even as they shape new meanings and calls to action. They grow out of nineteenth-century landscape paintings and mythologies of place that came to supplement if not supplant Marxist ideology in the Brezhnev era, and school curricula that enshrined Nekrasov, Turgenev, and Tolstoy. In the 1990s they promised settled ground beneath the shifting sands of market capitalism and the "bandits" who arrived with it.[18]

All of these examples—scholarly as well as popular—suggest a relationship of both affection and need, in which humans' dependence on resources (for fire, warmth, building materials) often exists in uneasy tension with more obviously *emotional* or symbolic associations. One mid-nineteenth-century commentator in the *Journal of State Properties* reproached fellow Russians he considered "tree huggers" with extreme *sylvo-philia*.[19] The nineteenth-century historian Vasilii Kliuchevsky, however, contended that Russians' primary attitude toward the forest was not affection but hostility, born of long centuries' backbreaking labor in a milieu that unendingly resisted their efforts at survival. "The Russian [never found] the forest anything but oppressive. There was too much of it, for one thing, in olden days: it blocked his road with its density, set its troublesome growths to fight his efforts towards formation of pastoral and arable land, and harbored bear and wolf to menace his livestock. . . . Only this can explain the Russian's persistently surly, or persistently contemptuous, attitude towards forest. It is something for which he has never felt genuine affection."[20]

All these claims—Billington's and Merezhkovsky's as well as Kliuchevsky's—are as expansive as the landscape they seek to think about; they need careful attention, at a closer scale than they have usually been given. My approach to these claims and the questions they raise is to take particular writers and artists as my guides—to follow them into their own particular woods. This involves selecting among a dizzying array of writers and artists who have in one way or another depicted Russia's European forest. My choice of texts has come over time to seem appropriate, if not inevitable: I lean much more heavily on prose than poetry, considering only in cursory fashion the ways in which verse and oral culture were drawn into prose accounts of the forest throughout the nineteenth century. My discussion of the visual arts (and of music) is similarly limited. I begin with Turgenev because his "Journey into Polesye" constitutes an extraordinary and important example of meditative nature writing and cultural commentary. I also begin with Turgenev because I have come to know his woods—an expanse of forest northwest of Orel that he imaginatively maps in both his "Journey" and in the *Hunter's Sketches*. Apart from these personal motives, I have come to feel that Turgenev is important for *Russian* writers as they have entered forests of their own. His model of beguiling simplicity—a narrative journey into place that is resonant with all sorts of philosophical and literary voices, which manages nonetheless to convince you of a kind of *presence to place* beyond all allusive citation: this represents an important Russian contribution to nineteenth-century nature writing, worthy of comparison—despite differences in tone and attitude—with Henry David Thoreau.

Russia's contributions to imaginations of landscape are also deeply indebted to a tradition invoked by the antiquarian and novelist Pavel Mel'nikov-Pechersky, whose epic accounts of the trans-Volga woodlands traffic in myth, folklore, legend, and vast affection for the local. Mel'nikov—whose novel is the focus of chapter 2—is certainly less well known to most readers than Turgenev, but his work constitutes an equally important contribution to imaginations of the Russian forest, one that had significant impact in the decades immediately preceding the Revolution. Where Turgenev's woodland is meditative and fraught with conflicting voices and allegiances, Mel'nikov's is a boisterous, mythologized landscape, shaped both by pagan Rus' and contemplative, monastic Orthodoxy. The artist Mikhail Nesterov and the populist Vladimir Korolenko both return at century's end to Mel'nikov-Pechersky's woodlands, but elaborate radically differing visions of this sacred landscape, in Korolenko's case with an acute awareness of the vulnerability of ancient orders, both natural and human.

Intercut with this history of affection and imagination is a very different account of Russia's European forest in the nineteenth century: chapter 3 of this study explores a geography not of abundance or limitless possibility but loss—focusing on journalistic and imaginative texts that registered increasing alarm at the deforestation of central Russia. I sketch that history by drawing on a range of nineteenth-century sources—journals devoted to forestry, agriculture, and hunting, and histories of Russian forestry written at the end of the century, sources written both for specialists and for a broad public. The Forest Question was widely discussed in Russian thick journals from at least midcentury, and various works of art and literature document a growing awareness of the issue as the century progressed and alarm at "national disasters" grew to near-apocalyptic proportions. The writers and artists who responded imaginatively began to elaborate an environmental ethic and an ecological poetics embedded in Russian cultural traditions. The question these texts and images raise is not just how writers and artists were influenced by scientists and foresters, but how Russia's writers and artists helped shape the rhetoric and response of publicists and scientific writers.

Tracking an evolving awareness of the ways in which human actions impinge upon what we know as the "environment" is *one* aim of this study, but not its sole or even principal one. *Environment* is in many ways a problematic word to use in the nineteenth century in anything like our modern sense, suggesting as it does a strong distinction between humans and their culture and what *surrounds* them; the term is only slightly less vexed than "nature"—which Raymond Williams declared was "perhaps the most complex word in the language."[21] Historians have tended to speak of conservationist impulses or proto-ecological sensibilities in eras that predate modern environmentalism as a social movement.[22] While chapter 3 offers an account of nineteenth-century Russian culture in which there is a growing recognition of the impacts of deforestation, the aim of the book as a whole is broader, situating that "environmental" story in a larger thicket of narrative and visual expression, a broader cultural imagination.

This study moves back and forth between narratives that are visionary and those that are skeptical, between optimism and irony, ecstasies of oneness with nature and the anxious desire to get *home*—to human habitation, culture, commerce, urbanity, as quickly as possible. The final chapter focuses on Dmitrii Kaigorodov, a writer and educator who is the most obviously environmental of the writers and artists discussed here. He is an intriguing and apt figure to end with, since he brings the latent ecological insights of Russia's literary tradition to the fore, in publications that are elegant fusions of poetry, natural history, and visual art. Writing in the decades immediately preceding the revolutions of 1917, Kaigorodov drew deeply and comprehensively on many of the threads and motifs of the nineteenth-century tradition. Enormously popular in his own day, an influential educator and inspirational observer of seasonal change and the natural world just outside one's door, Kaigorodov—like many of his colleagues at the St. Petersburg Forest Institute, where he taught forest technology—seemed poised in the early twentieth century to inaugurate a public culture of ecological concern, rooted both in scientific understandings and in Russia's poetry, religious traditions, and civic literary culture. That the Bolshevik Revolution interfered with that promise seems clear—and yet Kaigorodov, together with other figures in this study, has had enduring influence and resonance in often surprising ways, with stories that are largely waiting to be told.[23]

Lawrence Buell, in his study of the American environmental imagination, suggests that for most of us the sense of our place in the world rests at the level of unconsciousness, that "no one will ever be able to bring it to full consciousness in all its nuanced complexity."[24] Buell clearly sees the environmental project in part as an effort to bring to consciousness those attachments, both personal and cultural, that form the imaginative terrain of our actions in and toward the natural world. The role of art and literature in that project is to help us become better listeners, better lookers, more attentive to the world but also to our own impulses within and toward it. There is something here of the German philosopher Heidegger's notion of poetry as *listening*, a relationship to the natural world that various ecocritics have found provocative. As George Steiner puts it, "For Heidegger . . . the human person and self-consciousness are *not* the center, the assessors of existence. The vital relation to otherness is not, as for Cartesian and positivist rationalism, one of 'grasping' and pragmatic use. It is a relation of audition. We are trying 'to listen to the voice of Being.'"[25]

Many of the writers discussed in the pages below go into the woods and hear voices, which they then bring *back* with them, into their narratives. While some of those voices are human (the peasants of Turgenev's encounters, or of Mel'nikov's ethnographic explorations), others are not: it is the forest itself that "speaks." For the narrator of Korolenko's 1886 story "The Forest Sounds," *sound is the way into the woods*: "There was always sound in this wood—unchanging, drawn-out, like the echoing voice of a distant bell, like an inchoate memory of the past. There was always sound in the wood, because it was an old, slumbering pine wood, as yet untouched by the saw and axe of woodland profiteers. . . . It seemed as though a thousand mighty, muffled voices were conversing in the forest, shouting out fiercely about something in the darkness."[26] Both the narrator and the elderly peasant he encounters *hear* the wood and its stories of the past—stories Korolenko brings into his own narrative with the particular inflections of each man's telling. We hear something in the woods, and then try to articulate it in human speech. That shift from audition to narrative involves a complicated process of translation, *pere-vod* in Russian, carrying back across the forest boundary into the world of human culture and converse. This is perhaps always true of artistic creation, but it seems doubly—or more intensely—true of creation that begins in a natural context where humans sense, acutely, their smallness, where form and structure are difficult to grasp. The acute sensitivity to tactile, aural, and visual presence that David Abram finds in traditional cultures' interactions with their natural surroundings is, I would suggest, at work here as well—in the work of wordsmiths who are also deep listeners, attentive to the nuance of how landscape enfolds us, draws us in, impels us toward some understanding of a place's meanings.[27]

The writers and artists who are our companions in this foray into Russia's forests are *translating* for us, bringing back, carrying over into a common fund of stories and images the visions, or wisdom, or stories they have collected in the woods. Putting it this way, using the language of gathering and carrying over, is helpful to me in several ways, ways I would like to lay out before we proceed into the chapters themselves. Walking into a forest involves crossing a boundary, going from a place of relative light and spaciousness to a place that is darker, where paths may peter out or not exist at all. We confront, along the way, the edge itself; depending on how closely we stick to paths, we may also become aware of the process itself of walking and way-finding—the very unfamiliarity of terrain heightens our awareness of movements that are normally automatic. All of these are relevant both to the writers and artists we address here, and to my own situation as reader and "auditor" of these images and texts.

Ecocriticism as it is currently practiced in the United States has been intent on bringing *place* back into our discussions of literature, and as such has often made much of how a critic or scholar knows the place she or he is writing about. There is often an assumption that one should have experiential knowledge of place that goes beyond the text itself. And while I'm in large part sympathetic with that impulse—I'm deeply fond of walking, and in fact have visited most if not all of the places I wind up reading and talking about in these pages— the fact of being a non-Russian engaging in this process of thinking about Russia reminds me, constantly, that I am not "at home" here. The trope of *home*—homecoming, being at home on the earth, finding one's home, making a home—has also been central to ecocriticism.[28] But it is complicated (in ways that I think are all to the good, and in fact central to any vision of a world in which we can think critically and compassionately about words like *native, homeland, alien*) to write about places that one lives thousands of miles away from. What forms of affection or knowledge can I claim for a band of forest on the northwest border of the Orel and Kaluga districts? or for a tiny round lake to the north of Nizhnii Novgorod? or even for a wooded park in the "Venice of the North"? I am not native there, I am always at some level a stranger, I am crossing boundaries of ignorance and knowledge every time I enter. And yet . . .

And yet, these places are somehow deeply known to me. They are, as Anna Akhmatova put it in 1964, "ne rodnaia, no pamiatnaia navsegda." Not one's own, but remembered forever. In Akhmatova's wonderful expression, and in my own sense of translated affection and knowledge, lies the extraordinary power of art to create in us a *sense of place*, so that places we might never have seen before become "known" to us in some uncanny way. There is in this imagination of space a repudiation of time, since the place we have never been before (as Akhmatova puts it) is a place we already remember. How can we remember it, never having seen it? Because we have been there in story, in the words of someone who lived there, in the gift of what they brought over, across the boundary from "real world" into "real language"—the story that we have already lived in, the story-space where we have already traveled.[29]

All of this involves moving, going back and forth across boundaries, whether ecological or linguistic or geopolitical, and it involves a shifting back and forth between different attitudes and emotions. Walking is a perfect vehicle for this (as numerous authors, whether pastoral or urban, have known: Balzac was just as much a walker as Thoreau or Turgenev). And so it is no surprise that many of the narratives explored here involve lots of walking (Korolenko travels more by water), or that my own process as a writer has involved walking through dilemmas of structure and sequence. There is something deeper at work, though, I think, in the paradigm of *walking into the woods*, a common note in what Robert Bringhurst calls the "ecosystem" of a culture's stories about a given place.[30] There is that pause at the edge, the moment when entry seems daunting, or when the edge itself—called the *opushka* in Russian—is so captivating, so luminously filled with possibilities, that one is disinclined to leave that space for the interior. Three brief examples, before we enter.

Ivan Turgenev's brief sketch "Forest and Steppe" (1849) concludes his cycle of peasant stories, the *Hunter's Sketches*. It lays out in brilliant visual fashion the two great landscapes of Russian history. It also includes a passage that seems like a sketch for the story he was to work on over the next ten years, "Journey into

Polesye." That story is about a journey *into* a forest: Polesye is both the name for a particular forest, and the name of a certain *kind* of forest of scrub and bog. In "Forest and Steppe" Turgenev doesn't go in; he stays on the edge—the *opushka*. To follow the woodcock, he advises, you need not enter the "depths of the wood" but should instead "look for them along the edge," a place that despite its intense sensual pleasures—air like wine, springy ground, sparkling webs on "pallid sod"—inspires "a strange anxiety." The edge of the wood turns out to be more a place of memory and imagination than sharp-eyed attentiveness for birds to flush. Turgenev notes the anxiety and the impress of the past on his attention, and then moves on from his moment of hesitation at the forest's edge, from what he calls the heart's "convulsive wild beating."[31]

Over sixty years later Ivan Bunin stands at the edge of another woodland—Pskov Forest in far northwest Russia, at the border of the Mikhailovskoe estate that had belonged to Alexander Pushkin, where Russia's greatest poet had experienced extraordinary periods of creativity. Bunin stands at the edge of the wood, and we sense in his verse deep trepidation at entering a forest that is both a geophysical and cultural "ecosystem," a place already marked by words and stories:

> *It is dark in the distance, and the copses are forbidding.*
> *Beneath the reddish mast, beneath the pine*
> *I stand and slow my steps—on the threshold*
> *Of a world forgotten, but kindred.*
>
> *Are we worthy of our inheritance?*
> *It will be too dreadful for me there,*
> *Where the paths of fox and bear*
> *Lead to paths of fable.*
>
> *Where seeds redden on the snowball berry,*
> *Where rot is covered with rusty moss*
> *And dark-blue berries lie*
> *On the withered juniper.*[32]

The poet finally moves beyond the place of trepidation, into a place he calls *forgotten but kindred* (*pozabytyi, no rodnoi*—uncannily close to Akhmatova's epithets). His question remains unanswered: *Are we worthy of our inheritance?* For both Turgenev and Bunin, the edge and the wood are filled with memory, as vividly present as moss and berries and juniper. Inheritance is both woods and words; animals' paths become narrative lines, the edge becomes a place of invitation and dread. As Turgenev puts it, "Imagination lifts and hovers like a bird, and everything stands as if before your eyes, vividly alive." In these spaces of experience and articulation, the relationship between perceiver and perceived, between memory and presence, between what is remembered and what is not known, or still-to-be-known, becomes complex and weblike, less a matter of linearity than a form of traipsing back and forth over ground that is sometimes awkward and difficult, sometimes open and clear. The final boundary of human experience—the silhouette of a human body traveling through space—seems itself to break down, to become part of the landscape: either because our consciousness and heightened perception move out into the world of moss and juniper and birch, or because the smells and sentience of the vividly alive, densely encroaching world enter us. In either case, we feel less acutely—and perhaps also less comfortably—that division of human and "nature" that we tend on most days to live with.

Which brings us to our last figure standing on an edge, the *Self-Portrait from the Back* by Oleg Vasil'ev. Painted in 1971, now hanging in the Tretyakov Gallery in Moscow, Vasil'ev's canvas recalls the *Rückenfiguren* of Caspar David Friedrich—the turned figures who stand in contemplation of a natural landscape, often a forest, and who, in their acts of watching, seem to represent our own ambivalent sense of estrangement and longing. Friedrich's canvases are often of vast sublime landscapes, with tiny, sharply drawn figures standing in dwarfed contemplation of the vastness. Vasil'ev's canvas gives us a different scale and a different outline of human form against the surrounding world. In his self-portrait the human figure itself is in the process of disintegrating, shifting from integral form, set off against the landscape, to something our eyes cannot read as *separate* from what surrounds it. It's not just that we see no face here: the patterned light and texture of autumn leaves in a birch grove merge with the figure's head and shoulders. Vasil'ev's male figure is disappearing—or "losing himself"—in what still seems an act of motion *into*, rather than fixed contemplation *in the face of / in front of / before*. As we watch him disappear, we might think about other possibilities of meaning. This is a late-Soviet version of the *Rückenfigure*—so we could wonder just why the man is going into the woods. Is his entry a form of flight, the kind that Daniil Kharms describes in his 1936 absurdist fairy tale quoted as epigraph to this chapter? In that poem an unnamed man disappears into a wood, and the narrative voice shifts out of neutral in the final lines, with their request to *let us know* if you see him.[33] Stalin's regime provided ample reasons for someone to go into a wood and not look back, but Russia's forests have proved tempting for runaways from multiple regimes, both before and after 1917. In Vasil'ev's canvas, however, there is no sense of urgency or terror: there is simply the slow evaporation of human form

Oleg Vasil'ev, Self-Portrait from the Back *(1971). Reproduced with permission of the Tretyakov Gallery, Moscow.*

into a larger pattern of light, living organisms passing into stillness, human mobility moving toward the apparent stasis of leaf and ground.

Who are we when we enter the forest? What happens to our personalities, our languages, our histories, and our narratives? The essays in this book explore a tradition of writing and envisioning Russia's great European forest—diminished and vulnerable, but lovely and powerful and in many ways daunting to those who entered it on these explorations of an interior that is both national and cultural, biographical and intimate. They walk back and forth across boundaries of natural history and aesthetics, sentiment and sensory data, history and myth, politics and the personal. Following in their footsteps, I aim to track some of the legacies of that vast cultural imagination, bearing in mind my own foreignness to those places, but hoping (with some degree of humility) that my affection and powers of observation, as well as my own capacities for translation—bringing back meaning and language from that land which is not *my own, but remembered forever*—will serve me well, and keep us from getting lost.

1

Walking into the Woodland with Turgenev

> Perhaps we are all unredeemably "edge" creatures, never wholly at home either in the dark humid forest or the big open-sky country of the grassland, always struggling to convert both into [an] . . . idyll of shady oak groves dappled across a pastoral meadow.
>
> —Daniel Worster, *Nature's Economy: A History of Ecological Ideas*
>
> Regardless of all the polish, the culture and delicacy and westernizing—[Turgenev] was still a *Russian wanderer*.
>
> —Boris Zaitsev, *A Life of Turgenev*

THERE WAS A TIME—a time now consigned to medieval chronicles and the fragmentary memory embedded in proverbs—when much of European Russia was covered in woodland. By the nineteenth century many of the densest reaches of forest had shrunk and retreated northward: the lovely bands of green in Fedor Arnol'd's 1893 map show only a pale olive to the south, with a narrowing wedge "from 25–35% wooded" in the central regions around Moscow. While parts of the empire's western territory were still heavily wooded, the extent of forest loss in others was cause for increasing concern. One 1842 contributor to a Moscow journal of agronomy referred to an "olden day" of unspecified antiquity, when the Moscow region was covered in "ancient, immeasurable forests."[1] Ivan Turgenev, wandering among the fields and woodlands of his native Orel, some 210 miles south of Moscow, was struck in the late 1840s by how sparse the woodland was, how ill this boded for hunters like him: "In Orel province the last woods and thickets will be gone in five years or so, and bogs are all but forgotten; in Kaluga, on the other hand, the *zaseki* forests stretch for hundreds of *versts*, the bogs go on for miles, and the black grouse—that noble bird—hasn't yet taken wing."[2]

Turgenev's contrast in this story is between two adjoining administrative districts and their strikingly different landscapes: while the peasant serfs of Orel

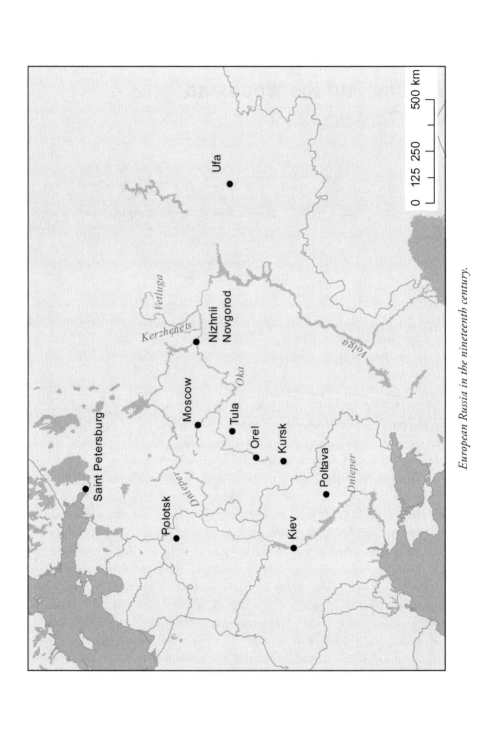

European Russia in the nineteenth century.

owe their masters labor, Kaluga serfs pay quitrent; Kaluga peasants live in well-built pine cottages, while the Orel village is a straggly affair with shoddy huts of aspen. The passage juxtaposes divergent lives without trying to nail down causality; it imagines a landscape in which one can wander quite quickly from poverty into relative well-being. Part of what distinguishes these landscapes is their trees: just over the border from the Orel *guberniia* lie the vast, ancient forests of Kaluga, while Orel is virtually treeless. Turgenev would wander across that border innumerable times both as hunter and writer; his 1857 story "Journey into Polesye" takes us west-northwest of his familial estate, into the Kaluga forests, deep into ancient woods.

"Journey into Polesye" was first published in the *Library for Reading* in October of 1857; Turgenev mentions the story as early as 1850, in a footnote to one of his *Hunter's Sketches*, "Singers"; he seems to have worked on it in fits and starts for years. At one point he considered sending it to his friend Sergei Aksakov for a volume of hunting sketches the latter was compiling; he refers to it periodically in letters to friends, sometimes as a story, sometimes as an "article." He finished it not in Russia but in France, and months later than he had promised the *Library* editor: he blamed gallbladder problems, and after he sent it off was beset by anxiety about whether it was any good. The history of the story's creation is interwoven with hunting trips to Polesye. The 1850 footnote promises a sketch of the "types" who inhabit the region: "Polesye is the name of a long band of ground, almost entirely covered in forest. . . . Numerous aspects of lifeway, mores and language distinguish the inhabitants of Polesye. Those who live in southern Polesye, near Plokhin and Sukhinich, two rich villages with manufactories, centers of local trade, are particularly noteworthy. At some point we will talk about them in greater detail" (4:239–40).[3] In August 1853 Turgenev spent several weeks hunting in Polesye, and once he got home wrote his friend Pavel Annenkov about the trip, using language that prefigures the story; the emphasis here is less on ethnography and more on place: "I've just recently returned from a fairly big hunting trip. I was on the shores of the Desna, and saw places that are in no way different from the way they were in Riurik's time; I saw endless forests, dense and silent—maybe a hazel grouse whistling or a black grouse rustling its wings as it comes up from the yellow moss, covered in berries and blueberries—I saw pines the size of [the Kremlin bell tower] Ivan the Great—you look at them and can't help thinking they feel their own enormity" (*Pis'ma* 2:173). Turgenev had the final title in mind as early as 1853 but also refers to it with a phrase that seems almost like an alternative title: "Peasants Shooting Bear in the Polesye Oat Fields." This is more description than title, but its link of agriculture and the wild is intriguing: the ursine tsar of the Polesye woods passes over into humanly created clearings and fields, helping himself to what humans have sown.[4]

In the original footnote to "Singers" Turgenev laid out a detailed geography: the forest of Polesye "begins on the border of Bolkhov and Zhizdrin counties, stretches through the provinces of Kaluga, Tula and Moscow, and ends at the Marino woods just south of Moscow."[5] There is a similar if less conspicuous exactitude in "Journey into Polesye": the narrator views the great wood from the banks of the "boggy river Reseta"; he sees laborers headed for the fair at Karachev, a small town between Bryansk and Orel; he is led by his peasant guide to a succession of woodland villages with uncannily allegorical names: first they go to Sviatoe—"Holy Place"—a village in a clearing surrounded by woods; and on the second day to Gar', an area whose name ("burned patch") stems from the fact that it was extensively burned ten years earlier. Many of these places we can still chart on contemporary maps of Russia.

The Polesye of the story is part of a forest that served in medieval Russia as a defensive line against southern invaders, the *zaseki* Turgenev refers to in "Khor and Kalinych." By the late nineteenth century (when an entry on Polesye was written for the Brokgaus and Efron encyclopedia) the forest encompassed more than a million *desyatinas*—or more than 430,000 acres—of woodland. Particularly in its northerly reaches the landscape was one typically found elsewhere: glacial deposits of clay, boulders, and sand were fertile ground for taiga, the predominantly pinewoods of the Russian north intermixed with birch, linden, and alder. Farther southeast—in the area closest to Orel Province—pines mix with oak, maple, and linden, in a forest more typical of central Russia. The *zaseki* forests of which Polesye was a part had lost their role as border fortifications by the time of Peter the Great (who decreed in 1723 that they be surveyed and replanted), but remained into Turgenev's day—and indeed into our own—as tracts of dense woodland. As one contemporary soil scientist puts it, "The remnants of the *Trans-Oka* defensive line are the largest block of broad-leafed forests not only in Russia, but in Europe. . . . While they lost their defensive function in the 18th century, the *zaseki* continue to play an important role today in 'ecological defense,' as preserves of plants and animals."[6]

Historians suggest that *zaseki* were being constructed well before the tenth century, as Slavic tribes migrated into the woodlands north and east of Kiev. While early inhabitants of these reaches (Finno-Ugric and Baltic peoples in addition to the Slavs) practiced slash-and-burn agriculture, they left the boundary woodlands standing, adding outer barriers of felled trees with crowns facing south to impede, if not completely stop, nomadic raiders on horseback. This thicket barrier (whose width ranged from a few yards to as much as thirty-seven miles) was augmented at intervals with fortified citadels; the natural woodlands just north of the line were both protected and replanted.[7] In the centuries before Moscow consolidated its power, each principality built its own line of defense; by the sixteenth century the *zaseki*, or *zasechnaia cherta*, had become one coordinated frontier (called "bereg"—shore—but also *zapoved'*) of almost twenty-five hundred miles.[8] The *zaseki* thus were places where Muscovites used natural vegetation to provide what geography had seemed *not* to give them: a natural barrier against invaders. They were also places of refuge; in the seventeenth century Bolotnikov—the leader of a peasant rebellion—hid in Polesye's dense, marshy woodlands. Turgenev's letters and the story itself play on much of this geographic and historical specificity; he seems to have regarded Polesye as wild terrain, redolent of a turbulent and complex history—different in important ways from the landscape of Orel Province, with its patchwork of woodlands, villages, and fields.

Turgenev's story confronts us with Polesye on page one, in a long passage that represents the forest as vast and forbidding. The narrative voice of that passage is intensely, indulgently emotive; this is prose that situates us in a place where "man" cannot be at home. Its lavish associations (an extended comparison of forest to sea, a personified female Nature who addresses man) are the opposite of a map or encyclopedia entry, or the terse account Turgenev gave of Polesye in the letter to Annenkov: "The forest we entered was extraordinarily old. I don't know if the Tatars had wandered about in it, but Russian thieves or Lithuanians from the Time of Troubles could certainly have hidden in its backwoods" (7:58). The beginning of the story that came out of that trip throws us into the woods in a gesture that feels almost like abandonment. Only at the end of the passage do we realize we have been listening to the remembered thoughts of an embodied narrator, a gentry hunter who is recounting his two-day hunt with a peasant guide. Turgenev's opening is deft, acute, and surely calculated: while the hunter will be led by a succession of peasant guides who know the territory much better than he does, we are in *his* pocket, led at least as much on a tour of his inner state as on a walkabout of Polesye. Like Caspar David Friedrich's solitary figures facing the landscape, Turgenev's hunter reminds us of the moment of perception, the fraught process of watching.

"The sight of the huge pinewood, embracing the whole of the horizon, the sight of 'Polesye' reminds one of the sea. And it draws forth the same impressions; the same elemental, untouched power spreads out broad and mighty in front of the viewer. From the depths of the ancient forests, from the immortal breast of the water the same voice rises up: 'I have nothing to do with you,'—Nature says to man,—'I reign, and you concern yourself with how not to die.' But the forest is more monotonous and mournful than the sea, especially a pine forest, everywhere the same and almost without sound. The sea threatens and comforts, it plays in all colors, speaks in all voices; it reflects the sky, which also breathes eternity, but an eternity that does not seem alien to us. . . . The unchanging, gloomy pinewood is silent, or moans dully—and in seeing it a sense of our nothingness penetrates deeper and more indelibly into the heart of human consciousness. It is difficult for a human being, the creature of a single day, born yesterday and sentenced today to die—it is difficult for him to bear the cold, indifferently directed gaze of eternal Isis; it's not only the reckless hopes and dreams of youth that grow still and die within him, caught by the icy breath of the elements; he feels that the last of his brothers might disappear from the face of the earth—and not one needle on these branches would move; he feels his solitude, his weakness, his irrelevance—and with a hurried, secret fear he turns to the small cares and labors of his life; it's easier for him in this world, which he himself has created, here he is at home, here he still dares to believe in his significance and power" (7:51–52).

The title of this story might be translated not as "Journey into Polesye" but "Journey into the Woodland"—a reasonable variant, since "Polesye" is both proper and common noun: it can mean a particular forest in central Russia, or a kind of forest one might encounter in numerous places. The two renderings get at something fundamental about how place works in the story. For years I read Turgenev's "Journey" without knowing or even thinking much about the particular place of its origin. But reading it that way, I've come to think, makes it less interesting, and also obscures for us a part of Russia that Turgenev wanted us to see. We are used, as readers, to thinking of Dostoevsky's Petersburg as a place that is both mythic and historical, a place where social realia and psychological hyperreality confront and confound each other. You can take walking trips of contemporary Petersburg and follow in Raskolnikov's footsteps. No entrepreneurs have (as far as I know) set up shop on the banks of the Reseta, but we could wander through these woods as surely as we can wander through what used to be slums along the Griboedov Canal. Turgenev's place is both real and more than real; there is a realist aesthetic and a gesturing toward allegory in the place names and predicaments of his Polesye. We lose a sense of that if we don't try to figure out his geography, a history of these woods that is both ecological and political.

The editors of the Soviet edition of Turgenev's work speak of this story as having to do with "man in nature"—*chelovek v prirode*.[9] In what follows I take that claim seriously, following its logic into a set of related questions. We have already broached the nature of the *place* where the story is set; the story also raises questions about just who that "man" might be: the Russian *chelovek* is closer to our *human being*, but the story's characters are in fact all men (leaving aside Isis and the personified Nature of the first passage). While the phrase "man in nature" is as generic as the "man" of the opening passage, the story as a whole makes distinctions among particular men and particular knowledges, particularities that are worth tracking. And if both place and character will be focal points of this chapter, so will the nature of Turgenev's narrative itself, a fictional form of nature writing that doesn't look quite like what Americans have come to expect from the category. We might call "Journey into Polesye" a hunting sketch, an ethnographic interlude, a quasi-allegorical travel piece, a fictionalized reminiscence, and all those terms would be right. It is also a piece of nature writing in the Russian style, establishing for subsequent writers (at least in the nineteenth century, and perhaps farther into the future), what it meant to write about nature in Russia. That Turgenev's story is rife with issues of class and the peculiarly bicultural nature of place in Russia is hardly coincidental: the landscape of Russia maps a world that a tiny Europeanized gentry awkwardly cohabited with a vast peasantry whose traditions of place and place-knowledge were radically different. Exploring the terrain of Turgenev's Polesye means stumbling against that knowledge almost continuously—even as we are repeatedly seduced by the stunning beauty of the place, translucent sap dripping down pine bark at midday, the oblique light of sunset on young birch, a landscape that is always inviting us further, into its web of sense and meaning.

* * *

THE OPENING PASSAGES of "Journey into Polesye" situate human lives in a quick series of vignettes that prefigure how evocative and open-ended the story will be, how attuned it is to the problematic of just who "man" is, just what "nature" is. The story begins with that long passage of the narrator looking out on an alien and dread-inspiring prospect; it quickly shifts to a narrative not of man but of men, of laboring men traveling rather than standing in awestruck contemplation. As the narrator stands on the bank of the Reseta, he sees a group of workers emerge from the forest with packs on their backs, led by an "old man of seventy, with white hair." One of the men stops to ask the price of gingerbread from an itinerant merchant with a "hawklike nose and mousey eyes" who is scornful of this "ignorant lot." The white-haired leader urges them on: "Hurry on, boys, hurry on! . . . It's a long time till we rest." The gingerbread merchant himself heads off, crossing over to the far side of the river. We are left on the near bank with our narrator, to travel deeper into Polesye. The anonymous band of workers—the narrator identifies them as diggers—moves in and out of the story "without speaking, in a kind of weighty silence" (7:52, 53). Except for the man who wants gingerbread and the elder concerned to make a distant place by nightfall, they do not speak: part of the varied life observed by the gentry hunter as he enters Polesye, these worker-walkers also seem like signs of something else—some not-quite-disclosed meaning that the story itself will play out.

Much of this gem of a story is concerned with seeing: it begins with that view of a vast and forbidding wood; it ends (almost) with an act of exquisite attentiveness that finds in an insect's quiet movements the way in which humans should live. In between those two moments we are led on a journey, in which a peasant guide acts as a kind of tracker, reading forest sign and guiding the narrator toward sustenance. In a story that is about moments of seeing, and about finding one's place in a difficult world, how can we not wonder just who these workers are meant to be—how, that is, we are to see them? These are men who dig; who labor; without time or money to stop for gingerbread. They are led through the woods toward a "night's rest" that is still far away. We might think of them as emblems of the kind of passage this story wants us to take, suggesting life as existential journey, but they also remind us, however indirectly, of the tension between reading them as emblematic of a universal human existence, and seeing their predicament as specific to place and time.

The elderly peasant who leads the diggers says their place of rest is still far away. The Russian *nochleg* literally means the place one lies down at night: the nineteenth-century lexicographer Vladimir Dal' begins his explanation of the word with examples of where one spends the night "in the field, in the forest"—and only then lists a "yard or house" where one might stay the night.[10] There is, in other words, no necessary assumption of shelter from the elements, or a permanent structure. You might lie down to rest without anything to cover your head or protect you from rain and storm. The central notion here, we might say, is cessation of movement, rest—rather than shelter or separation from the larger, nonhuman world.[11] Martin Heidegger connects the notion of dwelling with a built structure—but Turgenev's story and the notion of *nochleg* move us toward a more exposed, more vulnerable kind of encounter and resting *in the face of*, and encircled by, a natural world that is represented as a place of both beauty and indifference.[12]

The story's governing consciousness and angle of perception is the gentry narrator; he is the one who recalls seeing the "huge pinewood" from the banks of the boggy Reseta; he is the one who feels repulsed by an indifferent "Isis." His agonizing sense of being unrecognized by nature is the dominant emotion of the story's opening, and recurs at various moments on his journey inward. But he is not only an angst-ridden wanderer. Along with moments of intense subjectivity we find a realist's ability to describe the world, in language that can be extraordinarily atmospheric and supple. There are times in the story when the narrator sounds like a naturalist—or perhaps just a woodsman and lover of walks—as when he describes the feel—the sight, sound, smell—of the wood at midday: "Greenish moss all strewn with dead pine needles covered the earth; bilberries grew in dense clumps; the sharp smell of their berries, like the smell of muskrat, compressed one's breathing. The sun couldn't penetrate the high net of pine branches, but even so it was airless and not dark in the wood; heavy, translucent pitch dripped slowly, silently down the rough bark of trees like large beads of sweat. The motionless air, with neither shadow nor light, burned one's face. Everything was silent; even our footsteps weren't audible; we walked along the moss as on a carpet; Egor in particular moved without sound, like a shadow; even the brush didn't snap beneath his feet" (7:58). There is an extraordinary power of presence, observation, and articulate re-creation here; Turgenev's aesthetic is strongly visual, but not exclusively so: one feels the heat and beads of sweat and is aware of sound and its absence as part of the world into which this passage summons us. And then there is that briefest of similes—*like a shadow*—and we wonder if there is a metaphoric or literary resonance at work as well.

This hunter is also, in a sense, an ethnographer. Turgenev's first mention of the story refers to regional types, and his note about peasants shooting bear in oat fields suggests how wilderness and agriculture exist side by side. Both threads remain in the final story. The hunter is led through forbidding woodland toward a village called Sviatoe, a name that connects sunlight and the sacred; Turgenev's description of the village moves us from gentry consciousness toward Russian peasant culture and its symbolic of space, self, and other:

"The sun was already setting when I finally made my way out of the forest and saw a small village in front of me. Twenty homesteads or so clung around an old, wooden single-domed church, with a green cupola and tiny windows, whose pallor stood out in the evening dusk. This was Sviatoe. I went through the fence [*okolitsa*] around the village" (7:56). This first description of the village is followed by two bucolic sentences describing village girls meeting their livestock—pigs, cows, and sheep—as boys bring the animals back from pasture for the night. The next morning we are given one more brief bit of landscape, this time from within the village: "The forest made a dense blue circle along the entire horizon—there were at most two hundred *desyatinas* of plowed land around Sviatoe; to get to good land you had to go seven *versts*." The hunter and his guide Egor (and the boy Kondrat) set off for their day of hunting, leaving the clearing behind: "We made a lively trot through the clearing surrounding Sviatoe, but once we'd entered the forest, we dragged along once more at a walk" (7:57).

Turgenev creates in this account a landscape of circles. Within a forest that is itself a borderland we find another boundary, a circular one, marking the transition from the world of *dvor* (household or farmyard) and village to the world of the woods beyond. The boundary between village and forest is both visual and tactile, signaled by differences of vegetation and built structures. The village draws a circle around itself with its fence: the word Turgenev uses is *okolitsa*, derived from *okolo*, "around"—which is, if you think of it, an encircling word, with its series of *o*'s like an incantation. The circle of homesteads around a wooden church suggests an encampment of the human in the face of the greater-than-human world surrounding it. It is an inner boundary that echoes, in a way, the story's opening, when the narrator stood on the edge of the great wood. Here, however, we have a different edge, one that lies inside the encircling forest, one that (as the shepherds and girls remind us) must be constantly negotiated for peasant lives to persist.

The boundary between forest and village is one of the fundamental organizing categories of Russian traditional culture. The village is presided over by the spirits of human ancestors and their benign representative, the *domovoi* or house spirit; the forest domain is ruled by the *leshii*—a trickster figure who leads astray those who enter his world without taking appropriate precautions.[13] Symbolically and spatially, these are two distinct realms, corresponding in some sense to the dualism of "one's own" and "the alien"—*svoi* and *chuzoi*; and yet the peasant's acknowledgment that the forest was controlled by "other" forces did not prevent his going there.[14] The peasantry continued to enter into the forest, out of various forms of need. As Neonila Krinichnaia puts it, "Humans' interrelationships with the concrete realm of the forest, and with its spirit-*master* [the *leshii*], began with the . . . claiming of a given territory. . . . When a settlement grew from a forest clearing, and then turned into a village, the forest may have withdrawn, but it still interacted with the cultural space claimed by humans. It continued to be elemental nature, a chaos, where the sole organizing principle was its spirit-"master," along with other deities that had been engendered by him."[15] It is a vision of ongoing, dynamic relationship, an understanding of the elemental—or wild—as having its own governing principles: the two peasant men of Turgenev's story seem to grasp that pattern of relationship, each moving back and forth between forest and village in his own particular way.

Robert Pogue Harrison, in his magisterial *Forests: The Shadow of Civilization*, points out that human habitation has been associated since time immemorial with clearings—literally, with places of light. The historian Vasilii Kliuchevsky contended it was the difficulty of maintaining such clearings that drove Russian hostility to the forest: to practice agriculture in conditions like these means constantly having to push back the walls of woodland.[16] To mention hostility is to acknowledge the extraordinary difficulty of human life in these climates; Turgenev's Sviatoe, however, is placid and filled with light. The sun can warm the plowed land and reflect off the "tiny windows" of the church; the combination of agriculture and the church suggests a symbolic and symbiotic joining of life-giving light (*svet*) and what is sacred (*sviat*). This village with its geography of agri- and human culture represents a kind of *nochleg*—a resting spot—in the wood, one to which the narrator will want to return for sleep and nourishment.

Alongside this geography of peasant life we find in the story a series of allusions—resonances, echoes, half-citations—which suggest a very different frame of reference. These allusions belong entirely to the world of the narrator; they are part of his more European, literary culture. They begin with the opening passage with its reference to the "cold, indifferently directed gaze of Isis," its tone of anxiety and awe at a Russian landscape's version of the sublime. The story's Soviet editors point out a reminiscence of Pushkin that comes at a moment when the hunter is sunk in abject memories of a wasted youth (7:60), and there are surely echoes of Dante (in reverse) when the gingerbread salesman moves off across the boggy Reseta, and the narrator treks from a holy place of light to one associated with fire. Joseph Brodsky quipped that "since the 14th century, the woods have given off a very strong smell of *selva oscura*, and you may recall what that *selva* let the author of the *Divine Comedy* into." He has Robert Frost most immediately in mind, in an essay that begins with Auden's claim that American poets—unlike their European counterparts—confront the tree *as such*; Europeans must contend with a tree "made familiar by history, to which it's been a witness. . . . A tree stands there rustling, as it were, with allusions."[17] We might quibble about just how innocent of history American trees are, but Turgenev's story certainly gives us both: the forest "as such" and the one that is rustling with illusions.

The narrator's consciousness opens and closes the story; the center of "Journey" describes encounters with two peasant men. Critics of the story have tended to focus on the story's final epiphany, when the narrator watches an emerald-headed fly for more than an hour; they have had much less to say about these two men and the worlds they bring into the story. This peasant material is the aspect of "Journey into Polesye" closest to the *Hunter's Sketches*, which Turgenev had completed in the years he began thinking about this story: encounters with peasants are the fundamental pretext of those tales. Many of the *Sketches* are studies in contrast, with peasants presented as types of diverse character and response to the world. "Khor and Kalinych" and "The Singers" both operate on this principle—one that Turgenev was also to use in *The Inn*, a novella about peasant life and injustice, which juxtaposes the wronged but submissive Akim to a rapacious and opportunistic Naum. The contrast of peasants in "Journey into Polesye" functions in similar ways: Turgenev uses the two men to show different ways of negotiating the boundaries of village and woods—two different versions of "man in nature."

The two peasants of "Journey into Polesye" are Egor and Efrem; the first acts as the narrator's guide, the second they encounter on their second day of hunting. The first is likened to a deer, the second to the *lesnoi dukh*—the spirit who rules the world of the forest. Egor is a man of silence, Efrem is a rebel; Egor lives in Sviatoe and goes from there into the woods, while Efrem comes into the story from behind a tree. Both men become guides to a world that had seemed forbidding and unknowable to the narrator; both articulate forms of knowledge about place that are rooted in traditional life and culture.

Egor is presented to us as a man renowned for his hunting skills; he has brought down seven bears, and when we first meet him he is skinning (with a dull knife, Turgenev notes) one he killed the day before. Our sense of Egor derives as much from what we see of him as from what we are told about him; the narrator describes him as distinguished by measure, reserve, and silence. He is known as a *molchal'nik*—a man of few words—a silence underscored both by the description of him as possessing the "dignity of a handsome deer" and the ability to move in the woods without drawing attention to himself. Egor in fact seems to be as silent as the woods—Turgenev repeatedly notes how empty of sound this forest is. In all of this we get a sense of the man's imperturbable equanimity, despite the fact that his life doesn't go well. His wife takes ill, his children die, he can't shake the poverty that plagues him. The culprit in this—the narrator cites common wisdom—is his love of the forest: "a passion for hunting's no thing for a *muzhik*, whoever takes up with a rifle is a bad farmer" (7:57).

Efrem could not be more different. What we know of this man from the woods with the "strange face" comes from his brief interaction with the narrator and the boy Kondrat, who tells a string of tall tales about him. Efrem is larger than life, with an anarchic, disruptive character. This is not the silent man of the woods, or a man resigned to sorrow like Egor. Efrem's motto is both more rapacious and more impudent: his advice to Kondrat (who seems more taken with Efrem than with Egor) is to make his own mark, to be a survivor: "If you're timid you're done for; the one who's got guts is the one who eats" (7:64). Efrem is an outlaw and a trickster (Kondrat addresses him as a *shutnik*) who is disrespectful of authority—whether a clerical figure or, like Turgenev's hunter, a member of the gentry. It is as though Efrem somehow embodies the elemental, anarchic spirit of the woods, a spirit that is not without limits, however: he won't touch the wild beehives as sacred. His presence at village councils is respected— "No one makes a better decision than him. . . . He'll come in toward the back, have a listen, then say a word that cuts right through the matter and leave: and that word will have some weight to it" (7:65). Efrem suggests a value to the community of the kind of boundary-crossing he embodies; he also suggests that the elemental "chaos" or wildness Krinichnaia identifies with the forest is not without its own forms of restraint and authority.

Among other things, Turgenev gives us in these characters forms of knowledge about the woods. Egor reads the forest landscape. The narrator knows in a general way that the woods are old, but Egor explains that an earthen wall is not—as the hunter had thought—a place where birch was boiled down to make tar, but a thieves' town from generations ago. And Egor points out the trace of a paw on moss where the bear had dug for water, and on a tree where he had climbed in search of honey. Efrem, too, *knows* the woods in a way the narrator doesn't: he seems to know there is a fire in the direction Egor and the hunter are headed, and he knows where the wild bees' hives are (this is knowledge that bears have: their Russian name signifies *the one who knows where honey is*).[18] There is nothing mystical about such knowledge: grounded in traditional practices like hunting and hiving, this is knowledge that locals depend on, and which latter-day, more urban generations depend on someone else to teach them.[19]

Egor and Efrem are but part of a vast company of literary peasants: Turgenev's peasants as a group occupy a significant place in a history of representation that is ideologically laden, bearing the weight of many of the great debates that animated Russian society in the nineteenth century. By the time that Turgenev wrote "Journey into Polesye," the struggle over just who the peasant was—and how he (occasionally she) should be depicted—had become acute. For the Slavophiles the peasant represented the embodiment of Slavic Orthodox wisdom, a long-suffering but intact spirit that suggested to Russian intellectuals a developmental path other than European modernity. For Westernizers, on the other hand, the peasantry was sunk in ignorance and patriarchal violence; Western models of liberalism and scientific progress represented the only viable path for genuine Russian liberation and development. Both groups assume a connection between peasantry and the natural world, a connection that easily became inflected with Russian versions of Rousseau's Noble Savage. The peasant, in other words, became a kind of blank slate on which the dreams and aspirations of Russia's intellectual elite were written. Claims of knowledge or connection to the peasantry become common coin in Russian nineteenth-century writers, and representations of the peasantry often carry with them an implied vision of Russia and her future. Both Tolstoy and Dostoevsky elaborate complex mythologies of Russia's peasantry and its significance for the country's future. Revelations of peasant wisdom are life-changing for the heroes of both *War and Peace* and *Anna Karenina*. For Dostoevsky, the peasant's embeddedness in earth and the cycles of nature serves as an icon of natural redemption: the peasant Marei comforts a boy frightened by a wolf, making the sign of the cross and smearing his lips with dirt in a gesture that bespeaks the blessings of a peasant faith grounded in maternity and soil.[20]

Egor, Polesye's "Slavophile" peasant, plays the more obvious role in the story's dynamics. He figures both in its ending and in a crucial scene at the end of the first day, in which the narrator is thrust into a distraught sequence of memories: he and Egor have left Sviatoe and reentered the depths of Polesye.

Egor goes off in search of water, and the narrator is left alone. Now inside the great forest, he feels the presence of death, and a sense of having looked, as he thinks, "where man shouldn't"—a visual trespass he responds to by covering his eyes (7:59). His distress is apparently brought on by the terrifying silence of the forest, but also by the evidence of "traces" (*sledy*) of animal and human life, which Egor had pointed out to him; he feels what he calls his own impermanence: "Oh life, life, where, how have you passed and left no trace [*bessledno*]?" (7:60) The language of the episode is agonizing, interrogative, and more than a little artificial. The forest's airless darkness seems to infiltrate the man's own reverie: "The comrades of my earliest strivings came to mind. . . . Then shadows began to gather and close about me, it grew darker and darker all around, the monotonous years sped by, more and more airless and silent— and despair settled on my heart like a stone" (7:60). The breathless pacing intensifies to the point of rupture (or parody), as the distraught hunter tries to give himself advice and talk himself out of his panic: "Oh heart, to what end, why are you still regretful, if you long for peace, try to forget, school yourself in the resignation of final parting, to the bitter words *farewell* and *for ever more*" (7:61). It is Egor who startles the hunter out of this panicked spiral of emotion, with simple words and a simple gesture that seem almost comic in the context: "Here's your water" (7:61).

The abrupt shift moves us back into the realm of human company; the hunter acknowledges the "living speech" and "friendly call" and "powerful hand" that reached out to him when he had fallen into an "uncharted, dark depth" where only the "quiet and unending moan of endless sorrow" could be heard. Just in time, we are headed home: "Lead me," says the narrator to Egor—and we make our way back to the village, to human community and to the sensual pleasures of "thick cream . . . soft hay," and sleep (7:62). The passage ends with a gesture of *looking away* from the wood; the narrator's sense that he has looked somewhere he shouldn't explicitly echoes the Isis allusions at the story's beginning—but his plunge into memory and sense of abandonment seems punishment enough, as painful as anything the goddess might dole out. Looking at his past involves confronting what he has lost. Tellingly enough, the narrator's anguish is marked by literary allusion: his interior language echoes Pushkin's 1828 lyric "Remembrance" (*Vospominanie*), with its image of memory as a scroll: "I sat motionless and watched, watched with surprise and intensity, as though I could see my whole life before me, as though a scroll had appeared before my eyes" (7:60). Pushkin's verse is situated in nocturnal Petersburg; the poem ends with Pushkin declaring that regardless how bitter and repulsive his memories are, he "will not erase the mournful lines."[21] Turgenev's hunter has neither Pushkin's stoic acceptance nor his emotional restraint. We get the feeling that he would never have gotten out of his blinding funk if Egor hadn't come up with the water. The transaction is both psychological and ethical: the engulfing depths of memory are traded for literal drink, but there is also a symbolic dimension in accepting Egor's living water. There is a sense of communion with the real, present, literal man, and echoes of the magical "living water" of Russian folktales, which the hero is sent into forbidding woods to fetch (and whose securing depends on the help of others). And there is a shift from the excessive, clichéd rhetoric of the hunter's interior monologue to the simple, direct speech of the peasant Egor. In some curious but surely important sense the male peasant has replaced the great goddess. "Mother Nature" may reject the hunter, but the good peasant will give him cream and sleep.

Turgenev frames these encounters with the moments of watching that open and close the story. The opening frame looks out on the forest as a mass, from the relative distance and exterior vantage point of the Reseta bank. His reaction to this spectacle is to turn away from it. In a gesture that suggests he simply can't bear looking at the trees—or confronting his own mortality—the narrator mentally turns to the small cares of life, to a humanly made world, in which he feels at home (7:51–52). The final scene of watching in Turgenev's story, which comes just before its end, balances and in certain ways echoes this first panoramic vision, but at a radically different scale.[22] The hunter and his companions have finished their second day of hunting; they have ranged over the area known as Gar', and have come to a resting stop. Turgenev gives us a brief description of the surrounding quiet, the absence of heat, the "clear, gentle light" that rests on the leaves of a young birch. And then he describes an extraordinary, long pause. The narrator lies down on the road (the verb *to lie* is etymologically linked with the *nochleg* of the story's opening), and both watches and reflects on his watching.[23]

"I raised my head and on the very end of a slender branch I saw one of those large flies with an emerald head, a long body and four transparent wings, which the coquettish French call 'virgins,' but our unpretentious folk call 'bucket yokes.' For a long time, longer than an hour, I didn't take my eyes off her. Warmed through by the sun, she didn't move, only occasionally turned her head from side to side, shuddering her lifted wings . . . that was all. When I looked at her, it suddenly seemed to me that I understood the life of nature, that I understood its indubitable and evident meaning, one nonetheless still mysterious for many. Quiet and slowly paced animation, a lack of hurry and restraint of sensation and forces, equanimity of health in each separate being—this is its foundation, its changeless law, this is what it stands and endures upon. Everything that goes beyond that level—no matter whether above it or below—nature throws aside as unsuitable. Many insects die as soon as they experience the joys of love, which destroy the equilibrium of life; a sick animal disappears into the thickets and expires there, alone: it's as though he senses that he no longer has the right to see the sun that shines on all, or to breathe freely, he no longer has the right to live. And a human being who suffers, either through his own fault or that of others, should at least know how to keep silence" (7:69–70).

This passage has been of central importance to numerous readers of Turgenev, who have turned to the ending of "Journey into Polesye" as a way of thinking about aesthetics, nature, and incipient Russian ecological sensibilities. Robert Louis Jackson, in an essay first published in 1974, sees the passage as reflective of Turgenev's "balance, measure, harmony"—an "aesthetic of observation" that "begins with a vision of a real order and beatitude in nature." As Jackson puts it, "Journey into Polesye" represents the narrator's passage from "a painfully subjective" to a "properly objective perspective of Nature."[24] The story itself, he suggests, gives us an essential perspective on the author's aesthetic and worldview, one that acknowledges the conflict between nature's equanimity and human striving, but which ultimately resolves that contradiction in an "epic vision of nature-divine."[25] Tom Newlin, in an explicitly ecocritical essay, considers the passage as one of a number of moments of "affective awareness" emergent in Russian prose writers of the 1850s; what intrigues Newlin is the possibility that these moments of awareness—suggestive of a distinctively Russian contemplative epistemology—might be connected to a biocentric worldview, one that takes "nature more fully into account."[26] Newlin gives an astute and nuanced reading of these moments of "'affective' and potently saturated contact with the natural world" in Turgenev, connecting the passage from "Journey into Polesye" to others in Turgenev's literary prose and letters. For Newlin these moments suggest a way of *knowing* the natural world that is neither analytically dissective or subjectively oblivious of what is really *out there*.[27]

The contemplative delicacy of this moment is indisputable; it feels as though we have come to a calm, safe harbor after the turbulence of the story's opening and the narrator's second plunge into morose solipsism at the end of the first day. Unlike the abstraction and distance of the opening scene, we have turned here to nature in the small scale, and an undivided and patient regard. But I want to suggest that this epiphany—for that is surely what it is—is in some sense taken away from us. The emerald fly scene isn't the end: something else is. Turgenev offers us the moment and its wisdom, and then qualifies it in a dialogue that actually ends the story. The beautiful moment is just that—a moment—and we are left wondering, within the contexts of our life, just what it means and whether it's really something to live by.[28]

The story ends with the following dialogue:

> "What are you up to, Egor!"—Kondrat called out suddenly; he'd already gotten on to the carter's seat, and was playing and fidgeting with the reins. "Come sit down. What are you thinking about? Still about the cow?"
>
> "About the cow? What cow?" I repeated, and looked at Egor: calm and dignified as ever, he had in fact set to thinking and looked off somewhere in the distance, towards the fields that were starting to grow dark.
>
> "You didn't know?" Kondrat picked up. "His last cow dropped dead last night. He's got no luck—what can you do . . ."
>
> Egor sat silent on the carter's seat, and we set off. "Here's one who knows how not to complain," I thought. (7:70)

This is a wonderful and enigmatic ending: Egor is looking off into the distance. It is not clear whether he is actually looking *at* something, or simply off into an unfocused "beyond." Turgenev was fond of this visual stance, and of this kind of allusive and indirect closure. *On the Eve*, Turgenev's third novel (published in 1859), ends with a sequence that involves both heroic action (a Russian woman going off into the unknown to complete what her Bulgarian husband, a freedom fighter now dead, had begun), and a character looking off into an indeterminate distance: "Uvar Ivanovich tapped his fingers and looked into the distance with his mysterious gaze" (8:167). The quandary here—a narrative pacing that also records the author's uncertainty about just what lay in store for Russia—is whether the time has come for heroics, or if the spirit of inertia and gazing into an uncertain distance will continue.[29] The story "Singers" ends with a similarly gnomic call and contrast: the vast store of talent and emotion displayed in the singing contest at the heart of the story is left behind, and we hear a lone voice in a vast landscape, a boy being called home to a thrashing.[30]

Egor's gaze moves us off into a similarly indeterminate future, but we also note that he is looking back toward the fields: fields around Sviatoe, we might think, fields that represent agriculture, settlement, family, labor—and with a cow that has died, potential hunger.[31] We are already turning back from the lyric space of the hunter's epiphany toward the story of a man's life. The ending shifts the narrator's observations back into the complexities of social reality. It is as though the narrator, just minutes after his wonderful epiphanic moment, is being tested: if the law of nature suggests that he to whom wrong has been done shouldn't complain, then Egor—the logic would go—is fulfilling that law in not complaining. His silence is a kind of submission to "natural law."

Put in these terms, Egor is a hero of meekness—*smirenie*—one of the qualities of spirit that the Slavophiles identified with the Russian peasantry.

Turgenev's attitude toward this quietism of spirit was ambivalent: the heroine of *A Nest of Gentry*, published less than two years after "Journey into Polesye," is regarded as Turgenev's most Slavophilic character; while the author clearly has deep affection for the heroine Liza, who is possessed of both sustaining faith and an aura of spiritualized Russian nature, the plot of the novel denies the hero the happy ending he longs for. At the center of the novel the hero watches the world around him with the same profound equanimity of spirit that we find in the final epiphany of "Journey to Polesye": "[Lavretskii] descended into a kind of peaceful trance, that he didn't come out of all day long. . . . He sat beneath the window without moving, and seemed to listen to the flow of quiet life that surrounded him, to the occasional sounds of the country backwater" (7:189). This plenitude of nature has no counterpart in history: the hero is called out of contemplative union with the natural world into the disappointments and labors of life. The ethical and political costs of *smirenie* are also central in *The Inn*, published in 1855. The story treats *smirenie* with subtle but devastating irony. Akim, the main character, is an industrious serf who has established a small, successful business in a posting house; various characters manipulate a pseudo-theological language of submission to justify class status, taking the posting house from Akim since it turns out that the land (like Akim himself) in fact belongs to his mistress. In both these narratives Turgenev explores but finally undermines the supposed virtues of humility and equanimity before life's troubles. The virtues and delight of contemplative response to the natural world are not in themselves at stake; these are part of the deep tissue of Turgenev's writing, and of his evident response to the world. Contemplation of the natural world can bring with it a deep and restorative peace. What is at stake are the ways in which readers or characters analogize between an aesthetic response (the calm regard of the emerald-headed fly, or the lush nature of a Russian summer day in *A Nest of Gentry*) and ethics: *Does* "nature" set humans a rule for life? Should we live by a law of conservation of forces? Should Egor keep quiet, and not complain?

There is one further way in which we might read the closure of "Journey into Polesye" and its shift from epiphany to dialogue. Encounters with peasants often wind up confounding the narrator of the *Hunter's Sketches*, or acting as a kind of ironizing brake on his assumptions and moments of aesthetic reverie. Not infrequently these encounters force the narrator to confront his own privileged and ethically ambiguous status. In "Loner," the narrator takes shelter in a forester's hut and then accompanies him as he detains a peasant who is felling a tree illegally. The peasant claims he has been forced to it "from hunger." The narrator wants to pay the fine and let the man go. The forester, however, says he can't release him, and then reminds us that he (like the peasant) is a man *podnevol'nyi*—a man who is not free. The story moves us through compassion and ecological concern (isn't the forester protecting the forest?) toward a revelation of property relations and compulsion that also entrap the narrator. Does the forester serve the forest or a system of class privilege? The story leaves us with the question, rather than suggesting an answer.

Other stories from the *Sketches* give us similar examples of such narrative and moral complexity: In "Kasyan from the Beautiful Lands," a peasant companion interrupts quite unceremoniously the narrator's protracted reverie and description of a beautiful forest at midday, just as he is exclaiming how "extraordinarily pleasant" you feel as you watch without moving: "You don't move—you are watching: there are no words to express how joyous, and quiet, and happy you feel. You watch: that deep, clear azure brings a smile to your lips, innocent as the sky itself, as the clouds in the sky, while happy memories seem to wind slowly across your soul in their wake, and it seems more and more as though your gaze is drawn farther and farther into the distance, carrying you with it into that still, glowing abyss, and it's impossible to tear oneself from that height, from that depth."[32] The narrator's daydreaming is oddly reminiscent of Emerson's famous comparison of the watching self to a transparent eyeball: "Standing on the bare ground,—my head bathed by the blithe air and uplifted into infinite space,—all mean egotism vanishes. I become a transparent eyeball; I am nothing; I see all; the currents of the Universal Being circulate through me; I am part or parcel of God. The name of the nearest friend sounds then foreign and accidental: to be brothers, to be acquaintances, master or servant, is then a trifle and a disturbance. I am a lover of uncontained and immortal beauty. In the wilderness, I have something more connate and dear than in the streets or villages. In the tranquil landscape, and especially in the distant line of the horizon, man beholds somewhat as beautiful as his own nature."[33] Aside from the absence of quasi-theological language of "Universal Being" and "God," and Turgenev's greater investment in actually describing the world he sees, what is striking in the Russian is how he uses narrative irony to challenge what seems—despite Emerson's protestations to the contrary—the egotism of epiphanic merging with nature. Turgenev's narrator is brought abruptly back to earth and human community when his peasant companion Kasyan jolts him out of his reverie by calling him *barin* ("lord") and asking *how he can kill birds*. All illusions of a "tranquil landscape" without anyone else around, in which there is neither "master or servant," are destroyed—wittily, but destroyed. Kasyan's voice yanks us out of the world of Universalist Spirit to fraught ethics and the disruptions of culture and class: you might say we are torn from the transparent eyeball to a mote of conscience that disturbs our sight. The solitary voice in the bosom of nature gets recontextualized, or ironized, or at the very least humorously deflated. The syntax of interruption and question in this story asks us to confront just how it is that aesthetic appreciation of nature can coexist so blithely with hunting—or with the spectacle of poverty and destruction we have just been privy to.[34] As with the ending of "Journey into Polesye," the function of these moments is not to take from us the pleasure or deep peace of those moments of watching, but to complicate just how we understand their meaning. Kenneth Brostrom's characterization of Turgenev's "subtle elaboration of problems, not answers" makes of him a demonstrably modern writer; it also makes him an excellent chronicler of our problematic relationships with nature. The solitary wanderer who since Thoreau has been so fundamental to American nature writing is here replaced by a privileged loner who has to talk to peasants who (annoyingly) interrupt his aestheticizing reverie—and remind him of other ways of living in the natural world. It is a move toward irony, but also toward splendid complication of our relationships toward what we still call, with Emerson, "nature."[35]

* * *

"JOURNEY INTO POLESYE" is a story so densely allusive, so intensely emotional, so beautifully evocative of place, that the reader can easily be left speechless: baffled, perhaps, by just what the story means, but grateful for the experience—an experience that mirrors the journey of the narrator himself, ending with a cryptic koan of a conversation. I don't want to transgress here on that sense of gratitude, one that I myself feel each time I read the story. But I do want to return briefly to some of my opening considerations: the antiquity of the forest, its status as a borderland, as a place of both defense and refuge, and a place markedly different from the landscapes of Turgenev's home province.

Why does Turgenev take us into the forest? When the story was first completed, he considered including it in the *Hunter's Sketches*, but while it appeared in the 1860 edition, he took it out of later versions of the collection; it didn't fit. Part of why it didn't fit, I would suggest, is the landscape: Polesye was out there to the north and west, off in the region beyond Orel's nearly woodless spaces; it was a place less known, more wild, literally darker than the open fields and groves closer to home. The landscape of *Hunter's Sketches* is often closer to pastoral: even when Turgenev is reminding us of the miseries of Russian agriculture, it lurks as evidence of what isn't.[36] But pastoral is a middle ground that stands over against something wilder and less amenable to human culture: Turgenev's Polesye might seem to be this wilder place, where the narrator's encounter is not just with the peasant other but with the larger-than-human ground that holds men and women of all classes. The forest disrupts existing social relations between peasants and gentry—because Egor and Efrem know it better than the narrator does, because the forest recalibrates what knowledge and power are. And the forest brings with it those mythopoetic associations, a still-resonant forest of symbols, that make of this wild place a suggestive something more: Russian antiquity, thieves, the Time of Troubles, beehives, the *leshii* . . .

Forests outlive humans, often by centuries: if nothing else, Turgenev's story reminds us of this, with "places that are in no way different from the way they were in Riurik's time," suspending us sometime between 1857 and the ninth-century arrival of the Nordic prince who ruled Kievan Rus'. Coniferous trees do not seem to be subject to seasonality as we are, or even as the fruits of agriculture are; they seem unchanging in a way we aren't—the temporal counterpart of their physical enormity. They are bigger than us, and much older. Sensory complexity, too, is a natural feature of a sylvan landscape: trunks and underbrush complicate our sight lines, sound is muffled or indirect, smells may be generated by a huge number of different plants and animals, either present or vanished (like the smell of musk on a forest trail where moose or deer have been drinking before our arrival). Light, color, and temperature all shift as we move into and through a woodland; the clarity we associate with distance—an exterior vantage point—seems undermined; we are surrounded, and made to be aware of it.[37] It really is easier to get lost in a forest than a field. We can't see as far, and the light is indirect. So perhaps Turgenev takes us into the forest because it reminds us as no other place of the brevity and confusions of human life. There is a coincidence of what Anne Whiston Spirn calls "inherent qualities of landscape" and humanly invented meanings.[38]

What kind of story does Turgenev tell us? A story about anxiety and encounter, some tall tales, bits of forest lore and legend, a story about *seeing*. But what matters in this story most are its voices, which are multiple, layered, direct, and indirect: this story is surely the only place where Polesye peasants, Dante, and a Russian landowner who had studied Hegel could come together. It intertwines philosophy, natural history, ethnography, and does all this at a walking pace. The pace of the narrative is its own temporality (perhaps what Bakhtin would have called a chronotope), which records encounter, reminiscence, scraps of thought, moments of attention: Leslie O'Bell has suggested thinking of the *Hunter's Sketches* as poetic essays—and there is something akin to the essay in this "Journey" as well.[39] The story creates a space in which the temporality of trees and that of humans are brought together, along with all the resonances of Turgenev's prose—the narrator's memories but also the *cultural* memory represented by Dante or the *leshii* or the time when

Tatars and Lithuanians roamed these woods. What is brought together has something of the same confusion and complexity of the woods themselves, as sensory field and ecosystem.

In the story's final exchange Egor is looking back toward home, worrying about a dead cow. Like "Peasants Shooting Bear in the Polesye Oat Fields" his glance suggests tension, if not conflict, between farming and hunting, between cleared fields and the elemental world of the forest. The original work of the *zaseki* was to protect settled agricultural communities from nomadic raiders. Turgenev's biographer Boris Zaitsev suggests that the writer was, despite all his polish and Westernizing, still a "Russian wanderer." It is a resonant phrase, one that makes me think of this story in particular, with its wandering hunter and a restlessness—almost a nomadism—that is both physical and spiritual. Movement—what the narrator describes as "quiet and slowly paced animation"—is for the narrator part of the "changeless" law of nature. There is in all this a kind of intellectual restlessness as well, moving back and forth between the language of change and changelessness, pause and process. To hunt, for Turgenev, was to wander, but also to seek shelter, that *nochleg* fantasy of sleep and cream and comfort. Settlement offers protection, but it also demands someone's unceasing labor. "A passion for hunting's no thing for a *muzhik*, whoever takes up with a rifle is a bad farmer." There is a cost involved in trading settlement for wandering.

At the end of the story's opening passage, the narrator says that the specter of the vast forest drives humans to turn away, toward the small cares and labors of life, toward a world humans have themselves created, where they are "at home," where they still "dare to believe in their significance and power." Turgenev's great social novels might be seen as a turning away to a world "made by men"— although the greater horizon of cosmic time is never far away, and often frames his novels. In turning toward the great world of the forest, Russian writers and artists engage with many of the themes and dilemmas that Turgenev launches here: the complex moral and social geography of a society in which two cultures are mapped on one ground; the traditions of folk culture—both idealized and occasionally mocked or excoriated; the brutal legacies of property and class as they have fundamentally wounded humans' relationships to each other and to the natural world; religious and symbolic identities (both European and Russian) mapped onto space; the forest as locus of historical—often repressed—memory; the search for grounding—for *home*—in a culture that had come to be defined in terms of *homelessness*.[40] Turgenev's Polesye opens the territory up—in a narrative sense, at least, since he creates in his "Journey" a model of writing about nature that combines attentive observation, the inner voice of an educated man, and the symbolic legacy and oral tales of an indigenous tradition with its own relationship to the natural world. Turgenev's narrative registers an extremity of emotion, an understanding of the impulse toward nostalgia, and an intelligence that both engages and disengages from emotion in the process of discovering its truths. As a vehicle for reading the landscape—in its widest, most complex, sense—Turgenev's narrative seems a model of possibility.

2

Heart-Pine Russia

Mel'nikov-Pechersky and
the Sacred Geographies of the Woods

> Through this veil of forest
> Everything looks unfamiliar:
> As though an inaccessible land were arrayed
> in impenetrable mystery.
>
> —Antonii (A. P. Bochkov),
>   *Zelenetskii les: poema* (1850s)

> Are there still enchanted forests on the earth?
>
> —N. Boev, "Pictures of Forest Life" (1871)

READERS OF THE *RUSSIAN HERALD* in December 1871 would have discovered in its pages a series of narrative "pictures" of forest life by the now forgotten N. Boev. These sketches—presented as "episodes from an unfinished novella"—describe the adventures and encounters of an urbane, European-educated Russian by the name of El'novsky. His travels take him deep into northern Russian forests, into a landscape offered in symbolic counterpoint to the fractious, radical modernity of St. Petersburg. El'novsky—whose name derives from the Russian for "spruce"—returns to ancestral lands and encounters a Russian heartland filled with "real life" and "marvelous folk." As he is led into this world by an unnamed, bearded old man who emerges from behind a tree, the pictures Boev presents are a series of epiphanies intended for an urban audience, not unlike Mussorgsky's *Pictures at an Exhibition* (1874) in offering iconic vignettes of supposedly authentic Russian life, hidden away in a world both mysterious and uncannily familiar.[1]

While many of the central motifs of Boev's novella are ones we find in Turgenev's "Journey into Polesye"—the journey itself, a dense northern woodland, allusions to Russian history, a peasant who emerges from and disappears into the forest—"Pictures of Forest Life" is significantly shaped by a set of religious references that are largely absent in Turgenev's story. Boev's forest is associated with Orthodox monasticism and the hermit monks of medieval Russia—with Nil Sorskii and hesychasm (a spiritual discipline of silent, wordless prayer); a forest glade that resounds with the sounds of liturgical chanting; monastery "walls of unshakeable faith and temples of prayer"—*not*, Boev notes, the "proud" and blood-drenched castles of medieval Europe (or the penal colonies of the New World). In literal terms these woods are hundreds of miles northeast of Turgenev's Polesye; the symbolic geography of Boev's forest is farther still from the threatening woodland of Turgenev's 1857 story. The smoke of censers has replaced the veil of Isis.

Boev's story invites us into a woodland associated with authenticity and religious tradition. Turgenev's story, I have suggested, is all about *estrangement* from the world of the forest. Turgenev's allusions to a geography of habitation and healing are subtle and qualified: the dome of the village church is the barest of references to Orthodoxy, and what brings the hunter back to life is as much contact with nature (the emerald fly) as the kindness of a peasant. The symbolic resonance of these images is vastly more evident in a work like Boev's, which traffics wholeheartedly in a mythologizing of landscape that sees the salvation not just of individuals, but of Russia as a whole, in the return to a primordial, pure, Orthodox existence—miraculously intact in the vast woodlands of Russia's north. What I will be suggesting here is that works like Boev's—and particularly the epic *In the Forests*, by Pavel Mel'nikov-Pechersky—invite us into a landscape associated with religious tradition, ancient and unchanging mores, and an essential national identity that their authors view as critical to healing Russia's ills. These works (and a number of canvases by Russian artists in the same decades) suggest the existence of an intact *Rus'*—a stylized medieval appellation that refers to premodern Russia—providentially protected from modernity. These works trace a kind of *okolitsa* in the dense, boggy woodlands of northern Russia—the fencing of protective habitation and culture that encircled Turgenev's Sviatoe. The *okolitsa* boundary demands certain ritual obeisances when one passes through it: these authors and artists lead us into a world we might not find on our own, marking its difference with icons of sanctity, regional language, and antiquarian enthusiasms. As aesthetic objects and readerly experiences, these works always suggest that they—like the *okolitsa*—have a kind of incantatory power: those of us who enter them with a willing suspension of disbelief will be returned to life as miraculously as the fairy tale prince who drinks the living water.

This chapter will be primarily concerned with Mel'nikov-Pechersky's great epic, an encyclopedic novel of Old Believer communities, religious dissenters who had lived since the late seventeenth century in the northern forests beyond the Volga River. But we will also have occasion to look at some of the paintings that depict this sacred Russia in the woods, while later chapters will consider the work of writers and artists who followed in Mel'nikov's footsteps, invoking both a nostalgic mythology and a more modern skepticism about his landscapes. This body of work raises important and intriguing questions about symbolic associations with wilderness in Russia, and whether one can speak of a Russian *wilderness* in anything like the American sense of the word. These texts and paintings also raise compelling questions about the political valence of symbolic geographies of the sacred: while writers like Boev and Mel'nikov are patently conservative, espousing "retrospective utopias" that to some extent are Slavophile, the geography of righteous dissent and hidden endurance was also powerfully resonant for more progressive writers.[2] The afterlife of this symbolic geography in twentieth-century art and poetry has as often as not been associated with dissent and the survival of alternative discourses in the face of an oppressive state. The task of this chapter, however, is to investigate its nineteenth-century roots, and the various motifs and strategies that its progenitors employed.

* * *

JUST *WHERE* is this place called Holy Russia? Does it have actual, physical coordinates? Boev and Mel'nikov-Pechersky situate their sacred geographies on a map that is both literal and symbolic, in a region to the north of Nizhnii Novgorod, where the rivers Vetluga and Kerzhenets flow south into "Mother Volga"—but scholars have tended to view the *myth* of Holy Russia as aspatial, transcending any particular place or time. As David Bethea puts it in his study of apocalypse in modern Russian fiction, "Here was a spatial myth that existed no place." While Holy Russia might be associated with the folk, or with villages and monasteries, it became "something nonhistorical, transcendental."[3] "Holy Russia," according to Michael Cherniavsky, was "what remained, during the Time of Troubles, after Tsar and State and Church hierarchy were gone; it was the concentrated essence of Russia, visible when the form of Russia was destroyed. Hence, both on the transcendental and concrete levels Holy Russia was an absolute, immutable, because the land of salvation could not change except catastrophically, nor could the Russian essence change without losing itself."[4] As Bethea points out, however, Holy Russia came to be strongly associated with "preachers in the northern woods who burned themselves alive" in acts of protest at an ungodly tsar; or with "the underwater kingdom of Kitezh"—the righteous city of legend protected from invading Mongols by an act of divine intervention that submerged the city, intact, beneath the waters of a woodland lake. For Bethea, though, the idea of Kitezh becomes liberated from that particular tiny lake—Svetlyi Yar—where it supposedly lies.[5]

These authors point, quite compellingly, to a liberation of image from any particular place, a freeing that has arguably helped to make this imagery so powerful and long-lived. National iconographies may always work this way, in defiance of the impacts of historical change and modernization. "Amber waves of grain" may have been displaced by shopping malls, but they are nonetheless deeply and powerfully rooted in the American psyche. In Mel'nikov-Pechersky (and Boev), however, we see something rather different: an explicit, polemical association of one particular region with a sanctified wilderness, a *living, ancient Rus'* that draws on those images to which Bethea refers, but situates them geographically. These authors are intent not on divorcing image from place, but on reinforcing a literal link. They want their readers to believe that *this place is real*, and that even the most alienated of Petersburg intellectuals might find their way there. In doing this they attempt to reinvigorate a set of imaginative associations that have significant longevity in Russian culture (Cherniavsky dates the myth of Holy Russia to the dynastic crisis of the late sixteenth century), but which these authors make newly available to modern readers. In this they help to construct what Anthony Smith has called imaginative ethnoscapes, "endowing with a particular collective emotion a specific terrain. . . . What is at stake is the idea of an historic and poetic landscape, one imbued with the culture and history of a group, and vice versa, a group part of whose character is felt by themselves and outsiders to derive from the particular landscape they inhabit, and commemorated as such in verse and song."[6] As Smith so perceptively notes, these landscapes promise *emotional* security to those who engage with them; they are "models of nationality" created not primarily through ideas or policies but in images—with a resonance and longevity that outlasts changes of government and ideology (a point to which we shall return in considering Soviet and post-Soviet examples).

There is always the question, in these texts and images, of whether their authors are *creating* something or merely reinscribing what is already given. Does Mel'nikov create the riotous and holy backwoods of the trans-Volga, or does he merely recycle existing images and conventions? Are Boev, Mel'nikov, and Ivan Shishkin and Alexei Savrasov (two artists whose work we will look at shortly) *constructing* visions of a sacred backwoods or merely re-presenting icons that already exist? John Strickland, in a study of the Orthodox church's appeal to notions of Holy Russia and traditional identity, suggests that by the late nineteenth century, church authorities had "managed to gain influence in defining the symbols and imagery of Russian nationality."[7] This process of defining and recovery of national identity often involves returning to a preexisting well—the spring from which Egor draws in Turgenev's Polesye comes to mind. These texts, like the churchmen, or like tsarist bureaucrats who promoted particular versions of national identity, are returning to preexisting forms that they rearticulate for mass consumption. Like the traditions of icon painting and narratives of saints' lives that formed the backbone of Russia's traditional Christian culture, innovation takes place within the constraints of preexisting models. Vera Chaikovskaia has recently suggested that the endless return to "old models" in the interest of "new articulations" is at the base of Russian artistic consciousness.[8] The old gives birth to the new; the individual is embedded in potentially life-giving (or alternately stultifying) tradition. Context and reframing matter, but so does the appropriated convention. The evidence suggests that tradition can be as supportive of radical aesthetic innovation as it can be of mediocrity and the predictable.[9]

Part of what is at stake here is the fact that this landscape can be seen to already have stories associated with it. This presents a provocative contrast with our American sense of wilderness, long understood (wrongly) to be a blank page, a land without any history of human action. The associations of wilderness and demonic formlessness, or of Edenic abundance, that Puritans brought with them from Europe were projected wholesale onto this unknown landscape; native people's stories that had been associated with the landscape were displaced by immigrant cultures.[10] This is arguably different from what is found in these narratives and images of Russia's northern woods, in which authors present themselves as gatherers of traditional culture. Someone like Boev resuscitates references to monastic tradition that date back to the fourteenth century. Mel'nikov introduces legends that have storied these woods from the late seventeenth century (in the case of Old Believer traditions), and from centuries earlier, in his recounting of creation myths and agrarian rites associated with pre-Christian practice. Boev and his contemporary Pavel Zasodimskii both give us accounts of holy hermits and their activities among the non-Russian populations of the north, tales of benign conversions and the establishment of monastic institutions.[11] Artists paint monasteries deep in the woods, and images of Sergius of Radonezh, the fourteenth-century saint credited with the renaissance of Orthodox culture in the woodlands to the northeast of Moscow. There is never any question that this woodland could be a blank page; it is already deeply overlaid with stories—*zhitiia* (saints' lives), *predaniia* (legends), *letopisi* (chronicles), as well as folktales and oral poetry. This is a place of long settlement and long-embedded culture—in the sense that Russian peasants, Old Believers, and non-Russian populations have inhabited these forests for centuries.[12] The polemic intent of much of this writing is to remind readers of these roots and recall them to ways of living associated with these places.

Is this, then, wilderness? The American associations of wilderness and the absence of human shaping or activity are by now so fundamentally embedded in our sense of the word that we will need to pause and reflect before we answer (even though revisionist historians are now at pains to remind us that the world to which European settlers came in the fifteenth century had been intentionally shaped by native peoples for centuries[13]). *Wilderness*, of course, has strong religious connotations in the Judeo-Christian tradition, that body of associations that the Puritans brought with them to the New World. Our modern, environmentally charged sense of the word denotes a place in which there is neither agriculture or human habitation, a meaning still resonant with religious notions of fear and trembling or an aesthetic of "delightful horror."[14] That the vast tracts of northern Russian forestland are sparsely populated is never in question in these texts, but nor are they places that are without traces of human activity—witness the various stories and forms of legend I have just referred to. The Russian word most frequently used here is not the calque "*dikie mesta*" (wild places), but *pustynia*—which can mean both "place of little settlement" and "place of holy retreat."[15] These are places that are "empty" (*pustye*) of humans, but also places in which the monk or hermit can emulate Christ's sojourn in the wilderness, learning deep humility and eschewing the vanities of the world. As the monastic author of our epigraph puts it, "Country of silence! From hence / The passage is easier to the grave."

And what is the relationship between *nature* and the spiritual strivings of the monk or religious dissenter? Is this—as the Puritans, true to Gospel, maintained—a place of demonic temptation (Matthew 4)? Is man given dominion over a fallen earth, and charged by God to "replenish the earth and subdue it" (Genesis 1:28)?[16] The relationship of religious traditions to humans' attitudes toward nature has been a central question in environmental ethics in the last decades; it is also an implicit concern of Mel'nikov and Boev, with their imaginations of religion in a blessed, fertile landscape—and thus not irrelevant in a consideration of just what "wilderness" might mean in Russia. In an influential (if now broadly contested) 1967 essay, Lynn White suggested that the Judeo-Christian tradition bore primary responsibility for much of the modern world's misuse and destruction of the natural world.[17] For White, Christianity (which for him means Western, largely Protestant Christianity) is distinguished by an attitude of hostility toward the natural world and a suspicion of anything that smacks of animism or pantheistic association of divinity and place. Creation, in this account, cannot be blessed, and is always already fallen, a vehicle of damnation that humans must struggle to overcome. Does Russian Orthodoxy offer any particular antidote to this narrative of hostility and alienation? The artists and writers we are about to turn to suggest a very different affective and symbolic relationship; whether *official* Orthodoxy (as opposed to artists involved in myth-making) offers resources for a more ecological nature theology is to date an open question. Tatyana Goricheva suggests in a recent essay that "Russia did not fear the *pustynia*—that is, places not frequented by men. While western civilization experienced horror in the face of the 'wilderness,' in Russia they loved the emptiness, entering with it into a harmonious dialogue."[18] For now we turn to the artistic imagination, rather than to theological discourse—the locus in any case of Russia's most fecund religious imagination. What is the "Holy Russian Forest" in the works of these artists and writers?

* * *

"[IN THESE WOODS] there are neither insurmountable cliffs or rocky massifs. The birch and the pine slumber peacefully in these impassable forests, which muffle no sounds of a hunter's horn; shepherds, fishermen and trappers live peacefully, knowing no greed, killing only what is necessary; and the clumsy bear runs from man until he's wounded. . . . The forest river, full of fish, sounds bright and fast between its high banks. Villages and farmyards hewn from the powerful, ancient forest cluster peacefully along its banks. But already there rise white stone walls—and these aren't an adornment or buttressing of dwellings; they are walls of the unshakeable fortress of faith, temples of prayer—the golden domes of Russian monasteries."[19]

The landscape of N. Boev's quintessential Russia is an Edenic place of peaceful coexistence of man and beast, and of humans among themselves, infused by a kind of primitive, cosmic communitarianism (*sobornost'*) with the monastery at its center. Boev's contrast of monasteries with what *isn't* here (Gothic castles with turrets and chains and a general association with blood and predatory birds) is stock-in-trade Slavophile rhetoric, and recalls Ivan Kireevsky's polemical contrast of European feudalism, castles, and class conflict with the "solitary silence of [Russian] monastic cells."[20] Even the process of Christianization is for Boev bloodless, a matter of persuasion and peaceful surrender rather than violence: when monks come into the northern woods in the late fourteenth century they find a "peaceful, half-wild population" (as opposed to the *completely* wild population that European convict settlers found in the Americas). This half-wild population worships a great birch tree, but when the missionary cuts it down he does not attempt to defend himself from the "enraged heathen"—and they are immediately and miraculously won over by his act of nonviolent submission. Five centuries later the monastery he founded is a refuge in this "wild forest place"—"closely surrounded by its *ancient protectors* from wind and storm—old birches and pines."[21] The trees that once were worshipped have become the protectors of this holy place—and, one suspects, are still part of the aura of sanctity that extends beyond the monastery walls out into the surrounding woodland. What is more holy here, the trees or the monastery walls? Boev's rhetoric doesn't force us to make a choice.

Russian artists of the 1870s and 1880s were intent, as Chris Ely has argued, on creating images of Russia that would represent the distinct if humble contours and emotional appeal of their homeland. What had initially been an anxious recognition of Russia's *lack* of the kind of dramatic landscapes that Europe apparently offered (those landscapes that inspired sublime and horrified *frissons*) shifted in this generation to a sense of deep affection for what the poet Fedor Tiutchev called "this meager nature"—"the whole character of which consists, so to speak, in its lack of character." There is a sense in these artists and their advocates of discovering in the most humble and unassuming of landscapes something "sweet and dear" (as Dostoevsky put it)—something deeply Russian—something available to the Russian eye and heart that would seem unlovable to the foreigner.[22]

The "discovery" of distinctively *Russian* landscapes is obviously at work in a piece of prose like Boev's. The kind of nationalistic appeal he makes to a spiritualized landscape is also palpable in the canvases of various artists from the same period. These paintings play on some of the same associations we find in Boev—if more subtly, and with more compelling (and sometimes critical) understatement. We find in these canvases a process of sacralization that draws on references to the institutional church—monasteries and bell towers—but also alludes to folk Orthodoxy, and perhaps even to those "half-wild" venerations of trees the fourteenth-century missionary thought he had gotten rid of. They demonstrate, in other words, a refashioning of iconic references into a new symbolic geography, a forest landscape that melds the palpable, physical beauty of forest scenes with a sense of the sacred—embodied sometimes in a human figure, sometimes in a structure, sometimes in a natural place venerated as holy.

The work of Ivan Shishkin (1832–98) has become virtually synonymous with Russia's *dremuchie lesa*—impenetrable forests. Almost all of Shishkin's canvases from the 1870s show forests that are both vast and forbidding (in a literal sense: one searches for a way *out of* the dense growth of trees and underbrush), but they also not infrequently show evidence of human activity, activity usually dwarfed by the scale of the forest. These canvases imply that humans are simply incapable of making any real inroads on the woods: the forest is simply too vast, too huge, too insurmountable. *Thickets* (1881) gives us a woodland in which one is at pains to find evidence of human presence: the viewer's eye moves from the lush moss on a rocky foreground into the impenetrable darkness of a pinewood. This landscape seems genuinely *untouched*, and more than a little forbidding. This is Turgenev's Polesye (or Caspar David Friedrich's vast wood), without the human figure.

Other canvases, however, remind us of human activity: *The Felled Tree* (*Srublennoe derevo*, 1875), *Hives in the Forest* (*Paseka v lesu*, 1876), *Twilight, Sunset* (*Sumerki, Zakhod solntsa*, 1874), and *The Coniferous Wood* (*Khvoinii les*, 1873) all feature felled trees or tree stumps, some the work of beavers, within dense, healthy woodlands. The primary landscape is visited (and used) by humans, but not fundamentally transformed. For a sense of contrasting scale of human impact, we might look at American artists' paintings of the same period

Ivan Shishkin, Thickets *(1881). Tretyakov Gallery, Moscow. Image copyright Lebrecht Music & Arts.*

Ivan Shishkin, The Coniferous Wood *(1873). Reproduced with permission of the State Art Museum of Belarus, Minsk.*

in which the clearing activity of farmers heading west is represented: Sanford Robinson Gifford's *Hunter Mountain, Twilight* (1866) shows a human figure and horses who are tiny, but they are surrounded by a considerable swath of cleared land, where the felling of trees has pushed back the forest and established human habitation. There is nothing in Shishkin's canvases to suggest similar impacts or domestication in the Russian forests.[23]

Human *figures*—as opposed to evidence of previous human activity—are in fact relatively rare in Shishkin's paintings: *Countess Mordvinova's Forest, Petergof* (1891) is a famous exception, in which a seemingly ancient, bearded old man in peasant dress looks out at us from the base of a massive pine. The image suggests a "spirit of place"—perhaps the *leshii*-"master" of the forest who in some accounts is also its protector; or, less fantastically, simply an ancient soul who has grown as deeply into this ground as the trees themselves.[24] The shimmer of light from the top center of the painting—light filtering through pine boughs—gives a sense of the sacred, but in a way divorced from any explicit cultural or ecclesiastical reference. This kind of virtually pantheistic aura recalls what scholars have referred to as American painters' vision of a "natural church" in which the hand of God is visible within a sublime wilderness.[25]

Shishkin's *Holy Spring near Yelabuga* (1886), however, *does* refer explicitly to Russian religious culture(s)—both in its title and visual iconography: the foreground shows a largely dry streambed, with eroded banks, evidence of a felled tree, and two modest icon stands—small shrines that mark this place as blessed. A boy on horseback (judging by his clothes, a peasant boy) faces away from us as his horse drinks from a trough in the streambed; a male figure moves away in the middle ground of the painting, where massive pines part to create a footpath toward a village in the distance. What we see in that distance are low roofs and the bell tower of a church. The painting thus brings together on different ends of one axis both "official"—ecclesial—Orthodoxy, and "popular" religion with the forest spring. The trickle of water here is meager; in other canvases by Shishkin there is a more mystical rendering of woodland springs (without accompanying icons to mark them as officially holy), in which pools of water become repositories of light—often in contrast to the great surrounding darkness of the forest.[26]

The composition of Shishkin's *Holy Spring near Yelabuga* bears comparing with a painting from a decade earlier by Alexei Savrasov (1830–97), *At the Monastery Gates* (1875).[27] In Savrasov's canvas, our attention is drawn to the center of the painting, with its entryway (in a kind of *okolitsa*) at the top of a long flight of stairs. In the foreground we see a body of water, what seems to be a small pond, while in the distance—just behind a grove of tall birches and pines—we glimpse two bell towers. As in Shishkin's painting, our eye travels from the near ground, with its pool of water, into the distance and its church

structure. In each painting there is a parting of the woods—opening up to allow access to the circle of religiously marked space. The opening is more generous in Shishkin—we see his church better than we do Savrasov's, but it feels much farther away. And while the path to the church leads through a patch of deep darkness in Shishkin, Savrasov's canvas is suffused with light: the deep, watery light of the foreground pool, the bright, slender trunks of the birches on either side of the monastery gate, and the arc of a rainbow in the right background— as though the path that begins in the left foreground of the painting moves through the monastery walls into further regions of light and transfiguration, in a place that Savrasov can allude to but cannot represent.

Both these paintings exploit vocabularies of faith and practice not unlike what we found in Boev: the holy spring, the tiny figure, the wooded landscape, the domes of Orthodoxy are all aspects of what Chris Ely has called a "uniquely Russian" model of picturesque scenery, emphasizing monastic architecture as

Sanford Robinson Gifford, Hunter Mountain, Twilight *(1866). Terra Foundation for American Art, Chicago / Art Resource, NY.*

key to the "essence of Russianness."[28] Shishkin's canvas, though, is critical—showing us just how remote the realities of Russian life and poverty are from that picturesque ideal; no such critique is evident in Savrasov's over-the-rainbow sentiment. Shishkin's holy spring is almost dry—and it is a very long way back to the village with its church. The towering, robust pines in the middle distance are the painting's only evidence of health. The streambed is heavily eroded, and the horse the boy is on looks perilously sunken in the ribs. The sense of hope and promised transformation that we find in Savrasov (or in other canvases of Shishkin's, where the forest pools are deeper and more filled with light) is starkly absent here. While Savrasov works in uncomplicated fashion to "sanctify Russian space," as Ely puts it, Shishkin puts a similar iconography to critical use.[29]

These iconic landscapes provide an appropriate ground from which to shift our discussion to Mel'nikov-Pechersky's *In the Forests*—a work that more than any other in the nineteenth century celebrated the ecstatic, life-affirming energies

Ivan Shishkin, Countess Mordvinova's Forest, Petergof *(1891). Tretyakov Gallery, Moscow. Scala / Art Resource, NY.*

of the "slumbering forests" of Russia's north, with a sentiment much closer to Savrasov or the Shishkin of *Thickets.* Mel'nikov's epic account of folkways and religious dissenters enjoyed considerable popularity in the final decades of the nineteenth century, and was championed in the mid-twentieth century by Soviet literary scholars interested in its mixture of folk tradition and patriarchal religiosity in a region "beyond the reach of serfdom and bureaucracy."[30] Their interest was linked to shifting constructions of identity in post–World War II, post-Stalinist Russia, in which Russian nationalism—strongly linked to cults of nature and the village—increasingly displaced Marxist-Leninism.[31] For late nineteenth-century artists, writers, and composers, Mel'nikov's epic evoked a rich, intact culture that seemed still to exist within the depths of these remote but Russian forests; it suggested a world in which time stood still, a world permeated by legend and tale, a world in which the very language people spoke was rich with the syncretic agrarian symbolism of conservative Orthodoxy and still more ancient, pagan practice.

All of this gets jumbled into the roisterous, opinionated, gargantuan world of Mel'nikov's trans-Volga forests. It is a work that offers up myth and legend,

Ivan Shishkin, "Holy Spring" near Yelabuga (1886). Reproduced with permission of Kiev National Museum of Russian Art.

repackaging the scholarly antiquarianism of nineteenth-century folklorists, Slavophiles, and lexicographers—making of it something that would stir the imagination of fin de siècle artists as they turned to Old Russia for sources of visual and linguistic innovation. There is in Mel'nikov-Pechersky much

Alexei Savrasov, At the Monastery Gates *(1875). Reproduced with permission of the State Russian Museum, St. Petersburg.*

mythologizing, considerable ethnography, set pieces of nature writing that are sometimes delightful—and motifs of plot and character that readers of better-known Russian novels will recognize as familiar.[32] My intention in what follows is to be a tracker in these woods, to show the reader what we might see there. As with any close reading of a text (particularly with a novel as vast as this one), these are patterns of language and intent that strike me as important—not arbitrary to any compelling reading of the novel, but which might be extended and replaced by other readers with different questions. What interests us here is the geography of what Mel'nikov sometimes calls "Heart-Pine Rus'" (*kondovaia Rus'*)—that hard center wood that is old, close-grained, and virtually indestructible. His own novel is a dense, multibranched labor of love. What—we shall ask—is the geography of Mel'nikov's heartland, and what are the emotional and symbolic contours of this place in which territory and memory come together?

* * *

A FEW WORDS, to begin, about Mel'nikov-Pechersky, his popularity, and his controversial status within his own lifetime. Pavel Mel'nikov (1818–83), who wrote under the pen name Andrei Pechersky, spent most of his life in the middle Volga region, some 250 miles east of Moscow. Born in Nizhnii Novgorod, a flourishing market center situated at the confluence of the Oka and Volga rivers, he grew up in a tiny town in the forests he would later describe, in an atmosphere of "trusting patriotism," schooled at home by a French tutor; he later enrolled at Kazan University, where the mathematician Lobachevsky was rector (and where, just a few years later, the young Leo Tolstoy would enroll as a desultory student).[33] Mel'nikov's interests at university included the languages of "the east"—Persian, Mongolian, and Arabic—and a growing fascination with all things Russian, from carved and lacquered oaken tables to the peasant dress that contemporary Slavophiles affected.[34] Incautiously expressed opinions at a student gathering earned Mel'nikov an unpleasant encounter with tsarist police; a trip abroad was canceled, replaced by an assignment as village teacher in a remote village.[35] Such indiscretions didn't prevent Mel'nikov's entry into government service after completing his degree at Kazan; he was also to work as a journalist off and on throughout the 1850s.

The focus of Mel'nikov's work as a state official was Old Belief—religious dissenters who had separated from the official Orthodox church in the late seventeenth century in a dispute over reform of both liturgy and sacred texts, and state control of religious practice. By the mid-nineteenth century there were untold thousands of Old Believers living in scattered communities throughout the woodlands north of the Volga.[36] In his work as a tsarist bureaucrat, Mel'nikov was involved in the production of data and reports that were part of efforts to monitor and convert these religious dissenters. In 1854 he produced a major official report on the state of Old Belief in the trans-Volga region (the forested area north of the Volga that serves as the locus for *In the Forests*).[37] His work in preparation for this report involved extensive travel throughout the region that would later be at the center of his fictional work. In addition to being objects of unwanted attentions by the state, Old Believers were throughout the nineteenth century the focus of discussion and appropriation by various camps within the intelligentsia: for the radical intelligentsia in the reform decades of midcentury, Old Believers represented "Protestant" opposition and potential; for conservatives, on the other hand, Old Believers distilled Old Russian virtue and resistance to the West. Mel'nikov's own attitudes toward Old Belief were complex and, in the eyes of some, fundamentally hypocritical, since his measured admiration for community virtues was tempered (or contradicted) by his official destruction of Old Believer communities. Mel'nikov's bureaucratic work fundamentally discredited Mel'nikov's fiction in the eyes of many progressive intellectuals: as Vladimir Korolenko was to put it twenty years after publication of *In the Forests*, Mel'nikov "described [Old Believer communities] wonderfully—but he destroyed them even better."[38]

Bureaucratic work alone would certainly never have sufficed for the creation of Mel'nikov's enthusiastic epics of Old Believer life. Along with his official work, Mel'nikov began the antiquarian and ethnographic research that was to lay the foundation for his narratives of regional culture and history. A voracious collector of manuscripts and books connected with the seventeenth-century Schism within Orthodoxy (the "*raskol*") that gave birth to Old Belief, Mel'nikov traveled extensively throughout the middle Volga region, gathering materials and listening to stories.[39] He also befriended and corresponded with some of the leading historians and folklorists of his day—Vladimir Dal', the compiler of Russia's first modern dictionary, itself a marvelous compendium of regional usage, was a friend and mentor, as was the conservative historian Mikhail Pogodin.[40]

In the Forests was first published in installments during the years 1871–75, in the *Russian Herald*—the same journal that published *Anna Karenina* beginning in 1875, and, by the end of the decade, the opening sections of *The Brothers Karamazov*.[41] There were occasional hiatuses in the novel's publication, perhaps related to Mel'nikov's notorious inability to stop editing what he had written.[42] Boev's "Pictures of Forest Life" appeared in the *Russian Herald* in one of those months when there was nothing from Mel'nikov—leading one to wonder whether the editors didn't see it as a stopgap offering to appease readers' hunger for the Old Believer epic.[43]

For the generation that succeeded Mel'nikov's own, *In the Forests* was an unparalleled imaginative compendium of Old Russian lore and legend. Andrei Remizov, whose experiments in modernist reframing of traditional genres have led one scholar to compare him to James Joyce, said that Mel'nikov's novel had "opened his eyes" as a writer; the older author's exuberant use of folk voice and oral genres anticipates (within a still primarily realist aesthetic) Remizov's own experimental articulation of tradition. Remizov's *Sunwise* (1907) is in fact a whimsical stylization of the traditional Russian folk calendar that structures Mel'nikov's novel.[44] Mikhail Nesterov, another fin de siècle artist specifically interested in medieval Russia and Russian Orthodoxy, began his professional artist's life with illustrations for the cheap weeklies that began to appear in Russia in the 1880s, work that included scenes from *In the Forests*. Nesterov returned to the novel in the late 1890s with his *Taking the Veil*—which he insisted was "inspired" by but not an illustration of the work.[45] Nesterov, along with his fellow art students Levitan and Arkhipov, had "read and reread" the novel in the early 1880s, an eager enthusiasm that seems to have been shared by various artists in an age that went in search of Old Russia, the folk, multiple traditions associated with official and nonconformist Orthodoxy, and mystical versions of Russian identity.[46] John Bowlt sees in this search for roots a deep, troubled disaffection with the materialism and radicalism of late Imperial life; these journeys into Russian antiquity and a Russian folk interior were also quests for aesthetic resources that gave birth to the avant-garde. Thus Mel'nikov's epics and his encyclopedic knowledge of sectarians formed an important source of creative potential for Andrei Bely in his symbolist explorations of Russian religious culture, and Rimsky-Korsakov's musical legend of a mystically delivered Rus' draws on Mel'nikov's well in producing a synthetic, symbolist treatment of sacred geography.[47]

What is striking is how fertile the novel seems to have been for artists of Russia's Silver Age—and how notable in contrast is the oblivion into which the novel fell in subsequent years. It gets dismissed in D. M. Mirsky's 1926 *History of Russian Literature* as "not really first-class literature . . . disfigured by a meretricious pseudo-poetic style, imitative of folklore."[48] Dmitrii Chizhevskii gives it a few pages in his history of nineteenth-century literature—again noting Mel'nikov's language (more positively than Mirsky)—but calling his folkloric sources "dubious."[49] Hugh McLean, in his biography of Nikolai Leskov (who regarded Mel'nikov as his mentor in all things relating to Old Belief), refers to Mel'nikov's "bulky ethnographic novels . . . that try to get the maximum artistic mileage out of Russian *couleur locale*."[50] American scholars who have attempted to give the novel its due must labor against their readers' ignorance of the work they are discussing. Russian scholars have proved more receptive; two editions of the novel have appeared in recent years, one highbrow and one more popular. The cover of the first is a restrained green with Old Russian script declaring the title and author; the cover illustration on the second shows the lush bare shoulders and neck of a young woman with demurely downcast eyes, all against the background of—what else?—a pine tree and a wooden church.[51]

Thomas Hoisington and Veronica Shapovalov, whose critical work on Mel'nikov's novel has been enormously helpful to me, both insist on the importance of *place* and setting for the novel. For Hoisington, *In the Forests* is essentially a *romance*—"a transition form, standing somewhere between the idealism of the epic and the realism of the novel"—an "immense" work, which, like the companion volume published by Mel'nikov in the last years of his life (*On the Hills*), is distinguished by "*setting*, the *byt* [daily life and mores] of Trans-Volga merchants and religious sectarians, the description of a social, economic, and ethical structure quite unlike that found in the works of other nineteenth-century Russian writers." For Hoisington, setting is at least as important to the novel as the "underlying philosophy or message."[52] As Shapovalov reminds us, one of the points of origin of the novel was Mel'nikov's promise to "write down his stories of 'how people live in the woods, in the Transvolga region.'"[53] Characterized by Lydia Lotman as an "ethnographic novel," *In the Forests* weaves together "the life and myth"—*byt i mif*—of Russian folklife of the mid-nineteenth century.[54]

What these accounts don't say much about—perhaps because it seems too obvious to make explicit—is the *natural* setting of the work. "Nature" announces itself, however, both in the title and on virtually every page of *In the Forests*, and is so deeply bound up with lives, traditions, myths, and legends that one cannot really speak of the novel's overarching themes without thinking about woods, and paths, and seasonality, and agrarian proverbs, and boggy land you can easily get lost in. Mel'nikov's Russia is set deeply and inextricably into a magnificent and evocative cosmos—understood as both Christian and older-than-Christian, or pagan. In both cases, God (or the gods) work within and through a specifically, richly evoked natural world.

So just what *is* the geography of this cosmos—a word that might encompass both politics and religion? How does Mel'nikov imagine and construct this world? Where *are we*, when we read the novel? It is a novel written for urbanized literate Russians, which transported them *somewhere else*—an elsewhere they could situate on a map, but which they could only really travel to in his tale. In the pages that follow I explore the central features of Mel'nikov's geography, delineating its overarching structure (the trunk and major branches, if you will) and then suggesting some of the finer motifs and patterns of language that make this such a rich, often quite delightful, and emotionally surprising work. Some of Mel'nikov's pages are lovely and affecting (the death of a heroine whose soul is borne on in music and birdsong; descriptions of the forest at dawn; the sheer abundance and exuberance of his telling of local legend and lore). Some of them are laborious and obscure (the dizzying varieties of Old Belief and their mutual hostilities)—but these latter are in point of fact quite few. What captivates, though, is the total picture—a kind of cosmic, syncretic geography. This account will begin by looking at the overarching mythologies that give the novel its temporal and imaginative structure; we shall then explore some of the novel's central motifs, its own mythos of Heart-

Pine Russia: the woodland as refuge, as unchanging, as site of healing, and of a particular (and peculiar) language that Mel'nikov celebrates—and whose virtues he polemically defends. This local language is linked to the rich varieties of *song* in the novel, song that often seems to flow out of birds' mouths into young women's souls and voices. Finally, we shall consider how throughout the novel Mel'nikov stakes his claim to this *region* as the antidote to everything connected to the capital cities (echoing Boev's pointed contrast of "here" to "there"—Petersburg—with its scribbling intellectuals and pale, translated imitations of life). In this sense Mel'nikov's novel invites us to retrace the steps of Turgenev's alienated intellectual, beyond the *okolitsa*, into a heartland that might heal us with its rich culture and its promise of living water, and living speech.

* * *

THE STRUCTURE of *In the Forests* rests on two foundational myths, each of which is retold in the novel, providing a consistent frame of reference for the characters, the narrator, and for us as readers. The first of these is connected to the legendary city of Kitezh and Old Believers' accounts of how they came to the trans-Volga forests. This situates the action of the novel in the context of a sacred history of deliverance from oppression. But while this is mentioned first (on the first page of the novel), it would be misleading to say that it somehow has precedence over the other structuring myth of the novel, associated not with Old Belief but with the antecedent legends of this landscape. This myth belongs to "tipsy Yar"—the pre-Christian sky god Yarilo, whose cosmic eros informs the novel in myriad ways. The Yarilo legend gets introduced wholesale at the beginning of part 4, as the "tale of our forefathers about how the god Yarilo came to love Moist Mother Earth and how she gave birth to all creatures on earth."[55] The Kitezh legend is repeatedly presented in brief, as a refrain in the narrator's accounts of place, and in pilgrims' voices during a midsummer pilgrimage, when the bells and lights of the miraculously immersed, righteous city are supposedly audible (and visible) to the pure in heart (2:276–77, 288–89). Prior to that, Mel'nikov includes two extended tellings of the Old Believers' flight into the wilderness: led by a hovering icon, monks fleeing the siege of the Solovki monastery in the seventeenth century were brought through dense woodland to the place that would become their sacred refuge (1:298–99, 547). Just as the lake Svetlyi Yar hides the righteous city until the end of time, Old Believers wait out the reign of injustice in their hidden forest communities. The Yarilo legend is what Laurence Coupe has called a "myth of creation"; the Old Believer stories present what Coupe calls a "myth of deliverance." Both legends enter into and shape the narrative in various ways relating to temporality, place, character, and language.[56]

The sheer variety of forms and sources that Mel'nikov uses to present these tales—and to show their impact on his characters' lives—gives the novel what Thomas Hoisington has aptly called its "mosaic" character (not, I think, the "lack of compositional unity" that one Russian commentator complained of).[57] As a lifelong amateur historian and folklorist, Mel'nikov used a range of sources in creating this mosaic of tale and legend. The question of whether or not he may have done fieldwork himself long remained an open one: Georgii Vinogradov, in a 1936 article, argued that Mel'nikov's primary sources were written, and that the author himself had neither the temperament of a field ethnographer, nor (given his background as a tsarist bureaucrat) a reputation in Old Believer communities that would have made him welcome there.[58] Subsequent scholars have challenged Vinogradov, in part on the basis of new archival evidence, suggesting that Mel'nikov did in fact collect materials that went into the novel, and could well have observed some of the rituals he described.[59] No one would dispute, however, that the central and major source for the Yarilo myths (and for much of the assorted plant and place lore in the novel) was Alexander Afanas'ev's *The Slavs' Poetic Views of Nature*, published in Moscow in the late 1860s. While later scholars have been critical of Afanas'ev's mythological bent (a tendency to explain all current tales or practices as relics of ancient myth), this massive codex became foundational for Russians' sense of their past, and one can certainly read it for its *detail* rather than its argument. Afanas'ev's compilation of Russian folktales is still the childhood reading of Russians (and even some Americans[60]), and the "rich and diverse material" presented in *The Slavs' Poetic Views of Nature* filtered into broad consciousness through popular editions and textbooks.[61] As Vinogradov put it, Afanas'ev's rich lode of "rituals, the songs that accompanied them, legends, cosmogenic tales, magical poetry, etc., etc." was just what Mel'nikov needed for his epic novel.[62] It also seems likely that Mel'nikov was just what *Afanas'ev* needed to bring his voluminous presentation into more vivid imaginative form. The novel draws the language and tales in Afanas'ev's volumes—along with folk songs collected by Petr Kireevsky, versions of the Kitezh legend that had been published in the 1840s, and materials on folk holidays and superstitious rituals—into its memorable account of the "fermenting mix" (*zakvaska*) of peoples and place.[63]

The retelling of these foundational myths often frames sections of the novel. I have mentioned that the Kitezh myth is alluded to at the beginning of part 1; part 2 opens with an account of the mix of populations in the trans-Volga forests, and then introduces virtually verbatim the legend of how the Old Believers came to settle there. That legend is given a brief reprise near the close of part 2, which ends with a description of preparations for the coming holiday of Troitsyn Den' (Trinity Sunday). Women cut birch fronds to decorate a chapel (*not*, one of them insists, aspen or mountain ash, which are too "bitter, not sanctified"), and Mel'nikov informs us in a footnote that "both Old Believers and the Trans Volga common folk" believe you must cry for your sins during the Trinity vespers, enough so that each leaf and bud in your hands has at least one teardrop fall on it.[64] For Mel'nikov these holidays often disclose the energies of Yarilo, even before his legend is introduced in full. Part 2 ends with an exclamatory description of "tipsy Yar's" power ("Yarilo is walking among the folk, sparking passion and clouding heads")—and the opening of part 3 picks up right where the festivities had left off. This interweaving of what are, in essence, competing (or companion) myths—one Christian, the other pagan—establishes the "geo-cosmic" scale of the novel, threading it together with details of time, place, and plot.[65]

But are the myths *competing* or *companion*? The question has a long and vexed history within the study of Russian culture, where notions of what was long called double faith (*dvoeverie*) for years informed understandings of folk religion. By this understanding, the Russian peasantry had been nominally Christianized but continued to adhere to what were in effect pagan beliefs and practices—everything from agrarian rituals to house spirits and animist veneration of stones and trees. Afanas'ev himself certainly adhered to this understanding of folk belief, which was scholarly orthodoxy for his day.[66] Mel'nikov on the face of it seems to understand Old Believer Christianity as fundamentally *hostile* to the rituals and practices aligned with the "Yarilo" festivities and their remnants of pagan belief. Numerous times he reminds us that Old Believer elders forbid observation of folk rituals they regard as non-Christian (young girls want to "feed the house spirit" on the feast day of Efrem Sirin, to the horror of the older women).[67] After his exuberant telling of the Yarilo legends that were played out in the midsummer ritual of Kupalo, Mel'nikov is blunt: "These days folk don't burn Kupalo bonfires in the woods beyond the Volga. The Old Russian ritual has finally been destroyed" (2:275)—and then goes on to relate how Old Believer observation of midsummer at Svetlyi Yar has replaced pagan custom with Christian pilgrimage.

But the reality, even of Mel'nikov's novel, is vastly more complex—and doesn't suggest that the old (pagan) ways have been so completely obliterated.[68] Nor does Mel'nikov always suggest that they *are* pagan—since his descriptions of various syncretic holidays and rituals tend to use a blended language of cosmic, animist Christianity. "Among the Russian folk, especially in the backwoods, along with Christian beliefs and strict church rituals they hold firm to old rituals, and carefully preserve remants of belief in the joyful old Russian gods" (1:441). This is a world of both/and, not either/or. Old Believer girls break into the "inebriating song of Radunitsa [a folk holiday that coincides with Easter and celebrates the rebirth of Moist Mother Earth and the rising from the dead of the ancestors] breaking from the turbulent heart of Tipsy Yar throughout the fields and woods of Rus'" (1:467–68). An Old Believer elder falls into convulsions of grief at the sudden appearance of her old lover ("What kind of trial was this, what kind of demon was wracking Manefa's blood? It was Joyous Yar—his charms" 1:457); and an elderly Old Believer peasant tells a young man how to cure his anxiety with "nests" of birch branches wound tight by the wind—the "breath of God." All these suggest a world of human practice and emotion in which the line between the joyous god in the blood and the divine God who breathes upon and through the waters is not nearly as closely policed as some of Mel'nikov's church elders might hope. For Mel'nikov in any case there is a sense it which it doesn't matter; he is not after consistency but a faithfulness to his vision of the *zakvaska*—the ferment and mixing—of the backwoods. This is "ageless, heart-pine Rus'. . . . It stands there from ancient times, undefiled,—the way it was in our great-grandfathers' time, that's how it's been kept to our day. It's a kindhearted land, though it looks with anger on the stranger" (1:5). And it is a land in which Yarilo and Kitezh *both* inform a geography of the sacred.

The Yarilo legend that Mel'nikov tells is a fundamentally erotic conception of creation, one in which the cosmos pulses with irrepressible, life-giving energy. Among other things the story explains seasonality and the sun god's "abandonment" of his beloved earth: Moist Mother Earth begs Yarilo to take pity, "at least . . . on your favorite child, who answered your thunderous speeches with knowing words and winged speech. . . . He is naked and weak—he will be the first to die, when you deprive us of warmth and light" (2:271). In response to the mother's pleading, Yarilo grants humans the gift of fire. The father then departs, leaving his beloved Earth shrouded in winter snows. "Thus thought the old Russian folk about the passage from summer into winter, and about the origin of fire." And thus—according to Mel'nikov, following Afanas'ev—there began the series of celebrations associated with Yarilo/Kupalo, midsummer festivities of fire and fecundity, with their erotic license and legends of a time of unimpeded communication among all creation.

The calendrical structure of the novel as a whole is related to this account of the seasons, as the analogy of cosmic with earthly lives creates links between different orders of erotic encounter. The novel begins with Epiphany and moves through the traditional calendar to the feast day of the Kazan mother of God, weaving in an enormous body of legend and ritual calendar poetry that has grown up around agrarian and liturgical practice. Russia's traditional calendar interweaves a church year filled with feast days of Orthodox saints, and an agrarian cycle that relays the "elemental agrarian wisdom of the populace, a practical approach" to time and seasonality.[69] This calendar, as one scholar puts it, *humanizes time.*[70] The rich links between the two threads of culture create a calendar of seasonal change that is filled with human stories and observation. Each aspect of returning life in nature is keyed to some human action. At the "end of spring, the beginning of summer"—a day given the name of Peter Solnovorot (Peter the Sun-turner)—we mark a whole series of events in the natural world: the nightingales have quieted; the bees have returned; the gadflies have descended on the livestock; the men go out to spread manure on the fallow fields; the women have said the "cucumber prayer" invoking the forces of fertility when they find the first "golden newcomer"—the first flower on the cucumber plant (2:102–5). What frames these smaller stories is Yarilo's *skazanie*, or legend, which promises ultimate benevolence from the source of life; there is no punishment or expulsion from Eden in this tale—just the onset of winter, to be followed in time by the return of light and warmth. A similar sense of the goodness of life's cycles, and a corresponding acceptance of the round of life and death, inform much of what happens in the novel: the passionate couplings and uncouplings of the wealthy Patap's family; tales of travelers through the woods; even the legends that a healer associates with individual plants. The healer's imagery of mist-towels wiping the face of Mother Earth, or her invocation of a loving creator and a world full of wonders "created for man's use," places us still within a world in which humans are the beloved child, and the earth itself a place of transparent, abundant love and ultimate generosity.

The world of the Kitezh legends, on the other hand, moves us into a drama of righteousness and determinations of "fallen" and "saved" humanity. Here too, though, the divine intervener has smiled on the people of these woods, delivering the righteous Old Believers from death and destruction. These tales are told and retold in the novel: in part 1 and then again at the end of part 2 we are told the story of the Old Believers' deliverance into woodlands likened to the biblical Promised Land: Arsenii, a monk at Solovki, refuses to denounce the Old Faith—but rather than being taken prisoner by the tsar's forces who have come to enforce their reforms, he is led into the woods by an icon that hovers miraculously above the pines. "The trees made way before him, the impassable bogs dried up in his path, and an unseen power cleared away the fallen underbrush" (1:298). When the legend is reprised more briefly at the end of part 2, the analogy to biblical landscapes is made explicit: "Just as ancient Israel was led by a fiery pillar to the Promised Land, so the elder Arsenii was led by that Holy Icon into the Kerzhensk and Chernoramensk Forests" (1:547).

These legends of deliverance refer to the late seventeenth-century flight into the "wilderness" (*pustynia*) in defiance of the official church's forced introduction of liturgical reforms, which Old Believers regarded as transgressions of the true faith. The Kitezh legends, on the other hand, refer to an earlier act of deliverance. While there are several accounts of just why (and when) the city came to be submerged, the one Mel'nikov uses refers to an approaching Tatar army led by Batu in the late fifteenth century; Batu's forces quickly overcame Lesser Kitezh—but Greater Kitezh was delivered through an act of divine intervention.[71] Thanks to the prayers of the faithful, the city descended beneath the waters of Svetlyi Yar, thus escaping ruin at the hands of the "infidel." It remains there intact to this day (or so the legend goes) and will remain so until the Second Coming. Lake Svetlyi Yar itself is transformed by this event into its own kind of holy place, where those of pure and righteous heart can, on certain summer evenings, hear the bells of Kitezh and see the flickering of its icon lamps. Like the tale of an icon and miraculous deliverance, the Kitezh legend gets told several times in the novel, and in several voices—a process that seems not unlike what Mikhail Bakhtin called novelization, when a piece of text (with very specific generic markers) is inserted into a more novelistic narrative. There emerges from this a complex and to some extent ironic process of distinguishing among varieties of credulity—as when Vasily Borisych (a "progressive" Old Believer from Moscow) is dismayed by pilgrims' bizarre and creative spinning of new versions of the Kitezh legend, which he insists "aren't in the manuscript." Vasily Borisych is a sympathetic character, and some of the tale-spinners have dubious motives; but the quibble seems a bit beside the point, since *all* of the legends Mel'nikov's novel relates might seem, to the modern reader, to belong to the realm of creative fantasy.[72]

The paradisal quality of these forests relates both to the exuberant cosmic vision of the Yarilo tales and to the sense of refuge conferred by the faithful's deliverance from evil into a Promised Land. While there are instances of memento mori—a visit to the monk Sofonty's grave occasions a lovely, elegiac meditation on the landscape of death (2:28)—and various elderly religious women constantly shushing up rebellious Old Believer girls, Mel'nikov's descriptions of nature more frequently evoke a world that seems deeply and vibrantly alive. He occasionally turns the contrast of old and young to comic (even slapstick) effect. The group of Old Believer pilgrims makes its way toward a holy grave, through woods that are lush with flowers and birdsong: "The trees are all at the peak of their sap, the grasses all flowering and fragrant. No matter where you look, flowers, flowers and more flowers. Over there among the hardwoods is a small, dry glade." For Vasily Borisych, natural beauty bespeaks praise for the divine: "every breath is praising the Lord." But the ironically named elder Arkadiia can only scold, and interjects a sour reminder of the Garden of Eden and the serpent—implying that now all creation serves "the evil one" and not God. The pilgrims are obviously unmoved by her sermonizing—Vasily Borisych and one of the girls kiss in the middle of the woods—and when they are approaching the gravesite, Arkadiia goes *plop* into a bog: "the rotten plank broke in two, and the lady preacher went head first into the muck" (2:244–45). If the forest—as Vasily Borisych suggests—is the "book of God," then Arkadiia has just gotten a playful, divine scolding.

Both these bodies of legend are part of Mel'nikov's mythic Rus', what he locates in the novel's opening paragraphs as a place distinct, intact, and unchanging. All the elements of Mel'nikov's symbolic geography emerge in embryonic form in this prelude: topography and myth; legend and historical time; the distinctions of local language and regional culture; a tale teller who spins a spell with his own version of the locals' singsong vernacular; and a claim that *this is Rus'*—not just Old Believers, but some essence of what it means to be Russian, which stands "from ancient times, undefiled."

> The upper Trans-Volga [Zavolzhe] is a boisterous land. The folk there are free-wheeling, lively, capable and quick. That's how Zavolzhe is from Rybinsk as far down as the mouth of the Kerzhenets. Lower down it's not the same: there you get thick forests, the Cheremis meadows, the Chuvash and the Tatars. And still farther down the river, beyond the Kama, the steppe stretches out, the folk there are different: they're Russian all right, but not like in Zavolzhe. The population there are newcomers, but Rus' settled in the woods and bogs of upper Zavolzhe from long, long ago. To judge from the way folk speak—the Novgorod people settled there in ancient time, under Riurik. Legends of Batu's defeat are still fresh there. They'll show you "Batu's path" and the place where the invisible city of Kitezh lies in Svetlyi Yar lake. The city is intact to this day—with its walls of white stone, golden-domed churches, the stone palaces of the boyars and houses hewn of heartwood that doesn't decay. The city is intact, but invisible. Sinful folk can't see glorious Kitezh. It was miraculously hidden, at God's command, when the godless tsar Batu . . . went to battle Kitezh Rus'. . . . And to this day that city stands hidden,—it will show itself at Christ's last judgment. But on Svetlyi Yar lake, on a quiet summer evening, the reflections of the walls and churches and monasteries are visible in the water, the princesses' chambers and the boyars' palaces, the merchants' houses. And at night you hear the muffled, sorrowing sound of the Kitezh bells.
>
> That's what they say beyond the Volga. It's Old Rus' there: time out of time, heart-pine Russia. From as far back as when the Russian Lands came to be there have been no strangers settled in those parts. Rus' stands there from ancient times, undefiled,—the way it was in our great-grandfathers' time, that's how it's been kept to our day. It's a kindhearted land, though it looks with anger on the stranger.

Mel'nikov's opening settles Zavolzhe—the trans-Volga—into an aura of antiquity: the region is the child of ancient Novgorod, with a nod toward Riurik, called in the chronicles to bring peace to the Russian lands.[73] This is also a place associated with purity—a place with "no strangers." Given Mel'nikov's interest in the non-Russian population of the trans-Volga woods, it seems likely that the stranger to whom he is referring is not a non-Russian inhabitant of the woods, but a *Russian* from Petersburg or Moscow.[74] Finding a path into these woods is in some sense the task of the novel, a challenge for which the novel offers multiple models; Batu's path and the Divine way that opens before Arsenii are but two opposing examples of how people move into these depths. There is a similar narrative gesture at the beginning of Boev's "Pictures of Forest Life," when his narrator El'novsky must pause before entering, and is then "led in" by the old forest sprite who pops out from behind the tree. Arsenii's path delivers him; Batu's path leads him nowhere. Arsenii follows the miraculous icon, a pathfinding that is about submission and trust; the agency that clears a path is divine, not human. The "stranger" Batu, on the other hand, moves through the woods in an act of aggression and transgression.

People repeatedly get lost in these woods—sometimes intentionally. As one of the community elders puts it, "Those are some huge forests—it's so homegrown there that for fifty versts [kilometers] or so you'll not find a house or a road—you're lucky to find a footpath. That's the woods where dugouts are put up, in some of them there are hermits saving themselves, in others there are *muzhiks* forging coins . . . . That's the Vetluga for you . . . . And you thought they were only stripping bast out there?" (1:383) The Old Believers are frequently associated with pilgrimage—one of the most ancient forms of attributing sacred meaning to space—but there is also quite a bit of "strolling" (*gulianie*) that goes on in the novel, particularly on the Yarilo-related holidays: these are primarily erotic meanderings (the "mushroom wanderings" associated with Petr Solnovorot are a good example) that have the self-sufficiency of Russian imperfective verbs. Russian verbs of motion distinguish between movement in one direction and movement that wanders or circles back on itself. Old Believer paths are, like Christian versions of history, unidirectional; Yarilo's ways are endless, if joyous, repetitions.

Mel'nikov also reminds us that these are woods where people have come for centuries *in order to get lost*—outlaws, rebels, runaway serfs, and those peasants forging coins. Mel'nikov's Rus' is a place that harbors all these "bravehearts" (*udal'tsy*) who would otherwise be flogged or hanged. The Old Believers themselves ultimately fit into this category of courageous dissenters who know how to disappear at the right time: "The Khlynov priests wanted nothing to do with Moscow and her metropolitan, and their spiritual children wanted nothing to do with the tsar's *voevodas* [military governors]. . . . As soon as some emissary of the *voevoda* or a Patriarch's emissary appeared on the edge of the forest they'd leave their homes and head into the forest hideouts, where neither the *voevoda* himself or the Patriarch could have found them" (1:297). The intent of the Old Believers is to be invisible to emissaries of state power. There is in this no small irony, of course, since Mel'nikov himself had worked as a state-authorized demographer, whose task was to count and describe Old Believers so that they could be more effectively controlled. He celebrates here what had undermined the functionality of his work—not just the Old Believers, but the forests themselves, whose terrain makes movement incredibly difficult.

It is literally difficult to get through these woods—something that is brought home to the reader at various moments in the novel. For one thing, even Arsenii's legend notes that it is not just trees that need to part—you have to somehow maneuver the boggy ground, which is treacherous and virtually untrackable. The dangers of boggy ground get extensive treatment in Mel'nikov's description of a logger's cooperative, one of the novel's quasi-ethnographic "set pieces" that help to convey the rich variety of lives and labors within these forests. Here as elsewhere Mel'nikov is obviously fascinated with the abundance and exactitude of local language, which replaces the generic "bog" (*boloto*) with a precisely calibrated range of terms for water-saturated turf: "An expanse of hummocky bog [*kochkarnik*], covered with moss, extended for several *versts*. Meter-thick layers cover a deep, almost bottomless mire [*top'*]. It's called *mshava*—in other words, a mossy bog. It's grown over with thin, scrubby woods; your foot sinks into soft sphagnum mat [*zybun*], strewn with wild rosemary [*bagun*], floating star [*zvezdoplavka*], cranesbill [*mozgusha*], buttercup [*liutik*] and mat grass [*belous*]. The sphagnum mat shakes beneath the walker's weight, and sometimes there will be a sudden fountain of water for two or three steps from an air-hole your eye can't make out. It's dangerous to walk there, in an instant you'll fall into the depths of the bog [*bolotnaia puchina*] and be lost for more than a day" (1:193). To be fair, my thesaurus offers an impressive range of synonyms for "bog" in English: it is my own limited acquaintance with this particular landscape (and locals who know how to talk about it) that leaves me overreliant on "bog" and "mire."[75] Mel'nikov's powers of observation and experiential hydrology seem considerable, but then he shifts without pause into an account of the spirits who inhabit these boggy places, regarded by the loggers as "unclean" and "bewitched." The bog version of Russia's mermaid (the *bolotnitsa*) lures men to their death, and a bog-devil masquerading as a hermit entraps a holy elder. Mel'nikov summarizes these stories with a proverb—"It's no accident that since the old days people have said that demons lurk in quiet waters, and they breed in forest bogs"—and then quickly moves on to other "enemies" of forest

workers in the summertime: the insects. We have no trouble believing, later in
the novel, that an Old Believer elder could elude state officials for six weeks in
this labyrinth of water and floating sphagnum, protected as he understands it by
the mantle of the Lord (2:15).

What *doesn't* particularly seem to help those lost in the woods is a compass.
Just before the account of boggy ground, Mel'nikov has his band of Old
Believers, led by the enterprising, wealthy Patap Maksimych, set off in hope
of finding gold—fool's gold, as it turns out. Along the way they get lost in the
woods' deep drifts of snow; the man who is leading them—a "pilgrim" who
turns out to be a crook—reassures them that he has a compass (1:188). The
compass is of no help—and only later does one of the loggers explain that it was
because of the northern lights, clearly a form of magnetic interference, which
the loggers describe as "God's mysterious power."

Mel'nikov's account of the bogs exemplifies his interest in regional language
and legend, which he relates both to *knowing* a place and to *finding one's way*
in these woods. The compass signifies orientation via mechanical means,
disengaged from the kind of close observation and sensory knowledge (along
with "God's mysterious power") that enables men to find their way and survive.
Mel'nikov's shift from natural history to folklore in his account of boggy land
is an abrupt discursive shift for modern readers—but the implication is that
both languages have something to teach us about the place, and the spirit stories
may have functioned as the equivalent of warnings about treacherous ground.
Mel'nikov makes a lively and polemical defense of local language in a passage
that follows closely on the description of the bog, when the loggers talk with the
Old Believers about what had thrown the compass off—*not*, for Mel'nikov, the
severnoe siianie (a Russian calque of *aurora borealis*) but *pazori*—a Slavic term
that he vigorously defends in an extensive footnote. The note is worth quoting
in full:

> *Pazori*—the northern lights [*severnoe siianie*]. The folk don't know the word
> "northern lights." It's a fabricated word, artificial, thought up in a study, maybe
> even by Lomonosov himself, and he—a northerner himself—could not have
> been ignorant of the real Russian word, *pazori*. Northern lights is a literal
> translation of the German *Nordlicht*. In our country, every phase of this celestial
> phenomenon, so typical in Rus', is denoted by a particular, specific word. Thus
> the beginning of *pazori*, when a pale white light like the Milky Way starts to
> spread in the northern portion of the sky, is called *otbel* or *bel* [from the word for
> white]. The phase which follows it, when the *otbel* first takes on a rosy shade and
> then gradually grows redder, is called *zori* or *zorniki* [from the word for dawn].
> Usually after *zori* milky bands start to dart across the sky. That is called *luchi*

[*luch* = ray]. . . . if the phenomenon continues, the *luchi* grow red and gradually turn into bright *stolby* [columns], either red or of different colors. (1:210)[76]

The footnote is motivated by Mel'nikov's use of a term he presumably thought his readers might not understand (*pazori* is in fact not given in the Dal' dictionary)—but he also wants us to grasp the larger issue of using "real Russian" terms rather than calques from the German. We might read this as more evidence of Mel'nikov's national pride—written here into a kind of pedantic linguistic niggling. But it seems to me that it is more interesting than that; it is a defense of local language and the way it registers phenomena more precisely, and with more nuance, than the scientific term. Mikhail Lomonosov, a fellow northerner whose journey from a White Sea village into the heart of European science has become legendary, is emblematic here of the introduction of scientific knowledge (and language) into Russia, but also of a modernity that Mel'nikov laments as displacing the local. The passage itself isn't anti-empirical; in speaking of the loggers' names for the northern lights, Mel'nikov notes that they don't believe legends about the lights' foretelling war and upheaval. And the careful account of just how each phase of the lights looks reminds us that the language Mel'nikov records here is embedded in careful observation. It has come out of a world in which men working in the forest and staying there through long northern nights have *paid attention* and given things names. There is nothing obscure about the words and their roots, but Mel'nikov thinks we ought to hold on to them, as a form of memory—not only of culture, but of natural phenomena.[77] This passionate desire to retain native linguistic resources was one Mel'nikov shared with his friend and teacher, Vladimir Dal': "The time has come to value the language of the people [*narodnym iazykom*] and to develop from it a literate language."[78]

Much nature writing as we have come to know it values a descriptive accuracy identified with natural history; modern traditions of empiricism and realist writing, which gave birth to both the great Russian novel and American nature writers like John Bartram and Thoreau, assume the need to describe— and to use primarily the language of *visual* recognition. (Thoreau himself marks a trajectory from the dense, allusive language of *Walden* to the late writings, which are much closer to "natural history.") This descriptive language dovetails with the emergence of objective scientific prose, which makes the world available for even the least initiated, most urban reader.[79] Language of the sort that Mel'nikov uses works quite differently. His language gives us not so much the world itself as people's relationship to it, their stories about it—an environment "mediated through the unofficial folk wisdom" of the region.[80] Mel'nikov's account of the cucumber flowering in spring is a good example of this; what we are given is not a close visual description of the cucumber flower, but a woman watching for it, and the traditional epithet used to refer to it. The phrase has a wonderful lilting rhyme (*zolotistyi novichok, pervenkii tsvetochek*) and assumes a close parallel between the woman's body and the body of the cucumber: "Let my cucumbers hug as tight as my waistband, so there's no daylight between them!" (2:102) In some very basic sense, this is not Mel'nikov's language: it is stylized folkloric speech, a language whose authority is grounded in conventionality. Mel'nikov is, as one scholar has put it, a fundamentally *oral* author.[81] The "language thought up in a study" of someone like Lomonosov stands at some remove from the language in and of place that Mel'nikov celebrates as his model.

The oral quality of Mel'nikov's prose extends as well to the myriad instances when he introduces songs and singing into the novel. He does this in ways that are markedly different from someone like Turgenev—whose rendering of a contest in "Singers" is almost entirely about the way the men are singing, rather than the words of the songs.[82] Mel'nikov introduces text after text of song, and implies a kind of permeability between human voice, birdsong, and the air itself. Singing is important both to Old Believer domestic life and religious culture as Mel'nikov depicts it; one of the key characters of the novel, Vasily Borisych, is a choirmaster, whose presence in the novel introduces romantic intrigue, a sympathetically critical view of Old Belief, and a Muscovite outsider's delight at the natural beauty of the backwoods. Music is central to both Yarilo and Kitezh: "Tipsy Yar" is constantly breaking through young lovers' mouths and spilling out into the countryside; and Kitezh is known to the righteous through the sound of its bells at midsummer. It is no wonder that Rimsky-Korsakov and his librettist Vladimir Bel'skii found the novel inspiring, or that the first act of *The Legend of the Invisible City of Kitezh and the Maiden Fevroniya* weaves birdsong, a woman's voice, and incantatory healing in a forest glade.[83] In the novel, the lover Aleksei's "waves of new passion" are first manifest as a headlong gallop, and then are "resolved" (a term that has musical applications—*razreshilis'*) in a song that is at first "loud, impetuous, full of despair and hopeless sorrow, then gradually quieted and finally died out in barely audible murmurs of quiet sadness and love" (1:499). Aleksei grows silent, but the birds of the forest seem to pick up the song: we move from "complete silence" to the call and response of an oriole, a wren, and a robin. "Somewhere in the distance a nightingale clicked," and before we know it, Mel'nikov is leading us into a lengthy description of all the nightingale's trills and runs: "First he *zapulkal*, then he *zaklykal* like a glass bell, showering out a fine silvery patter, then he *zaplenkal*, set off on a '*iulin-knock*,' clicked loudly, and flowing out with a rilling fife, shut up."[84] Aleksei's passionate song morphs into one of Mel'nikov's virtuosic linguistic riffs. In other passages, the transition from human song to birdsong is less elaborate (and less challenging to translate). The death of the young, lovesick Nastya is described as the progress of a girl's soul into sky-borne birdsong:

> Nikitishna came in. In one hand she was carrying a glass of water, in the other a censer with embers and incense. She placed the glass on the open window, so that the soul might have a drop to drink as it flew out into the sky. . . . Nikitishna censed three times before the icons, and then over Nastya's head. Evprakseia the lector came in with a book, stood by the icons, and began quietly to read the text appointed "For the departure of the soul . . ."
>
> Nastya breathed more quietly and less frequently. Soon she began to fall completely quiet.
>
> At that moment, out of nowhere, a robin started gently and mournfully singing her song; the free song of a lark poured out louder and more resonant from the skies. . . . A light breeze lifted and lightly stirred the window curtains.
>
> . . . For five minutes they kept deep silence. . . . All one could hear was the mournful earthly singing of the robin, and the joyous song of the lark as it soared in the heavens. (1:514–15)

A scene like this works on readers' sentiment to create an aura around the dying Nastya—but also to emphasize a kind of synaesthetic sense of the holy. The scene describes "institutional" religion (the lector, her book, the prayer, the incense), but also folk religious practice (the glass of water and the notion of the soul's literal thirst); and it suggests a kind of cosmic lamentation, in which the voice of the prayer reader is joined by the birds who both grieve and rejoice. Scenes like this are intended to move the reader in multiple senses (we shed a tear at Nastya's death and are given a glimpse of her entry into some cosmic, more eternal life; it is a good example of how the novel is deeply associated with *women's* stories). But it also works on the reader's multiple senses: smell, sound, and touch are all active here, with incense, song, and breeze. Scenes like this are good examples of how Mel'nikov sacralizes place, drawing on clusters of cultural reference that are bundled around resonant and affecting moments of plot. Other moments give us more visual landscapes, that also convey an aura of silence and deep calm: a morning after snowfall becomes almost a genre painting of quiet, well-disciplined labor as women clear snow, haul wood, and gather for morning prayers (1:337); or another early morning, with the sun rising over Maria Gavrilovna's house, a "golden sickle" over the "heights of the distant dark-gray wood" (1:485). But in his descriptions of soul-filled song, one gets a glimpse of why this author's evocation of sacred place would have held such interest for a generation of symbolist artists. There is a kind of proto-liturgy of the cosmos here, with all the "smells and bells" of rich syncretic tradition(s).

One is in fact tempted to describe these moments of soul-filled singing as acts of fictional *incantation*, summoning up a supposedly lost world that Mel'nikov has found for us, but also promising to work on its readers as a form of *healing*. I suggested earlier in this chapter that one of the fundamental narrative gestures of Boev's story is the entrance of a Europeanized Russian into terrain in which he is symbolically healed. Sickness and healing turns out to be a central concern of Mel'nikov's novel: physical sickness is associated in the novel with emotional or psychic disturbance—and accounts of healing introduce a rich lode of lore about healing plants and folk medicine. The elder Manefa falls into convulsions when she discovers that her former lover Stukolov is part of a counterfeiting ring; Aleksei is beset by a sense that the patriarch Patap will be the cause of his death (and given the advice we noted above to wear a "wind nest" from a birch tree); Nastya, as we have just seen, dies when Aleksei abandons her; and Maria Gavrilovna pines away when Aleksei leaves the village and she fears he has abandoned her, too.[85] Each of these plot developments becomes the occasion for a discussion of Old Believer attitudes toward health, the body, and healing (the community is scandalized when Maria Gravilovna calls in a doctor to treat Manefa). The most vividly drawn and extensive discussion of healing involves the local *znakharka*, or traditional healer—Egorikha. The scene is worth our attention for several reasons: it compellingly links the novel's cosmic and Christian vocabularies, and it also presents a holy figure who bears comparison with other saints and healers in Russia literature—particularly with Dostoevsky's Zosima. Mel'nikov's Egorikha, like Dostoevsky's elder in *The Brothers Karamazov*, combines an ecstatic affection for the creation with an Orthodox Christian vocabulary—and while her presence in this novel is in no way as central or developed as Dostoevsky's Zosima, they both represent the authors' visions of what religious tradition has to offer the modern world. Whether or not their offers of healing are effective within the world and plot of their respective novels, the authors present them as models of wisdom that *readers* are in need of.

As Rose Glickman points out in her study of peasant women healers, peasant culture distinguished healers (*znakharki*) from witches (*ved'my*) by the source of their powers: healers "derived their powers from God or his entourage of saints and performed only beneficial, curative services," whereas witches "negotiated with unclean spirits."[86] The Old Believer community is suspicious of Egorikha and regards her as a witch; but it is immediately clear in Mel'nikov's description that this "tall, graceful woman . . . [with] a bright cotton kerchief on her head and a bast-wood basket on her shoulders" is not evil. In fact, Egorikha herself distinguishes between healers and witches using the terms Glickman cites, insisting that her work is grounded in God's spirit: "Those who are kind come from God, those who are dark are from the evil one. Nothing can displace the mysterious power of God, and the dark power of the evil one can be vanquished with God's power" (2:187). Egorikha is distinguished by her kindness, her knowledge of the natural world, and her constant supplication to divine powers, both to God and the Mother of God, using both Orthodox prayers and an invocation of Moist Mother Earth.[87]

Egorikha's advice articulates an ecstatic apprehension of divine goodness and immanence in the creation. The healer has come out before dawn's light to gather herbs on Saint Tikhon's day, when according to folk wisdom therapeutic properties are at their height. "See how our little sun is getting close, soon folk will start to get up. . . . Today's St. Tikhon's day, it's quiet, our Moist Mother Earth is kind. . . . And the sun flows quiet across the sky today. . . . And from this day on the songbirds will grow quiet. . . . The quiet light of God's glorious saint shines bright today! . . . Because of that light all the grasses are filled to the full with nectar, and right up till St. Ivan's day they're filled with healing nectar. . . . You can't let today's morning dew go by. At first dew on Tikhon's you must pluck up grasses and root up roots, gather flowers" (2:186). Her rambling commentary is sprinkled with traditional folk epithets, and once more draws primarily on Afanas'ev: "Believe me, my beauty, there's not a single blade of grass on the moist earth that wasn't created for man's use. In every grass, in every flower the Lord has put His great mercy. . . . The world is full of His wonders, and there is no end to His love for man. . . . Aren't we the sinners, who live in anger and strife? . . .But He is merciful, suffers all, covers all with his love. . . . Let's go a little quicker, the mist is lifting, the dew is washing the face of Moist Mother Earth. . . . Look what towels are carried along the sky. Moist Mother Earth is drying off with them" (2:186–88).[88]

Gathering herbs on Saint Tikhon's day, Egorikha reminds us both of the saint and of the Russian word for *quiet*—*tikhii*—all of which Mel'nikov wants to connect to the curative, cosmic goodness that the healer seems to embody as a spirit or genius of place. The genius of this place (indeed, of the larger place of Mel'nikov's novel, Heart-Pine Russia) is that it does not change; its vitality is linked to the seasonal measure of time; it embodies the *quiet* of nature and spirit but also the erotic, creative powers of Yarilo; it makes use of the creation without abusing it. Boev's Russian forest is, like Mel'nikov's, a place of human labor and productivity, but also a place sacralized by association with monastic tradition, contemplative prayer, Russian saints, and liturgical chanting. Mel'nikov's forest is more energetic, an energy derived both from the entrepreneurial spirit of characters like Patap, and from the irrepressible cosmic energies of Yarilo and company. There is that sense of *zakvaska* in Mel'nikov, a frothy fermenting brew that to some extent derives from the clash (occasionally comic) of cultures. The very enormity of Mel'nikov's vast epic, its gargantuan appetite for character and language and tall tale and multiple genres and competing religious traditions— all suggest a fecund universe of "Heart-Pine Russia" ready to burst forth and revivify a country that has lost contact with it.

* * *

DAVID HARVEY, A contemporary cultural geographer, has argued that "place" is determined through a complex process of differentiation, in which our sense of location is created in contrast with some *elsewhere*, involving a difference that takes on symbolic and ideological weight. This seems particularly germane to thinking about the final decades of the nineteenth century in Russia, and the ways in which the forest came to be associated with religious traditions, dissent, and potentials for renewal. Mel'nikov's Heart-Pine Russia is a topographical and environmental location, but it is also a cluster of attributes and images that cohere in juxtaposition to other places, primarily to cities. A symbolic topography that associates the essence of Russia with certain righteous figures and spiritual topoi works imaginatively *in contrast* to the fallen worlds of Russia's capital cities— associated with modernity, Europe, and the fractiousness of ideology and intellectual life. The Moscow of Mel'nikov's novel is a "place of sorrow," of false authority, or an image of biblical damnation: "You folks in Moscow, with your paunchy hypocrites and wolves dressed up in sheep's clothing, you've not even heard of the wonders that happen here—and we simpletons have seen them with our own eyes. . . . What's your Moscow to us? Lives big, spits high, wants nothing to do with God. . . . Thrice-damned Babylon!" (2:258)

The rhetoric of Boev's story is virtually the same: his narrator writes back to Petersburg in a gush of revelation at the contrast between *here* (the Russian backwoods) and *there* (St. Petersburg): "Dearest Grandfather! I'm very, very grateful, dearest friend, that you sent me here. Just think of it, other than you, no one understood me. All I heard was the same thing: 'It's a backwood, depressing! what are you going to do there?' 'I'd go abroad,' 'There's nothing there to live on' . . . 'Is it far? Where is it on the map? Oh my God!' and so forth and so on. Do we really intend to live forever in Petersburg and Moscow? Will we really never know—neither we nor our children—what is happening in our backwoods? . . . Can it really be that no one has felt this unsettling rumble that calls us to real life, instead of staying contented with fantastic phalansteries and communes? Will we really sit forever in copying offices and editorial rooms—just the same as copying offices? Russian life is beginning to ferment around us, *our* Russian forests are sounding, but we're going to translate revolutionary brochures and drag ourselves abroad, all the while laughing and deriding everything that's ours."[89] The people of Russia's capital cities literally *cannot see* the wonders of a world that, but for the efforts of writers like Boev and Mel'nikov (or painters like Savrasov and Shishkin) would remain *invisible*. The trope of invisibility is of course central to the whole myth of Kitezh: the righteous city can no longer be seen with the mortal eye; it is visible only to the righteous, and only on certain days of the year. This aura of righteousness, and of privileged seeing ("They who have eyes to see, let them see") communicates itself in Mel'nikov's pages to the whole of this region: "We simpletons have seen [these wonders] with our own eyes."

Boev's hero maps the intellectual life of post–Reform Russia, the post-1861 world of intelligentsia enthusiasms with "phalansteries and communes"—models of progressive life drawn from French Utopian Socialists whose "revolutionary brochures" may well be the ones El'novsky is lamenting. His psychic grid sets translations and "imitations of life" in opposition to the *real life* of Russia's backwoods, a world that El'novsky's friends can't imagine except as absence and lack of amenities. They literally don't know where it is on the map. Boev's geography mirrors the kind of superheated ideological landscape of Dostoevsky's novels of the 1870s, particularly *Demons*, his account of a cell of radicals drawn into an imbroglio of murder and violent politics of the will. In a recent account of the novel's geography, Anne Lounsbery has argued that the radicals' mentality is shaped by their sense that all meaning derives from *elsewhere*; the provinces are for them just what El'novsky's friends think they are—a place of absence, lack, and negativity. Their submission to control from "elsewhere" is part of what underpins their moral and intellectual arrogance; they have no sense of self, no moral compass—they are adrift and wholly dependent on others' directions. Lounsbery points to motifs of *invisibility* or *illegibility* in this symbolic geography: "The denizens of Gogol''s *gorod N* keep their eyes trained on a distant center (whether Petersburg, Moscow, Paris, or someplace else) because there is nothing local that *signifies*. And in fact in many nineteenth-century Russian texts, the provinces are represented as a place where it is hard to make sense of things, a place where meanings are more likely to dissolve than to coalesce."[90] Dostoevsky's revolutionaries are fundamentally ungrounded—working, terrifyingly enough, to install a socialist future, a *utopia* (no place) that for Dostoevsky becomes conflated with *dystopia* (bad place). Mel'nikov and Boev imagine places of intact community, organic health, and vibrant religious traditions, in which an idealized past seems to have been miraculously preserved, retrospective utopias that function as antidotes to nightmares of urban modernity.

For David Harvey, the emergence of such symbolic, contrastive geographies is related to the history of capitalism, and to modernity's increased pace of dislocation. "We worry," he writes, "about the meaning of place in general and of our place in particular when the security of actual places becomes generally threatened."[91] Post-1861 shifts in class relations, rural life, and in the landscape itself (the kind of deforestation that accelerated in the 1860s and '70s, and which we explore in our next chapter) may well underlie the dreams and nightmares we find in Mel'nikov and Dostoevsky. Victor Vinogradov, writing in 1936, linked what he calls Mel'nikov's "reactionary Slavophilism" to *genuine regret*: "The idealization of old ways of life, the images of what doesn't change, the poeticization of folk-poetic tradition—are not only aspects of the author's narrative form, but expressions of genuine regret, genuine sadness at the retreat and death of the old world." In the Soviet context there is a terrible irony in Vinogradov's scholarly comment, since by 1936 Stalin's program of forced collectivization had instituted draconian changes in the whole structure of rural life. There is a sudden flash of recognition in a sentence like this. One wonders whether Vinogradov himself didn't feel some of that *genuine* regret at the "death of an old world."[92]

Larisa Lotman, writing in 1964, suggested that the hero of Mel'nikov's novel is the "population of a whole region."[93] The overall impact of *In the Forests* is to convey a vital and vibrant culture of place, a complex human community in which institutions have not been able to repress the energies (one wants to call them both organic and orgiastic) that still animate humans and the wider creation. The very disarray and abundance of the novel is in the spirit of Yarilo: it is embracing, encyclopedic, enthusiastic. The ironies of impending extinction are of course intense: Mel'nikov creates this canvas of vibrant culture at a moment when much of it is dying—either thanks to the works of his own official hand (in the case of dispersed Old Believer communities), or due to the eroding effects of an increasingly skeptical modernity. As he himself put it in an 1875 speech to the Society of Lovers of Russian Literature: "We must seize the day. . . . We must gather these precious fragments [of Russian antiquity and folklore] while there is still time, while it is still possible—not only beliefs, not only legends are disappearing before our eyes: the Russian way of life is changing."[94]

Mel'nikov's forest encompasses both the myth of creation and the myth of deliverance, both Yarilo and Kitezh, both natural time and divine intervention—just as it encompasses both "mythology" and "everyday life." The popularity of the novel probably had something to do with this catholicity of intention and inclusion; it is a *generous* novel more than an ideological one— and in that affable disinclination to be ideological lies perhaps the other secret of its success. The novel, we might say, is an escape: like the God who separates the forests, or covers Kitezh, Mel'nikov as a writer carries his readers away from the ideological contentiousness of late nineteenth-century Russia. He evokes a place in which the *real* Russia remains intact, a place far away from compromised sites of overheated intellectual and political debate.[95] His detractors felt this was a privilege he hadn't earned; his association with tsarist bureaucracies that had persecuted Old Belief up until the mid-1850s disqualified his authority as a writer. But for others—and for Mel'nikov himself—the provinciality of the novel becomes a badge of pride and legitimacy, linked to its mythos of a place through which Russia might still come to its senses.

The symbolic and affective geography we have been tracking in these pages has continued to be powerfully resonant into the twentieth century and post-Soviet Russia. Suffice it for now to mention the official Soviet writer Leonid Leonov, whose work follows a trajectory from clear-cut to conservation in Russia's forests. His "production novel" *The River Sot''* (1930) starts in woods filled with monasteries and cosmic energies, a forest landscape that seems to come straight out of Mel'nikov-Pechersky, but in a grotesque, parodic form. Leonov's novel celebrates Soviet industrial transformation of that landscape: pulp mills replace monastery walls, rational planning replaces the chaotic disorder of the backwoods. By the 1950s, however, Leonov was advocating a very different developmental politics: his *Russian Forest* (1953) critiques Soviet forest policy, narrating the symbolic birth of its hero, Vikhrov, at a forest spring deep in the northern woods. The spring is presided over by an elderly peasant who might have stepped right out of the pages of Mel'nikov or Turgenev. We are back in Polesye, with Egor offering us "living water." Leonov's evolution continued with the century, and by the early 1990s he was contributing a foreword to a volume of essays on Russia's archetypal forest saint, Sergius of Radonezh: in his brief remembrance of prerevolutionary pilgrimage to the Trinity monastery founded by Sergius, Leonov joins symbolic forces with authors celebrating a national saint who for some had become an emblem of preservation of Russian nature and public health.[96]

W. J. T. Mitchell, in a recent essay on notions of holy land and their imbrication in Palestinian-Israeli politics, cautions that all narratives of memory are also exercises in forgetting: "While it is clearly important, then, to retrieve the memories and excavate the depths of landscape, one must register as well the sense in which landscape is all about forgetting, about getting away from the real in ways that may produce astonishing dislocations."[97] Part of what the reader *forgets* in reading Mel'nikov's novel is that the forests of his day were rapidly disappearing. I suggested above that Mel'nikov's novel is subject to the ironies of impending extinction; that extinction extended not only to human communities, but to the forest itself. As we shall see in the following chapter, in the period when *In the Forests* was published, there were increasingly frequent and increasingly alarmed accounts in Russia's major journals of the "national calamity" of deforestation. The forests in Mel'nikov's pages stretch endlessly, almost eternally, into a vague and distant north. His intrepid band of loggers rise with each wintry dawn to cut down trees, and the wealthy patriarch of the novel builds his fortune on utensils made of wood. But the notion that this vast source of livelihood (as well as legend) could somehow *disappear* is wholly foreign to the novel.

It was not, however, foreign to the readers of the *Russian Herald*, who were increasingly treated to laments over the economic and agricultural impact of rampant, undisciplined cutting. What emerged in the 1870s and '80s was a kind of incipient ecological awareness, first noted by hydrologists and foresters, then taken up by writers and artists already possessed of pantheistic sympathy for Russia's woodlands. That Mel'nikov does not—with one brief exception—mention any of this is perhaps indicative of the very different function he understood his novel to have. In a startling and completely anomalous digression, the chronicler-mythologer of Russia's trans-Volga has this to say about Russian agrarians' attitude toward the forest: "The Great Russian is a died-in-the-wool enemy of the forest; his work is to cut, to burn, to ruin, but not to plant trees" (1:303). Mel'nikov leaves it at that. The authors to whom we now turn are more inquisitive, less sentimental, and more urgent in their descriptions and diagnosis of what they saw as an alarming—if not apocalyptic—destruction of the great forests of European Russia. It will come as no surprise to learn that one iconic instance of their alarm is a painting that shows a procession of the cross, *not*, as in Boev or Mel'nikov-Pechersky, progressing through deep forest—but against a recently denuded hillside, leaving humans to a desiccated and violent landscape.

Ivan Shishkin, The Coniferous Wood *(1873). Reproduced with permission of the State Art Museum of Belarus, Minsk.*

Alexei Savrasov, At the Monastery Gates *(1875). Reproduced with permission of the State Russian Museum, St. Petersburg.*

Ilya Repin, Procession of the Cross in the Kursk District *(1883). Tretyakov Gallery, Moscow. Scala / Art Resource, NY.*

Ilya Repin, Summer Landscape (1881). Study for Procession of the Cross in the Kursk District. *Reproduced with permission of the Tretyakov Gallery, Moscow.*

3
Geographies of Loss

The "Forest Question" in Nineteenth-Century Russia

> The forest! the pictures and lush images one
> imagines at the word, the poets who have turned
> their thoughts toward that mysterious world,
> where the dendrometer measures tree trunks with
> anti-poetic exactitude, and the inexorable forester
> makes cuttings, sight lines and measurements
> of reserve plantings! But one doesn't hinder the
> other.
>
> —A. S., "Dilletantism in Forestry" (1851)

> Our papers have taken hold of one issue, which
> gets trotted out as soon as there's not a lead article
> ready; that's the "forest question." Holy Russia,
> they say, is cutting down its slumbering forests,
> leading the population to certain death—there's a
> theme written about with volume and frequency
> for some time now.
>
> —F. Treimut, "Is It Profitable for the Owner of
> Woodlands in a Forested Region to Introduce
> Rule-Based Forestry?" (1871)

TURGENEV'S *HUNTER'S SKETCHES* begin with a recognition of loss: "The last woods and brushwoods in the Orel region will disappear in five years or so, and the bog lands are already long gone." "Khor and Kalinych" is not *about* the loss of woodlands, but embeds its story of human lives in a quietly alarming geography of disappearance. We don't normally think of the stories in this way, but what we would call environmental concerns are in fact frequently apparent in the *Hunter's Sketches*. As Alec Paul notes in his survey of the stories, "there is uncontrolled clearing of woodland and draining of marshes, while water-supply dams are falling into disrepair, boundaries and land ownership are changing, and even factories are making an appearance."[1] Turgenev is not openly polemical about such devastation, but it is as much a part of his central Russian landscape as are his descriptions of summer heat and a shady bank for fishing. A grove of lindens has been spared the "ruthless axe of the Russian peasant" in "My Neighbor

Radilov"; gentlemen hunters in "L'gov" bring down a vast number of ducks, far more than their party can manage to take home—and then stand neck-deep in pond water with duck corpses floating around them when their leaky boat finally sinks. Turgenev's gaze in these stories is as unsentimental as it is open to the extraordinary beauty of central Russia; a natural disaster (a bitterly cold and snowless winter) fells a whole forest of trees, but then the human stewards of the land don't know how even to make use of timber that now rots on the ground, "like corpses" (4:214).[2]

In 1841, six years before Turgenev began publishing the *Hunter's Sketches*, the Moscow-based *Journal of Agriculture and Livestock* presented to readers the translation of a speech by a German forest statistician, Gottlob Koenig, calling for the conservation of woodlands. Sergei Maslov, the journal's editor and a leading advocate of agricultural innovation in Russia, appended his own words of alarm at the end of Koenig's speech: the worsening landscape of deforestation, forest loss and its negative consequences, applied to Russia as well.[3] Within the year Maslov's journal would publish additional articles focusing on Russian deforestation and its potential consequences for domestic economies, agriculture, and trade. Writing in 1842 about the forests of the Moscow region, Karl Tseplin (identified only as a "member of the Moscow Society of Lovers of Agriculture") connected his description of the present day with a dire prophecy: "There is extremely little done to care for forests here. However nature grows them, that's the way they're used. They're cut down and no one thinks about planting them again. That's why there's insufficient wood, and why it's getting more expensive. That inadequacy will be more and more apparent as the years go by, until something is done about ensuring that woodlands are cared for, that they are replanted and improved."[4] The call to protection had sounded, a call that combined alarm at shrinking stocks of fuel and building material with a sense of the less tangible values of woodland. Over the next four decades that call would continue to sound, in ways both explicit and subtle, in lyrical descriptions and scientific debate. The Forest Question would come to occupy a major place on the pages of Russia's major journals; in state commissions and bureaucracies; in the pages and on the canvases of her literary and visual artists. The texture and tenor of that question encompassed a broad range of concerns, both environmental and social: authors debated issues ranging from how forest loss affected hydrology to whether the Imperial government should limit landowners' rights to use of their woodlands; they encouraged the introduction of "rule-based" [*pravil'noe*] forestry and rebuked various groups for barbaric destruction of woodlands.[5] Over the course of the century, the wooded landscapes of European Russian changed radically; in their imagination of that change and their response to its impact, a broad range of Russians—both scientists and artists—created a geography of loss that is both documentary and visionary.

The anonymous author of "Dilletantism in Forestry" proclaims to his readers that *poetry and measurement don't hinder one another.*[6] *Poetry* for A. S. is constituted by "pictures and lush images" of a mysterious world, while measurement is the domain of the forester, a way of knowing with "anti-poetic exactitude." There are at least two kinds of seeing evoked in this account, one the realm of imagination and the mysterious, the other associated with technology (the dendrometer), planning, and use. A. S.'s insistence that the two *don't hinder each other* seems almost surprising, or naïve, linked to the prelapsarian world of 1850s Russia, before the culture wars of a new generation drew battle lines between poetry and science, pleasure and utility, temples and workshops. In the 1862 novel *Fathers and Sons*, Turgenev's iconoclastic hero Bazarov insists that nature "is not a temple but a workshop"—presumably articulating a generational shift in views of the natural world. For many of the men we consider in this chapter, however, the operative assumption is that "pictures and lush images" have roles to play along with more quantitative inquiry in coming to know, and protect, the forest; the forests of Russia are to be valued for reasons both material and spiritual; and the forester, with his dendrometer, is an agent not of destruction but of knowledge, planning, and conservation—opposed not to the dreamy poet but to the wanton destroyer of woodlands. Just who the wanton destroyer *was* sometimes entered into the discussion—peasants, merchants, Jews, post-Emancipation landowners all take their turns as object of denunciation. But for the writers who turned their attention to the Forest Question, including those whose primary allegiance was to professional forest science, the "poetic" was an essential aspect of why and how one should value this landscape.

And what of the dendrometer, which A. S. calls "anti-poetic"? This small device with the non-Russian-sounding name (Vladimir Dal' calls it a *lesomer—tree measurer*) is an instrument used to calculate the height and diameter of standing timber, part of a system developed by German foresters in the eighteenth century; the system is a more mathematical version of earlier strategies that divide woodlands into sectors based on projected years to maturity—if a tree needs seventy years to mature, your woods should be divided into seventy plots, cutting only one plot in any given year, to ensure what has come to be called sustained yield.[7] Gottlob Koenig, the German forest scientist whose speech was published in the *Moscow Journal of Agriculture and Livestock*, had helped develop mathematical formulas for those calculations: his speech begins with woodlands' value for the "habitability, life and well-being of peoples," makes a careful review of the hydrological and climatic impact of forest loss, and then ends with very different arguments for why conservation is essential:

> We [foresters] must behave with [trees] as with living beings, and not look at them as a mass which occurs mechanically, that can simply be divided into woodlots according to short-sighted accountants' instructions; for the growth of trees is founded on supremely subtle, deeply hidden mysteries. We have so far studied very few of these secrets of nature, and our knowledge, defining in formulas and figures the path of sylvan life from one generation to the next, exposes its shakiness in the paltry growth of forests through which nature takes revenge on each of our actions that are not consonant with her law. . . . There can be no doubt that the mysterious bonds of nature link the fate of men with the fate of trees, not only through the satisfaction of our material needs, but morally as well—in the influence of these living beings on men's well-being. Where forest disappears, drought and wasteland take their place.[8]

In Koenig's speech, the forester and the poet, far from being at odds, seem rather to have become one.

This chapter sets out to trace some of the complexity and nuance of the nineteenth-century Forest Question. I begin by sketching in broad terms the Forest Question's central themes and strategies, and then suggest some of the ways in which a rhetoric of love, alarm, and protection came to inform both imaginative literature and visual art. To do this is to remind ourselves of the extent to which artists and forest scientists occupied a common space, both geophysical and symbolic: even when they disputed terms, there was much that they held in common. While the intention of many of those involved was to change legal regimes and management practices, they also aimed to change public opinion and the human heart, and to that end drew not so much on statistics as on evocations of deeply known, much-loved places.

* * *

THE SPECTER OF FOREST LOSS, soil erosion, impeded river flow, and shifting climate that Koenig described for Germany had also come to haunt the Russian imagination by the early 1840s, leading to the creation of state commissions, ministerial reviews, learned societies—and increased attention in the periodical press. The British geologist Roderick Murchison visited Russia in 1841 and is reported to have expressed to Nicholas I his surprise at "the speed with which forests are being destroyed in Your Highness' delightful country." The remark has entered the history of the Forest Question as a kind of benchmark for its inauguration. P. I. Zhudra, outgoing president in 1884 of the Moscow branch of the Forest Society, quotes Murchison (and exaggerates just how long ago he was in Russia) as a way of foregrounding the longevity and extremity of the problem of deforestation.[9] The central regions of Russia, Zhudra laments, are now waste and scrubland, and "so called forests" have for the most part been decimated in the most "barbaric fashion." But while Murchison's remark may have lent an air of authority, or desperation, to the debate, Russians themselves had been calling attention in steady, sustained ways to shrinking woodlands, rising prices, impending disruption of trade, impacts on agriculture, and a host of other grim consequences. While the pace of forest exploitation increased dramatically in the wake of the Emancipation of 1861, the decades preceding saw sufficient loss of woodland to cause alarm.

In 1837 an Imperial commission was charged with studying how deforestation might play a role in distressingly low water levels on the Volga River; that commission concluded that loss of woodlands in the region *probably* was the cause, but felt it "premature" to institute new legal restrictions on the cutting of watershed woodlands.[10] The debate continued, however, in the *Journal of the Ministry of State Properties*, and in the Moscow Society of Agriculturalists, where Sergei Maslov was presiding secretary.[11] Among periodicals that addressed the forest issue, a central role was played by the *Forest Journal*, which began publication in St. Petersburg in 1833 as the first forest periodical in Russia, published by the Society for the Promotion of Forest Management, an organization founded in 1832 and merged in 1845 with the Free Economic Society, the "oldest and most influential economic society in Russia."[12] The *Forest Journal* continued publication through the century, with a hiatus of twenty years (1851–71), after which its audience and scope changed as forestry itself became increasingly professionalized.[13] From 1833 through 1851 the *Forest Journal*'s primary intention was "helping landowners undertake rule-based forestry, through provision of useful information on forest sciences and new discoveries in this realm."[14] Bimonthly issues offered landowners and estate managers an array of perspectives and information on woodlands and agriculture. Section headings for the journal in the 1840s included silviculture, forest technology and taxonomy, entomology, natural history, zoology, and botany. For more leisurely reading, issues included accounts of hunting exploits and reports of extreme weather events, as well as miscellaneous entries on gardening, beekeeping, and forest-threatening pests.[15] Numbers regularly included reports from abroad and accounts of deforestation and forestry challenges in both European countries and the New World.[16] Throughout the 1840s there were periodic contributions to forest statistics, with regular "field reports" from crown forests and private estates throughout European Russia.[17]

Articles in both the *Forest Journal* and the *Journal of Agriculture and Livestock* lamented loss of woodland and called for better management of forestland. The titles don't mince words; one typical example from the *Forest Journal* in 1841 proclaims "A perspective on the state of forests in Russia generally, the main reasons for their exhaustion, and a method to eradicate this evil."[18] A contribution to the *Journal of Agriculture and Livestock* in the same year lamented the loss of woodlands in the Moscow region and an attendant scarcity that was driving up the cost of fuel: "In earlier days a large part of the Moscow *guberniia* was covered with ancient, immeasurable forest. . . . That was indeed a golden age for landowners, peasants and residents of Moscow."[19] Koenig's speech ends by pointing to Persia and various Mediterranean countries as evidence of arid landscapes that had once been fertile, suggesting the possibility that landscapes have already changed radically for the worse. Sergei Maslov's afterword counsels finding out just when—and for what reasons—Moscow's forests began to be destroyed; he refers to wood hunger in the wake of Napoleon's departure from Moscow, as the inhabitants began to rebuild the city that had burned: "short sighted observers imagined that Moscow's woodlands were limitless."[20] Taken together, these writers suggest a growing understanding of how quickly and radically landscapes could change, and how great the *human* role in such precipitous change could be. That recognition would strengthen over the course of the century, both in Russia and elsewhere: in the United States, George Perkins Marsh cataloged observations of profoundly altered landscapes, both in his home state of Vermont and in the countries of Europe and the Middle East, which he had visited while serving as U.S. envoy to Turkey in the 1850s. "Even Russia," he wrote, "which we habitually consider as substantially a forest country, is beginning to suffer seriously for want of wood."[21]

Commissions and periodicals throughout the following decades debated both the impact of deforestation and what should be done about it. In the early 1860s, Fedor Arnol'd argued adamantly in the *Journal of the Ministry of State Properties* for the role of forests in protecting agricultural land. Arnol'd, a forest specialist who would later become a professor of forestry at the Forest Institute and the Petrovsko-Razumovskaya Academy in Moscow, drew on German and Russian examples of silted rivers and impeded transport to argue for the "detrimental influence of forest destruction" on hydrology.[22] Russian scientists continued to debate the role of forests in hydrological systems, and to what extent woodlands were implicated in climate and patterns of moisture. The Emancipation of 1861, in the meantime, ushered in an economic revolution that was to have profound impacts on Russia's European forests. The scale and pace of deforestation increased with startling speed. "Never have our forests been so ruthlessly felled as at present, and in a huge region stretching along the tributaries of the northern and central Volga—a region that one imagines might furnish fuel and building material for nearby districts in perpetuity—there is precious little timber of good quality."[23] Arnol'd and his contemporaries acknowledged the difficulty of getting a clear sense of just how much woodland was disappearing, and conditions were in any case chaotic; in the aftermath of the reform landowners sold almost 30 percent of lands they had held before Emancipation; their sales of cutting rights were at least as destructive, "while landowners had only the foggiest notion of what they were selling."[24] In 1864, still at the beginning of his broad-reaching reforms, Alexander II charged his minister of state properties with a study of how best to protect privately owned woodlands.[25] Just over a decade later a ministerial report, "On the Protection of Woodlands of Importance to the State," acknowledged the need for action, but balked at imposing limits on what private owners did with their property.[26] In April of 1877 the Imperial Society of Naturalists convened a commission to consider the science of the question.[27] And in publications as diverse as the *Russian Herald*, the *Voice*, and Fyodor Dostoevsky's *A Writer's Diary*, the fate of Russia's forests—and their impact on human lives—continued to be debated. As one historian of Russian forestry puts it, "the *forest problem* had taken over public consciousness. You could barely find a newspaper or journal that didn't present endless evidence of the catastrophic state of the forests."[28]

Writers like Turgenev and Mel'nikov-Pechersky, along with writers for both broad and more specialized readerships, give us a vivid sense of the communities whose lives depended on Russia's European forests. Nineteenth-century Russians of all stations depended heavily on wood for fuel and building material, and peasant communities used wood as raw material for craft objects either for home use or trade. Mel'nikov-Pechersky's trans-Volga communities produced an array of implements of daily life—everything from spoons to saucers out of native linden, items shipped out to markets along the river, and from there throughout Russia.[29] One 1844 account of an estate owned by the Stroganovs in the Perm region enumerates fifty-one categories of products for their own use from local forests—everything from linden bark stripped for peasant shoes and birch for canisters, to tar, elm ashes, and willow bark.[30] Game, honey, berries, mushrooms—all were essential and sustaining "gifts" of the forest economy, access to which was granted (or denied) by tradition and law. The symbolic rituals of rural life also depended on woodlands, including seasonal rites that trained foresters found unnecessarily destructive, since they involved gathering the boughs of young birches to decorate homes and the village church.[31] In August of 1868 a lengthy article on Russian forestry appeared in the *Russian Herald*; the author, Aleksandr Rudzkii, was a young forester who would later take a position at the Forest Institute in St. Petersburg. In his survey of the economics of Russian forestry he noted how little other surrogates had come into use in Russia, with little or no coal used for heating, and much less iron and stone used in building than in European countries. In Russia's most southerly, sparsely forested provinces, manure and straw replaced wood as a source of fuel, with ruinous effects on agriculture—Russian soils, as Rudzkii put it, being far less inexhaustible than "perennial optimism" wanted to believe. Europeans routinely expressed amazement at how overheated Russian dwellings were—Rudzkii compares them to hospital wards—and industry and the development of railroads had begun to consume greater and greater quantities of wood.[32] Ivanovo, a textile center northeast of Moscow, was often called the "Russian Manchester"—but, as Rudzkii puts it, were the economic activity of Ivanovo to equal that of the *real* Manchester, it would need six times more wood than existed in the whole of the Vladimir *guberniia*. Russia had not, as yet, accessed the resources of coal that would fuel its own version of the industrial revolution, although an 1871 contributor to the *Transactions of the Free Economic Society* suggested that coal would "boil the soup and fire the stoves" of our grandchildren, and that warnings of wood hunger were, "thank God," premature.[33]

Rudzkii wields the dry prose of economic statistics in order to estimate the reality of just how much woodland Russia actually has at its disposal—claiming, in a manner that was surely intended to startle the reader, that Russia is a country *extremely poor in wood* (458). His claim is based both on careful analyses of existing statistics and a consideration of the geography of Russia's forests: the sparsely populated provinces of the north are home to the vast preponderance of woodlands, while central and southern regions—with the bulk of the population and most rapidly industrializing urban centers—are starved for wood. Gauging just how much of European Russia was forested was no simple task: Rudzkii uses figures amassed by Arnol'd but concedes that they are highly inexact, including "a mass of bogs, lakes, wastes, ravines, roads, clearcuts that have not grown back, and other non-forested areas within the region designated as forest."[34] Russia could without doubt make better use of its existing resources, but given the "lamentable lack of management," Russia abuses and exploits an essential but limited resource: "We get from our woods only a tiny portion of what they might give if the owner [*khoziain*] were more attentive and educated" (459). Despite the caution and conservatism of his estimates, Rudzkii's conclusion is quietly apocalyptic: "The day is not far off when, with the growth of population and the development of industry and continued lack of forest management, the present lack of wood will take on the proportions of civic disaster" (465).

At the time he wrote his "Notes on Russian Forestry," Rudzkii was working as head forester on a newly organized model forest in the Penza region, and on various privately owned woodlands, positions he would keep until 1878, when he became professor of forest management at the St. Petersburg Forest Institute.[35] He had grown up in the Chernigov district northeast of Kiev, where his father was a county forester.[36] After training at the Forest Institute, Rudzkii spent two years traveling in Germany, France, Holland, and England, a customary rite of passage for young Russian foresters. These travels became the occasion for Rudzkii's first efforts as a writer, when his "Notes on Contemporary European Forestry" appeared in the *Journal of the Ministry of State Properties*.[37] When he returned to Russia in 1863 he made a tour of the forests of European Russia. Offered a position at the Petersburg Forest Institute in the mid-1860s, he turned it down, wanting instead to increase his experience with practical forestry.[38] His essay in the *Russian Herald* draws on his awareness of European forestry and industrial development but is also keenly attentive to the particularities of Russian forests and the sociocultural conditions that shape their use and abuse.

Rudzkii was one of many professional forest scientists and publicists who contributed to broad public discussions of the Forest Question in the decades after 1861. While scientists continued to debate just how woodlands, hydrology, and climate were related, other contributors engaged questions regarding community and state control over privately held woodlands. The Russian state's earliest efforts at forest protection were instituted under Peter I, in a series of measures intended to restrict access to mast pines essential to the Russian navy. Though Peter was hailed by one commentator as "Russia's first forester," his often-draconian measures for protecting woodland recognized no distinction between privately held and state woodlands; setting fire to protected forests or felling oak for building purposes was punishable by death.[39] This lack of differentiation between private and public woodland led, suggests Enessa Istomina, to a view among the public of "forest resources as state property."[40] That situation changed radically under Catherine II, with an affirmation of private landowners' rights to "make the best use of all of their woodlands." Woodlands, as Istomina puts it, came to be regarded in the wake of Catherine's statute as "profit-bearing property."[41] Contributors to the *Forest Journal* and men like Rudzkii tended to use the term *pravil'noe lesnoe khoziaistvo* in calling for better management; their appeals were to landowners' self-interest, but as Rudzkii and others pointed out, a variety of economic factors after 1861 worked against keeping land in forest. Given the disincentive of the market, Rudzkii turns to other considerations that might keep a landowner from selling his woodlands, including obligations "as landowners, capitalists, fathers or, finally, citizens."[42] For much of the nineteenth century, defenders of Russia's forest would work to challenge the notion of woodlands as subject only to individual control, seeking instead to argue a higher claim, one grounded in the forests' essential role in common life, and the averting of "national disasters."[43]

Brian Bonhomme has suggested that "to a degree perhaps unparalleled in the west, private forestry [in Russia] came to be reviled by influential members of the major forest societies—and even within the Forest Department itself—as a continuing and primary threat to good forest management and to the existence of the forests themselves."[44] Rudzkii's 1868 essay does not challenge private forestry per se, but insists on the "urgent necessity for the government to become involved in private forest management, in order to stop the immoderate destruction of one of the main sources of people's well-being."[45] His claim is that forests need to be seen as a particular *kind* of property, one whose use (or abuse) bears consequences for the community as a whole. While certain kinds of property brought with them the right of both use (*jus utendi*) and abuse (*jus abutendi*), this must not be the case with woodlands: "If the product being abused is necessary for common life, and if its abuse threatens to lead to national disasters, then only a weak and insecure state would fail to limit personal rights in the name of the common good" (453). His argument would be echoed a decade later by Iakov Veinberg, a Moscow educator invited by two Imperial societies to review current understandings of deforestation's impacts on hydrology and climate. In a series of articles written for the *Russian Herald*, Veinberg made a comprehensive review of the current science and also argued for limitations on private property rights, in order to protect resources whose destruction would endanger the whole community: just as the state is justified in protecting an individual from the negative or injurious actions of others, so is it bound to limit freedom "in those cases when the capricious, merciless and irrational destruction of private woodlands threatens (or may subsequently threaten) a whole region with calamity."[46]

In his 1868 essay Rudzkii noted ruefully that *moderation only comes with the experience of need* (454). Conservation of a limited resource would only come when sufficient numbers of people—or sufficiently powerful—had felt the impact of its loss. The most significant legal action regarding the forest taken in the nineteenth century was the 1888 Law on the Protection of Forests, signed in April of that year by Alexander III. The law uses the language of "destruction and exhaustion" to establish jurisdiction, grounded in an assumption of "state and societal need."[47] The law's jurisdiction extended to all forests of European Russia, whether private or state-owned; it established certain woodlands as protected based on a series of considerations, all premised on an understanding of the forest's role in preventing erosion, stabilizing sandy soils, and retaining moisture that would otherwise compromise river systems and agriculture. Restrictions on certain kinds of activity—including clear-cuts that would threaten the forest's ability to regenerate—were extended to *all* forests, not just those deemed protected. The law charged local commissions with determining just which woodlands were to receive protective status, and the Forest Department of the Ministry of Agriculture and State Lands with enforcement. Clearly informed by scientific and legal discussions of the preceding decades, the law aimed, suggests Enessa Istomina, as much to modernize Russian forestry as to preserve Russia's forests, and to enforce what concerned voices had been calling for over the past four decades: *pravil'noe lesnoe khoziaistvo*—literally "rule-based" forest management, a term that bears some comparison with what we understand as *sustainable* forestry. Growing awareness of forest loss, of silted rivers, eroded banks, and arid fields seems to have shaped a perception of what Rudzkii had called "need."

How effective was the law? What did it accomplish? While the pace of cutting continued virtually unabated, the losses would undoubtedly have been still greater *without* the law—given the intensified growth of industry and population in the final decades of the Russian Empire.[48] The law did curtail some destruction—and if it didn't live up to its intentions, argue Istomina and others, it was because it was ill enforced, because it included numerous loopholes, and because Russia lacked both personnel and the body of knowledge that could have undergirded its fine intentions. In *Russian Forest* (*Russkii les*), a handbook of forestry written for a broad public two years after the law's passage, Fedor Arnol'd declined in principle to lay blame for the "sad contemporary state of forestry": "One wants to avoid discussions of the rapacity of the Russian wood manufacturer, or the wastefulness of woodland owners, the ignorance and incompetence of Russian forestry specialists, and finally of the Russian peasant's low level of culture—perhaps better put as the low level of the Russian peasantry's inclination to adopt new and unfamiliar cultural strategies. The printed word must be honorable and truthful; but the reasons for the sad state of contemporary forestry lie considerably deeper than those superficial layers, breeding grounds for wastefulness, rapacity and piquant judgments about our ignorance and cultural incompetence."[49] His words make clear where blame had tended to fall—but Arnol'd himself chooses to look forward with guarded optimism, hoping that the knowledge he proffers will combine with citizens' care for the forest: the passions aroused by the law will die down, and "in the current generation of youth will remain only a feeling of gratitude for their fathers' first step to preserve a national treasure."[50] Istomina suggests that the law's most significant legacy was its inculcation of conservationist and ecological outlooks in public consciousness: Arnol'd and his generation gave Russia a legacy of scientific work that delved more deeply into the interconnections of climate, hydrology, and woodlands—and established the notion of "monuments of nature" that became foundational for protected lands in both Russia and the Soviet Union.[51]

Arnol'd's *Russian Forest* begins by characterizing the country's woodlands not in scientific language but with the languages of folklore and popular Orthodoxy. The "Russian Forest," Arnol'd suggests, is really *two forests*: the first is made up of the "broad woodland regions of the north and northeast European Russia, Siberia and the Caucasus mountains," dense and unified, intersected only occasionally by bogs, lakes, and cultivated land. These are the "kingdom of almost wild forest, little acquainted with the strength and power of cultured humankind," forests more accustomed to "reigning supreme in the realm they occupy than submitting to the conditions of the surrounding world . . . impassable either on foot or by cart, strewn with downed trees, clothed in gray mists, silver frost and moist, shaggy moss." This forest looks with indifference on the "tears and sorrow of humans, and grants its products to them unwillingly."[52] Arnol'd goes on to call this forest Russia's "northern colossus"—noting that *this* is what most foreigners think of when they think of Russia's forest.

But for Arnol'd there is another forest that is more truly Russian, one that is long-suffering, generous of heart, and self-sacrificing. "The dispassionate foreign gaze only sees [in this long-suffering forest] the normal traits of an invalid and starveling compared to European forest beauties, but the Russian soul must give it his due and call *this* forest *his own*." It is this familiar, beloved, suffering forest that is closest to the Russian's heart: these are "tame forests, or at any rate they've grown accustomed to humans"; these are the forests that every educated Russian has visited at least once in his life, and about which so much has been written of late. "[These forests] are being ruthlessly cut down and even wholly destroyed, thanks to ambition, greed, and perhaps simply the faintheartedness of people— in a word, this is that long-suffering forest whose situation of late has become so threatened and miserable that the government at long last acknowledged the need to offer its powerful hand in aid, to take it under its protection, and to take steps for its defense."[53] Arnol'd draws here on what A. S. called "poetry" to stir in his readers a desire to protect and preserve. A similar impulse led Aleksandr Rudzkii, a decade after his "Notes on Russian Forestry," to proclaim the *affective values* of forests: where his 1868 essay had marshaled economic discourse for a broad audience, this essay—published in the newly revived *Forest Journal* for an audience of professional foresters—suggests that the "value" of woodlands goes far beyond the monetary or quantifiable: "Forests are useful to man either directly—in what they produce—or indirectly: they satisfy our feeling of beauty; they influence the country's climate; they influence the fertility and inhabitability of surrounding areas; they are of socio-political significance; they influence other forms of culture."[54] While Rudzkii, Veinberg, Arnol'd, and other scientific writers acknowledged the nonutilitarian, affective significance of Russia's forests, Russia's artists and writers were increasingly aware of—and moved by—scientific, legal, and economic understandings of how Russia's forests were vulnerable to the forces of greed and destruction. In the decade preceding the promulgation of the 1888 Forest Law, the forest question would occupy a central place in Russia's cultural imagination, as writers, artists, and citizens grappled with the meaning for human and natural communities of the destruction of their European woodland. In doing this they would explore, from their own vantage points, how "poetry and measurement" might not hinder each other.

* * *

RUDZKII CONCLUDES his 1868 essay with an affirmation of the power of public opinion, *obshchestvennoe mnenie*. "In conclusion let us add that in addition to various administrative institutions, there exists a powerful and, moreover, cost-free means of administrative oversight. We are speaking of public opinion. This form of oversight is thus far little used in Russia. Although its use is accompanied with challenges and is not without danger, nonetheless public opinion may serve as an excellent means of oversight, for those who know how to use it."[55] Rudzkii's comment embodies the optimism and sense of potential of the Reform period in Russia, with its growing sense among professionals that public discourse (*glasnost'*) and civic action might effect positive change.[56] The fact that the Forest Question—along with all those other questions of late Imperial Russia—got raised at all in broad-circulation journals suggests the extent to which writers felt it was a matter that needed broad and multifaceted response. Commissions and legal proposals were part of that—and so were the kinds of opinion and consciousness that Istomina and Rudzkii refer to. The relationship between forms of writing traditionally called *publicistics*—the popular science and management advice of the *Forest Journal* or the *Russian Herald* accounts of hydrology and deforestation for a broad, nonspecialist audience—and the creative work of Russia's poets, artists, and prose writers, is complex, a matter less of influence than of a broad cultural and environmental context, in which both scientific writers and their artistic contemporaries draw on bodies of information and resonant images, along with their own experience of landscape and change. In the decade and a half before the promulgation of the 1888 law, educated Russians might have encountered the Forest Question at every turn: while Mel'nikov-Pechersky and Tolstoy published epic treatments of rural life and forested landscapes in monthly journals, the Petersburg Forest Society was established and restarted publication of the the *Forest Journal*; the botanist Kliment Timiriazev gave public lectures on "The Plant as a Source of Strength"; and Pavel Valuev, in the Ministry of State Properties, issued a report "On the Protection of Woodlands of Importance to the State."[57] The apocalyptic landscape of deforested Russia had become an icon of publicistic writing at least as much as of literary work, so that tones of alarm could easily give way to sarcasm: "Holy Russia, they say, is cutting down its slumbering forests, leading the population to certain death."[58] Iakov Veinberg begins his 1879 account of the forest's significance in nature not with geography and botany but with "imagination": "The forest couldn't but make a profound impression on human imagination, thanks to the cool and mysterious shadows of the pinelands, the imperturbable stillness that reigns there. The forest presents itself to the poetic mind as something mysterious, loftier, something that exists apart, indifferent to human affairs. Winds rock the heights of the giants, but are powerless to break them; the sun's rays penetrate the forest glade only weakly, one barely feels the winds and rain. Many beings give birth and die there; and sometimes a mysterious sounding and speaking sounds hence."[59] Russia's "poetic mind" represented forest destruction in these decades in both negative aesthetic and idyllic vision, marrying both to an emerging ecological understanding and to the vexed Russian politics of class.

Ilya Repin's 1883 canvas *Procession of the Cross in the Kursk District* is to my mind the starkest image we have of nineteenth-century deforestation in Russia, powerfully suggestive of a connection between the cultural imagination and the work of scientists and journalists who were both documenting and decrying the destruction of Russian woodlands. Repin's painting is not normally thought of as an environmental image, or a reflection of the Forest Question. For generations of viewers and critics, it has been an icon of social protest, one that focuses on the inequities and hypocrisy of post-Emancipation Russian social order. The painting's evident social critique made it the subject of both praise and blame, its "manifest message . . . a mordant judgment on conditions in the countryside some two decades after the Emancipation."[60] The painting is a prime example of denunciatory realism, illustrating the ways in which Russia's realist painters, the Itinerants, used their art as a vehicle of conscience and consciousness-raising.[61] Soviet critics lavished attention on the diverse representatives of Russia's privileged and her poorest—cripples, beggars, itinerant pilgrims polemically contrasted with plump merchants and still plumper priests.

Seeing the painting in this way is compelling, but it pays scant attention to the role of landscape in the image—or, to be more precise, the *absence* of landscape—what Elizabeth Valkenier calls "the alienation of people from the natural surroundings."[62] Repin's canvas shows a vast crowd of Russian humanity, enacting one of the central summer rituals of Orthodox village life, a procession of the faithful led by an entourage of priests, icons, and banners.

The crowd of peasants, merchants, beggars, and pilgrims moves along a long, dusty diagonal. Repin painted the scene as a series of horizontals—the mass of humanity with their dark bodies at ground level creates the

Ilya Repin, Procession of the Cross in the Kursk District *(1883). Tretyakov Gallery, Moscow. Scala / Art Resource, NY.*

horizontal nearest us; the sky and hillside in the background create another. The great diversity of Repin's rendering of the earthbound crowd draws the viewer's eye, but so do the figures who stand out above them. Rising above the crowd are eight or so figures on horseback, and if our gaze moves beyond them into the background, we are confronted with a bare and dusty hillside, with stumps of recently cut timber and brush, a hillside where a forest used to be.

There is no indication in the painting of just why this procession might have been taking place, although both regular saints' days and irregular climatic events led local clergy to institute processions of the cross. Similar rituals took place in nearby regions in times of poor harvest and drought: an 1869 description from the city of Orel—one hundred miles north of Kursk—cites three yearly processions: one for the Feast of the Assumption, one to pray for deliverance from cholera epidemics, and one (celebrated July 20) for relief from drought.[63] In the late 1880s and early 1890s, Vladimir Korolenko's accounts of drought conditions and famine in the central Volga region similarly describe processions of the cross—popular responses to climatic conditions that seemed beyond human control.[64] Ilya Repin's painting, in any case, situates the procession not in a pastoral landscape but in a world that seems ravaged by both natural and human forces.

Early sketches for the painting date from 1877: the first of these focuses on human figures involved in an altercation over who will carry the icon; the second, produced in 1878, situates the procession deep in an oak wood.

The 1878 sketch is lush, almost bucolic; Aleksei Fedorov-Davydov—one of the Soviet Union's most distinguished art historians—suggests that the sheer *visual* pleasures of landscape threaten to swamp the "ideological" in this version.[65] This sketch in fact recalls the world of Boev's 1871 "Pictures of Forest Life" with its sense of idyllic harmony between ritual procession and a natural world that seems blessed. Boev's description is itself a narrative icon of sacred landscape, with the urban observer standing entranced as a religious procession emerges from woods and then passes on, leaving an echo of "familiar, prayer-filled singing" in its wake.[66] Repin's sketches for the *Procession* veer from satiric to elegiac, as though the painter himself was unsure how to depict an event so complexly evocative of changing village life. Leo Tolstoy, when Repin showed him a sketch of the work in the early 1880s, urged him to make more explicit his own relationship to what he was painting: when Repin told Tolstoy that his job was to "represent life," the writer pushed him on whether he "love[d] or hate[d]" the rituals he was depicting.[67] In the summer of 1878 Repin had visited his childhood home in the Kharkov region of southern Russia (now Ukraine), thinking to revisit beloved places; instead

Ilya Repin, Procession of the Cross in an Oak Forest: Presentation of the Icon *(1878). Reproduced with permission of the Tretyakov Gallery, Moscow.*

he found deep provincial torpor and a ruined landscape: "The only ones who aren't sleeping are the local exploiters, the *kulaks.* They've cut down my favorite oakwood. . . . Now it's just bare land, covered with stumps."[68] Those stumps dominate another plein air sketch from 1881, and we see them in the final painting on the hillside beyond the crowd of believers, above the backs of police on horseback. One of the police prepares to strike a woman in the crowd: the whip—which elicited outrage from contemporary reviewers—is potently reminiscent of the axes that would have felled those hillside oaks.[69] In Repin's landscape of post-reform Russia nothing is sacred; the forces of violence that assail human society are also at work destroying oaks, which in the earlier version suggest fertility, shelter, and authentic faith. The sense of organic unity and correspondence between human and natural worlds has yielded in the final painting to grotesquerie and violence. Fedorov-Davydov in fact suggested that the *absence* of landscape is part of what makes the painting so powerful, as though we as viewers are assaulted by the arid emptiness of the land. What had once nurtured human communities now turns against them. Meanwhile the procession moves on—oblivious of the ravaged landscape where a kind of Eden used to be.

Ilya Repin, Summer Landscape. *Study for* Procession of the Cross in the Kursk District *(1881). Reproduced with permission of the Tretyakov Gallery, Moscow.*

Repin's painting draws powerfully on traditions that imagine an animate relationship between humans and woodlands. The analogizing of trees and humans, and the assumption that humans can communicate with animals, woodlands, and natural phenomena, are ubiquitous features of Russian folk song and poetry. What modern critics have called anthropomorphism is here a legacy of animistic imaginations, locutions that came to fascinate ethnographers and poets in search of folk perceptions of the natural world.[70] The nineteenth-century historian and ethnographer Nikolai Kostomarov refers to folk songs "addressing the forest as a being capable of participating in human feeling," while the silence of a grove far from a peasant's native place brings forth deep anguish. The implication is not just that humans and trees talk to each other, but that such communication is sustained by common lives and shared places.[71] Alexander Afanas'ev's *Poetic Views of the Slavs on Nature*—so central to Mel'nikov-Pechersky's *In the Forests*—includes a lengthy section of creation stories in which the first humans are created from trees. The number of nineteenth-century poets who imagine human-sylvan converse is quite likely a list of *all* nineteenth-century Russian poets—although certain writers' claims to authenticity are more heavily linked to traditions of folk allegory.[72] Aleksei Kol'tsov's 1837 poem "The Forest" ("*Les*") memorializes the death of Pushkin with a figurative likening of the great poet to a slumbering wood, whose noble speech has been silenced. The poem metaphorically connects the forests themselves to mythic *bogatyrs*: both warriors and walls of forest have—like the poet—been staunch defenders of Russia. Nikolai Nekrasov's 1858 "Sasha" includes an extended lament for a violently destroyed forest, a destruction that leaves a mother jackdaw crying frantically for her children, who have been thrown from their nest. Nekrasov's verse makes the clear-cut into a battleground, his woodsmen into rampaging conquerors, and the fallen trees themselves corpses. The poem elaborates a linkage between violent acts against nature and similarly violent acts against humans, rehearsing in its heroine Sasha a highly sentimental, outraged reaction: the phrase *"plakala Sasha kak les vyrubili"*—"Sasha wept as the woods were cut down"—has become both a much-anthologized cliché and a rallying cry for forest activists in the late twentieth century.[73]

Oaks are associated with righteousness and authority in multiple cultural traditions, including Russia's: Ivan Shishkin's *Among the Spreading Vale*—like Repin's *Procession of the Cross*, first displayed at the 1883 Itinerant exhibit— shows a monumental oak, standing in a vast landscape of fields and light, reaching almost to the top of the canvas against a broad, empty sky.[74]

Shishkin's oak is in a sense an image of what has been destroyed in Repin's painting.[75] The painting's title is taken from Andrei Merzliakov's popular folk song, which begins by invoking the "powerful beauty" and loneliness of a solitary oak, then shifts into the singer's lament at loneliness in "a strange land."

Ivan Shishkin, Among the Spreading Vale *(1883). Reproduced with permission of the Kiev National Museum of Russian Art.*

The lyrics link the oak and the lonely singer's voice, offering the image of a great oak on a broad upland as an image of the "dear homeland," an image that is the anguished singer's only solace. The oak almost has a voice here: like Kol'tsov's poem, Merzliakov grants sentience to the natural world; we understand our own emotions of anguish and longing for home in terms of the great tree's solitude.[76]

Ilya Repin, L. N. Tolstoi Resting in the Forest under a Tree *(1891). Tretyakov Gallery, Moscow. Image copyright Lebrecht Music & Arts.*

Repin's 1883 painting gives us, in contrast, an image of Russia abandoned to violence, lacking the upright dignity of authority represented both in peasant culture and in literary tradition by those towering oaks. A decade later, when Repin produced a series of paintings of Leo Tolstoy, he represented the writer in various settings that emphasize his connections to peasant culture, labor, and the natural world: several of those paintings show Tolstoy in the shadow of his beloved trees—including one in which the writer is recumbent on a bed of last year's leaves, a dark brown trunk extending upward from his white-capped head.

The composition suggests he has become rooted there, his dignity and authority nourished by the same source as the trees'. Tolstoy takes on an oak-like quality in these paintings, as if Repin—dismayed by the apocalyptic spectacle of violence, hypocrisy, and destroyed woodlands, all of it undermining the very possibility of health, whether natural or human—found solace in these images of dignity and fertility.

Repin's images of Tolstoy scything, or standing barefoot in a freely rendered greenwood, or reading at the base of a great shade tree, are both consolation and calls to action. Perhaps—Repin suggests—the scythe could replace the ax, or the policeman's whip.[77]

Tolstoy himself provides our second example of artistic Russia's "response" to the Forest Question, one that began in the years of his youth and stretches, in some sense, into our own day—since some of the trees he planted are still standing.[78] As a young man Tolstoy had, like many other landed sons, cut and sold his woods to pay off debts. The family estate he inherited in 1847 had been left to fall into disrepair by its purported managers; the peasants of Yasnaya Polyana ("Clear Glade") were ruined, and much of the woodland had been cut down.[79] Tolstoy's initial reaction to the inheritance was to continue the profligate ways of his predecessors; in a letter of February 1849 to his brother Sergei he is desperate for cash: "I need as much money as possible, firstly in order to live here and secondly in order to settle up my debts in Moscow. If there's not enough grain to provide me with another 800 silver roubles on top of the 250 and 500 which I've already written about, for goodness sake sell Savin wood, and if that's still not enough, get another advance from Kopylov, less interest. If you sell Savin wood, the first condition must be: all money in advance."[80] Tolstoy's journey to the Caucasus and his service in the Imperial army there and in the Crimean campaign inaugurated a set of profound personal changes, however—the beginning of his career as a writer, and a growing desire to forge a life at Yasnaya that would embrace labor and family. From 1856 until his death over fifty years later, Yasnaya Polyana was to be the wellspring of Tolstoy's creativity and ground from which to critique a rapidly modernizing Russia. Sustained, well-considered reforestation of the estate was part and parcel of his life there,

Ilya Repin, Leo Tolstoy Barefoot *(1891). Image copyright Lebrecht Authors / Lebrecht Music & Arts.*

an activity—what was surely a *vocation*—that gave visible evidence of the ways in which Tolstoy sought to challenge an ethos of destruction. Konstantin Semenov, who worked as forester on the estate in the twentieth century—by which point it had become a museum and *zapovednik*, or conservation area—spoke of Yasnaya as "a great book of life, of the agrarian labors and creativity of Tolstoy. *One needs to know how to read it.*"[81]

Tolstoy's work on the estate both restored that particular place and created the imaginative space in which to write *Anna Karenina*, a novel that among other things considers woodlands and their role in human tales of greed and grace. Tolstoy and his wife, Sofya Andreevna, were actively involved in the work of practical forestry, planting, thinning, and constructing drainage ditches.[82] Semenov estimates that Tolstoy increased the amount of orchard land from tens of hectares to 40 (about 100 acres), while expanding woodlands on the estate from 174 to 440 hectares—some of which he planted, while others he left to return naturally to forest. In doing so he "transformed the natural environment of Yasnaya Polyana, turning arable land, the slopes of ravines, and unwooded banks of the Voronka river and its tributary the Kochak into wooded plantations." His efforts at replanting took him in 1857 to Frants Maier, an innovative agronomist and pioneer of steppe forestation who worked as manager of the Shatilov estates near Tula. Tolstoy consulted with Maier on methods of field division and came home with over seven thousand seedlings to plant at Yasnaya—including spruce, pine, and linden.[83]

Tolstoy's engagement with the woodlands of his estate and the surrounding regions also included a brief foray into public policy: in 1857 he drew up a proposal for restoration of the *Tulskie zaseki*—those bands of dense woodland into which Turgenev's hunter had wandered in "Journey into Polesye."

Tolstoy's proposal aimed to shift responsibility for forest management and conservation to landowners rather than the state. As Semenov puts it, "Tolstoy wasn't proposing anything particularly new when it came to the technology of planting. He proposed that cleared woodlots be temporarily used for agricultural uses, with the idea that the user would return them to the forest district in 7 to 9 years, planted with seedlings or young stock, as previously agreed. What was new was something else. Since he had no faith in the Forest Department bureaucrats, Tolstoy proposed attracting 'independent entrepreneurs' to do the planting; they would be drawn by the possibility of using the land."[84] In late October of 1857 Tolstoy presented his proposal to Aleksandr Zelenyi at the Ministry of State Properties; both that meeting and one later in the week with the minister himself, M. N. Murav'ev, left Tolstoy feeling he had spoken badly and botched his chances. The proposal wasn't accepted, and perhaps wasn't even considered seriously. Tolstoy's fellow writers, in the meantime, regarded

Map of Yasnaya Polyana showing the Tula zaseki *just to the north. From K. S. Semenov,* Zapovednik: Ocherk-putevoditel'. *Tula: Tul'skoe knizhnoe izdatel'stvo, 1956, 94.*

his efforts at both practical and political forestry as nothing short of folly, a distraction from his *real* work as an author. Ivan Turgenev and Pavel Annenkov traded letters expressing amazement at Tolstoy's plan "for reforesting the whole of Russia." Turgenev, Nekrasov, and other Petersburg literati might recognize and even condemn the loss of Russia's forests, but Tolstoy's attempts at practical husbandry struck them as ludicrous. "There's a man for you! With excellent legs on him he absolutely must walk about on his head. He just recently wrote Botkin a letter in which he says, 'I'm very pleased I didn't listen to Turgenev, didn't just become a *penman.*' In response I asked him just what he is, then: an officer? a landowner? etc. Turns out he's a forester! I only fear he doesn't break the back of his talent with all this jumping about."[85]

As it turned out, the back of Tolstoy's talent would be strengthened rather than broken by the heavy lifting he engaged in at Yasnaya—activities that ranged from establishing schools to scything to felling wood, all of which nourished his lifelong passion *not simply* to be a "penman." While Turgenev imagines planting trees to be at odds with writing novels, for Tolstoy there is a vital link between the planting, the ministerial proposal, and the novel written over fifteen years later. *Anna Karenina* engages deeply with questions of responsibility, fidelity, and labor—in relationship not simply to matrimony and family but to place and coming generations.

Tolstoy's work on *Anna Karenina* began in earnest in 1873, by which point the concerns with forestry that had motivated his 1857 proposal had become widely acknowledged.[86] The ruined and deforested estate that Tolstoy had inherited in the late 1840s was in some sense a harbinger of the rampant destruction of woodlands and further impoverishment of the peasantry that would follow the 1861 Emancipation.[87] While his 1857 proposal for the *zaseki* hoped "independent entrepreneurs" might respond to incentives, *Anna Karenina* leaves us wondering whether Russia's landowners are up to the task. The depiction of Stiva Oblonsky—Anna's brother—as an unfaithful husband and bon vivant hardly suggests that responsibility for the country's forests should be lodged with such a likable but careless spendthrift. Tolstoy's alter ego Konstantin Levin expresses sharp disapproval of Stiva's decision to sell off his wife's woodlands in order to cover his debts. It is not just that Oblonsky has no knowledge of the forest itself (he has not "counted the trees," as Levin puts it); he is squandering an inheritance that is moral as well as material. " 'The fact is, you are giving the forest away,' said Levin gloomily." As he puts it in a conversation near the end of the novel, "I always feel I'm making no real profit out of my work on the land, and yet I go on. . . . One seems to owe a sort of duty to the land."[88] The notion that forms of obligation exist both to the land and to future generations underpins Iakov Veinberg's arguments in his 1878 discussion of decreasing water levels in Russia's rivers and springs: "We must make intelligent use of the earth's surface as we transform it, and not capriciously and selfishly change it, in such a way that we extract the utmost temporary benefit for ourselves, leaving nothing in the future either for ourselves or for future generations. . . . If our forefathers had thoughts of us in their early cultivation of the earth's surface, then our obligation is to have concern for our descendants." The novelist and the publicist echo each other here, with an understanding of responsibilities that curtail the kind of "caprice" and immediate gratification that Stiva Oblonsky so enjoys. One's thoughts and cares must extend beyond the self, in a continuum of concern that takes a much longer view.[89]

Tolstoy's environmental ethic in *Anna Karenina* is linked to his senses of obligation to family and community—an ethic that is finally inseparable from that "duty to the land" he senses is at odds with the ethos of modernity. In an exchange at the novel's end, Levin commiserates with a neighboring farmer about the seeming absurdity of their efforts: both men resist the advice of a neighboring merchant to cut down their lindens, which would fetch a good price. Levin and his friend resist those farmers—like this merchant, or like Vronsky, Anna's lover—who want to "turn agriculture into an industry," a notion that was not entirely new, even in Russia. In his preface to the Russian 1830 translation of Albrecht Thaer (considered the father of agricultural science and rational agriculture), N. S. Mordvinov had suggested that agriculture be viewed "as a factory that produces grain instead of cloth and other articles. Consequently, agriculture is subject to the same laws as those that govern other forms of industry."[90] Levin and his friend will be planters of orchards, rather than harvesters of lindens—trees associated in Russian culture with memory, and here with traditions of labor and place. "We work without making anything, as though we were ordained, like the vestals of old, to keep some sacred fire burning." While the language he uses suggests a priesthood of the earth, for Levin as for Tolstoy it is a life discipline in which labor becomes service to both land and family. Tolstoy's anti-industrial land ethic comes close to what Wendell Berry calls *good husbandry*: understanding the relationship of humans to the natural world as a relationship of long-term, multigenerational obligation, a kind of marriage to place that sees relationship in terms of complex responsibilities and pleasures.[91] The pleasures of both field and forest are many in Tolstoy's novel, including the deep quietude of hunting and the novel's final epiphany of life's meaning, when Levin "ran off to the forest once again, lay down under some aspen trees and began thinking, almost in a kind of ecstasy." For his contemporary Dostoevsky this is a paradigmatic moment: Levin is the eternal seeker who "runs off into the woods and groves."[92] But Tolstoy's celebration of these moral and psychological clarities is tinged by awareness of the vulnerability of Russia's forests both to spendthrift landowners and distant bureaucrats. Karenin, the novel's betrayed husband, is a state bureaucrat charged with the administration of distant lands, for whom complex machinations and power politics obscure any vivid sense of the realities of an actual place. As we shift in the novel away from Levin's literal, physical labor at an estate he knows so well, we find Karenin preparing a bureaucratic campaign against existing policies on irrigation and indigenous peoples—policies surely linked, in Tolstoy's mind, to the broader consequences for land and community when deracinated bureaucrats displace local knowledge and control.[93] We find ourselves back in the company of a younger Tolstoy, wanting to vest responsibility for Russia's natural resources in local landowners who have *counted their trees*. Between Stiva Oblonsky's blithe ignorance and Karenin's imperious will to control, Konstantin Levin and his woodlands stake a delicate but impassioned claim for the need for intimate knowledge of place, and principled husbandry that sees individuals (whether trees or humans) in terms of their larger communities of health and well-being.

The "forest question" is for Tolstoy fundamentally linked to the moral dramas of his characters, and to the complex psychic and moral challenges of his own privilege. In 1910, the final year of his life, Tolstoy received an anguished letter from a man named Luzinov, a forest warden in the Nizhnii region struggling with his role as enforcer of laws that criminalized peasants poaching timber. "There are many peasant communities near the county forest [*narodnaia dacha*], where much of the population is in desperate need of firewood and wood for building, and some of the peasants, driven by need, decide to enter the county forest in order to cut a load of firewood or logs for building, for what is absolutely necessary. . . . It sickens me to see these poor folk, when they pour out their soul before the judge, but state regulations mean they throw him in jail and write out a warrant. Your heart simply breaks when you have to go and demand money, make an inventory of their possessions and set a date to sell their pittance. . . . I haven't the strength to carry out all the warrants, of which almost 200 have piled up over the past ten years, and I keep finding ways to put off demanding funds, which are supposed to go for charitable causes. What sort of charity is financed with extorted funds? You'll not do good by doing evil. But that's what I'm made to do: take from one and give to the other. And I'm convinced that it shouldn't be done. It's a great sin!"[94]

The question clearly crystallized the whole painful topic of landownership and class privilege for Tolstoy. His answer is unequivocal: "You are right, conscience does not allow one to take part in such things as demanding money from poor peasants, or throwing them into prison because they want to take back even a small part of what has been taken from them. Ownership of property is theft. And therefore taking wood in someone else's forest is the small thief's theft from the bigger one."[95] Here both Tolstoy and the warden see the forest in primarily *communal* terms, as a resource necessary for human life, access to which has been denied. In the final decades of his life Tolstoy clearly understood himself to be one of those "bigger thieves"; what Levin in *Anna Karenina* calls duty to the land is not necessarily displaced here, but qualified by the scandal of a common resource expropriated by a landowning class. How was Russia to protect its woodlands when the forces of social inequality conspired with greed, population growth, and industrialization? Tolstoy's 1910 letter suggests that a land ethic—or protection of the forests—must also protect those communities least empowered and most dispossessed. But his blunt statement of what by this point seems to him indisputable ("Ownership of property is theft") doesn't indicate just how the loving knowledge and care that Levin had envisioned might extend into a more radical reshaping of access.

In February of 1876, the month in which the fourth section of *Anna Karenina* appeared in the *Russian Herald*, another group of Russian writers began what would become a spirited exchange about the Forest Question and its significance for Russia's future.[96] Nikolai Petrovich Zalomanov, an agronomist who went on to write widely, and critically, about efforts to "rationalize" Russian agriculture, delivered an address before the Society of St. Petersburg Agriculturalists, a group whose efforts since its founding in 1863 had been directed at assisting landowners in the practical management of their estates.[97] Zalomanov's speech drew responses from both Fyodor Dostoevsky and Evgenii Markov, a minor novelist and estate owner from the Kursk region.[98] In his speech, Zalomanov made the claim that it wasn't deforestation that was causing drought, but drought that was causing deforestation. He went on to suggest that advice to remediate the situation by planting trees would in fact only make the situation worse.[99] The exact impacts of forest loss on soil moisture, microclimate, and river systems continued to be debated: in the following year both Aleksandr Voeikov (climatologist and member of the Russian Academy) and Iakov Veinberg would write major reviews of the science, and understandings of the relationship between loss of forest cover and soil moisture would continue to evolve in the coming decades. Zalomanov's speech was, however, concerned with practical forestry, and his proposal seems to have been controversial enough to draw spirited rebuttals from both Markov and Dostoevsky.[100]

Markov begins his essay by challenging Zalomanov's science: the over-whelming consensus, Markov insists, is clear.[101] Citing both European specialists and a broad array of nonscientists, Markov draws on scientific and lay observation regarding the causes of drought, and then moves on to draw one more in our series of "catastrophic" pictures: "A whole continent the size of Europe, known to us as the breadbasket of Russia, is shaved as bald as an old man's head; a decade of droughts destroys our agriculture; people are impoverished; the government is impoverished; a century of European experience and the exacting results of diverse sciences are unanimous in confirming the dire impact of deforestation"—and Zalomanov denies it all. As Markov quotes him, Zalomanov had given an almost parodically narrow definition of forests in his speech: "forests are vertical *breillage*"—that is, containers of moisture. Markov's is a different sort of account, describing forests in terms that involve hydrology, climate, agriculture, and economy—but also spiritual well-being and community life. "Thus we expand the question of deforestation, taking it from economic to social and ethical ground. We defend and celebrate the forest not only as a repository of firewood or retainer of moisture, but also as a great temple of nature, in which the laborer of the field gains insight, takes his leisure, and is elevated in spirit—a temple in which he feels, thinks, contemplates and takes his rest." But this "temple" is fast disappearing. Markov offers place names as evidence of landscapes that have been lost, including seven villages whose names refer to lakes that are no longer there. In one of the essay's more striking passages, Markov announces that *nature no longer exists* in the lives of deforested peasants. What is lost isn't merely harvest and firewood, but a whole way of life, which Markov describes in miniature: "Amidst his inhospitable, wretched field, in his straw hut, with his straw feed, in clothing that might as well be made of straw, the peasant is now an impoverished tenant in the village. He has nothing: he's obliged to buy everything or get it on the side. . . . Without nature man is less moral and more dull-witted than the man in whom natural feeling is still alive. . . . Thus deforestation, as we see it, inevitably turns village dwellers into a second proletariat. . . . The village without the refreshing breath of nature will be exactly the same inhospitable and wretched urban quarter of coarse and agitated indigents." In a way not unlike Repin's suggestion of a landscape that has been violently destroyed, Markov's is an inserted description of a world from which "nature" has been removed.

Markov's parting vision, however, balances the idyllic against the dystopian. He wants to leave the reader with the "gratifying picture" he remembers from a visit to the farm of a Mennonite named Kornis, a "hospitable host who was the very image of an honest and hard-working Puritan. . . . His hamlet was alive with green and joyful groves, amongst which one saw the well-kept Dutch-brick structures of his home, barn and sheds. A narrow stream, that rare apparition among the steppes, snaked among the fields, with trees planted along its ambling course. Wherever one looked one saw joyous, joy-bringing islands of green, small but already mature groves. 'All about us was bare steppe, when my father got here,' Kornis told me. 'Everything you see was planted by my father and me. My father wanted the field where he worked to bring him joy: that's why he planted trees all about. There was no stream here—we planted the dry bed with trees, constructed small ponds, and now we can catch small fish.'" Here, says Markov, is evidence of what "rational labors" (*razumnye trudy*) and love can achieve. The Mennonite farmer has turned saline soils and bare clay into a "grapevine, a fertile garden, shaded southern groves." Unfortunately, laments Markov, this is an exception: "All our overlords [*bary*] can do is cart off invaluable forests by the thousands of acres, forests that really belong not to them but to the whole people, the whole region, what has grown over centuries. They've left us our native land, which once ran with milk and honey, almost as dead as the deserts of Syria or Edom, punished by God for their historical sins." Markov's pastoral vision—and the biblical language of his devastated counter-landscape—works to help us see, feel, and long for a way of life, one that he implies may be realized through human labor. His presentation of the idyllic landscape is allied to the world of civic action, and to an appreciation of focused, well-organized human labor. Markov's nature is a "temple," but it is one in which humans must also be good workers—and his forests are conceived not as property that can be wholly controlled by individuals, but as a kind of natural legacy of "centuries," belonging "to the whole people."

Dostoevsky's response to Zalomanov's speech came a few months later, in a June 1876 column entitled "My Paradox."[102] He begins with the so-called Eastern Question, but this is little more than a pretext, and he turns almost immediately from war in the Balkans to the "paradox" of his title, which has to do with the endlessly discussed (not least by Dostoevsky) question of Russia's relationship to Europe, and whether those who repudiate Russian backwardness and look to Europe for models of development and behavior weren't in fact profoundly "Russian." Dostoevsky's example is the literary critic and socialist Vissarion Belinsky—a man who criticized Russia at home but in European socialist contexts was critical of European culture. Europeans, Dostoevsky claims, hate Russians, whom they see as destroyers of civilization, as a "horde of savages, a band of Huns, ready to fall upon ancient Rome and destroy its sacred shrines." That the "majority" of Russians in Europe have declared themselves liberal is, Dostoevsky concedes, a "strange fact." What interests him, though, is the *why* of that fact, and thus begins a circling around of the question of Russians' purported destructiveness, and just *why* they destroy: just for the hell of it, or for some other reason? The question remains unanswered, and Dostoevsky moves on—to educated Russia's ignorance of Russian realities, and finally to the inability of society to reach any sort of consensus when presented with pressing "questions."

It is in this context that the "Forest Question" enters Dostoevsky's stream of paradox and provocation. The Eastern Question elicits a "clamor of discordant voices—but so do any one of the

> hundreds, the thousands of our internal and everyday, current questions: how uncertain everyone is; how poorly our views are established; how little accustomed we are to work! Here we see Russia's forests being destroyed; both landowners and peasants are cutting down trees in a kind of frenzy. One can state positively that timber is being sold for a tenth of its value: can the supply

last for long? Before our children grow up there will be only a tenth of today's timber on the market. What will happen then? Ruination, perhaps. And meanwhile, try to say a word about curtailing the right to destroy our forests and what do you hear? On the one hand, that it is a state and a national necessity, and, on the other, that it is a violation of the rights of private property—two opposite notions. . . . The matter will drag on for a long time. Someone made a witty remark in the current liberal spirit to the effect that there is no cloud without a silver lining, since cutting down all the Russian forests would at least have the positive value of eliminating corporal punishment: the district courts would have no switches to beat errant peasants. This is some consolation, of course, yet somehow it is hard to believe: even if the forests should disappear altogether, there would always be something to flog people with; they'd start importing it, I suppose. Now the Yids are becoming landowners, and people shout and write everywhere that they are destroying the soil of Russia. A Yid, they say, having spent capital to buy an estate, at once exhausts all the fertility of the land he has purchased in order to restore his capital with interest. But just try and say anything against this and the hue and cry will be at once raised: you are violating the principles of economic freedom and equal rights for all citizens. But what sort of equal rights are there here if it is a case of a clear and Talmudic *status in statu* above all and in the first place? What if it is a case not only of exhausting the soil but also of the future exhaustion of our peasant, who having been freed from the landowner will, with his whole commune, undoubtedly and very quickly now fall into a far worse form of slavery under far worse landowners—those same new landowners who have already sucked the juices from the peasants of western Russia, those same landowners who are now buying up not only estates and peasants but who have also begun to buy up liberal opinion and continue doing so with great success? Why do we have all these things?[103]

A passage that begins by lamenting lack of consensus and the "clamor of discordant voices" continues with a confounding tissue of attributed remarks, quoted opinions, and outraged defenses of private property. Birch rods, soil exhaustion, trees being cut down in a frenzy: some of this passage's motifs and concerns make their way into Dostoevsky's last and greatest novel, *The Brothers Karamazov*—the anecdote about birch rods is given to Fyodor Karamazov, and various characters in the novel are engaged in frenetic efforts to generate cash by selling forests. The narrator introduces one of the brother's guardians as involved in a property dispute with the local monastery over woodland, and the petty tyrant who presides over the village of Mokroe, where Dmitrii Karamazov is arrested, seems in fact to illustrate Dostoevsky's point about "a state within a state" (*status in statu*), in which little has changed from the pre-Reform era: exploitation and drunkenness reign, destroying both human lives and the natural world.[104] The 1876 column seems determined to agitate the reader as much as possible: even embedded in his characteristic strategy of quotation ("they say"), the implication that Jewish landowners are exhausting not just the soil but the peasant himself is incendiary—although Dostoevsky does admit that peasants themselves are actors in this drama. They too are "cutting down trees in a frenzy," rather than waiting to be flogged by newly invented, surrogate switches.

Strikingly enough, Dostoevsky engages in this column with some of the very issues we have been tracking in these pages: "curtailing the right to destroy," "ruination," "violation of the rights of private property." The discursive refrains of a decades-long debate surface in Dostoevsky's column and leave us with a series of painful, pointed conclusions: "how uncertain everyone is; how poorly our views are established; how little accustomed we are to work!" Dostoevsky's rendition of the "clamor of voices" forgoes the idyllic ending of Markov's response to Zalomanov; there is no hardworking Mennonite farmer in Dostoevsky's world to stabilize either the literal or the metaphoric soil of Russia's future. And underlying the whole discussion there is the uneasy, unanswered question of just *why* Russians are so destructive. Where other authors (Rudzkii, Markov, Tolstoy) suggest economic factors, market incentives, lack of knowledge, and greed, Dostoevsky hints at a kind of existential impulse to destroy, a near pathological drive to exterminate the very source that nourishes. Our only hope—if we read back through Dostoevsky's lamentations—is for "certainty; well-established views; and hard work." Neither Dostoevsky's narratives nor his publicistics give us images of just how this might be accomplished.

This does not, however, constitute Dostoevsky's last word on forests and the forest question in Russia. In addition to brief allusions to ravaged landscapes and scurrilous landowners in *The Brothers Karamazov*, he returns to the subject in one of his most beautiful and elusive stories, "The Dream of a Ridiculous Man," published in the April 1877 installation of *A Writer's Diary*. Markov ends his apocalyptic warning with an idyllic landscape of labor and possibility; Dostoevsky's "Ridiculous Man" revisits some of the motifs of "My Paradox," offering a vivid and visionary counterpoint to the violence and cacophonous voices of that column.

"The Dream of a Ridiculous Man" records the dream journey of a disenchanted, near-suicidal resident of Petersburg to a blissful world evocative of both Edenic beginnings and a promised Future Land. The story is dense with allusions to Dostoevsky's own utopian longings (and critiques), and to literary sources as diverse as Swedenborg, Dickens, and Rousseau. The disenchanted

"Ridiculous Man" travels to this *elsewhere* and experiences a kind of prelapsarian cosmos, a form of being in which humans have not yet separated themselves from the more-than-human world. The Ridiculous Man becomes agent of a second fall into violence and discord, but before the fall, Dostoevsky gives us a visionary rendering of woodlands, and of a language shared by trees and humans: "They showed me their trees, and I could not understand the intensity of love with which they regarded these trees: it was just as though they were speaking to creatures like themselves. And, you know, I may not be wrong in saying that they spoke with them! Yes, they had found their language, and I am convinced that the trees understood them."[105] The Ridiculous Man's intuition of a common language is part of his fantastic journey to a world that looks a lot like the Greek Isles of antiquity. He has arrived on these shores from a wretched, disputatious Petersburg, in which he is indifferent to everything and understands no one (a Petersburg, we imagine, filled with the "clamor of discordant voices" from "My Paradox"). He wakes up to a world before Babel, before men have stopped being able to speak not just with each other, but with other parts of creation. The Ridiculous Man arrives on this blessed isle and is greeted by the trees themselves: "Tall, beautiful trees stood in full splendor, and their countless little leaves—I'm convinced of it—welcomed me with their gentle, calming rustle and seemed to be whispering words of love." What it means to be in paradise is to be held in this landscape in which we are "greeted" by trees and their audible affection (952).[106]

Dostoevsky's story ends with religious and ethical (rather than political) advice: *You must love others as you love yourself; that's the main thing. . . .* He has returned with a vision, but has lost the words to articulate it: "But how we are to build paradise I do not know, because I do not have the words to express it" (960). And yet he promises us that he will go out into the world to preach and teach. The ending grounds the potential for civic change (*kak ustroit'sia*) in Christian love and the *living image*. While we may register skepticism as to just how the cacophony that Dostoevsky so engagingly renders is to be overcome by compassionate love and attention, it is worth considering that his visionary story also moves us back into an unmediated, intimate relationship to *the trees themselves*. The predominant landscape of Dostoevsky's 1876 *Writer's Diary* is ravaged, carted off, as violently destroyed as the hillside of Repin's painting from a few years later. The landscape of the Ridiculous Man's dream, on the other hand, is visionary and deeply sensual: if we think of this story as a tentative "resolution" to the fractiousness of the "Forest Question," then what it suggests is that we return *to the trees themselves*. From that love, from that awareness and deep presence, will come—somehow—a resolution and end to destruction.

The Ridiculous Man's dream lifts him out of modernity and then returns him to it, transformed. For the story's narrator, "science" is part of the fallen world, the lapsed world in which humans have forgotten the language of the trees, after humans have become cruel and animals have fled from them, after humans have begun to separate from each other, to distinguish between "mine" and "thine." "At that point science made its appearance among them" (957). This connection of scientific inquiry to the fall from grace and the idyllic condition of oneness with the natural world owes something both to European romanticism and to more-local animosities between poetic idealism and scientific materialism. It assumes that the kind of intuitive, transcendent converse that the Ridiculous Man experiences will be destroyed or fractured by analysis and reason. This is not, however, the vision that Markov had held up—a vision of common calamity that both traditional knowledge and scientific understanding might be brought to address.[107]

What we encounter in Dostoevsky and Markov's responses to Zalomanov are not so much different imaginations of the forest, as different imaginations of how civic discourse and spiritual values might be related, and of the role that science might play in our understanding of and actions in the world. The Ridiculous Man's final words are closer to deep ecology than to legislation; it bears remembering that even today, in our own situation of cacophonous voices warning of climate catastrophe and extinctions, there are those who argue that legislative action is insufficient, that only a profound change of heart will prevent wide-scale environmental destruction. Yet from the "cacophony" of late 1870s discussions of the Forest Question, legal action did emerge, action that significantly reshaped how private landowners could use woodlands whose importance for the public good was broadly acknowledged. Taken together, these offerings of scientific, civic, and literary discourse offer support for Istomina's conclusion that one of the most important accomplishments of nineteenth-century forestry was the "engendering of forest protection and, more broadly, ecological outlooks in societal consciousness."[108]

Aleksandr Rudzkii's claim that *moderation only comes with the experience of need* is an observation that underpins much of what we know as environmentalism: the challenge for those who perceive problems in advance of widespread "experience of need" is to make loss palpable, to help the broader public *imagine* and *envision* that which seems not yet to have touched their lives. Tolstoy, Repin, Dostoevsky, and Markov draw on and develop an array of modes and genres in their imaginative exploration of the Forest Question: their work uses folk traditions and Aesopian language; scrutinizes social relations and questions the morality of private property; constructs landscapes that are both apocalyptic and blessed; adopts tones that are alternately prophetic and poetic.

The possibility of some deep converse between humans and trees is never far from these men's creative consciousness, as is the almost axiomatic assumption that woodlands have roles to play that are as "spiritual" as they are material. They draw on bodies of scientific knowledge, made accessible to a broad public readership by forest specialists, agronomists, geographers, and climatologists who understood the need for broad public discussion—and who clearly felt it their responsibility as scientifically trained citizens to bring specialized knowledge to bear. Here as in other spheres of Russian public life, the trained specialist understood his profession in terms of public service. But it is equally striking that, at least in writing for the thick journals, these citizen scientists drew with ease of familiarity and clarity of conscience not just on scientific consensus, but on the languages of poetry and spiritual well-being.

In the following chapters we explore some of the ways in which artists and writers in the final decades of the nineteenth century revisited and reenvisioned the forest—embedding their awareness in existing cultural traditions, but increasingly alert to a changing, endangered landscape. By no means are all these writers and artists "environmental" in their impulses. And yet we discover in their woodlands an intensified awareness of change, of class, of destruction and loss. Vladimir Korolenko revisits Mel'nikov-Pechersky's Heart-Pine Rus' with a greater attention to the conflicts between modernity and "anarchic" tradition and the ways in which rational forestry imperils an ancient order. Mikhail Nesterov's stylized images of Holy Russia offer another kind of return to Mel'nikov's "Holy Wilderness"—but suggestive of the ecological potential latent in Slavophile mythologizing. It is, finally, Dmitrii Kaigorodov, a late-Imperial forest scientist turned anthologist of poetry, who forges the strongest link between the aesthetic and the environmental, producing enormously popular books of natural history that marry the traditions of nineteenth-century writing and art to an explicitly environmental ethic.

4

Jumping In

Vladimir Korolenko and
the Civic/Environmental Imagination

> . . . unless I now
> Confound my present feelings with the past,
> Even then, when from the bower I turned away,
> Exulting, rich beyond the wealth of kings
> I felt a sense of pain when I beheld
> The silent trees and the intruding sky.
>
> —William Wordsworth, "Nutting" (1800)

IN JULY OF 1890, less than twenty years after Mel'nikov's epic novels were published, Vladimir Galaktionovich Korolenko (1853–1921) set off with his two nephews to retrace the older writer's journey into the heart-pine woodlands north of Nizhnii Novgorod on the Volga. The writer and his young companions traveled up the Vetluga River on a boat called *Sweetheart* (*Liubimchik*), then made their way overland to Lake Svetloyar, supposed site of the miraculously saved, eternally hidden Kitezh. They returned to the Volga down the meandering Kerzhenets. Along the way Korolenko talked with loggers and fishermen, with one of whom he spent a night seining for river fish; he heard the tale of a beloved foundling adopted by grieving parents whose son had died; he clambered up a steep, overgrown path to an Old Believer cemetery; he overcame suspicion and resistance to strangers in riverbank villages; and he picnicked with the abbot of a much-diminished, nearly ruined Old Believer monastery. The narrative of the trip, which Korolenko titled *In the Wild and Empty Places*, is both travelogue and cultural history, observation and personal reflection, local yarns and the musings of an urbanized, modern Russian. The prose is as fluid as the rivers Korolenko traveled, shifting easily from the description of an unexpected rapid-shoot (where they had anticipated a portage) to polemic revisitation of places made famous by Mel'nikov-Pechersky. Korolenko's title plays on the word *pustynnyi*—which can mean either "desert/wilderness" (*pustynia*) or "hermitage" (*pustyn*); it is also related to the Russian word for empty—*pustoi*.[1] These backwoods are both full and empty: full of legend and cultural significance, but increasingly *empty* of the communities that had once flourished in them (and on the pages of Mel'nikov's epic). They are abandoned now in part because of Mel'nikov the bureaucrat—who had, as Korolenko puts it, "described very well, but destroyed even better."[2] The journey takes Korolenko into a literal place, but also into the mythologies of Russia: in a voice that for the most part reserves judgment, he engages seriously the onset of modernity and change, sacred legacies and incipient disruption, what he calls the "dream of a people" and the "dark, silent forests, filled with ghastly memories and the graves of the murdered."

Korolenko's *In the Wild and Empty Places* is worth reading for a variety of reasons, not the least of which is its wonderful mix of wistful appreciation for the past and bemused relief at its passing. Generically, Korolenko's nonfiction— what Russians have traditionally categorized as *publicistics*—comes close in this narrative to what the American reader understands as "nature writing," combining vivid depictions of regional geography with ruminations on the relationship between humans and the natural world. As A. Derman put it in an astute essay written almost a century ago (he is commenting on a passage from *In the Wild and Empty Places*), "This is more than a picture, more than a strategy for depicting the vitality and expectant qualities of nature; it is a particular, unique perception of the inter-relationship of humans and nature, highly typical for the artistic and humanistic world view of the author."[3] Description and rumination, in other words, are a way of *thinking* about "nature" and the human. Korolenko's narrative considers human character, ways of knowing and relating to the natural world, and the ways in which preconceptions, or what we might call pre-*visualizations*, structure our understanding of various phenomena. The trans-Volga forest becomes for Korolenko a place of imaginative and documentary interaction, his journey into this landscape an occasion for a kind of citizen's reporting on life in the interior. American nature writing is often situated somewhere between tourism and pilgrimage: while much nature writing combines narratives of journey and exploration with natural history, numerous foundational texts of the American tradition employ a rhetoric of awe and veneration conventionally associated with faith journeys and religious sites.[4] The pleasure and usefulness of Korolenko's narrative lie in the intelligence with which he negotiates the shoals of "naïve faith" and a touristic gaze that wouldn't see half of what he sees. For someone interested in just what nature, or wilderness, or the forest itself *is* for Russians, there can be no better guide than Vladimir Galaktionovich.

Korolenko was born into what was, for his time, a multicultural family: his father was Ukrainian and an Orthodox Christian, his mother a Polish Catholic referred to by one biographer as a "luminous angel" in a large family where two nationalities, two faiths, and three languages (Polish, Ukrainian, and Russian) coexisted.[5] His father was a bureaucrat whose honesty and refusal to take bribes made him a "Don Quixote" to his son.[6] Born in Zhitomir, one of two intellectual capitals of Jewish life in the Pale of Settlement, Korolenko was thirteen when the family moved west to Rovno, and in later life the author would return to eastern Ukraine and settle in Poltava. As an adolescent, Korolenko was the family dreamer, with visions of becoming a lawyer and advocate for social outcasts; prevented by the Russian educational system from entering university (he had studied at a so-called "real" school, which prepared students for practical careers with a curriculum focusing more on the sciences), he enrolled instead in the Technological University in Petersburg in 1871, transferring two years later to the Petrovsk Academy in Moscow, where he entered the school of forestry.[7] It was here that Korolenko studied with Kliment Timiriazev, one of the most important scientists of his generation. Korolenko in fact worked for Timiriazev, producing illustrations for his lectures on botany. An enthusiastic follower of Darwin, Timiriazev did foundational work on photosynthesis, which earned him recognition throughout the European scientific community; he was, moreover, an ardent supporter of progressive causes in late nineteenth-century Russia, and gave public lectures on "The Life of the Plant," which made him widely popular.[8] While Timiriazev, like his student turned writer, was a staunch defender of intellectual freedom, he was to differ from Korolenko in his unqualified support of the Bolshevik regime in 1917.[9] In 1913, Korolenko recalled Timiriazev with affection, both as a teacher ("you taught us to value reason as a sacred thing") and as a source of moral support. Arrested in 1876 for delivering a letter of protest to the academy's rector, Korolenko and those held with him could hear their teacher's "independent, conscientious" voice in the adjoining room. "We didn't know just what you were saying at that moment, but we knew that all that was best in what we felt obscurely and imprecisely drawn to found resonance in your soul, but in more mature form."[10]

As with so many other young people of his generation, the guiding vision of Korolenko's youth was to *serve the people*, a quasi-religious call to abandon privilege and immerse oneself in the lives and tribulations of Russia's rural masses. The readings that underpinned Korolenko's protest activities as a student were the central texts of Russian populism: Bervi-Flerovskii, Lavrov, Tkachev, and Mikhailovsky. For a subsequent generation of Soviet biographers, the label "populist" became a term of condescension, since Russian populists, from the Marxists' standpoint, had not adequately understood the predetermined march of history toward socialist revolution.[11] Populists and Marxists in late nineteenth-century Russia disagreed over the inevitability not just of revolution but of capitalism in Russia, with populists of widely varying stripes holding out the possibility that Russia might evolve along a different path of economic development. Korolenko's life path, thanks to the government's draconian measures, was to lead him into exile, first in the Vologda region of Russia's European north, and then in the distant northern reaches of central Siberia. The experience of "wilderness" for Korolenko, as for so many generations of Russians, came not as a form of pioneering exploration or solitary Thoreauvian retreat, but as punishment meted out for freethinking and illegal association. Landscape, climate, and distance were tools of the state, not vehicles of self-determination.

The unwillingness to live by anything other than ideals of human justice and dignity landed Korolenko in exile; it was also to be a lifelong hallmark of his writing, whether publicistics or fiction. Years later, at a banquet honoring Korolenko before his departure from Nizhnii to Petersburg, one of the speakers put it this way: "Justice—that is what is written on Vladimir Korolenko's banner, as a writer and as a public figure. He is everywhere before us as a *knight of the just cause*."[12] Simon Karlinsky once referred to Korolenko as the "one-man civil liberties union" of late Imperial Russia, intervening in a court case in which members of an ethnic minority in the Viatka region had been falsely accused of human sacrifice; documenting the ravages of hunger during the drought years of 1891–92; and decrying capital punishment. Tolstoy, himself near death in 1910, wrote Korolenko that his essay opposing the death penalty had brought the older writer not merely to tears, but to sobs of gratitude and admiration.[13]

Korolenko's years in exile shaped him in fundamental ways. The years there strengthened him physically—he returned from ten years' exile "a tempered fighter."[14] He took pride in his capacity for physical labor—he learned to make boots, to sow and harvest, to hunt and to fell trees. Most important for our purposes, he came into direct and difficult contact with communities living in the vast and forbidding Siberian taiga, or boreal forest. For Korolenko as for Dostoevsky forty years earlier, Siberia offered the young idealist an education in life and human psychology. His exile to Yakutia in north central Siberia effected for Korolenko a fundamental qualification in varieties of romance—both with "the people" and with wilderness. Writing in 1893 to Anastasia Piotrovskaia, a young writer and activist who had turned to him for advice, Korolenko reflected on how the years in Siberia had affected him: "In earlier years both I and many of my comrades constructed a whole program of life on the proposition that the *narod* is made up first, of essentially good people, and second, that the masses are capable of demonstrating the genuine greatness of that people. That was what we both expected and believed. Now, I no longer think that—or to put it better, no longer think *that way*. You already know a bit about my biography: I lived in exile in a chimneyless hut with peasants, sewing boots in order to live. I sat in prisons, walked with parties of convicts, and plowed land for three years with those same peasants. Over the course of that time I saw how my former views vanished. At first it seemed that there was no longer any point in living. But in fact, there was in that proximity to the people much that was invigorating and gave me courage! After it all, I said to myself that *Thou shalt not make any graven images* is a very great truth, and that *the people*, as we often imagine it to ourselves, singular and indistinguishable, with one countenance, doesn't exist. What does exist are millions of people—kind and evil, noble and base, pleasant and disgusting. And within that mass—I believe this deeply—goodness and truth are more and more widespread. And what that means is that one should serve goodness and truth. If that means that one can move along with the masses (which does sometimes happen)—well enough; but if one must remain alone, then so be it. Conscience is the sole master of one's actions, and there is no need for idols. But given all that, it's well to remember that we are, generally speaking, closer to the heights of happiness and joy, and that they, generally speaking, are closer to the very depths of suffering and need. And in that light many of the masses' "faults" are significantly mitigated. But the task is still the same, since goodness and truth in any case join hands to lessen suffering, so that human lives could be filled with joy, instead of pain."[15]

Along with this shift to a still deeply humane, but much more complex, view of the Russian people, the landscapes of Yakutia gave Korolenko a sharpened sense of human relationships to the natural world. Mark Azadovskii, the Soviet ethnographer, published two fine essays on Korolenko, both characterized by deep affection for the Russian champion of civil liberties. For Azadovskii, Korolenko's experience of the Siberian landscape was of a fundamentally *alien* world. While this stemmed in part from Korolenko's own status as an exile—an "alien"—in the landscape, Azadovskii suggests something more complicated at work as well. The writer's experience of the wild reaches of the Lena River as it flows north among forbidding cliffs leads at first to a kind of conventionally sublime reaction. But Korolenko isn't standing there alone, like Turgenev's initial narrator or a romantic figure out of Caspar David Friedrich: he is accompanied by a local Russian coachman, whose family have made these wild parts their home for generations. The awe and romance of Korolenko's initial reaction is countered by the coachman's mournful response. As Azadovskii puts it: "Korolenko looked with rapture at the grandeur and beauty of the harsh, rocky shore, and it seemed to him that he had never in his life seen anything more beautiful than this spectacle; but standing beside him was a different observer—a resident of these magnificent cliffs, the frontiersman [*stanochnik*] Frol. Our fathers were lured here by these rocks—he said, and in his face the author read something 'close to hatred.' Another outpost resident, the naïve dreamer Mikesha, also denies this beauty. 'No, he said in his naively broken version of the central Lena dialect,—*Belom svete khorosho*. It's good beyond the mountains. But us, here . . . what are we living for? Guarding the striped posts. . . . The striped posts and the gray rock and the dark woods.' These feelings, stemming as they do from human sorrow, destroy at their core the artist's romantic inclinations, rendering impossible any surrender to the unfettered contemplation of, and union with, nature. And then along with these moods comes something else, that powerfully nourishes them: the mood of the exile, of a man torn from his native land, from the delights of a different nature, one that is filled with light and tenderness."[16]

For Azadovskii, this moment betrays something essential about Korolenko's sense of the natural world. Nature for Korolenko is always inextricably linked to human lives—to human work, human politics, and complex human emotions. In the passage above, even the coachman's negative reaction ("close to hatred") betrays Korolenko's interest in the link of what Azadovskii elsewhere called the "psychological and the social." As in his other narratives of place, *In the Wild and Empty Places* will focus on working landscapes, men and nature, forests and rivers, and how humans live there. Korolenko will track the connections generated by labor, story, legend. The telling strategy of Korolenko's prose is the one Azadovskii points to: multiple points of view, voices that balance off against the romantic's impulse, creating what Richard White said all good nature writing needs—"irony, satire, paradox and history"—all of which "exist *because* the world is a serious place."[17] Korolenko discovered in Siberia complex conditions of human coexistence with a difficult natural world, and artistic strategies for rendering those complex conditions—in which longing for "union with nature" is always complicated by other voices, by irony, paradox, and history. What the sublime landscape *doesn't* become in his Siberian stories is something like Ansel Adams's American West or John Muir's Alaska, a landscape that suggests a divinely preferred promise of national glory.

Korolenko's strategy is not unlike the one we noted in Turgenev's "Journey into Polesye," with its counterpoint of voices and cultural reference. There is in fact a strong continuity between the work of Turgenev and Korolenko, one noted by various critics—though more often it is a matter of kindred lyricism that they note.[18] When he returned to European Russia in 1885, Korolenko settled in Nizhnii Novgorod, where Mel'nikov-Pechersky had died two years earlier. Korolenko's writing in the late 1880s included reportage, travel writing, literary ethnography, and something very close to "nature sketches" of the American variety. The best-known of his short stories is "Makar's Dream" (1885), in which a Russian peasant who has "gone native" is transported from the gritty poverty of his life as a hunter in the vast taiga into a cosmic vision of souls traveling toward their encounter with "the Great Toyon."[19] But along with the short fiction about his Siberian experience, Korolenko also wrote a series of stories and quasi-ethnographic accounts that focus on the landscape of European Russia. M. G. Petrova notes that Korolenko's interest in "observing the people" often led him on summer excursions: in *Following the Icon* (1887) Korolenko and a friend spend several weeks on the path of a wonder-working icon as it makes its way from Nizhnii to the Oranki monastery, south on the road to Arzamas.[20] The summer pilgrimage, with its assortment of pilgrims, drunkards, old women, and "shriekers" (peasant women afflicted by seizures), seems at times like a thick description of Repin's *Procession of the Cross in the Kursk District*. There is the same sense of heat and drought, the same fascination with the multiplicity of types and extremity of contrasts that such a procession might offer. But there are also moments of extraordinary stillness and beauty, when Korolenko's talents as a lyricist of nature come to the fore, and passages of commentary, in which the political and economic history of monastic holdings figures as background to the human drama of piety and need. "The Forest Speaks," a short story written the year after his account of the pilgrimage to Oranki, echoes Turgenev's "Journey into Polesye" quite explicitly, but in the opening passages of "The Forest Speaks" Turgenev's terrifyingly silent woodland has been replaced by a forest whose sounds are a language of memory and witness. The story is an account of violence deep in the woods of the Ukrainian *Poles'e*, with an old man recalling exploitation, rape, and murder from the days of serfdom. Korolenko's forest becomes an ally of ultimate justice, sheltering peasants who take revenge on violent masters, and preserving the memory of injustice in a kind of sylvan witness to truth.[21]

Narratives like these prefigure *In the Wild and Empty Places* in their sensitivity to setting and in their endless curiosity at the diversity of human life. What Korolenko seems to have taken from Turgenev was not simply the mixture of social critique, natural history, and depictions of peasant life, or the elder writer's blend of humor, lyricism, and social protest. The open-ended form of works like *Following the Icon* or *In the Wild and Empty Places* suggests a reworking of Turgenev's hunting sketches with their wandering observer and interlocutor of human life in place. Korolenko does not seem to have been a hunter; but the walker's—or canoer's—sketch turned out to be an ideal form for representation and reflection, with an unobtrusive narrator who is less of a *barin*—a "lord"—than Turgenev's was. In her introduction to the German translation of Korolenko's *The History of My Contemporary*, Rosa Luxemburg suggested that "unlike Turgenev, the elegant and perfectly groomed aristocrat, [Korolenko] was no silent observer. He finds no difficulty in mingling with people, knowing just what to say to make friends and how to strike the right note."[22] During the years when he lived in Nizhnii Novgorod, Korolenko spent his summers wandering the length and breadth of the region—sometimes on foot with a pack on his back, sometimes by boat or steamboat. Despite encroaching electrification and the coming of the railway, the Nizhnii district was still a place of "untouched corners and slumbering forests, forgotten villages and religious minds untouched by 20th century skepticism." Korolenko wandered

Korolenko's sketches of Lake Svetloyar. Lake Svetloyar *(top) and* The Chapel at Lake Svetloyar *(bottom). From V. G. Korolenko,* Sobranie sochinenii, *vol. 3 (Moscow: Gosudarstvennoe izdatel'stvo khudozhestvennoi literatury, 1954).*

the backroads "in the same way that botanists, geologists and zoologists go on excursions for their material."[23] He took notes of his own impressions and conversations with those he met, and he drew sketches, all of which then became the raw material for his literary work.

In the Wild and Empty Places captures some of the sense of spontaneity and fluidity of field notes or a traveler's diary; we often find Korolenko referring to the process of jotting down his thoughts by the evening campfire, and the twists and turns of the meandering Kerzhenets seem an apt analogue for the freedom of his own ruminations as they move downstream. In an essay published in March 1888, Korolenko describes the "role of literature" as a kind of riverman's pole, something with which we navigate lives that are defined not by stasis but by change. Korolenko is polemicizing with Hippolyte Taine's overly deterministic understanding of the relationship of art to life: literature is not merely *reflection*, says Korolenko, however powerful the influence of place and climate may be on human culture. Art, he insists, involves the play of imagination and demands a "point of view" that alone can lead to *hidden paths*. "Logical thought," whatever its virtues of speed and precision, leads all too easily into quagmires. "Life," Korolenko insists, "is inconstant; it flows continuously from the forms of the past into those of the future, while the *present is a kind of fiction*, a concept we invest with some of the past and some of the future, whose interaction and struggle we call the here and now."[24]

The imagination at work in the sketches of *In the Wild and Empty Places* is both Korolenko's and that of the people he talks to; there is a sense of discovering in the pilgrims and woodsmen and fisherfolk of Russia's backwoods yarns, and visions, and a "people's dream." Within a few years after the writing of this narrative, much of European Russia—including the Nizhnii region—would be plunged into a devastating famine, a disaster that was both "natural" and political. That disaster—which we would call *environmental*—became the focus of another of Korolenko's reports from the field, *In the Famine Year*; the tone of that narrative would be more urgent, its exposures of Russian corruption more unstinting. *In the Wild and Empty Places* comes before that environmental apocalypse, ruminating before the drought and famine on how human communities exist in relationship with place, giving us both field notes and a *point of view*, grasping with the guide pole of the imagination the deserted utopias and resonant shorelines of the "present" of this place, the intermingling and struggle of future and past.

* * *

IN THE WILD AND EMPTY PLACES begins with a series of humorous exchanges with the captain of a riverboat, who tells Korolenko that they are "absolutely leaving in an hour" and then says he has plenty of time to go into town and back—which will take an hour and a half. There is a lot of riverside kibitzing and lethargic inactivity where you would expect the bustle of departure: another steamboat comes and goes, and the *Sweetheart* is still sitting calmly at the wharf, with no sign of steam from the engines. There is much humorous business about riverboat competition, timetables, and fares, with Korolenko's boat going nowhere; and then he confesses to us that he is a man who is not in a hurry: "I love country roads" (113). The humorous beginning resolves in a fond evocation of back roads and narrow-gauge railroad lines, and of Russians who are all "a little bit romantics"—for whom the loss of the past is all the more regrettable because it is unclear whether Russia even has a past (114). "They say we have no past! Well what of it. . . . We're that much sorrier for what we lose: the mist is that much more mysterious and thick."[25]

Our sense of Korolenko here is of a gentle, good-humored romantic with a fondness for slow going, who only gradually announces a "more particular aim" for his notes. That aim is to explore one aspect of the supposedly nonexistent Russian past that is fast disappearing: "these quiet forest retreats, where the dream of a people about a longed-for invisible city slumbers above a shining lake, where the dark Kerzhenets winds through slumbering forests, along with the dead and dying cloisters" (115). The narrative gets launched as a journey into a landscape of the past, a journey that tries to balance sentiment with critique and an ever-present sense of the incongruities of Russia's road in the other direction—into modernity. Korolenko's boat leaves in fifteen minutes—but there is still plenty of time to get to town.

What Korolenko discovers in these "empty" parts are people: this is a populated (if sparsely), working landscape, where we meet barge haulers, fishermen and trappers, aging Old Believers, and a Polish forester—all of whom absorb Korolenko's attention and come to constitute the forest world he maps for us. The barge haulers on the *Sweetheart* are headed back upriver after having finished a log drive. They banter with the ship's captain and give him much more advice than he wants about how to navigate the river channels: "Here, on their native Vetluga, on their own Vetluga steamboat, they feel at home. They relate to the Sweetheart with jovial indifference, frequently giving directions to the helmsman from where they sit." These are, as Korolenko puts it, the most "numerous, most burdened by labor, and the least valued children" of Mother Volga.

Like his fellow populists, or like his contemporary Maxim Gorky, who wandered the Volga and described its laborers and eccentrics, Korolenko is fascinated with these workers and their stories. He listens in as "Wolf"—reputed to be a champion storyteller—tells a tale of "not so long ago, in a kingdom not so far away, in fact in this very one where we are right now" (119)—which turns into a machismo fantasy of wish fulfillment (the ugly wife drops out of the story; the tsar's daughter turns into a horse). The term "Wolf" is one Korolenko has heard from "statisticians in Nizhnii": "A *wolf* is someone who has no household or steady trade. . . . In winter he makes for town and the dross houses; come spring, when the rivers open, the sun warms the earth and the forests put on their new foliage, the wolf heads out into the woods beyond the Volga. Here he's got no means of getting real work, and his pride—and the fact that he's used to a kind of wild independence—won't allow him to take handouts. So he wanders around the woods where he came from, hunting or fishing, or doing some petty thieving when the opportunity presents itself." The Wolf's tale—whose misogyny Korolenko finds disturbing—fades off into tales of the haulers' encounters with the *leshii*, or forest spirit, the one whose name should not be spoken. There is a sense of quiet, heat, a fading day and the dense darkness of night. Korolenko shifts effortlessly from the Wolf's story into the atmosphere of the forest:

> Evening quiet moves along the Vetluga. It feels pleasantly cool. Stars glint in the light mist, now and then the slender sickle moon cuts out from a cloud lifting heavily from the forest. Every day somewhere they're saying prayers in fields grown parched from heat, and every evening the same cloud rises in the moonless sky, standing there like a deceptive spirit; it disappears toward morning, without even a trace of dew on the grass. Today it's heavier; you can feel a light mist in the air; the woods are burning somewhere, and a smoky shroud swirls along the horizon all day long, floating in the sky and seeming to thicken with moisture. There's something enervating in these hints of rain amidst stifling exhaustion. (118)

Within the year these regions would be struggling with devastating famine; here we register only drought and the futile longing for rain. Two years later Korolenko (like Leo Tolstoy) would try to ameliorate the situation of starving villages, traveling to a region south of Nizhnii with two objects in mind: to participate in relief work and to write an account of "what famine looks like." When he wrote that account, he would look back on these summer days of heat and drought in 1890: "Over the past two years, wandering about in more or less these same places, I've had the chance—as an accidental observer-writer—to take note of dire warnings. With a kind of systematic ruthlessness, which involuntarily prompts one to think superstitiously of conscious intentions and vengeance, nature has been stalking man. Again and again the deacons came to dried-out grain fields to say prayers, icons raised high, but the clouds stretched out across the scorching sky, waterless and miserly. From the bluffs in Nizhnii you could constantly see fires and their smoke in the woods beyond the Volga. The forests burned all summer, igniting on their own; over the winter fire concealed itself in the underbrush, died down under the snow, and then started up again the next spring, as soon as things dried out, and moved in flaming circles until the next winter. I remember how for weeks at a time from Nizhnii you could see pillars of flame above the woods on the horizon, above a thick mat of dark smoke. During the day smoke roiled like a murky sea, and at night it was as though unseen arms were lifting kindled brands to the sky."[26]

In the Famine Year begins with the weather and moves on to a multifaceted examination of regional politics, government policy, and human suffering. *In the Wild and Empty Places* is also attentive to the seamless interconnection of human lives and natural places, but in ways so subtle, and so *assumed*, that we might not notice it: it is implicit in the labor these men do, whether logging or hunting or fishing; in the *leshii* tales, which remind the listeners that those who work in the forest are always at the mercy of some powers greater than themselves; and in Korolenko's registering of sounds that emerge from the woods on either side of the river, which often seem to echo or "speak" to the men on the boat. At one point it feels to Korolenko as if the stories the men tell are actually *coming from* the forest: "The steamboat moves past these sleeping woods, and it seems as though someone was prompting Efrem's fantastic stories from in there, from the whispering, dark-green wall" (120). There is a kind of leveling, or embedding, of consciousness and stature in terms of those surrounding woods: these men aren't "heroic" figures of the Paul Bunyan variety, but nor are they downtrodden, broken men, like the barge haulers in Repin's famous painting (1870–73). They seem to have the same inscrutable, indeterminate strength as the deep forests from which they have come.

There is in Korolenko a strong lyrical strain; whatever spirits have lived in these woods seem to have fled or retreated, but their spell lingers: at one point a fisherman named Stepan tells him that "in the old days, there were lots of spirits in the woods, all sorts of 'em. But now, see, it's like this: there's more houses, they've built churches—and *he*'s gone farther into the woods, that's how we see it" (154). The "he" here is the *leshii* (whose name you don't pronounce, unless you want a nasty encounter), and the story about him explains his disappearance by the incursions of human civilization. For Stepan, though— and for Korolenko—there is still a sense of magic about the woods. Stepan goes on to tell "Vladimir" how he was fishing one night and suddenly heard a noise in the forest: at first he thinks it is a wood spirit, and then sees a "black healthy-sized thing" passing along the shore. "I see it moving along, but just what it is I can't make out, it's so dark right there by the woods. Suddenly it goes plop into the water, right into the whirlpool. I looked at the water, at a place where it was light, and almost passed out: there's a head of antlers swimming toward you, and were those antlers something awful! . . . I crossed myself and rubbed my eyes, and what do you think—a moose! And not just one but two. The other one stayed on the shore, turned toward me, wiped its snout and then cried out to its pal. That's what I'm telling you, Vladimir, just like language, only you can't make out the words" (154).

There's a language being spoken in these woods, but neither the fisherman nor Korolenko can understand it. In his account of a night's fishing ("*Na sezhe*"), what captivates Korolenko is the *silence* of the setting. He and Stepan are sitting on a small platform in the middle of the river; the stream has been blocked off so fish will have to swim through a small opening beneath the platform. The net falls "with a hissing sound" into the dark river. "At first you can see how it flows out with the current, the openings in its mesh showing white; then it's as though some unseen hand grasped it and pulled it toward the depths." Stepan hands Korolenko the threads that reach to the river bottom where a long pole anchors the bottom of the net: "They remind me of reins that have harnessed the black depths. . . . I could feel each thread separately, and they quivered in my hand like strings. . . . At once there was a link with the depths. The threads quivered, heaved, and strained as if some invisible figure in the depths was playing on them like a musical instrument. . . . My nerves involuntarily tensed. . . . One wanted to stay absolutely still, to talk as quietly as possible" (153).

Korolenko's language here suggests something—in the river, in the woods—that is both still present and yet has disappeared. This lament for lost presences becomes something of a cliché for late nineteenth-century writers, Russian elegies for what Max Weber famously called the "disenchantment of the world."[27] Turgenev, in his 1878 "The Nymphs," imagines a landscape from which the gods have fled. When he cries out that "Pan has risen!" Diana and a whole suite of nymphs appear, only to vanish when they see a cross and bell tower in the distance.[28] Mel'nikov, as we have seen, understood the exuberant animist celebrations of traditional culture to have been repressed by Old Believer elders. Korolenko's rendering of this mystery seems significantly different, however: in Turgenev, there is a decadent feel to his regret, couched not in the vernacular of Russian folklife but in the aesthete's allusions to classical antiquity. Mel'nikov is so enthralled with his epic canvas that the reader could be forgiven for simply not *believing* that these folk and their revels don't exist anymore. They do, on his pages. For Korolenko, this hovering but elusive presence becomes emblematic of *that which cannot be spoken*, or that which resists modernity and reason. Compared with Mel'nikov, or Nesterov, whose images of Mel'nikov we shall discuss in chapter 5, Korolenko is less sentimental, more willing to represent the violence of this "mysterious" world. There is a drunken brawl at one of the

Sweetheart's stops on the Vetluga (125), but there is also the brute force of the Russian peasant's relationship to the forest, which Korolenko is quite explicit about toward the end of his narrative. There is also the metaphoric "violence" of hunger and vulnerability, a country that is literally *dying of thirst* throughout the whole journey. What makes Korolenko's account so compelling is his ability to suggest mystery and the ineffable *along with* hardship, loss, and even a kind of situational boredom: a young girl in the final river settlement he sees is apathetic and listless, clearly desperate to be somewhere else. When Korolenko goes off into a reverie (he may be asleep) about mysterious sounds and something emerging from the deep to overturn the platform, the fisherman Stepan is the one who jolts him awake, alarmed that something is caught on the net that will destroy the whole contraption if it gets caught on a snag. It is the peasant Stepan who returns us to reality and the literal.[29]

Korolenko is not immune to the desire for the heroic; his portrait of Stepan begins with humor: the man can barely stand up, he is so tired. He has been sitting out night after night fishing—to no avail, according to his wife. Korolenko's final image of him, though, is larger than life, and comes after they have wrestled what turns out to be a huge fish from the river. "'Will there be rain, will God send it our way?' Stepan wonders, crossing himself and once more sitting down on the platform. . . . The words settle into my memory, a final impression of my first night on the Kerzhenets. I finally get settled on the uncomfortable planks. . . . The depths lap beneath me, mysterious, black, bottomless. . . . And when I rouse from light sleep, I see Stepan's figure. It's huge, rising above the forests, his head lifting away toward the phosphorescent clouds where they gather thicker and thicker. . . . In his hands Stepan is holding the reins, and with them he's driving the river (156).

It is a wonderful image, fantastic and *visual* in a way that much of Korolenko's writing is; it gathers together the longing for rain and the need for sustenance and the tireless labors of a sleepy man whose fatigue has now left him and settled on the writer. Like the loggers and the Wolf, and like the woodsman Aksen later in the journey, Stepan knows the natural world through his labors. There is that tactile link (holding the reins of the river, hauling the fish onto the boards) between his body and the body of the world, and the visual magic whereby Stepan's head becomes the clouds that will finally give rain.[30]

These transactions back and forth between metaphoric and literal elements (water, river, lake, rain, tears) are part of what Korolenko does so brilliantly; it is how he hangs on to the middle of the river, a narrative position from which the locals aren't quite sure if he is friend or foe. When Korolenko and his nephews leave the Vetluga and the *Sweetheart* behind and head for Lake Svetloyar, they head into Old Believer country, into terrain in which he is greeted with the fundamental suspicion and mistrust that centuries of persecution have made second nature. Rebuffed at one point by the caretaker of an Old Believer cemetery, Korolenko realizes that he should have come "either as a powerful enemy or a confederate," bringing either the state assessor's bell or the coreligionist's respectful greeting. Then Old Believers would have known how to receive him. "But I came with neither one. I brought with me only my powers of observation, and the hermitage coldly closed me out, sensing in me perhaps that new, third thing, encroaching on the old faith. . . . And 'more bitter than the first will be the last.'" Old Belief had survived persecution; "it won't survive indifference" (168).

Compared with Mel'nikov's portrait of Old Belief, Korolenko's is more skeptical than elegiac. These are the "empty" places of his narrative, places on the edge of extinction, places that are dead and dying. The fanaticism and apocalyptic impulse to immolation and ritual castration—aspects of sectarian culture that so fascinated the literati of turn-of-the-century St. Petersburg—are replaced in Korolenko's narrative by a death of quiet oblivion, a kind of exhausted irrelevance.[31] There are no longer any *communities* here, just aged individuals, a few women on a riverbank who won't speak to him, and wild-eyed ascetics who exchange tales on the banks of Lake Svetloyar. The dugout dwellings near peat bogs and under the vast roots of shore trees are empty now, and the path to a hillside cemetery is almost invisible. Old Belief seems to have sunk—like the city of Kitezh—back into a landscape that will hide it forever.

What draws Korolenko to these woods is a "people's dream"—the Kitezh legend—of two worlds coexisting in one place. Korolenko's account is that of a lyric ethnographer, relaying the various tales of the city (many of which are familiar from Mel'nikov's novel), but also capturing in vivid prose the psychological and symbolic essence of the legends: "Two worlds stand above Lake Svetloyar: one is the real world, but unseen; the other is seen, but unreal. And they flow one into the other, they cover over, and penetrate each other. The false, illusory world is firmer than the true one. The latter glimmers through its watery shroud only rarely, opening briefly to the pious gaze before it disappears. And once more the crude deception of bodily sensation takes over" (131). We are led up to Svetloyar in a counterpoint of expectation, disappointment and re-enchantment: on the writer's first trip by the lake, we are told, his driver stopped, pointed toward the lake, and Korolenko thought, *that's it?* A tiny, unassuming lake, round and ringed with birch. "What? This is Svetloyar? woven round with the legend of the unseen city, where people of varied belief converge—from Perm, sometimes even from the Urals—to set up their icon cases, to pray, to hear the mysterious bells of Kitezh and stand firm for their faith in dispute? . . . From stories, and even from the descriptions of Mel'nikov-

Pechersky I had expected to see impenetrable forests, narrow paths, places hidden and dark, with the cautious whispering of the hidden, wilderness places." On his second visit, though, he is won over by the lake's "magical simplicity" and its "own, distinctive charm." He tries to remember what the lake reminds him of, and realizes that he is thinking of very old, very primitive icons.

> Bright little lakes like this, and rounded little hummocks and birches like these, show up on old, old icons of unassuming manner. A monk kneels in a round glade. A green oak wood had approached him on the one side, as if listening in on the words of human prayer; and in the background (if there is a foreground and background in such pictures) within green banks as in a chalice, is a tiny lake just like this. The awkward hand of the pious artist knows only simple, naïvely correct forms: an oval lake, round hills, trees that form a ring, like children for a folk dance. And over it all the air of "mother-pustynia," the very thing these simple-hearted supplicants were seeking. (129)

"Mother-*pustynia*" is the sacred wilderness that is the "people's dream"—what they come seeking in these backwoods, in this perfectly round lake. Korolenko settles us into its spell with his description—as though he himself is painting an icon for us to contemplate. But it is almost immediately taken away from us, with a gesture that verges on violence: "The forests have been cut down now, roads have been cut through the glades, the hermitages have been destroyed, the mystery is breathing its last. Tilled fields have crept up to the 'sacred lake,' you hear harness bells along the highway, and see cockaded figures in carriages. Kitezh's 'mystery' lies exposed at the side of the highway, clutching to the opposite bank, hiding in the shadows round the tall oaks and birches.

"And it too is quietly breathing its last" (130).

It is worth thinking for a moment about Korolenko's use of an icon in this description. He reminds us of the ways in which experience is governed by expectation, and the tension between how we imagine something beforehand (often based on descriptions of it) and then experience it in an actual encounter. But he also reminds us of the role of icons in Orthodox culture, and their *sacralization* of creation. Landscape as such is not an important element in traditional icons, which focus on the divine image and likeness in human form. But in Korolenko's remembered, naïve image, landscape becomes central. The icon in Orthodoxy entails, of course, both a specific theology and particular cultures of devotion, or ways of seeing: the icon "portrays the divine beauty and glory in material ways which are visible to physical eyes," representing in visible form the reality of divine incarnation. As Leonid Ouspensky puts it, "The nature of holiness is to sanctify that which surrounds it. . . . This is the beginning of the transfiguration of the world"—what had been destroyed by human pride and the ensuing "cosmic catastrophe."[32]

In an understated but powerful way, Korolenko gives us both the "transfiguration of the world"—with trees that listen in on a monk's silent prayer—and "cosmic catastrophe," when the perfect beauty of a woodland lake is destroyed, and the "mother wilderness" is left violated by a roadside. One of the acts of apostasy that lies at the emotional and symbolic center of Dostoevsky's *Brothers Karamazov* is the desecration of an icon: the drunken father Karamazov tramples an icon of the mother of God underfoot, in an act intended to provoke his deeply religious wife. The original act of desecration is then *repeated*, when the father tells the story to his son Alyosha, apparently having forgotten just who Alyosha's mother was.[33] There is something of the same "doubling" of destruction in Korolenko's account, since both the landscape itself and our image of it are violated; Korolenko's reference to the "mother" wilderness suggests that here, too, an image of sacred motherhood has been trampled upon. The holiness of the lake derives not from any particular aesthetic quality, either picturesque or sublime, but from a certain quality of attention that has been brought to it—and perhaps from its very lack of ostentation. And what has happened to it now? The final paragraph shifts out of iconic vision to something closer to documentary or journalistic prose. Korolenko's language suggests violation, what one almost wants to call rape— with the "mystery" (a feminine noun in Russian), or what Korolenko earlier called "mother-*pustynia*" lying "exposed at the side of the highway" and hiding in the shadows.[34]

The power of Korolenko's language derives in part from the abruptness of his shift from sacred, simple beauty to a destroyed and ravaged place. The verbs, tellingly enough, are past tense plurals—they tell us what has happened, but they don't tell us *who did it*. Korolenko's intent here is not, though, to rail against modernity. He has considerable sympathy for the *place*, but his feelings about the people who once lived here are more complex. Old Believers in Korolenko's account display "much naïve feeling, but little living thought." There is no one here to compare with Stepan, or Wolf, or the woodsman Aksen. There is a deaf elder who hears the bells of Kitezh, which he says remind him of his childhood village. There is a fiery-eyed pilgrim who quotes chapter and verse. And there is an old man quietly fishing, who tells Korolenko the story of a local man who has disappeared—vanished, everyone is convinced, into the underwater kingdom of Kitezh. (Korolenko's telling of the tale leaves us wondering if he was actually murdered.)

In *Following the Icon*, mentioned briefly above, Korolenko's interest had been less in the icon itself (which is left undescribed) than in the varieties of devotion granted it, and the cultures of veneration that follow "after the icon." In *In the Wild and Empty Places*, Korolenko seems more attentive to the image itself, and to problems of representation and expectation; the icon affords him a chance to present an idealized rendering of the world, but it also gives evidence of the ways in which Korolenko is interested in how images interact with reality—an attentiveness that may well have been shaped by his own practice as an artist.[35] In *In The Famine Year*, Korolenko would begin— after his description of forests burning to the north of Nizhnii—by pondering the question of *what famine looks like*. The question is not merely academic, Korolenko insists, since the public's willingness to believe in extremity of hardship hinges on what they think "famine" looks like: "I know what the reader expects from a correspondent in the famine districts . . . a concentrated, vivid picture which will immediately force him, the urbanite, to live through and feel all the horror of famine, that would melt his heart and get him to open his purse. . . . I know that the reader of these pages will more than once ask with surprise: but where is the famine? the famine that should shake us, and turn us inside out? *Famine is when mothers devour their children*—so wrote one gentleman just recently. . . . Finally, we must learn to acknowledge and see popular misery and sorrow where not one mother has eaten her child. . . . Famine has been sneaking up to us amidst this heat and smoke, amidst this drought; it was among us, it moved among the villages for two years already, but we didn't notice it, because so far not one mother has eaten her children" (101–2). A passage like this suggests a growing understanding on the writer's part of the challenges of getting people to *see*; and it suggests a shrewd understanding, both psychological and political, of what is at stake in an image of the world. How to get people to see an "apocalypse" that doesn't look like what they are expecting?

Perceptual psychology, and a kind of implied ethics of sight, are also central to Korolenko's account of Old Believer communities. Old Belief, as Korolenko presents it, is possessed of a desire to see through or beyond the phenomenal world into some other reality—a world of righteousness visible only to the elect, a "second world" that exists alongside this one. It is as though the *actual* world has no significance, or is a snare and delusion. Korolenko reminds us of the counter-phenomenology of the Kitezh legend and Old Belief:

> There stands to this day the city of Kitezh in the small, round-shaped lake Svetloyar, pure as a tear. Hidden from human eyes are the houses, the streets, the boyars' mansions and the walls with embrasures, the churches and monasteries in which "there are a great multitude of holy fathers, shining forth in their lives like the stars in the heavens or the sands of the sea." And to our

sinful, unenlightened gaze it seems there is but forest, and lake, and hills, and boggy ground. But that is only the illusion of our sinful nature. In reality, "in truth," here stand in all their beauty the grand palaces, and gilded chambers, and monasteries. . . . And whosoever is able even partially to see through the veil of deception, will see at the lake's bottom the glittering small flames of processions of the cross, gilded banners held high; and a sweet ringing is carried over the smooth, illusory waters. Then all grows quiet, and again only the oak groves whisper.

So two worlds stand above Lake Svetloyar: one is the real world, but unseen; the other is seen, but unreal. And they flow one into the other, they cover over, and penetrate each other. The false, illusory world is firmer than the true one. Only rarely the latter glimmers through its watery shroud, opens to the pious gaze and then disappears. And once more the crude deception of bodily sensation takes over. (131)

Whatever irony may have informed Korolenko's response to Old Belief, this passage is also deeply lovely, evoking from the "sinful, illusory" world great beauty, and a mystery that is defensive of our trespass upon it. Korolenko's response to Old Belief is bemused but not unkind, and it is worth noting its fundamental difference from what we find in his contemporary Zasodimskii, whose ethnographic account of the northern forests depicts Old Believer communities as bastions of ignorance that are ravaged by syphilis.[36] Korolenko's response to his conversations with Old Believers is perhaps best summed up in the action that ends the "Svetloyar" section of the narrative. After talking with an old man who is fishing on the banks of the lake—and teasing him about whether the fish he hopes to catch will be "real" or "illusory"—Korolenko decides to go swimming. His final response to Svetloyar, in other words, is to *jump in*.

I felt like swimming. I walked a ways away, so as not to disturb the kind man pulling illusory fish from the seeming lake; I undressed near a shed with a boat tied to it and plunged into the water with relish. The high, calm sky was above me. A small golden cloud faded in the ruddy, dying light. Beneath me was the enigmatic depth, bottomless and mysterious.

. . . Once I'd taken a deep breath, I went straight down into the depths. It was cold, the water was very dense. There was an involuntary feeling of mystery and awe. . . . I'm quickly carried back to the surface . . .

. . . I give it a second try. This time is more successful, I go deeper. The water is even colder and pushes upward like a spring, but I still manage to feel an object of some sort with my foot. The branch of a tree. It slips out from under my leg, but there's a second and a third. It's like the tops of a drowned forest. I'm hanging among them in the deeps, dense and dark. More effort. A ringing in the ears. I'm quickly carried up to the surface, and breathe deep chestfuls of air. (143)

There is something archetypal in this jump into Lake Svetloyar: the sheer physicality of it is wonderful, as is Korolenko's description of what he feels—the tactile (deep, cold, airless, leg-stretching) shock of his dive, the lung-bursting plunge into a different element. Korolenko doesn't touch bottom when he dives in (the lake is, indeed, quite deep), but he does make physical, literal *contact* with this lake that is so mythologized—both in Old Believer folklore and in later appropriations of it by literate, intelligentsia Russia.[37] Those tales and legends interest Korolenko, but so does the lake itself; he has a tactile desire to grasp the realities of this place, and also a kind of trickster's desire to poke gentle fun. There is a footnote (provided by Korolenko) that suggests the lake is volcanic in origin. Scientists still dispute its provenance; what is interesting, though, is Korolenko's relegation of geologic discourse to a footnote, as though even that naming doesn't get at the kind of reality his dive gives him. Present-day pilgrims to Svetloyar frown on those who come there to swim; on a visit in the summer of 2007 our guide (an ecologist from a nearby *zapovednik*, who was a rich source of both botanical lore and local legend) explained that families out swimming on a hot day have nowhere else to go. But for pilgrims the lake's water is sacred, and should be gathered or touched only for ritual purposes—not for the sheer pleasure of a hot day's swim. Korolenko's jump into the clear, cold water seems a similar act of trespass, or perhaps it is simply a physical "confession" that he is there as an observer, not a pilgrim.

The breadth of Korolenko's interest in this narrative is also evident in his attention not just to the forest, but to forestry. The landscape around the lake, we remember, is *exposed*: "The forests have been cut down . . . , roads have been cut through the glades. . . . Tilled fields have crept up to the 'sacred lake'" (130). Korolenko builds here not just on the contrast of desecrated landscape and sacred icon, but on the difference between what he sees—a treeless landscape—and Mel'nikov's descriptions of supposedly lush forest. What Mel'nikov left out, Korolenko brings into focus. The forested northern banks of the Volga River had in fact been intensively cut throughout the decades preceding Korolenko's visit to Svetloyar, with consequences for river travel and agriculture that led to the formation of Imperial commissions and alarmed calls to action: "Never have our forests been so ruthlessly felled as at present, and in a huge region stretching along the tributaries of the northern and central Volga."[38] Korolenko calls our attention to how physical changes have altered a mythologized landscape, but he also gives us a portrait of "modern forestry" as it was being practiced in the backwoods, an on-the-ground report on "rational use" of forest resources.

The penultimate section of Korolenko's narrative is devoted to his encounter with a woodsman by the name of Aksen, a "bear man" (*medvezhatik*—the term refers to the numbers of bears he has killed) who canoes past them and later hails the writer and his nephews from the shore, where they share a night's campfire and conversation. Aksen is another one of the characters that anchor Korolenko's account of his journey; he comes to represent a kind of paradigmatic "peasant" attitude toward the forest—in contrast to a Polish forest manager (Kazimir Kazimirovich) whom Korolenko had met a few days earlier. As Korolenko sits dreaming by a bonfire on the riverbank, he recalls Kazimir Kazimirovich and his forest, which is a rational manager's dream of order and planning. He and the Pole had stood on the belvedere of the manager's house and looked out on the woods; what they saw was an almost geometric landscape:

> He had built himself a wonderful, comfortable little nest in his government house. . . . This little house stands on the edge of the village, on a steep slope. You can see the river from here, and the meadows beyond the river, and beyond the meadows there are woods and then more woods. . . . Light and dark green, deep blue and violet against the distant horizon—they spread into the distance, hiding within themselves the meanders of the Kerzhenets. . . . In places they were hewn through by straight cuts . . . regular blocks [where] young saplings, evenly trimmed, hugged close to the tall, old forest. . . . And when I looked out on all that from the belvedere, the forester's house seemed to be the center from which, and to which, all this order moved. (188)

Aksen, on the other hand, doesn't fit into this rationally managed world: government regulations are disrupting his beekeeping, and he complains bitterly and with sarcasm to Korolenko about a situation in which a man can't kill a bear or take linden bark without checking first with some official. Aksen is the archetypal *muzhik* (a peasant, particularly an uneducated one), whose relationship to the forest Kazimir laments: the peasant will fell centuries-old oaks for acorns; he will skin hundreds of trees for bast, and to clear a small section of woodland he will burn hundreds of hectares of forest. From the Pole's belvedere—literally an "open sided gallery that commands a fine view"—he and Korolenko look out *over* the woods. What they see is "government property" (as Kazimir puts it) and "wood resources," an "order which has left visible traces amidst the elemental chaos of the forests" (188).

The distinctions that Korolenko is getting at here are fundamental, and the stakes are huge. What Korolenko lays out are differences in culture, temperament, and language, differences that will, he implies, have real consequences for the forest itself. Aksen represents deeply embedded peasant mentality and practice; Kazimir, on the other hand, suggests modernity, order, and an almost domesticated woodland. In writing these pages Korolenko may well have been thinking of the forest law that had been completed just two years earlier. The 1888 "Law on the Protection of Forests," as we saw in chapter 3, established guidelines for harvesting practices, which it was hoped might curb the destructive practices of post-Emancipation decades. The law represented an attempt on the part of the state—informed by the discourse of specialists and landowners—to frame the rationale for government intervention in a resource hailed as "our national inheritance."[39] But somewhere beneath the *belvedere*— that "beautiful view"—of bureaucrats and specialists lies the vast abyss between visions of rational management and a peasant mentality that viewed the forests as a "gift from God." Korolenko's meandering conversations thrust him smack in the middle of this discursive abyss. After a rambling and in some ways frustrating conversation with Aksen, Korolenko muses again on the Polish forester's vision of rational order:

> I found myself remembering the conversations on the forester's balcony, and his stories of plans for "rational forest management." So it turns out that this whole forest world, spread out at my feet, lost in mist and smoky blue along the broad horizon, rotates calmly, magnificently, in orderly fashion about the center, moving gracefully from chaos to order and harmony. Here on the sand bar of the river, after Aksen's passionate talk, that "rotation" seemed not quite so graceful. . . . Something was groaning and struggling under the axes. The sight lines were being cut into the living, raw earth of age-old popular understanding. (197)

Aksen makes Korolenko reconsider the view from Kazimir's house; but what Aksen tells him doesn't lead him wholly to discount the dream of symmetry and rational planning. Aksen's stories are about beekeeping and disputed claims to trees on government land; he is a tapper of wild hives, and the taxes have gone up—and to challenge them he has engaged a city lawyer who Korolenko is convinced is a shyster. We (and Korolenko) may in fact share Kazimir's concern that the peasant's traditional manner of laboring in the forest does serious damage: when Korolenko started thinking back to his conversation with the Pole, his sense was that "the Russian himself" doesn't make a good forest manager, that he is "too close to the views of his people. . . . The Pole is more cultured and restrained, his 'civilized' views on property are firmer and more consistent" (189). What Aksen's rambling monologue reminds Korolenko of is just how wide the gap is separating rational order and the "chaos"—not so much of the forest itself as of a way of life the woodsman represents. Aksen's beekeeping suggests to Korolenko an analogy of humans and bees, which he pursues to its disquieting conclusion:

> Like this creature of God, [the forest world has] settled among the wilds, without direction or orders, it's gotten settled and swarmed, and is linked to the conditions of its existence by a thousand unseen threads. . . . And then the axe of a government forester pounds on the trunk of the hive, and the hard-working creature buzzes and frets and gets agitated. . . . There's an axe hanging over the forest world's ways of thinking, too—and wild, elemental, immediate forest truth, born somewhere in ancient unconsciousness, protests in the name of elemental laws that rule in the forest kingdom. . . . And since for people of the forest the whole of God's world is the forest, where every one of God's creatures must swarm according to the simplest of laws—the same for a woodland hive and for a forest commune—well now, a man of the forest finds this "little Kazimir" has designs on the whole world order. (198)

Korolenko's conversation and his musings suggest a conundrum from which there is no easy exit. Aksen resents government officials and is certain that the "good tsar" of legend will intervene against oppressive bureaucrats. His stories get increasingly "fantastic"—and Korolenko concludes that he and Aksen are simply "speaking different languages." As fascinated as the populist writer is by this woodsman, he represents a world and mentality that stumps a man who in many of these pages has advocated "good thought" and the benefits of civilization.

We are left with the feeling that the "elemental chaos" of the woods won't surrender to rational management without a struggle; but we are also left wondering just what would be best *for the woods.* Kazimir's even sight-lines and well-trimmed plantings? Aksen's bees and individual contests with bears? Toward the end of their conversation both men grow quiet, and in the silence of human language, the forest "whispers." Whatever it might have to say remains incomprehensible to humans. To a modern reader this might seem like a moment in which Korolenko is advocating a "voice" for the forest itself, seeking to grant the natural world the kind of agency and standing that some modern environmental ethicists and activists have sought.[40] Korolenko's position is never, though, one we might call "conservationist." His concerns throughout this narrative are with human lives and actions, with how labor grants what Richard White calls "bodily knowledge of the natural world."[41] To say this is in some sense to return us to Korolenko's vision of Stepan on the river, his head rising into the clouds, his hands "driving" the Kerzhenets with his fishing-seine reins. I suggested there that this image reminds us of the complex and deeply physical relationship of men and women to a landscape in which they labor. Kazimir's comment about waste suggests a less charitable view of the outcomes of that labor. Our postmodern concerns tend to be with the impact of human labor on the environment; Korolenko and his contemporaries would likely have stated it differently, wondering about the impact of environment on human labor and dignity. Nature, as Korolenko put it at the beginning of his account of the famine, is *stalking* humans, with a relentlessness that drives them to superstitious attributions of evil intent. The writer's accounts of lives in place always take politics into account—corrupt bureaucrats, tax laws, and the perennial inequities of class and power. But there is also a sense in which his operative assumption is of a nature that is at best erratically benevolent, that will always in some sense represent an enemy of human aspiration. Korolenko's position, it seems to me, is somewhere in between the late nineteenth-century determinists with whom he polemicized, and someone like Gorky, whose heroic representations of laborers and wanderers turn too easily to Soviet rhetoric of triumphant humans subduing a hostile but malleable natural world.[42] Kornei Chukovsky reproached Korolenko for being too "hopeful," but there is a strong measure of environmental realism in the writer's depiction of humans' profound dependence on unpredictable forces of nature. Nonetheless, between Aksen's bees and Kazimir's geometry, Korolenko leaves us wondering if there might be another way.[43]

The ending of this narrative brings us back to human community, to the bustle and barges of the "civilized" Volga where the Kerzhenets flows into it. It is a moment of enormous relief and great delight for Korolenko; the last stretches of the wild river have been *too* wild for him, have induced an attack of *toska*—melancholy—and anxious boredom. Their last contact with human community is at a forest station, where Korolenko talks with a forester's wife and watches their "apathetic, bedraggled" daughter bringing the family cow home. From then on they are surrounded by "real wilderness," impassable tracts of boggy land and woodland streams. Rabbits watch them from the shore with their "round, naïve eyes"; kites circle above them; Korolenko suddenly shoots at an eagle watching them from a great height, and then wonders why in the world he thought to kill the "old bird." He observes the "silent, elemental drama" of the death of trees, great carcasses of pine and spruce submerged along the bank in what Korolenko calls a "graveyard of trees." When they camp at night and Korolenko turns to his notebook, he confesses a profound longing for human company: "Within these dark, silent forests, filled with ghastly memories and the graves of the murdered, of those who have submitted to the martyr's crown of fire; beside a river scattered with corpses of trees, beneath the sound of forest heights that converse in incomprehensible voices—to meet with a human being, in whom you'll find when needed both fellow-feeling and a helping hand, with whom you can speak in the language of humans, and not of the woods—that is indeed something more than our casual encounters and hat-tipping acquaintances. . . . But there was no one to wait for, and I fell fitfully asleep, listening to the wild cries of some forest predator, to the pathetic wails of his victim, to the meek rustling of a tentative rain as it hit against the leaves" (206).

Passages like this suggest just how different Korolenko's sense of "wilderness" is from our conventional American understanding of the word. Korolenko isn't fleeing human company, but inviting it, all along the way: he is curious and generous with everyone he meets, even the suspicious and guarded Old Believers. He is a conversationalist and democrat, eager to hear stories, aware that his encounters will teach him something not just about this neck of the woods, but about Russia itself. Change comes to these parts slowly, but it comes. There are steamboats and increased taxes and empty settlements where Old Believers once lived; there is the violated landscape of a sacred lake; there are the orderly sight lines of a model forest.

In an 1893 letter to the populist Nikolai Mikhailovsky, Korolenko insisted that "we need to look forward, not backward, we need to resolve our doubts by seeking solutions from positive knowledge, not by suppressing those doubts within ourselves."[44] I have leaned hard on a sense of ambivalence and paradox in this account of Korolenko, but I see no alternative. In his 1888 essay on art, Korolenko insisted that "if life is movement and struggle then art, as a faithful reflection of life, must represent that same movement and struggle of opinion and ideas."[45] The "struggle" that Korolenko represents in the forest narrative is not only external and economic, but his own struggle about the fate of the region, and about Russia as a whole.

Korolenko's commitment to looking *forward* is balanced in this account of a river journey by his affectionate, disarming openness to a place and its people. Like Turgenev in "Journey into Polesye," there is a shift away from sublime landscapes and the romantic's monologue of encounter, into a world of labor, legend, conversation, and complication. There is something, however, more *modern* in Korolenko—related perhaps to his less-privileged status, or his Siberian sojourn and the forms of physical labor he undertook, or simply to his living fifty years later, in a period that saw the beginning of Russia's twentieth-century revolutions. To a far greater extent than Turgenev, Korolenko maintained a powerful presence and voice in the political life of his country, until the end. Korolenko's final contribution to public discourse provides in fact an interesting commentary on the extent of his "environmentalism"—if in fact we want to call it that.

The great environmental crisis of Korolenko's middle life was the famine of 1891–92. While historians have not necessarily written about the famine in those terms, it seems plausible to see it in that light, as a disaster with roots not merely in natural forces but in human choices and structures of land ownership, agricultural practice, and the distribution of wealth. Korolenko's 1890 account of his river trip does *not*, as I have noted already, turn into an argument for conservation. His feelings about what we call "wild" nature—those uninhabited reaches of the Kerzhenets—are deeply ambivalent; he is a creature who longs for companionship, a man of the village more than the backwoods. But throughout the narrative, he registers in complex and profound ways the interdependence of human and natural lives, both imaginatively and literally. And his account of the radically different worldviews of the forest manager and the bear-man Aksen lays out the difficult terrain on which any sustainable forestry would need to be constructed.

In the preceding chapter I argued that Russia's writers and artists were increasingly aware, by century's end, of the dire consequences of the rampant felling of their European forests. Environmental tragedy, in nineteenth-century Russia, got articulated as *narodnoe bedstvie*—popular disaster: the philosopher Vladimir Solovyov, writing of the drought and famine in the same years as Korolenko, addressed literate Russians with grim warnings of the consequences of their inability to grapple not just with the growing desertification of Russian soil, but the failures of Russian agriculture and the wretched level of education among the peasantry. In a remarkable series of essays written in the early 1890s, Solovyov called the educated public to account, warning them that the *real* "enemy from the east" was not military but environmental. Like Korolenko, Solovyov is watching the weather. In "Enemy from the East" he makes clear he has been following discussions of drought and deforestation: "Even though the spring floods this year were considerable, all the same, not only in the southern half of Russia, which is completely denuded of forests, but even in those locations where I'm now writing (the boundary between the Moscow and Zvenigorod districts), the ground has been so dry from mid-May that after measurable rainfalls the moisture is retained only for a few hours."[46] In their tracking of weather and reading of scientific sources, both Korolenko and Solovyov were calling the Russian public to civic and environmental accountability, a restructuring of land law and agricultural practice that might mitigate the potentially apocalyptic consequences of inaction.[47]

Korolenko's final word on environment, culture, and civic action comes in a remarkable document, a series of letters that he wrote to the Soviet commissar of education, Anatolii Lunacharsky. Lunacharsky had invited Korolenko to write them, and promised to have them published in the Bolshevik press, but he reneged on his offer; written in 1920, they were published in Paris in 1922, but not in Russia until the late 1980s.[48] The pretext for their writing was a series of executions of peasants, accused of hoarding grain during the Civil War; Korolenko had written empassioned pleas against capital punishment before the Revolution, and was dismayed to have to continue this campaign under the new order. The letters are an anguished and passionate plea for freedom: freedom of the press, freedom of conscience, freedom and integrity of judicial process. They are also a passionate defense of imagination over what Korolenko calls "schematicism," using language that harks back to his essays of the 1880s, when he warned that rigidities of logic lead into quagmires, and that "people possessed of a strong feeling for life don't write utopias."[49] Rigid attachment to Marxist doctrine, Korolenko writes in 1920, has blinded the Bolsheviks to the realities of Russian life: imagination alone, in the context of a free press, would enable those in power to understand the complex realities of a vast country[50]. What concerns Korolenko in the final letters is the looming specter of famine. The Bolsheviks, with their "schemes," have won out over capital—but they have also destroyed the productive forces of society; and for Korolenko, this "victory" constitutes a complete defeat "on a broader and more important front"—in which humans do battle with the "hostile forces of nature." "Years ago, in my book *In the Famine Year*, I tried to depict the mournful condition to which autocracy had led: huge areas of the Russian breadbasket were going hungry, and those pangs of hunger intensified. What we have now is worse: *the whole of Russia* is struck by famine, beginning with the capital cities, where there have been cases of death from famine on the streets" (166–67). Korolenko returns to hunger a few pages later in his description of Poltava, where the ideological extremism of war communism leaves soldiers shoeless and hungry. His description of the consequences of that hunger is lengthy and unsettling: "Just two weeks ago a Red Army unit was headed out of Poltava toward the front. The *shtab* stationed them just beside my apartment. . . . In the yard of the house where I live there are several walnut trees. This attracted the soldiers. . . . It's hard to describe what happened. They climbed up on the trees, broke the branches, and gradually got into a frenzy of haste, rushing like children, the soldiers starting grabbing firewood, bricks, and stones to throw at the trees. . . . All of the trees were torn apart, and the Reds only left after a ceremonial speech by their commander, about how the Red Army was going to build a new society" (176–77). This is Wordsworth's "Nutting," but over a century later, married to ideological intransigence and a famished, frenzied, resentful soldiery.

Korolenko's description shows us his undying concern for human well-being: he and others from the house were concerned that the soldiers would break windows, which would then be impossible to fix. There is also bleak exasperation at the absolute gap between dreams of a new society and the destruction of the present, along with a distraught sense of what is happening to the soldiers themselves—not just their hunger, which drives them to destroy the trees, but their loss of an "impulse to labor," which Korolenko refers to earlier in his expression of dismay at the extent of theft more generally. The passage is, in general, grim reading, shadowed by our own knowledge of the history of famine, lawlessness, and destruction in the Soviet Union. As with the trees that were leveled in the background of Repin's painting, that violence was directed against both humans and the natural world. The famine that Korolenko had witnessed in 1891–92 would not be the worst one. He would not live to see the genocidal famines in Ukraine, famines in which Stalin's state turned the "hostile forces of nature" against a whole people. Korolenko died in December of 1921. His letters to Lunacharsky did not enter the Soviet narrative of his life. But like all of what this remarkable man wrote, they are a legacy of which the Russian people should be proud.

They are also a legacy of writing about place, labor, economics, culture—together with natural conditions, climate, and soil—that is a model of what such writing can be. Is this "environmental writing"? While Korolenko studied with one of the greatest Russian natural scientists of his day, he did not finally choose science as his métier, finding instead that Russia's tradition of committed writing would allow him a broader vehicle, not just to *reflect*, but to create and perhaps to change society. Change, as he observes in the *Letters to Lunacharsky*, involves both men's souls and human institutions. Scientific language, or the close observational qualities we associate with natural history, are not noticeably important in Korolenko's prose. What is important is a kind of communitarian discourse, in which a wandering, open-hearted, and open-eyed *observer-belletrist* records what he sees, opens his own imagination to the figures and stories of those he meets, and registers his own skepticism when it seems appropriate. The visionary and the pragmatist stand together in Korolenko—sometimes they are two people (as in the passage above the Lena River that Azadovskii cites), sometimes they are side by side in his own voice. What seems most admirable about this "one-man civil liberties union" was his willingness to *jump in*—whether into the waters of Svetloyar, or into villages ravaged by a famine that some refused to see. His ability to see both beauty and hardship, both the "icon" and its destruction, his sense of a quasi-mystical connection to nature that rides together with a recognition of how, in fact, the forces of nature *could be* hostile: all of this makes of Korolenko a splendid "guide pole" in our own negotiation of what it means to change souls and institutions. Or, to put it less figuratively, what it means to nurture civic discourse, to care both about nature and human lives.

5

Beyond the Shattered Image

Mikhail Nesterov's Epiphanic Woodlands

> To attend is to imagine. . . . It is the image—
> enlivening or atrophying attention—that escorts
> the world to us.
>
> —Richard Niebuhr, "The Strife of Interpreting: The
> Moral Burden of Imagination" (1985)

IN 1890, THE SAME YEAR that Korolenko published *In the Wild and Empty Places*, the artist Mikhail Nesterov (1862–1942) completed what would be the first of a series of paintings devoted to Sergius of Radonezh, Russia's "forest" saint, an Orthodox hermit whose life of sanctity and labor within the northern forest had become emblematic of moral and political rebirth. Nesterov is a painter whose work is almost synonymous with a certain kind of sentimental Slavophilism; his prerevolutionary work was dominated by a lyrical vision of religious figures in a northern landscape, creating a version of what Vladimir Lenyashin, curator at the Russian Museum in St. Petersburg, has called "Russian National Romanticism."[1] As such, his canvases both evoke and have been constitutive of a Russian variant of what Anthony Smith terms "ethnoscape"—a "particular stretch of territory" associated with events that have shaped communal identity, a landscape invested with "powerful emotional connotations and cultural meanings."[2] Nesterov's landscapes with religious figures evince a nostalgia for Russia's medieval, monastic past on the eve of revolution; his paintings can seem inseparable from the reactionary patriotism and resistance to change of the final decades of Romanov rule. And yet they also have a compelling contemplative quality, imagining as they do an ideal relationship between humans and the surrounding world. As Smith himself notes, ethnoscapes function in part through their offer of "emotional as well as physical security"—perhaps at no time more powerfully than in periods of rapid change.[3] This no doubt suggests one reason for the longevity of the paintings' popularity. Nesterov painted, among other things, the Kitezh myth; scenes from Mel'nikov-Pechersky's novels of Old Believer life; renderings of monastic life in the Russian north; and images of Sergius. His Sergius series takes us into an "ancient" Russian past in a way that makes that past seem immediate and contemporary: a boy meeting a cowled

Mikhail Nesterov, The Boy Bartholomew's Vision *(1889–90). Tretyakov Gallery, Moscow. Image copyright Lebrecht Music & Arts.*

figure by an oak tree is Russia's most famous saint, but there is nothing in the painting (except its title) to tell us that this is the fourteenth century; there is something utterly familiar and everyday (what Russians would call *bytovoi*) in this encounter of the domestic and the divine.[4]

Nesterov's paintings of Sergius are important to imaginations of the Russian forest for several reasons. For one, they are vivid renderings of a figure associated with the monastic settlement of the forests of northeast European Russia, re-creating for late Imperial Russia a vision of place and sanctity. They have retained an extraordinary popularity within Russia, becoming emblematic of national identity and religious traditions, and projecting an image of hallowed land.[5] Compared with Korolenko's ethic of "jumping in," these paintings are both more contemplative and more nostalgic, less troubled by the ironies or compromises of modernity. "Mother Wilderness" is neither ravaged nor empty in these images. But these paintings have, as do Korolenko's narratives, their own ecological ethos, one grounded in precisely that contemplative stance, a way of looking at—and being in—the world. Tom Newlin has suggested a synchronicity of the holistic, contemplative gaze of poets and natural historians with *sobornost'*—a notion of organic union, a kind of mystical merging of the individual within a larger whole—that the Slavophiles of the 1840s took as distinctive of Russian culture.[6] For Newlin, *sobornost'* has both phenomenological and ecological implications: a way of seeing and experiencing the world is at stake. For John Chryssavgis, a contemporary theologian, Eastern Orthodoxy's unique offering to environmental questions is similarly its particular culture of *seeing*, grounded in the icon, the central devotional element of the Eastern church. For Chryssavgis, the icon offers the modern world a way of overcoming what he compellingly calls our "autism" as regards the natural world: "The world of the icon not only presupposes a way of thinking and demands a way of living, but also offers new . . . perceptions of the world around us. . . . Our generation is characterized by a behavior that results from an autism with regard to the natural cosmos: a certain lack of awareness, or recognition, causes us to use, or even waste the beauty of the world. . . . We have disestablished a continuity between ourselves and the outside, with no possibility for intimate communion and mutual enhancement."[7] In other words, we do not really *see*, do not really *attend to* the world in which we live; the icon—as an image that calls for a particular kind of attention and openness—offers the viewer a practicum in attending to the world. As Chryssavgis's title suggests, the icon moves us *beyond the shattered image* of a suffering world; in contemplation of the "unshattered" image both world and viewer will find the potential for healing.

What Newlin and Chryssavgis are proposing is a culturally embedded way of seeing that in shifting the way we see the world changes our relationship to it: what is suggested here is a form of attention that reestablishes "communion," overcomes "autism," and returns us to continuity and a different ethics.[8] Attention, attentiveness, and action are knit together in these visionary claims. Nesterov's paintings are not, however, *icons*, in the strict sense of the word; they are easel paintings grounded in Russian religious traditions, both ecclesiastical and popular. One of my arguments here will be that they nonetheless encourage in us precisely the kind of attentive regard that Chryssavgis is talking about, that they represent a re-envisioned creation, in which humans' relationship to the natural world has overcome a fallen state of violence and separation. They do that by drawing on a wide array of traditions—artistic, literary, and folkloric—and on many of the myths and legends of the forest *ethnoscape* that we have already examined in preceding chapters. Elena Polenova, an artist and a friend of Nesterov's whose work on traditional crafts helped shape the "rustic organicism" of fin de siècle art, longed to produce a series of paintings that would "express the poetic views of the Russian people toward Russian nature."[9] Polenova's phrasing echoes *The Slavs' Poetic Views of Nature,* the title of Alexander Afanas'ev's compendium of legend and mythology that had been so important to Mel'nikov-Pechersky in his forest epic.[10] Poetry, national culture, ways of seeing, and religious tradition all come together in Nesterov's images of a forest saint, in ways that connect ethnoscape to a vision of human and natural worlds transfigured. What is transfigured in Nesterov's paintings is not just humans (become saints) or nature (returned to its Edenic state). It is rather the *relationship* of humans and the creation that seems transfigured, evoking an icon of possibility whose implications are ecological and ethical as well as spiritual.

These observations move us well ahead; first we must attend to the paintings themselves, and their creator. The first and now most famous of Nesterov's Sergius paintings was painted in 1889–90 and exhibited at the Peredvnizhniki (Wanderers) exhibit in 1890. *The Boy Bartholomew's Vision* shows two figures encountering one another near an oak tree, in a meadow in which the grass is starting to turn from green to gold. In the distance we see lowland between two hillsides, both of them gold and green with birch and spruce. A wooden church with two small onion domes—their Orthodox crosses just visible atop them—emerges from the woods; the church's porch, or entrance, is partially concealed by the boy's head in the foreground. The boy stands just to the right of dead center; behind him there are two young trees, one a birch (we recognize it by its lightly mottled white bark and its few remaining gold leaves, which look like globes of light), the other a mountain ash or *riabina*. In the middle ground, between the meeting place of the two figures and the background with the church and forest, there is a dirt path—large enough for a cart, with ruts that still have water glistening in them. The past, the rebirth of Russian religious identity, the gift of the Word, the manifestation of the Holy Spirit beside an oak, a boy who would go on to build monastic settlements deep in the "slumbering forest" that we see in the distance: all this is made *present* to us here, in a canvas that has none of the trappings of historical painting, but settles instead deeply into the aura of what seems a blessed landscape.

Our attention in the painting is focused largely on the two human figures: the boy in the center, with his hands clasped before him, his clean white shirt, and a look of absolute simplicity, lack of fear, and a kind of acquiescence to the moment, and a black-robed elder who stands directly beneath—almost merging with—the oak tree with its dried brown leaves and lichens along the trunk. We identify this dark, faceless figure as a religious of some sort—both because of the crosses visible on his hood and back, and because of the faint nimbus around his head (an aspect of the painting that elicited strong criticism from numerous contemporaries, who felt it betrayed the "realism" of the painting).[11] The dark figure holds something in his hands, a vessel that we assume to be religious in meaning. Just behind him on the oak tree, a bit below the level of his head, a small square is affixed: while American viewers might not immediately identify this, Nesterov's contemporaries would certainly have known it to be an icon—darkened and obscured by age, but still a holy image. The icon hanging on the tree may have drawn the boy—or the old man—into prayer; it also stands as a reminder of the cultural practice of marking natural spaces with religious images.[12] And perhaps this icon is the key to the whole painting, which is in its own way an "icon" of religious calling and blessed creation.

This is a painting that makes one want to stand as still as the figures represented in it; a painting deeply embedded in various narratives (the canonical *Life* of a saint and the history of a culture), and yet also a painting that seems self-sufficient, for which commentary and context would be superfluous. It was painted in the same year as Korolenko's journey, with its drought and impending hardship, and yet the painting's vision of plenitude and nourishment—both material and spiritual—seems light years away from apocalypse, whether political or environmental. It is a painting, as Vasilii Rozanov put it, in which we *almost see myths, and the mythological, coming into being*. Or, as Rozanov's and Nesterov's contemporary Sergei Makovskii put it, where we glimpse the *epiphanies of a people*, a "smile from a distant shore."[13]

It is, I will confess, a painting that both moves me and gives me pause. On the one hand, it seems to offer a vision of reconciliation and relationship *in potentio*—not just between the two human figures, but between humans and the natural world. It is, I have come to think, an icon of Eucharist, a situating of culture within the breast of nature, a vision of what we take as binaries (forest and field, youth and age, beginning and end, prayer and labor) reconciled. In all of this it is an *icon*, not a photographic image; an ideal, not a document. It invites us into its still, simple space with a promise of growth and movement. All of these are indices of that "epiphany" that Makovskii is referring to—indices and epiphanies we will come back to explore more carefully. But the painting also troubles me—and here I become a more skeptical, perhaps more Korolenko-like viewer: painted in years of political reaction and repression, in a period in which the Imperial government and official church manipulated religious symbols and popular emotion to their own ends, the painting can seem an obfuscation of the real and difficult world—a world of famine and poverty and felled trees and damaged earth. Nesterov brings us away from the vision that Repin presents in his *Procession of the Cross in the Kursk District*, with its various brutalities and its overarching ecological disaster. He brings us back into the shade of oaks (which in Repin have been felled), back into the "old, old icons of unassuming manner," before *mother pustynia* has been ravaged.[14] Nostalgia lures us with the promise that we can go home again. Is Nesterov luring us with false promises?

Just what myths do we see "coming into being" in Nesterov's paintings? Rozanov himself points to the prayer-filled quality of the artist's easel paintings, their representation of what is for Rozanov the heart of religion, the soul's movement in spontaneous prayer, which, he contends, gives us the *living matter* of religion, as opposed to the *nature morte* of ritual and genre scenes. The mythology of Nesterov's paintings is for Rozanov connected to Orthodoxy and the specifics of Russian landscape, an undifferentiated plain that is quieter and "smoother" than the history-wracked Alps of European identity.[15] This is a landscape in which the soul is quieter and history is saved from conflict, as though a country's topographic features map its historical fate. (We recognize in this a geography akin to Boev's Slavophile juxtaposition of blood-drenched castles and Orthodox monastic bells.) Rozanov's essay in geographical/spiritual determinism seems more than a little bizarre, given the year in which it was written (1907): there is perhaps a powerful urge toward wish-fulfillment in his imagination that Russia would live out a pronouncement he attributes to Montesquieu: "Happy are those people who have had no history." What Rozanov wants to imagine is a Russia incapable of aggression, in which crusades are replaced by pilgrimage, colonialism by deferential exploration, and revolution by dynastic election. The tectonic cataclysms of 1917 were only a decade away, the first revolution was two years past; Rozanov's "mythologies" seem more fantastic by far than Nesterov's elision of famine and drought.

What Rozanov presents is as much his own mythology as Nesterov's: a Russia defined by prayer and quietude, in which the very landscape is a guarantor of protection from conflict and strife. Sergei Makovskii, writing two years later (1909), similarly identified the religious as the essence of Nesterov's gift; but for Makovskii, Nesterov is most successful as an artist when he joins Orthodoxy to something older and more "pagan." Much of this essay is directed *against* Nesterov's official icon painting, work he did with Victor Vasnetsov in the Cathedral of St. Vladimir in Kiev.[16] For Makovskii, these explicitly religious images are "sentimental and literary," spoiled by "ideology"—by an overdose of *ideas*. Nesterov is brilliant, says Makovskii, when he succumbs to an intuitive feel for beauty, when he grasps in painterly terms the "spirituality of slavic Christianity" as it mixes with "the pagan dream of animate nature." In doing this, claims Makovskii, Nesterov grasps something deep and poetic in the "epiphanies" of the Russian people; this is when he intuits the "smile" from that other shore.[17]

The sources of Nesterov's Sergius paintings are multiple—if we think of sources not merely as visual antecedents but in terms that are broadly cultural, biographical, and locational. Those sources are first of all hagiographical, rendered both visually and verbally. The canonic *Life* of Sergius was written by the fifteenth-century monk Epiphanii the Wise; a version in modern Russian (as opposed to the archaic church Slavonic) had appeared in 1885, compiled by the Hieromonk Nikon. Nesterov would have known and internalized the stories of Sergius—as well as those of many other Orthodox saints—from a wide variety of sources, both liturgical and published. The canonic *Life* found its visual counterpart in a rich tradition of icons, which Nesterov would have known from earliest childhood. But the sources for the painting are artistic as well as religious, including Nesterov's training and friendships in the world of Russian art and travel abroad; its sources are situated within the renaissance of interest in Russian national culture at century's end, and the official cult of religious national identity.[18] Finally there are sources of the painting in the place where it was begun—Abramtsevo, an artist's colony situated in the countryside to the northwest of Moscow.

Nesterov himself was born in Ufa in southeast European Russia, where the forest-steppe region gives way to open plains just south of the low-rising Urals. The family were merchants; he was the tenth of twelve children, only two of whom survived beyond childhood.[19] The remembered landscapes of his early years are summer gardens filled with ripe berries, apple trees—"each one is an acquaintance, how can you keep from checking if the apples are ripe?"—a birch tree his father had planted. The vast open plains of the southern Urals were not, however, the landscape that Nesterov would memorialize in his paintings: "How good is God's world! How fine is my birthplace [*rodina*]! And how could I not love it dearly, though I'm sorry I didn't grant it more attention and energy, didn't depict its beauties so that others might come to love it."[20] The artist's acquaintance with the more northerly landscape that came to dominate his paintings began at age twelve, when he was sent to Moscow to study. Within a few years his teachers had recognized his artistic gifts and recommended that he transfer to art school.[21]

Nesterov's formal training began in Moscow with the realist Perov, but from there he went to St. Petersburg to attend the Academy of Arts, a locale he found alienating in the extreme. "My soul frequently fled back to old-fashioned Moscow, to a city whose Russianness I felt acutely amidst the half-foreign chill of St. Petersburg."[22] He began his painter's career with work that was historical and largely narrative; what he produced in the 1880s for the newly popular illustrated weeklies was "bread and butter" work, genre paintings of Muscovite Russia and illustrations of Pushkin's folktales in verse. That early work also included illustrations of Dostoevsky's *Brothers Karamazov* and of Mel'nikov-Pechersky's novels. The critic and memoirist Sergei Durylin estimates that Nesterov did as many as a thousand illustrations for publications like *Niva*, *Vsemirnaia illiustratstiia*, and *Raduga*; years later Nesterov would comment, "I did illustrations because I had to eat and drink."[23]

The moment of aesthetic transformation in Nesterov's art, what changed him from an undistinguished illustrator and artist of historical scenes into an iconographer of the Russian landscape, was the personal crisis occasioned by the death of his wife, Maria, in childbirth in 1886. Nesterov himself put it this way: "Love for Maria and the loss of her made me an artist, gave to my work the content it had lacked, both feeling, and living soul, literally everything that came to be valued, that people still value in my art."[24] As Abbott Gleason notes in his essay on Nesterov's work, immediately after Maria's death the artist "produced several emaciated figures of angels and tsarevnas that strongly, if gropingly, suggested the explicit religiosity of his later work."[25] Nesterov's mature work, its "explicit religiosity," its inwardness (often suggested in his treatment of eyes and the gaze), and its frequent focus on female religious figures, is all related to this early and apparently lifelong grief.

In addition to the powerful emotional stimulus of this loss, there were other forces at work in Nesterov's movement toward explicitly religious canvases. The aesthetic and religious thought of the age was remarkably open to and interested in feminine faces of the divine, apparent in the attitude of receptivity and androgyny in many of the painter's religious figures.[26] By the late 1880s, Nesterov had strong associations with a group of artists working at the Abramtsevo estate, whose intense interest in Russian folk and religious traditions paved the way for avant-garde experiments with form and color in the early twentieth century.[27] The ecstatic religiosity and synthesis of pagan and Orthodox Russia found in Mel'nikov-Pechersky's Volga novels were also sources of inspiration and specific imagery. Those novels seem to have evoked for the artist both feminine spirituality and a particular landscape, along with nostalgically envisioned Old Believer communities. In a letter of 1896 to the critic Alexandre Benois, Nesterov describes various projects—including a painting of Old Believer life ("so poetically described in the works of A. Pechersky") and material for his Sergius cycle, which had taken him to monasteries in the Moscow region.[28] The letter suggests the extent to which the two different subjects—Old Belief and Sergius—coexisted in the artist's work of the 1890s, interconnected visions of "Old Russia" and its landscapes. Nesterov was captivated by both *In the Forests* and its sequel *On the Hills*, which he (along with his fellow art students Isaac Levitan and Abram Arkhipov) devoured in art school: "They were enthralled by the poetic pictures of Russian nature and old-fashioned Russian life."[29] Nesterov's first treatments of subjects drawn from Mel'nikov-Pechersky, executed in 1888 and published in the illustrated weekly *Niva*, are not unlike his drawings of pre-Petrine Russian life, with a cluttered attention to historical detail.[30] His later Mel'nikov paintings—which he insisted were not illustrations but rather *infused* by the novels—are elegantly stylized and carefully composed, usually focusing on female figures within an iconic Russian landscape. *On the Hills* (1896) sets a delicately curving female figure above a panoramic landscape of a similarly sinuous river and hazy distance; *Taking the Veil* (1898) and *Kitezh City* (*In the Forests*) (1917–22) give us a wooded Russia of spruce and birch, still-as-glass water, and traditional wooden structures.[31] In both these later paintings there is an almost ritualistic sense of figural organization, more obscure in the Kitezh painting than in *Taking the Veil*, where the procession of women with long tapers is explained by the title. In the Kitezh painting slender young women in white and black sit clustered on the ground, or in upright, trancelike postures, at the edge of a glassy lake; a powerful woman in brocade and red dominates the left middle ground, a massive pine trunk rising behind her as though through and out of her body. Behind the cluster of seated women we see Nesterov's signature birches, which in *Taking the Veil* become the silent companions of the ritual of women's lives. The birches of that painting frame the procession in a way that seems funereal.[32] The Kitezh painting, on the other hand, is more enigmatic: are the women guardians of some mystery? held prisoner by the powerful, almost witchlike figure in red? caught up in some grief either for themselves or at some other loss? Bearing in mind Nesterov's own caution against reading the paintings as straight illustration, we are left wondering. One commentator suggests that what we see in the painting is "Rus"—an "enchanted world, in harmony with nature, but vanished forever, like the legendary city of Kitezh." This makes of the women an allegory for Russia itself, and pushes us to see the image in terms of revolution and civil war. Whatever we make of this particular iteration of figures in an iconic landscape, it is striking how frequently Nesterov returned to this visual cluster with its carefully composed symmetries of natural and human form. The Civil War–era vision of Mel'nikov's women suggests the continuing significance for him of a book he first read thirty years earlier.[33]

The landscape of these paintings, and their statuesque, almost archetypal figures, link them to the artist's Sergius cycle, which he began in 1889. During late spring and summer of that year Nesterov traveled to the capitals of European art, a journey that quickened his affection for Russia's understated landscape. He saw the Austrian Alps in terms of painterly conventions: "I stood enthralled by the window, concealing my sense of ecstasy. There it is: *abroad*; there they are: *Tyrolean hunters* in green hats with feathers, which I'd first seen in the paintings . . . of German artists. How unlike Russia it all is—poor, gray Russia, loved to the point of heartbreak."[34] The trip would also educate his eye in contemporary European painters' handling of form and space. When he arrived in Paris, he quickly made his way to the World Exhibition, happy that his weeks in Rome and Florence had honed his sense of what he needed to see and what was superfluous. The

Mikhail Nesterov, Taking the Veil *(1898). Russian State Museum, St. Petersburg. Scala / Art Resource, NY.*

Mikhail Nesterov, Kitezh City: In the Forests *(1917–22). State Art Museum, Nizhnii Novgorod. Image copyright Lebrecht Music & Arts.*

revelation of his Parisian stay was Jules Bastien-Lepage (1848–84), whose every work was "an entire volume of wisdom, kindness and poetry." Best of all was his *Joan of Arc.* On July 22 Nesterov describes the painting in a letter to his family: "Joan is in a country garden, lost in thought, thinking of her poor motherland, her beloved France, and at just this moment of ecstasy and pure patriotism she sees among the bushes and the apple branches the shade of St. Louis and two martyrs." Two days later in another letter home he is once again writing about Joan, focusing now on her eyes: "Joan of Arc's eyes truly see something mysterious before them. They are light blue, clear and calm."[35] For Nesterov this painting of Joan in a moment of epiphany was vastly superior to the mass of technically proficient but "not particularly profound" French work.[36] Mornings he spent visiting the exhibit halls devoted to particular nationalities (not surprisingly, he was drawn to the Pre-Raphaelites[37]), but every afternoon was spent in careful contemplation of Joan. Years later, in his *Memoirs*, Nesterov was still struck by the French painter's achievement: "The whole effect, all of the power of *Joan of Arc* lay in its extreme simplicity, naturalness and in that unique and unparalleled *expression in the eyes* of the shepherdess from Domremi; those eyes were the artist's particular secret."[38]

Bastien's Joan is rendered in earth tones of muted brown and gray, the color of her skin and clothing like the bark and leaves of the apple tree, or the stucco and tile of the small farmhouse visible behind her. As is so often the case in Nesterov's own work, human and sylvan figures echo each other in color and form; Bastien-Lepage's visionary saint is seen head-on, her left arm outstretched and open-handed, head tilted ever so slightly to the left, the gesture suggesting a kind of contemplative, trancelike choreography. Realistic in its attention to the details of country life and the fertile disarray of a garden at harvest, Bastien's painting brings into this carefully observed quotidian world emissaries of another reality: behind Joan and hovering just above a swift for winding yarn we see two other figures, one a diaphanous female angel with a halo, the other a massive androgyne, perhaps an angelic figure for Joan's own future transformation.

The other painter who impressed Nesterov in Paris was Puvis de Chavannes (1824–98), a salon painter who also exhibited with Impressionists and post-Impressionists, and whose work had a major impact on the early twentieth-century avant-garde.[39] Puvis's frescoes in the Pantheon included a series of panels devoted to the patron saint of Paris, including one of Genevieve as a child praying in a delicate pastoral landscape. Nesterov recalled later that Puvis's panels "transported me to Florence and Ghirlandaio's frescoes in my favorite Chapel of Santa Maria Novella."[40] Puvis's emphasis in his murals is on decorative form, images that Jennifer Shaw argues "provoked in critics a vision of the French landscape as a nourishing, maternal power."[41] Puvis's rendering of figures who "often appear lost in silent contemplation" must also have captured the Russian artist, suggesting fundamentally different strategies to approach the evocation of spirituality, without the depth of field evident in Bastien-Lepage's canvas.

Jules Bastien-Lepage, Joan of Arc *(1884). The Metropolitan Museum of Art, New York. Image copyright © The Metropolitan Museum of Art / Art Resource, NY.*

What is striking about these two artists, from the perspective of Nesterov's own paintings of saints and epiphany, is the way they articulate space, and the relationship of figure to ground. Bastien-Lepage's canvas has a kind of depth and fullness, with the young Joan appearing to move into some unseen reality even as she embodies stillness. Puvis, on the other hand, is renowned for his rendering of flat, friezelike space, a quality of decorative flattening that became pivotal for painters like Gauguin and Picasso; Jennifer Shaw comments on the extent to which Puvis's landscape (in the 1891 *Summer*) establishes a "contrast between background and foreground," between that which is inaccessible and that which is "disturbingly present" and "part of the painting's language of dream."[42] Nesterov's reference to Ghirlandaio is astute, catching as it does the classical impulse in the French artist's work. Puvis drew inspiration from Florentine frieze paintings for his depiction of landscapes as a series of horizontal bands, creating images in which the relationship between figures is not acknowledged by the figures themselves, but is instead created by "the flow of abstract, decorative rhythms created by their postures and spatial relationships"—something William Robinson connects to the sense of isolation and "withdrawal into silence" in Puvis's paintings.[43] Such differing approaches to the representation of figures within the landscape, either in profile or full face, and of varying fields of depth, are evident in Nesterov's paintings of Sergius, and in his subsequent series of friezelike canvases that depict momentous encounters within a stylized Russian landscape. These are differing resolutions of a problem that is at once technical and, for want of a better world, "philosophical": how human figures are situated within the landscape. Bastien-Lepage's Joan suggests an epiphanic intermingling of reality and the divine, human and natural form, indebted to naturalistic recession and the creation of a sense of depth. Puvis's resolution brings humans and natural forms together in a more schematic, horizontal frame. These visual lessons would return with Nesterov to Russia. As he left Paris and began the journey home, he wrote of sensing "something being born within me, a living necessity, an obligation to say something of my own, that something within me was already beginning to move, like fruit within a mother's womb."[44] Midwife to this strikingly feminine creative process would be the landscape northeast of Moscow.

The previous summer Nesterov had befriended the artists of Abramtsevo, including Elena Polenova. Polenova, sister of the artist Vasilii Polenov and head of the estate's carpentry workshop, was contemplating a projected cycle of illustrated *skazki* (traditional Russian fairy tales), busy in the meantime with carefully observed, delicate miniatures of the natural world at Abramtsevo. Polenova had shared with Nesterov the idea of creating an illustrated *Lives of the Saints* in a popular edition, and had done a quick sketch of the youth Bartholomew's vision of a monk in the forest.[45] As important as these conversations and paintings was the landscape. After his return from Paris in 1889, Nesterov rented a peasant *izba*—a traditional one-room log cabin with a mammoth stove for heating and cooking—in the village of Komiakin. The village—some thirty miles northeast of Moscow—was near the Trinity monastery founded by Sergius in the fourteenth century. From the village Nesterov set out for daily walks, in a terrain that was to become the Russia of his paintings. "The area around Komiakin is very picturesque; all about there are forests, spruce and birch in wonderful combinations. I wandered for days on end. Three *versts* away is Abramtsevo, where I stopped in more and more frequently."[46] By the next summer Nesterov would be living at Abramtsevo, in rooms made available to him by Elizaveta Mamontova, one of late Imperial Russia's great patrons of the arts. It was here that Nesterov ultimately found the landscape of Bartholomew's encounter: "Once, from the Abramtsevo terrace, my eyes were unexpectedly presented with such truly Russian beauty: wooded hills to the left, the Aksakovs' Boria stream winding beneath them, the distance blushing rose, a bit of smoke, malachite cabbages in a garden closer in. A golden grove on the right. A few changes and additions here and there and you've got a better background for Bartholomew than you could possibly imagine. I set to work on the sketch, which turned out well, and looking at the landscape I was filled with a sense of its genuine 'historicity.'"[47]

Nesterov's account of discovering this landscape is striking: the original gives the landscape an agency that almost seems awkward in English, with its Russian beauty *presenting itself* to a receptive artist. The emotion that fills him as he works on the painting suggests a vision as powerful as the one he would depict in the painting, or that Bastien-Lepage had rendered in his *Joan*: this is an epiphany of Russia, that links landscape, emotion, and what Nesterov here calls *historicity* (*istorichnost'*). As important as the golds and greens of birch and spruce and those wonderful "malachite cabbages" is the emotion connected to a sense of what this landscape has meant for Russia, a meaning condensed in the figure of Bartholomew, the youth who would become the great Saint Sergius.

And just what does Nesterov mean here by *historicity*? I suggested above that Nesterov's painting effaces time's passage, presenting this historical subject as though it were happening in the immediacy of a well-known landscape. Nesterov achieves that sense of timelessness with the simplicity of his human figures, whose clothing shows neither antiquarian detail nor evidence of machine modernity. Bastien-Lepage's *Joan* claims a similar immediacy, with its simple French barnyard that looks as much like the nineteenth as the fifteenth century. Historical time is less important in Nesterov's canvas than seasonal, or natural time: we are more aware, I think, of the autumnal atmosphere—or of the contrast of youth and age—than of any particular century. There is none of the antiquarian detail of academic history painting or of Nesterov's English precursors, the Pre-Raphaelites. The *historicity* derives from the landscape itself, not from the markers of human culture; what Nesterov seems to have in mind is how the landscape, joined to his own intense emotion, makes the past *present and immediate*, linking the artist's emotions with those of an encounter centuries earlier.

The qualities of immediacy and essential timelessness are linked here, aura-like, with Sergius of Radonezh and the Russian land. Those same qualities would shape the central themes of a public address given by the historian Vasilii Kliuchevsky within a year after Nesterov's painting was exhibited. Sergius's significance for late nineteenth-century Russia was at the center of a broad array of official observations of the five hundredth anniversary of his death in 1892. In July of 1888, the Orthodox church joined forces with Alexander III to celebrate the millennium of the baptism of Rus'; the anniversary of Sergius's death offered a similar opportunity to celebrate a signal moment in the history of Russian Christianity, and to stage an extravagant display of Orthodox piety. John Strickland has called these well-orchestrated public celebrations "pilgrimages to the past," designed to shore up Orthodoxy as the foundation of Russian national identity at a time when secularization, religious diversity, and political radicalization increasingly challenged traditional understandings of Russia.[48] Processions of the cross, festal liturgies, and public speeches were intended to celebrate Sergius's legacy for Russia, drawing implicit connections between the saint's life during a period of Mongol rule and his role in liberating the Russian people from bondage. The luminaries who shared the lecture platform with Kliuchevsky situated Sergius's life in terms of Orthodox theology and the history of Russian monasticism. The celebrations as a whole, however, focused on Sergius's service to the Muscovite state—and by extension, to Imperial Russia. "In the Jubilee speeches and mass-circulation brochures, but also in an array of serious scholarly works, Sergius emerges as the inspiration behind the victory at Kulikovo [when Russian forces gained an important victory over Mongol armies], the unifier of Russia, the founder of autocracy, etc."[49] As Scott Kenworthy notes, "the meanings ascribed to St. Sergius emphasize the core elements of national myth" reasserted in Alexander III's reign: "the glorification of Muscovy's medieval past, the unity of the Russian people in Orthodoxy and autocracy."[50] Kenworthy goes on to remark that it is "unclear to what extent the meanings imputed to the memory of the saint by its interpreters [were] understood and embraced by the mass of people who participated"—and notes a similar difficulty in knowing how "secular society and civil leaders" responded. In reading Kliuchevsky's address, with its vision of Sergius and Russia, we are presented with an intriguing set of contexts for Nesterov's visual rendering of the celebrated saint.

Kliuchevsky's speech, delivered at the Moscow Theological Academy on September 25, 1892,[51] takes the listeners from the monastery that Sergius had founded back into the "trackless wilds" of fourteenth-century Russia. The historian begins his account by lamenting that there has been no constant chronicler sitting by the monastery gates, someone who might have described the stream of pilgrims who have come over those centuries to "bow to St. Sergius' grave" and then to return from here to all the ends of the Russian lands.[52] Kliuchevsky then gives us his own imaginative rendering of that stream of pilgrims: "monks and princes, lords and simple village folk" paid visits to the saint while he was still alive (388). That same diversity is what one finds today: political leaders come in moments of public crisis, simple folk come in times of sorrow or joy. What fascinates Kliuchevsky in this river of humanity is *what has not changed*: the composition of that "stream"; St. Sergius himself;

and the *emotion* experienced by those who come to his grave. "That emotion has no history, just as the movement of time stopped long ago for him who lies in that grave" (388). Kliuchevsky isn't quite suggesting that *Russia* hasn't changed in the last five hundred years: "Old concepts have dried up, and new ones have broken through or risen to the surface." But within that record of change certain feelings have stayed the same. The "deep content" of Russian political and moral life is somehow present in the silent thoughts and experiences that centuries of pilgrims have brought to Sergius's grave. Ask one of the pilgrims today what Sergius was in his lifetime, and few will be able to answer, writes Kliuchevsky. Ask who Sergius is for them, today, and each will give a "firm and judicious" answer.

What Kliuchevsky presents, in other words, is a kind of timelessness and immediacy that is uncannily like what we find in Nesterov's painting. The historian's account is also deeply linked to place, to those "trackless wilds" that stretched north and east of Moscow. Kliuchevsky's Sergius is a man of strength and quiet spirit, whose physical labors and unswerving moral sense become exemplary for a people who had, as he puts it, "cowered" in the region between the Oka and the upper Volga, constrained by Lithuanians to the west and Tatars to the south. Sergius and his disciples are "fearless pathfinders," opening new ground to the northeast, what Kliuchevsky calls the Volga-Dvina watershed. For Kliuchevsky, Sergius initiates the rebirth of Russian society not on the battlefield, but in the woods. "The monk fled the world and went into the trans-Volga forest to save his soul, and the layman followed on his shirttails and with his help began a new, Russian world in that very woodland. Thus the Great Russia of the upper Volga was created through the amicable labors of the monk and the peasant, both shaped by the spirit that Saint Sergius breathed into Russian society" (398).

The Volga-Dvina watershed that Kliuchevsky maps is a world positioned between two rivers, one flowing north into the White Sea, the other south toward the Caspian. The rivers here are not vehicles of transport, however, but protectors of a renascent culture, boundaries within which the forest—Nesterov's mix of spruce and birch—becomes a haven for both monastic life and agriculture. For Kliuchevsky, the northern monastic wilderness plays an equally central role in the formation of national character: it gave "practical schooling in good conduct" and developed "the ability to give the whole of one's self to a common cause; the custom of hard work, and the habit of strict discipline in one's activities, thoughts and feelings." His wilderness was a place of "labor, thought and prayer." The implication, for Kliuchevsky, was that this image of renewal (spiritual, moral, and political) had something to say to late nineteenth-century Russia, that the forests of the northern watershed might offer a symbolic well in whose waters Russians could find moral rebirth. Sergius distills the essence of that place. The timelessness of emotion associated with Sergius, and Sergius's own continued relevance despite historical change, are offered as promises of renewal, grounded in "amicable labors" and a union of "labor, thought and prayer." This essentially quietist vision seems as mythic and idealist as Rozanov's smooth and undramatic place.[53]

Nesterov's Sergius paintings were not conceived as direct responses to these events, but were produced in the midst of this wide-ranging celebration of Orthodoxy and medieval Russia. He attended the 1892 celebrations at Trinity monastery, and reproached himself for *not* having heard Kliuchevsky's "extraordinary speech" in Moscow: "I didn't participate wholeheartedly enough in the Monastery's celebration of Sergius—above all I missed the chance to hear Professor Kliuchevsky's extraordinary speech"—a speech he seems to have heard about from fellow painter Victor Vasnetsov.[54] By 1892 Nesterov had completed and exhibited his *Bartholomew* canvas, and had begun work on the second of the cycle of paintings of Sergius produced in the decade from 1889 to 1899.[55] Why was he so drawn to the saint? While the public celebrations of 1892 emphasized Sergius's service to the state, for Nesterov there were much more personal, intimate connections. As a young child Nesterov had been sickly, enough so that his parents resorted to various traditional cures to revive him—everything from tucking him into the warmth of the great Russian stove to laying him in snowdrifts. In his memoirs the artist recounts one early childhood memory when he was in fact taken for dead, laid out for burial with an icon of Tikhon of Zadonsk on his chest. But Nesterov unexpectedly awoke and returned to health: "Mother joyfully gave thanks to God, attributing my resurrection to the intervention of Tikhon . . . , who—together with Sergius of Radonezh—was particularly loved and revered in my family. We felt a closeness to both of these men of God who entered, one might say, into the daily round of our spiritual life."[56] Fedor Troitskii, priest at the church of St. Sergius in Ufa, was a family friend, who paid visits to the family home at Easter time, and presided over Nesterov's courtship with his first wife. Troitskii himself was an "artistic soul"—he had painted all the icons in the cemetery church. "They were very primitive, but for some reason that didn't offend the eye."[57]

Nesterov seems in fact to have taken a vow as a young man to paint Sergius's *Life*; in 1896 he speaks of finishing one of the paintings in his Sergius cycle as a way of "lifting from myself the vow I took to paint the *Life* of blessed Sergius."[58] Was the vow in some way connected with his wife's death? The language suggests something more than artistic interest, or even personal religious commitment. All we can say for sure is that the project lay close to his heart, and whatever obligation he might have fulfilled in finishing the cycle, the interest—perhaps obsession—with Sergius lasted throughout his life, far on into the Soviet period, when his reputation was built around portraiture of leading intellectual and scientific figures. As with Polenova—who contemplated a visual rendering of the *Lives of the Saints*, and Vasnetsov, whose icon of Sergius was painted for the small church on the Abramtsevo estate, Nesterov's interest in Sergius may have coincided with the celebration of 1892, but it went far beyond official attentions.[59]

Canonic icons of Sergius are traditionally of two kinds: the saint is represented either in a simple frontal view or "portrait," facing the viewer and standing alone; or he is depicted in one of a series of episodes (those "icon episodes" that Nesterov refers to) drawn from his *Life*. Icons of the second category, known as "hagiological" icons, shift attention to the "feats . . . that transfigure a person"; in these icons, Oleg Tarasov suggests, the didactic function of the icon predominates.[60] All icons are highly conventionalized, following patterns handed down over the centuries: portrait icons show Sergius as a mature, bearded figure in a simple brown cloak; the hagiological icons display the saint's portrait at their center, surrounded by an outer square of smaller images, which proceed in clockwise fashion around the portrait, giving visual evidence of the stages of a holy life. Nesterov's paintings draw on different episodes of the *Life*, and constitute in spirit if not form an equivalent to the hagiological scenes of traditional iconography: we imagine reading them in sequence, around a central portrait icon of the blessed saint. *The Boy Bartholomew's Vision* (1889–90) depicts, as we have seen, the moment when the young boy encounters a monk, an encounter described in Sergius's *Life* as both transformative and revelatory, turning the boy who everyone thought couldn't read into someone possessed of grace-filled gifts. *The Youth of the Blessed Sergius of Radonezh* was conceived in 1892 and completed in 1897; the painting shows a now adolescent Sergius standing in a glade with a large bear recumbent at his feet. This episode too is drawn from the *Life*, exemplifying the saint's peaceful hospitality to all, including a bear with whom he shares his Lenten meal. The third painting, *The Labors of the Most Revered Sergius* (1896), is a triptych showing Sergius at three different points in his life, building and sustaining his monastic community. The fourth canvas, *The Most Revered Sergius's Blessing of Dmitrii Donskoi for the Battle of Kulikovo* (1897), is the most public and "patriotic" of the series, depicting the saint's blessing of the Muscovite prince who would go on to win an important battle over Mongol forces on Kulikovo field. This scene comes closest to the "public" Sergius of the 1892 celebrations, and differs markedly from the rest of the cycle; Sergius here is one figure among many in an almost overcrowded frieze, in which the spikes of raised spears create a stockade between the foreground figures and the wooded landscape behind them.[61] Finally, a

Hagiological icon of Sergius Radonezhskii. Russia, Yaroslavl School, c. 1640. State Art Museum, Yaroslavl. Image copyright Lebrecht Music & Arts.

simple, portrait-like image of Sergius from 1899 represents the saint—adult but not yet old—standing at the center of a square landscape that distills the motifs and mood of the rest of the cycle: a simple monk in white muslin robe and brown cloak, holding his staff and prayer beads, shod in peasant bast shoes, Sergius looks directly at the viewer with an intense and disarming gaze. This is the least "episodic" of the cycle, and was perhaps for Nesterov the portrait—the essence—that could stand at the heart of his own devotion of painting.

Taken together, these paintings constitute an extraordinary meditation on saintliness, begging comparison with great narratives of Russian literature—Dostoevsky's portrait of the Russian monk in *The Brothers Karamazov*, with its gentle, wise, ecological Zossima; or Tolstoy's own version of a saint's life, his "Father Sergius"—a monk who relinquishes monastic isolation for a holy life of domestic labor and poverty.[62] What Nesterov brings to this re-visioning of sanctity is a quality of epiphany, and a vision of how human figures *fit into* and interact with creation.

The Boy Bartholomew's Vision shows us the moment recorded in Sergius's *Life* in which the boy receives the "gift of letters" from a "certain black-robed holy father." As in any hagiographic account, the author is at pains to demonstrate the trajectory of a life that will become an image of God's glory: the boy who has had trouble learning to read is destined to be given the gift of letters not through his own efforts but through grace. Bartholomew is sent by his father to look for horses who have run astray (the hagiographer reminds us of a parallel with the story of Saul in the Old Testament). But Bartholomew is led instead to search for "greater things" and encounters an elder standing beneath the oak "in tearful prayer." Once the elder finishes praying he sees the boy and understands "in the eyes of the Spirit" that Bartholomew is a vessel of the Holy Spirit. When he asks the boy what he wants, Bartholomew answers that more than anything he wants to be able to learn to read. The elder's response is to pray, and then to offer the boy a bit of the holy Prosfora; in giving him Eucharistic bread, the elder urges him to "open your mouth, child, and eat": what he gives may seem small, he says, but its sweetness will be great; it will give him God's grace and an understanding of the holy scriptures. So the boy eats, and is given a "sweetness" like "sweet honey." When the boy pronounces with joy that "Of this is it written: 'How sweet to my throat are your words!'" (quoting the Psalmist) he seems already to bear witness to the miracle of grace: in the encounter with this stranger he has, indeed, received the Word.[63]

Nesterov's painting of this moment is delicate, resonant, and prayerful. He described the scene in a letter to N. A. Bruni in a manner that is atmospheric and pointedly minimalist: "It's a gray autumn day, getting toward evening, a spruce forest stands on the hillside, no breeze to rustle the smallest leaf on the young mountain ash and birches scattered on the sown field, you can see a long way, you can see a stream and the neighboring village. Beyond the woods you can see the parish cemetery, where the bells are calling to vespers. . . . Bartholomew has been walking through the fields for quite some time. His father has sent him in search of the horses. He's tired, he wanted to sit down by an oak, he comes closer, there's a kind elder standing beside it. He's praying. After praying the elder called out kindly to Bartholomew, blessed him, comforted him and gave him a piece of the Body of Christ, and then together with Bartholomew set out for his father's house."[64] The delicacy of Nesterov's canvases is often related to seasonality, and this one is no different. We are in the fall of the year, but

Mikhail Nesterov, The Youth of the Blessed Sergius of Radonezh *(1892–97). Reproduced with permission of the Tretyakov Gallery, Moscow.*

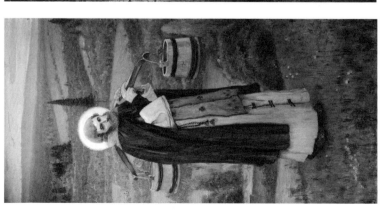

Mikhail Nesterov, The Labors of the Most Revered Sergius (1896). Reproduced with permission of the Tretyakov Gallery, Moscow.

Mikhail Nesterov, The Most Revered Sergius's Blessing of Dmitrii Donskoi for the Battle of Kulikovo *(1897). Reproduced with permission of the Tretyakov Gallery, Moscow.*

before the signs of nature's vitality and abundance have vanished. The grass has not yet withered with frost, there is still hay to be gathered in the fields below, and a bright green crop of late cabbage is waiting to be picked in the distance. The palette is muted and autumnal. The boy himself is delicate, the line of his chin almost frail, his eyes a bit sunken and dark. In fact, Nesterov's model for the painting was a young girl.[65] The delicacy of the painting derives from the frail, androgynous child at the center, and from the sense of abundance about to end; but that frailty is balanced by the powerful dark figure and the oak, which offer longevity and hope. Along with the fragility of the world there is a sense of strength and endurance.

The painting's cultural resonance derives both from the hagiographical *Life* and from associations with folk traditions and the stylized simplicity of village life; the canvas gives generous evidence of the kind of animistic sense of the world that Makovskii saw as Nesterov's greatest gift. The future path of the saint's life is hinted at in the rutted road back toward the church, and perhaps even in the bridle that the boy holds—the absent horse may allude to the soul.[66] These pictorial motifs suggest movement and spiritual journey; they are how Nesterov gets narrative into a still image, but also how this quiet landscape can seem so filled with vitality and the potential for change. The boy's life will be changed by this encounter; he will become the man who walks down that path

Mikhail Nesterov, The Most Revered Sergius *(1899). Reproduced with permission of the State Russian Museum, St. Petersburg.*

we see in the middle ground, toward the founding, first, of a hermitage, and then a monastery, that will indeed grow up amidst the great northern forest. His life in the forest will be celebrated as a life of reconciliation: the great bear will come to him in gentleness, and the labors of the monks will become a form of prayer.[67] The threatening and frightful powers of the wild will not so much be tamed as entered into covenant with: and so in this painting we see the church placed not in the middle of a meadow, or a village, but straddling the *edge*—that boundary of the cultivated and the wild that had so terrified Turgenev's narrator. But there is nothing terrifying here.

Our sense of reconciliation in the painting extends as well to the dark figure and the oak tree. The oak hovers over and protects both youth and age. And what is the oak in the painting? A mark of antiquity and strength and righteousness, but also a reminder of "pagan" venerations of the natural world. Boev's traveler into the forest discovers legends of Orthodox missionaries to a people who had worshiped the tree in the northern forest. Mel'nikov repeats like a litany the jovial saying about the trans-Volga folk: "They lived in the woods and they prayed to the stump, got hitched by the fir while the devil spirits sang."[68] In a letter of June 1889, Elena Polenova expresses delight at an old woman's rhyme that repeats this folk proverb verbatim; she had heard it in one of the villages near Abramtsevo: "Our place is as backward as can be, we're benighted folk, we were born in the woods, we prayed to the stump, and never learned to speak right."[69] In Nesterov's painting the tree and the holy elder become one block of righteousness and strength. This is among other things an icon of the founding of culture: for the author of Sergius's *Life,* the saint's great Trinity monastery had become a beacon of Orthodox religious culture. Here is the moment it flows from: a boy and a man, in a field, by an oak. Culture here is placed not in opposition to nature, but in its midst.

Finally, prayer. The painting is filled with prayer in a number of senses: the account in the *Life* has the elder standing in prayer beneath an oak; Nesterov adds an icon, and the boy himself stands in an attitude of prayer. But the atmosphere of prayer extends beyond the two human figures. The two young trees behind the boy also seem caught in a moment of grace-filled contemplation, as though they, too, stand in supplication, waiting to receive Eucharist and grace from the oak. There is something uncannily reminiscent of Korolenko's description of the green wood in "old, old icons" that has approached the saint on one side, "as if listening in on the words of human prayer."

To speak of trees praying, or listening in on human prayer, to represent trees as part of a Eucharistic transaction and moment of blessed relationship, shifts language away from the categories we tend to think of as modern. Critics have long noted this about Nesterov: I. Nikonova suggested that Nesterov was more interested in *inner* states than the outer trappings of historical setting,[70] and Fedorov-Davydov repeatedly noted the *contemplative* quality of Nesterov's painting, suggesting that in the Bartholomew vision "the whole of the landscape is prayerful."[71] This is perhaps part of that holistic quality of *sobornost'* that Newlin mentions—a "vast organic union" in which *all* of creation (not just humans) is brought together. Part of what enables this sense, in Nesterov's Sergius paintings, is the stillness of the saint himself, who becomes a focal point for our own attention, and whose presence in the landscape seems to radiate calm, that lack of aggression that Rozanov and Kliuchevsky refer to.

But we can say these things because in most of these paintings, Sergius isn't *doing* anything.[72] The 1896 triptych *The Labors of the Most Revered Sergius* is strikingly different in this regard, since it depicts the saint at a variety of labors: in the central panel Sergius is on one end of a double-handed saw, the sleeves on his monk's gown rolled up, one powerful hand grasping the saw handle, the other bracing himself against a foot-wide log—perhaps a felled spruce like one of those we see in the distance. In the narrower left panel we see Sergius hauling water, a yoke and two buckets over his shoulder, with the familiar landscape of woods and fields behind him; to the right we see the saint in a winter landscape, carrying a basket of bread down a lane, a church and two tall spruce behind him. Each of the side panels can be seen as having both literal and figurative, or theological, significance: Sergius bearing water recalls one who bears the yoke of Christ, but also someone who draws from the living water for his community and people. Sergius's distribution of morning bread reminds us of the "true bread" of Eucharist and Christ's body. The focal point of the triptych, however, is the figure of Sergius in the central panel.[73] Both visually and ideologically this is the heart of the image: here is the demanding physical labor of building a structure where before there was only dense forest. The saw and the fresh-hewn log remind us of the transition from "nature" to "culture" implicit in the narrative of the three panels, read left to right. The left panel shows Sergius in what is still an unbuilt landscape; the right panel shows him now within human community, the plumes from chimneys suggesting warmth and shelter from the obvious cold—but with spruce standing there still as witnesses to a larger, natural world. The saint sawing logs shows us how we go from "creation" to the humanly built. As the art historian Durylin so wonderfully puts it, in this panel of a now-elderly Sergius, the "only desert remaining is the one within"; Sergius's face is filled with a deep sorrow. Is this, Durylin wonders, because the woods are now gone?[74]

What is intriguing about these paintings is how they represent labor, and how Sergius's *work* becomes a form of *prayer*. Boris Zaitsev, the émigré novelist and critic, saw in Sergius the essence of Russian Orthodox spirituality, precisely in his relationship to labor and the earth. Saint Francis for Zaitsev is typical of Western sanctity: filled with ecstatic "exaltation," his disciples did not work but begged alms. "The Blessed One from Assisi didn't feel the earth under his feet. All his brief life he flew, in radiant ecstasy, *above the earth*, but he flew *to the folk*, with his preaching. Labor, and the love of work, which is the root of attachment, did not exist for him. Sergius, in contrast, spent fifty years, quietly, in the depth of the forest, teaching through example, *in the silence of his action*."[75] For Zaitsev, Sergius is an icon of labor, love, and what he calls "attachment"—*prikreplenie*—which also suggests *strengthening* (*krepkii*). The quiet of his actions is the practice of work that has become prayer, a *strengthening* that joins him physically and spiritually to the earth, and to the forest in which he worked out the consequences of his encounter with the Word.

The Labors of the Most Revered Sergius are also, then, images of devotion, within a monastic economy for which all work is prayer. What the paintings suggest is blessed labor, in which the physical acts of cutting, hewing, measuring, lifting, laying logs one on the other—like the acts of drawing water or baking bread—are not acts of aggression or offenses against the world, but ways of entering into grace; or to put it in more secular terms, ways of knowing and using the creation that do not destroy it. Does human use of the world necessarily destroy it? Does cutting the tree for warmth and shelter violate the wilderness? Does the fact of human labor fundamentally undo the holistic union—the contemplative *sobornost'*—that seems possible in the contemplative moment? Nesterov's canvases of Sergius laboring suggest, I think, otherwise.

These images of a man *laboring* in the landscape return us to a tradition of figures in the landscape that reaches back into nineteenth-century Russian landscape painting, with its idealization of peasant figures. Both Cathy Frierson and Chris Ely have argued that by the final decades of the century landscape painters had largely *removed* human figures from their paintings, in part because images of the peasant had become too contentious, and the realities of the village had changed. By removing figures from the landscape, Ely suggests, artists were able to create the illusion of looking at the world through the eyes of the peasant himself. "These paintings offered urban viewers the opportunity . . . to partake of the peasant perspective, to see what the *narod* [the people] saw. In this way, images of Russian landscape became a ground of common perception, an imagined locus from which it was possible, for a fleeting moment, to bridge the abyss that still divided Russian society."[76] As Frierson sees it, painters shifted toward a lyrically rendered natural world in which human figures were either absent or peripheral; the "critical realism" of an earlier generation moved elsewhere, to urban scenes.[77] Nesterov's landscapes qualify this process in interesting ways: his triptych in particular renders Sergius as a peasant, with the labors of building made to seem as natural as the landscape itself.

Not all the paintings in Nesterov's Sergius cycle succeed, and it is worth considering the one that Nesterov himself called a failure: *The Youth of the Blessed Sergius of Radonezh*, which he labored over from 1892 until at least 1897.[78] The painting shows Sergius in a woodland glade, the site of his hermetic retreat in the years before the Trinity monastery had been built; the young saint is standing, and recumbent at his feet is a bear. The bear is massive, partly hidden behind the folds of Sergius's cassock. Its coat is a mottle of dark and light, just like the landscape of Nesterov's painting: this bear seems almost to grow from the earth—or perhaps to be returning to it, sinking back into the underworld of hibernation that will soon come upon him. Sergius on the other hand stands, just off center of the painting, the nimbus of his sanctity creating a luminous bull's-eye against the light, newly hewn wood of the chapel behind him. As in so many of Nesterov's images, there is a patterning of dark and light, sylvan and human form: the saint's figure lifts from earth like the birch and spruce behind him, in contrast with the painting's darkness: a block of shadowed green in the left background, a green pool on the right, the black-brown of the bear's coat. Each of these patches of dark suggests some kind of depth, passages into darkness that the sentimentality of the canvas otherwise seems oblivious of.

The inclusion in this canvas of another sentient being—the bear—makes of it a more complicated image, since the "nature" to which the saint is relating is not merely the landscape (however animate some may argue that to be), but a creature with its own, wild will. The scene, as we have noted above, comes from the *Life*, and recounts Sergius's sharing of his meager fare with a hungry bear. Images of Sergius and the bear circulated in cheap editions of the saint's *Life*, one of which shows him sitting just outside his woodland retreat, watching placidly as the bear eats a morsel of Lenten bread. Vladimir Lossky describes Sergius's encounter with the bear as indicating the restoration of the "normal order of the universe where the whole of nature, united round man, obeys God," quoting the fifteenth-century author of Sergius's canonic *Life* to the effect that "when God dwells in a man and the Holy Spirit rests in him, all is subject to him."[79] But neither in the popular editions of the saint's *Life* nor in Nesterov's canvas is there any sense of Sergius as *master* of the animal. The bear is the most iconic of Russian animals, a symbol of Russia itself, and a constant companion of peasant life: a healer and entertainer at village markets and fairs, the bane of peasants' farming efforts, the pigeon-toed honey-lover of folktale, a remnant of ancient beliefs and shamanic practices. In peasant culture bears were in fact associated with Sergius himself, his autumn feast day coinciding with the bear's traditional entry into hibernation. Jack Haney, in his study of Russian folktales, notes that the traditional celebration of the bear's "return to the underworld" took place on September 25—Sergius's feast day and the day of the 1892 celebration—a conflation Haney sees as evidence of Sergius's replacing "the bear as mediator between the Russian peasant and the gods."[80]

Sitting placidly at the feet of Nesterov's still-young Sergius, the bear looks, however, more like a rug—or a panda—than a shamanic animal who can negotiate life and death. By the time that Nesterov painted *The Youth of the Blessed Sergius*, bears were not merely figures for traditional Russia; they had become the subject of zoological and ethnographic inquiry, and an Imperial edict issued in 1866 had banned the traditional bear comedies that brought wandering bears into far-flung villages. As he began work on the painting,

Nesterov several times visited the Moscow zoo, where he did sketches from live animals. Founders of the zoo had aimed at pedagogy rather than entertainment, hoping for a "better class of spectators" than those found at Shrovetide fairs, where bears would have been paraded to gawking crowds. But when funding flagged, the Moscow zoo repeatedly changed hands between entrepreneurs and scholars; by the time of Nesterov's visits in the early 1890s it was a shabby place, beset both by monetary and climatic challenges.[81] Both the zoo and the 1866 edict are markers of modernity, with its fundamentally changed relationship to this most "Russian" of creatures.[82] All of this, one senses, contributed to the awkwardness of execution in Nesterov's attempt to render the relationship between the saint and his totemic animal.[83]

Much later in life Nesterov was to pronounce the painting a failure. "Sergius needs to be taken out. . . . He didn't come out right. . . . And the bear—is like a set design or something from Mikhailov's Siberian Fur shop—even though I went to the zoo, when I was painting him. But the landscape—now that's another matter. That, I think, came out well."[84] Nesterov's friend and biographer Sergei Durylin gives a more enthusiastic account of the painting, an account in which we sense a kindred spirit drawing from a failed work its imperfectly realized

The Most Revered Sergius Shares His Lenten Bread with the Bear. *Zhizn' i chudesa prepodobnago i bogonosnago ottsa nashego Sergiia Radonezhskago i vseiia Rossii chudotvortsa s istoricheskim opisaniem Sergievoi lavry i ee okrestnostei v kartinakh (Moscow, 1889).*

potential: "In all of his sketches Nesterov eliminated the touching feeding of the bear by the hermit—he strengthened the motif of luminous friendship between man and beast, friendship that the surrounding world takes delight in." And in his comments on the final painting, Durylin points to the significance of Sergius's placement *outside* his cell, with the significant implication that he lives *in the forest*, rather than in a built dwelling: "you're not even sure he needs the cell—he is to such an extent with nature, in nature, and somehow included, taken up into nature."[85]

As interesting as Durylin's defense of the painting—he challenged the art critic Stasov's dismissal of its "stylized, Byzantine landscape," insisting that Nesterov's landscapes emerged from "loving study of the Russian forest"—is his final acknowledgment that the painting's imperfections derive not from the separate elements but from their *relationship*. Evidence suggests that Nesterov struggled with Sergius and his bear even as he painted it: he radically reduced the painting's size at one point, and took to heart the criticism of fellow painters and the lukewarm response of Pavel Tretyakov. His allusion to the fur merchant and the Moscow zoo suggest a fundamental disparity in time frames and worldviews may have contributed to his difficulties: the worlds of commerce and captive nature are fundamentally at odds with the vision of reconciliation the painting aimed to represent. There was perhaps too great a tension between the idealization of Russia's past, a time when humanity was supposedly "more in tune with the natural world,"[86] and the reality of modern zoos, with their mix of spectacle, confinement, and degradation of both humans and animals. One wonders, too, if the motif of *feeding*—which as Durylin points out, Nesterov chose *not* to represent—was not fraught, even for an artist so removed from contemporary politics. Elena Polenova notes in a letter of October 1891 that she is going to participate in an artists' benefit to aid famine victims, organized by her brother Vasilii. Begun in that same famine year Nesterov's image of a saint and a hungry bear seems haunted by the need for material rather than spiritual bread.[87]

Durylin and other painters who saw early versions of the painting also pointed to more technical, compositional failings—failings that illuminate, I think, why some of Nesterov's paintings can convince us of "intimate communion" and what Chryssavgis calls the overcoming of autism—while others don't just fail, but become monuments of oppressive, kitschy nationalism. What these observers pointed to was the awkward relationship of the human figure to the landscape, a canvas in which the relationship between human and natural form was no longer in balance. There is a sense both in their comments and in Nesterov's response of seesawing back and forth between trying to perfect Sergius's face and retouching the landscape: Nesterov repainted first

Mikhail Nesterov, The Boy Bartholomew's Vision *(1889–90). Tretyakov Gallery, Moscow. Image copyright Lebrecht Music & Arts.*

Mikhail Nesterov, The Labors of the Most Revered Sergius (1896). Reproduced with permission of the Tretyakov Gallery, Moscow.

the Sergius figure, then the grove of trees, and ultimately began the whole painting over again, in a smaller format.[88] He withdrew the painting from competition for the Peredvizhnik show in 1891, then felt a new burst of inspiration after the Sergius celebrations and Kliuchevsky's speech in 1892, spent a month sketching in the region where Sergius had lived as a hermit, all the while intermittently continuing his work in Kiev with Vasnetsov on the frescoes of the Vladimir Cathedral. But when the painting was finally shown it was controversial and met with misunderstanding or disdain by many of the other artists.

Other paintings from the Sergius cycle almost convince us of another way of seeing, of the possibility of a renewed creation in which human predations and passions can grow still, without denying the sensory, indeed sensual, magnificence of the world. *The Youth of the Blessed Sergius*, on the other hand, *doesn't* convince us; the failure seems connected not so much to the way the realities of the world reinstate themselves as to the inner dynamics of composition. Various commentators have noted that the animating challenge of Nesterov's early career was the relationship of figure to ground, a problem that is both technical and existential: the painterly composition and rendering of space must find a way to join the human figure to the landscape—and Nesterov's paintings were always, as Fedorov-Davydov put it, not "merely" landscapes. They were religiously inspired paintings of contemplative "immersion" in the natural world, narrative paintings in which the relationship of humans to nature are part of the landscapes' "profound philosophical problematic."[89] His most successful paintings are those in which we feel that relationship of figure to ground not merely as a matter of painterly composition, but as a vibrant, melodic, and tactile exchange.

Nesterov's paintings from the decade before the 1917 revolution too frequently present a static frieze, rather than space that seems to hum with relationship. *Holy Russia* (1905), his most explicit rendering of Orthodox Russia as ethnoscape, is stagey and static; there is no real relationship between the landscape (which has become mere backdrop) and the human figures. *In Rus'* (1915–16) is similarly flat and programmatic: a crowd of witnesses, many of them identifiable as famous writers and cultural figures, stands to the right as a young boy in peasant tunic and bast shoes advances ahead of them. The background landscape—a vaguely rendered "northern" meeting of water and wooded hillsides—is a kind of shorthand for what Nesterov could count on us recognizing as his "Holy Russia." If some of Nesterov's canvases show us the birthing of mythologies, these show us the mythic grown inert and lifeless. They are ethnoscape turned to political ends, responding defensively both to the Revolution of 1905 and to World War I. In a compositional sense, these paintings suggest a retreat from the painterly potentials that Nesterov discovered in Paris in 1889: Bastien-Lepage's ecstatic Saint Joan represents mystical experience in a spatial field that conveys depth and the interpenetration of cosmos, creation, and the human. Visually, this means that there is a complex, felt relationship between Joan, the apple tree, and the angels— even the winding swift seems to have some part in it. Puvis de Chavannes, on the other hand, resolves the relationship of figure to ground in a very different way: flattening space in a decorative, stylistically simplified neoclassical tableau, his paintings work against the kind of relationship that Bastien's both expresses and invites. As William Robinson puts it in his discussion of Puvis's *Summer*, "None of the women in the lower right [of the canvas] acknowledges the others' presence; they [have] withdrawn into silence," with little overlapping or interaction. We are left, says Robinson, with a sense of isolation, along with the monumental grandeur of his vision.[90]

The static friezes of Nesterov's late Imperial work too often give us a sense of stagey pamphleteering, an elegant *tableau vivant* that is paradoxically dead. That powerful emotions could be elicited and transacted across the "fourth wall" of the canvas is clear from Nesterov's memory of an excursion as an eight-year-old to the theater in Ufa to see a play called *Parasha the Siberian Girl*. Nesterov describes for his reader the visual impact of its opening moments: "Before one's eyes there was a decorated curtain. It rose, and it was as though I was bound to the scene, transfixed by the unexpectedness of it all. . . . Before me was a real forest, a real spruce forest, with snow falling in great flakes, snow was everywhere, as though alive. In the forest stood a poor girl; all of her unhappy adventures found an immediate response in my small, impressionable heart. . . . How touching it all was: Parasha's sorrow, and the forest, and the deep snow—it all seemed more real to me than reality itself, and it was perhaps this very moment when some of my artistic passions and revelations were born."[91] At their best, Nesterov's canvases invite us across the flat proscenium into an imaginative and emotive world in which we are *touched*. He convinces us that we know this place, and that we ourselves might be known in it. He convinces us that it is something more than *landscape*—that it is a beloved and intimately shared *place*, a world, as Lucy Lippard puts it, that we have a sense of knowing not as tourists and spectators, but from the inside out.[92]

* * *

IF I RIDE my bike out six miles or so into the Maine countryside from my house, I come to a roadside I have come to think of as Nesterov country. It is an unassuming meadow edged with spruce and birch and pine, slanting down and away from the road and then up onto a hillside in the distance. Two years ago, in early spring, I took my camera with me one day, trying to capture something of that hovering quality of expectant birth that so many of Nesterov's canvases possess. Northern springs are fragile and wholly unpredictable: the birch begin to leaf out pale against the almost black-green spruce, ferns unfurl on the forest floor, curls of asparagus green through last year's fall of brown leaves. This particular bit of Maine reminds me of Nesterov because of its marriage of woodland and meadow, the rhythm of old, massed trees and slender young ones, the way it feels as if there is a *way into* the landscape, even though there is no evidence of a path. Nesterov's paintings have made this particular corner of my homeland *familiar* to me; I have stopped to take it in—to pause and be a contemplative before I shift back into movement and passage.

When I stop today the landscape is subtly changed, and not only because it is July: the firs in the foreground—looking like an unkempt acre of Christmas trees—are now almost eight feet tall, and the meadow behind them is growing in with birch and maple. There is a sky-blue Chevy and a red motorboat on a trailer abandoned among the Christmas trees. I stand in the shade under a big maple and drink from my water bottle; while I'm drinking a local farmer comes down the road on his tractor, waving as he goes by. It is haying season, and everywhere there are wisps of grass and bits of twining vetch, tossed in the breeze and scattered on the asphalt. Across the road from Nesterov there is an abandoned New England boundary wall, heavy stones routed from unforgiving soil that must have been tilled for as many years as the farmer could take it, before he moved on—elsewhere—and let the maple and oak take back his land.

One measure of the *success*—if we must call it that—of a painting must surely be how it reorients our own faculties of sight. Icons of the visible world become imprinted in our imagination and memory, so that their rendering of the "external landscape" becomes forever part of our "internal landscape."[93] We carry them with us, like talismans of a possible world, and a *possible relationship to it*. Farther down the road as I ride today there is a big stretch of land that has been cleared, five acres or so of stumps and brush. It is right beside a small dairy farm, and it might be that the farmer has decided to expand his pasturage—but more likely, these days, he has tract housing in mind. I stop there, too, and think of Repin and his dusty hillside, icon of an all-too-familiar world in which woodlands are pulled down with little regard for long-term consequences. Looking at the barren field, I am glad to have Nesterov's talisman with me, the knowledge that there are corners of the world where the sentient birches stand and wait, leaning in toward my figure in the landscape, waiting with me for a blessing, or for the spring.

Nesterov's landscapes are icons of relationship. At their best, they open up a remarkable window—as icons do—on a transfigured world, in which human figures are but one part of a blessed cosmos. At their worst, they become prosceniums of self-quotation, in which the forms of a landscape are no longer present as *companions*, but become signs in an allegory of nation. Maine landscapes are as susceptible to commodification and mythology as those of any place—Russia included. The pitted asphalt road I ride, with its Christmas trees and overgrown meadows and pastures with cows and piles of drying brush, is as quotidian and undramatic a landscape as anything one finds in Nesterov; it is not the *rocky coast of Maine* that tourists come to see. It is not a proscenium to be admired, but a field to be entered into, a place to be loved.

To a striking extent, in reading critics' reactions to Nesterov's paintings, one has a sense of reading a kind of eco-theology: their accounts of these canvases proclaim a kind of cosmic liturgy, a communion of the human and more-than-human. His paintings invite viewers—whether Russian or American—to try to find language for this transfigured vision he presents. I am reminded, interestingly enough, of the claim that icons long played the role of "theological texts" for Russian Orthodoxy, that "the deepest religious experiences and ideas of ancient Russia were expressed not in words but in colors: in her religious painting."[94] Sergei Durylin—whose life trajectory had carried him from prerevolutionary radical politics, through symbolist circles and the study of architecture, into priesthood and then to prison under Stalin—could by 1976 wax ecstatic, presenting a remarkable example of discursive freedom at a time when American scholars would surely have shied away from anything this deeply subjective: "Looking out from the canvas was a dear, frail face with large eyes, and this face of a young Russian man brought together that *love, peace and joy* that was poured out everywhere around—in the benevolent silence of the bear, in the singing bird, in the bright triumph of May springtime that suffuses everything: trees, leaves, grasses, moss. The young hermit has withdrawn into this Radonezh wilderness not to retreat from voices of joy or to hide from the eternal call to true being. Quite the contrary. He has come here, to this native wilderness, in order to hear more clearly the never-ending voice of that joy, which is shared by all of nature. In the murmur of this green that returns to life the hermit hears a carillon of eternal being."[95]

In the following and final chapter of this study we turn to Dmitrii Kaigorodov, a forest scientist and literary naturalist who did more than anyone else in late Imperial Russia to turn Russians' eyes and hearts to the world outside their windows, the woodlands close at hand—whether in St. Petersburg or a village outside of Kursk. Kaigorodov's enormously popular essays in natural history, his calendars of place and enthusiastic advocacy of field trips and local phenology are all deeply informed by many of the same things we find in Nesterov: love of "motherland," the languages of Orthodoxy, folk tradition, and

Russian poetry—which he weaves into his anthologies on birds and Russian forests. All of this is packaged in an elegant aesthetic that was accessible to Russia's growing middle class. In Kaigorodov such elegance is married to a scientist's knowledge of the dynamics of botany, climate, and what we would call forest ecosystems. Kaigorodov's work, like that of his contemporary Nesterov, gives abundant evidence of his delight in a blessed and much-loved creation, and his scientist's (and artist's) faith that deep attentiveness—a *renewed way of seeing*—could lead to an ethic of greater care. Kaigorodov in his own way creates as much an "icon" of *native nature* as did Nesterov, working to overcome that "autism with regard to the natural cosmos" that Chryssavgis speaks of: "a certain lack of awareness, or recognition, [which] causes us to use, or even waste the beauty of the world." With his attention to scientific understandings and awareness of an urbanizing and industrializing society, Kaigorodov draws these traditions of Orthodoxy, poetry, and folk culture away from Nesterov's iconic past, toward a modern sensibility that serves as ground for an explicitly environmental ethic.

6

Measurement, Poetry, and the Pedagogy of Place

Dmitrii Kaigorodov and the Russian Forest

Up! up! my friend, and clear your looks,
Why all this toil and trouble?
Up! up! my friend, and quit your books,
Or surely you'll grow double.

—William Wordsworth, "The Tables Turned"
 (1798)

Mud in garden and yard there's lots of
Already sightings of Kaigorodov
Spring has sprung.

—Student folklore

THE VERSE IS GOOD-NATUREDLY IRREVERENT. The librarian at the Forest Academy first copied it down for me on the back of a request slip, once she knew I was interested in the father of Russian phenology who had also been a professor of forest technology. It was, she said, student folklore, a rhyme about Dmitrii Nikiforovich and his legendary wanderings about the neighborhood. Lev Razgon cites it as well: a Soviet-era memoirist and gulag survivor who wrote a loving appreciation of Kaigorodov in 1983, Razgon thought of it as a parody of the phenologist's strolls. Kaigorodov died in 1924, but the memorial ditty seems to have stuck; remarkably enough, the park where Russia's most famous phenologist went on his daily walks has changed very little. Tucked behind an elevated train track on the north side of St. Petersburg, in an area that bordered industrial suburbs in the early twentieth century, the sprawling grounds of the Forest Academy make a leafy oasis for lunchtime strolls, a surprisingly quiet woodland amidst the concrete and car-choked roadways heading north out of the city. There is an elegant classical main building that reminds you you are in Petersburg; and then there is a functional brick box behind it, which reminds you it is the twenty-first century. The grounds themselves are well tended, boasting over a thousand species of trees and shrubs; the park was founded in 1827 and has survived not only revolution and civil war but the siege of Leningrad and temperatures as low as minus forty-five degrees Fahrenheit (–43°C).[1] There are native species and species from East Asia, and even a few from the Rocky Mountains—as though the forests of the world have sent their own genteel ambassadors to this most Europeanized and densely built of Russian cities.[2] In April of 1917 Lenin's momentous arrival from Finland would have taken him just by Kaigorodov's strolling ground, the columned building and the quiet park. In Russia it is not only walls one wishes could talk. Wandering through the park on a chilly morning in June 2004, I only half appreciated how much these silent companions might have to say. Kaigorodov's legacy is carefully filed away in the academy library, but the genius of the place isn't just on those sheets of paper.

St. Petersburg is the last place you might think to look for forests. This northern city is a monument to human will and engineering, a city of quarried stone and felled timbers built on a river delta. For Mel'nikov-Pechersky's Old Believers Petersburg epitomized moral betrayal and cultural suicide. Their legends of miraculous intervention and protective submersion are antitheses of the tales of watery destruction that beset petty clerks and militant intellectuals in Peter's city.[3] Dostoevsky's Ridiculous Man must flee the city to remember the

St. Petersburg Forest Technical Academy, August 2011. Author's photograph.

possibilities of human converse with, and within, the forest. The Admiralty at the center of St. Petersburg is an elegant reminder of Russia's naval power—and of a prowess that paradoxically drove both the destruction and conservation of Russia's forests: Peter himself, as Nikolai Zobov put it, was the country's "first forester," his draconian laws the first efforts to preserve—for state use—stands of oak and pine.[4] By the late nineteenth century the men who articulated the need to practice sustainable forestry and an ethic of conservation were centered not in the woods of the trans-Volga, or Turgenev's Polesye, but in a suburb of St. Petersburg. Dmitrii Kaigorodov—professor of forest technology, painstaking phenologist, popularizer whose essays on birds and weather and forests were read throughout the empire—walked and wrote from his house in a suburb called "Woodlands," imploring his countrymen to love, to learn, to protect.

Many of the texts we have examined in this study are about journeys—journeys into a relatively distant, sometimes exoticized hinterland that becomes both emblematic and symptomatic of Russia. The journeys involve hunting for woodcock, looking for lost animals, following in the footsteps of other writers, wandering in philosophical and historical terrain; they occasion epiphanies and encounters and despair, cross boundaries that are both literal and metaphoric. Kaigorodov, however, is the first writer we have encountered who takes us into the woods for their own sakes, who takes us out *simply to have a look*, to learn about the dynamics of growth and health using the language of botany and silviculture. His essays don't deny the vastness of Russian geography, and in particular its woodlands, but the woods he takes us into are almost always close at hand, woods familiar to his readers from childhood and daily walks, right outside the door of even his most urban readership. The differences of location and intention are bound up with the genre of these sketches, and with their author's profession: Kaigorodov was a scientist, and he is more purely a natural historian than Turgenev or Korolenko or Mel'nikov-Pechersky, all of whom include passages of attentive observation but assimilate them to larger projects—ethnography, philosophy, cultural critique. Kaigorodov presents his readers with sketches of Russia's "native nature" intended to entertain, educate, and elicit ethical reactions—to promote a response we would identify with an ethos of conservation.

Dmitrii Kaigorodov sits in an important and intriguing way between the worlds of Imperial Russia and Soviet modernity, between the traditions of village and woodland, and more-urbanized experiences of the natural world. As an academic he helped educate forestry specialists who would advocate for sustainable yield and conservation under Stalin; he also established a kind of popular natural history that continued to entertain and educate in the Soviet era, with *Calendars of Nature* and *Chats about the Russian Forest*. He inspired nature education in primary schools, brigades of birdhouse builders, and excursion-based pedagogy for both children and adults. The first phenological section of the Russian Society of Lovers of Nature Study was named for him in 1925. All of this hints at Kaigorodov's role in sustaining an ethos of affection and care for the natural world in the Soviet era. But, like Kaigorodov himself—deeply religious, gifted amateur musician and painter, enthusiastic gardener and teacher—the ethos and aesthetic of his writing and worldview grew in the soil of nineteenth-century Russia; his essays honor and call on many of the writers and artists we have examined in these pages. Kaigorodov was educated by men whose understanding of modern forestry came from Germany, and his models as a natural historian included German writers like Adolf Brehm and Emil Rossmässler, but his essays and sketches are compilations of verse and image that pay homage to nineteenth-century Russia. The contemporary Ukrainian environmentalist Vladimir Boreiko calls Kaigorodov's influence on conservation efforts in the Russian empire "enormous." For Razgon as well, writing in 1983— three years before Chernobyl, but with broad and growing awareness of the environmental disasters accumulated under Soviet power—Kaigorodov was a model of someone who had seen nature as "the source of a full and harmonious human life. He sought to convince everyone, not just specialists, of the necessity of studying natural phenomena, which so enrich our hearts and minds. . . . The living world must be protected and cared for not only for its utility, but because the impoverishment of that world means the impoverishment and extinguishing of the whole of our life, as well."[5] For both late- and post-Soviet environmentalists, Kaigorodov is part of a usable past, a legacy of Russian conservation thought that their essays sought to publicize and build upon.

"The forest! the pictures and lush images one imagines at the word, the poets who have turned their thoughts toward that mysterious world, where the . . . inexorable forester makes cuttings, sight lines and measurements of reserve plantings! But one doesn't hinder the other."[6] Kaigorodov's life and writings are a kind of case study exemplifying this claim, quoted in one of the epigraphs to chapter 3 of this book; his legacy into the twentieth (and now twenty-first) century raises intriguing questions about how habits of place, poetry, and pedagogy can survive in an indifferent or hostile world. Before considering that legacy, however, we need to know who Kaigorodov was, why the "Kaigorodov style" and the genial professor's phenological walks were so popular with Russians in the final decades before war and Revolution. In what follows I introduce the reader briefly to Kaigorodov and his writing, considering in particular the essays on woodlands and phenology that were so centrally important to the man and his career. We shall also reflect briefly on Kaigorodov the educator and anthologist, with his passionate advocacy of what modern educators would call place-based pedagogy. In closing we shall consider how Kaigorodov faded from view—one more instance of forced decanonization—and how he started to make a comeback in essays by late Soviet environmentalists.

* * *

DMITRII NIKIFOROVICH KAIGORODOV was born in 1846 in Polotsk, in present-day Belarus', where his father taught mathematics at the local military academy.[7] In a memoir of childhood published when he was almost sixty, Kaigorodov spoke of his father's garden as the "cradle of my love for flowers, trees, birds—for all of nature—a love that has brought me so much joy and so many of the brightest days of my life!"[8] The father of that sketch is an enthusiastic amateur gardener, someone who prunes and plants and instills in his son both a love of nature and a sense of the pleasures of work: it is easy to read into this brief sketch the passions of the adult forester for education and attention to seasonal change. Kaigorodov's father seems in fact like a model environmental educator, raising a son who knows the shapes of seeds, varieties of apples, and different birdsongs, who joins in the father's garden work as a form of delight-filled learning and play. And while he doesn't mention it in the memoir, Kaigorodov surely also learned from his father that it was possible to combine the compatible incompatibles of "measurement and poetry": here was a mathematician who spent his leisure hours working in his garden.

Kaigorodov studied at the same Polotsk military academy where his father taught, graduating at age nineteen to serve in the artillery corps. After training as an artillery engineer in St. Petersburg, he served two years in Poland, where his interest in natural history grew.[9] In 1867 he returned to Russia as an officer at the Okhtinsky gunpowder factory, located just east of Petersburg on the Okhta River. It was a surprisingly auspicious location for someone with Kaigorodov's interests. The territory of the factory had been laid out in the mid-eighteenth century along the Okhta, just a few miles east of where it flows into the Neva; some 5,747 hectares (22 square miles) were designated forest preserve, with the understanding that the woodland would ensure an adequate supply of fuel for the munitions factory, and in 1868 approximately a third of the territory was transferred to the Ministry of State properties to be used as an experimental forest for training foresters. In later years Aleksandr Rudzkii would be the forest's director.[10] The factory itself played an essential role in Russia's drive for military prowess, its production of powder closely linked to the city's shipbuilding and naval fleets. Buildings were well separated to avoid disaster in the event of an explosion at one of the blocks: between 1720 and 1872 there were ninety-two explosions at the factory, one in August of 1858 so strong that it broke windows in Smolny monastery and the Tavrichesky palace (in central Petersburg).[11] In the 1880s the factory was the site of experiments on smokeless gunpowder undertaken by the Imperial ministry with the aid of the chemist Mendeleev; by the first decade of the twentieth century the factory had upward of 1,000 workers, and by the beginning of World War I the number had risen to 2,820, "men, women and boys."[12] R. V. Bobrov, in his account of Kaigorodov's years at the factory, suggests an idyllic suburban setting more like a village than an urban agglomeration. But is there any reason to believe that conditions here would have been particularly more idyllic than those found in other rapidly expanding enterprises in the city? One Soviet source dates the beginning of revolutionary activity at the Okhtinsky factory to 1874, when an underground library was established and a clandestine circle organized by the People's Will, a radical organization committed to the violent overthrow of the tsarist government. The attraction for revolutionaries of working at a munitions factory seems obvious; the group plotting to assassinate Alexander II apparently got its materials here.[13] It is unclear whether the young artillery officer would have been at all aware of worker unrest; in any case, Kaigorodov's interests were leading him away from the factory and toward the forest reserve.[14]

The production of gunpowder and munitions was by and large a seasonal undertaking, and that fact (along with the physical disposition of workshops for powder production at some distance from each other) made it possible for Kaigorodov to spend increasing amounts of time doing what he loved best— roaming the woods and fields of the Okhtinsky reserve. Realizing that his calling lay elsewhere than in the ever-more-efficient production of explosives, Kaigorodov enrolled at age twenty-three in the St. Petersburg Forest Institute (in those years called the Agronomical Institute), a shift that meant moving north and slightly west, to the Lesnoe ("Woodlands") neighborhood on the northeast outskirts of the city. Fedor Arnol'd was a professor there, Aleksandr Rudzkii a slightly older student who was soon to become one of Kaigorodov's colleagues.[15] In 1872 Kaigorodov defended his Kandidat's thesis ("The Production of Acetate of Lime [acetic acid] from Pulpwood as an Example of Small-Scale Forest Industry in the Yaroslavl District") and then spent two years abroad (at the Tarand Forest School in Saxony, and the forestry department of the Zurich Polytechnic) before returning to Petersburg. In 1875 he became chair of forest technology at the Forest Institute, a position he occupied until 1905.[16]

In the late nineteenth century the area around the Forest Institute was a popular location for summer homes, but by the first decade of the twentieth century industrialization was beginning to creep north: the Aivaz machine factory—where lightbulbs were first manufactured in Russia—was built on the north side of Lesnoe, a sprawling industrial complex that by 1914 employed six thousand people.[17] For the first two decades of his tenure at the institute Kaigorodov lived in an apartment on-site; in 1903 he and his wife finally undertook the design and construction of their own home, modestly elegant, in the northern modern style, with a capacious garden where Kaigorodov grew flowers.[18] The house still stands on the north side of Petersburg, a twenty-minute walk to the institute. The regular morning walks that inspired the verse epigraph to this chapter took place year in, year out, in a meandering path that took in the institute arboretum and, in later years, the "Golden Pond" across from his home. From this placid corner of the empire, in a neighborhood of summer houses that was beginning to be industrialized, the kindly professor described for Russians the nature that was close at hand.

From 1872 until his death in 1924 Kaigorodov wrote prolifically and spoke frequently in public, in a wide variety of genres and on a range of themes— almost all connected in one way or another to Russia's forests. Collections of his regular columns became books on birds and Russia's forests, and readers for schoolchildren; he wrote essays on fishing, on pedagogy, on nature curricula and the importance of taking children outside on field trips; he wrote on weather and its influence on living organisms, and he periodically contributed to debates on animal welfare. His lexical excursion into the forest terminology of the dictionary of Vladimir Dal' links Kaigorodov the philologist with Kaigorodov the naturalist. He translated the English animal enthusiast Eliza Brightwen, who, like Kaigorodov, wrote nature sketches and stylized fairy tales. He wrote an extended essay on Tchaikovsky and nature. And alongside this staggering array of essays and enthusiastic excursions into pedagogy, music, ornithology, and memoir, he wrote academic articles on a parasite noted on aspen lumber (1870); a method for retarding wood rot (1875); dynamite as a means of uprooting stumps (1877); and the relationship between tree ring width and the relative weight of spruce pulp (1900).[19]

In addition to his scientific and creative writing, Kaigorodov began in 1883 to write regular brief columns for *New Times*, a major daily newspaper published by the same house that produced his books. Those columns provided readers with details about the process of seasonal changes in and around St. Petersburg. Week by week, readers would be informed of temperatures and weather for the days just past, what had come into bloom, and what birds had appeared. These phenological notes turned out to have enormous resonance with the paper's readers, who began to respond to his columns with letters of their own, telling him about the progress of spring or fall in their own locales. Recognizing the possibility for a broader network of observation, Kaigorodov in 1895 published announcements in a series of papers, asking for readers to send in their own observations. The response was enormous: by the time of his death Kaigorodov had received something like twenty-three thousand letters from correspondents throughout Russia—all of which (as one laudatory account puts it) he apparently responded to.[20] It is this aspect of Kaigorodov's work that earned him the title of "father of Russian phenology." While Kaigorodov wasn't the first Russian to keep records of seasonal change, he was the first to create such a huge network of observers, taking advantage of an emerging technology—the daily newspaper—to link amateur phenologists throughout Russia.[21] The network of citizen-observers was later institutionalized in the Kaigorodov Commission of the Russian Society of Lovers of Nature Study.[22]

While this impressive array of publications includes a variety of forms—from scholarly article to brief observations and memoirs of childhood—the form he seems most to have loved was what he called the "*beseda*" (chat). The term suggests informality and the back and forth of conversation, rather than a structured academic lecture. Like other scholar scientists of his generation interested in broad public education, Kaigorodov frequently lectured, and not only to his students at the Forest Institute (the text of his course lectures on forest technology was published by the institute in 1900). His first public presentation was in 1872 to a workers' group, called the "Lovers of Enlightenment," at the Okhtinsky powder factory. Kaigorodov's talk was titled "The Flower as a Source of Delight."[23] Mikhail Tkachenko, a student of Kaigorodov's who later edited a memorial volume dedicated to him, suggests that the structure of what became known as the *Chats about the Russian Forest* was inspired by the German author Emil Rossmässler, but also notes that "in the elegance of his writing and the poetic feeling of his understanding of the forest the author surpasses his German mentor."[24] Kaigorodov's predecessor in the chair of forest technology at the Forest Institute, Nikolai Zobov, had published a volume of *Chats on Nature*—a volume whose subtitle indicates it was intended for "reading in villages and hamlets"; the chapters discourse "on the earth, the sun, the stars, plants and animals."[25] While Zobov is often paternalistic in his address, in Kaigorodov's hands the style of the chats becomes distinctly less formal, even intimate: he has the ability of all good teachers to address his pupils as people, to engage them and elicit their own abilities of perception and reflection. He isn't so much conveying information as he is teaching them to see and understand.

The sketches and tales that brought Kaigorodov fame first appeared in family magazines—*Family Evenings*, the *Spring*, the *Plaything*—aimed at the slowly expanding Russian middle class in the final decades of the nineteenth century. Critics writing in the 1860s had frequently lamented the fact that works of natural history published in Russia weren't about *Russian* nature.[26] By the late 1870s that charge could no longer be made, in part because of journals like the *Spring* and the *Plaything*. Founded by leading members of Russia's literary-cultural intelligentsia (both male and female), they offered a mixture of translated and Russian literature along with essays in natural history by leading academics.[27] *Family Evenings* had the explicit support of the Empress Maria Fedorovona, and published a great deal of "translated sentimental and moralizing literature."[28] The *Spring* and the *Plaything*, however, showed a much greater intellectual range, if not daring, in their list of authors—including professors Modest Bogdanov and Nikolai Vagner (professors of zoology at St. Petersburg and Moscow universities), Vsevolod Garshin (whose parable-like stories are cris de coeur by a man drowning in an empire of corruption and violence), and Nikolai Uspenskii, who wrote unvarnished sketches of rural poverty that drew praise from Russian radicals. The journals were resolutely committed to a program of moral formation and scientific enlightenment: many of Kaigorodov's essays originally appeared in the *Spring*, in the company of verse by Russian poets like Polonskii and Pleshcheev; translations of Aesop's *Fables*, *Tom Sawyer*, and *Jane Eyre*; and essays in natural history by Bogdanov and Vagner.[29] Like their better-known elders, the thick journals that were the main drivers of Russian public life in the nineteenth century, these journals for families and children are fascinating windows into evolving sensibilities, anthologizing the "cultural and social indicators" of the final generation of Imperial Russia.[30]

Many of Kaigorodov's writings are themselves small anthologies, gatherings of different sorts of knowledge and wisdom brought loosely together in service of a particular topic. They quote poets and folk sayings, describe plant structure and qualities of soil, refer to traditional use and economic value; sometimes they include inserted stories, or mention childhood games and seasonal observation. That mixture—the sketches' energetic variety, conveyed in a conversational tone that creates a sense of immediacy and curiosity—is at the heart of what readers and critics have meant by the "Kaigorodov style." A major contributor to that style is its visual presentation, the illustrations that accompanied Kaigorodov's essays—initially in more modest form in *Family Evenings* and the *Spring*, then, as if in full flowering, in separate editions published by Devrien and Suvorin. These editions of Kaigorodov's sketches and stories have a visual and pictorial diversity that matches the profusion of botany, ethnography, and verse of Kaigorodov's delivery. In a brief foreword to *Nature All Around Us*, his "Reader for Schools and Families," Kaigorodov alludes depressingly to conventional textbooks: "Readers like this should in no way convey the sterility of textbooks. Since their aim is to encourage the development of a feeling for nature, they themselves should as much as possible be infused with that feeling (love draws forth love!)."[31] *Love* is the watchword here, a feeling that will form the basis for knowledge, and through knowledge for care.

Chats about the Russian Forest, published in multiple editions by Suvorin between 1879 and 1910, contains several different kinds of images.[32] There are botanical drawings of the kind one would expect to find in a volume of natural history: plates that segment the living tree into its various parts—shoot, flower, leaf, branch—each individually identified and referred to in Kaigorodov's text. Botanical drawings like these would have been familiar to Kaigorodov from his childhood reading: the big volume of Brehm's *Thierleben*, images from which were used in Kaigorodov's *From the Feathered Kingdom*, and the compendiums of both Emil Rossmässler and Gotthilf Heinrich von Schubert.[33] Such drawings are often quite lovely to look at, but they represent a way of looking at the plant that is analytical and to some extent counterintuitive.[34]

Elements of the tree are laid out against each other with little regard for scale, and while the illustrations might be used for certain kinds of identification, they do not give a holistic sense of the tree. Alongside botanical drawings we find several other kinds of image in Kaigorodov's *Chats*: full-page reproductions of landscape paintings by Ivan Shishkin (who admired Kaigorodov's writing); Kaigorodov's own photographs (also full-page) of individual trees from the arboretum at the Forest Institute; individually drawn trees intended to illustrate rates of growth or the decay of lower branches on a pine (these also the work of Kaigorodov himself); and finally, perhaps the most striking signature of the whole volume, elegantly drawn miniatures that open each chapter, presenting the first letter of the chapter's first word as an illuminated capital that is also a tiny woodland world.[35]

Elaborate illuminated capitals were a standard feature of late nineteenth-century publications, but those in the Suvorin editions of Kaigorodov's essays are particularly lovely. Earlier versions published in *Family Evenings* also have ornate capitals, but those capitals are more often than not schematic—a *putto* carrying the letter *C*—with no thematic connection to the sketch itself. The letter itself is the clear visual focus.[36] The Suvorin edition, on the other hand, gives us a series of illuminated letters that are delicate and detailed. They are almost always woodland scenes, sometimes of wild forest, sometimes of park or agricultural land, with visual references to human activities and structures. The letters themselves must be sought out in these tiny landscapes, deciphered and read among natural forms. The focus here is not on the letter but on the total image, an amalgam of natural setting and letter that is also a kind of game of hide-and-seek. The *K* that opens the chat on oak, for example, emerges from a woodland edge where two human figures have gathered hay in a large stack; a scythe and rake lean against a tree (which doesn't seem to be an oak) in the foreground. The human tools and a protruding branch make the two arms of the *K*, while the tree's trunk forms the letter's backbone. There is a basket at the base of a tree—perhaps a witty

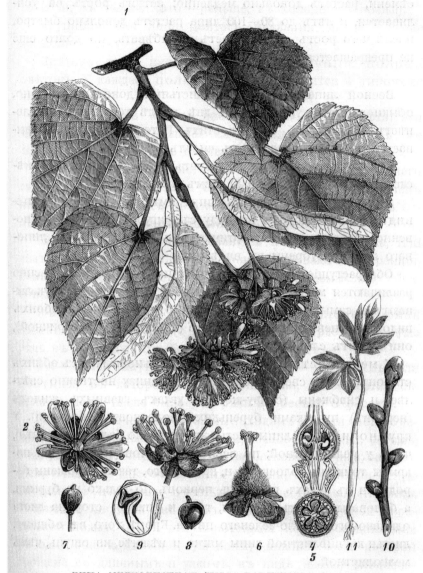

Рис. VIII.

ЛИПА МЕЛКОЛИСТНАЯ (TILIA PARVIFOLIA, Ehrh).

1. Побѣгъ въ цвѣту. 2. 3. Цвѣтокъ со стороны и сверху. 4. 5. Завязь въ продольномъ и поперечномъ разрѣзѣ. 6. Пестикъ. 7. Плодъ. 8. Тоже, въ продольномъ
поперечномъ разрѣзѣ. 9. Продольный разрѣзъ сѣмени. 10. Конецъ побѣга съ поч-
ками. 11. Всходъ.

Small-leaved linden (Tilia parvifolia). Botanical illustration from D. M. Kaigorodov,
Besedy o russkom lese, vol. 2 (St. Petersburg: Izdanie A. S. Suvorina, 1893), 47.

allusion to the word for basket in Russian, which begins with a *K*: *korzina*. The whole image is presented as something worth looking at—not just an elaborately decorated letter, but a tiny world, which both adult and younger readers could enter in the imagination. There are eighteen chapters but only thirteen illuminated capitals, since two of the letters (*C* and *B*) repeat several times. The willow gives us a moonlit night, what looks like a pine with a sickle moon creating a luminous *P*; the chapter on Siberian trees— larch, cedar, and fir—has a child standing on a swing hung between two tree trunks to make an *M*—the composition balanced to the left by a pastoral scene with a riverbank full of shady trees. The chapter on elms depicts a woman sitting with her back against a pine tree, in what look like deep woods: one slender trunk has fallen against another one—the way trees do—so that its diagonal between two larger trunks makes the Russian И. Some of these are pictures of repose, some of work, some have no reference to humans but include birds, a swan, a pond lily. They are all lovely, and create a visual tone that seems marvelously suited to Kaigorodov's voice and manner in the sketches.[37]

Chats about the Russian Forest gathered in one volume sketches that had first appeared in *Family Evenings* in 1879–80. In his foreword to the first edition Kaigorodov said he hoped the essays' botanical information would be used "for forest excursions." The book is both proto–field guide and something more, with generous and accessible botanical information that allows the reader to understand what he or she encounters in the world. It is divided into two sections: the first focuses on the coniferous or "red" forest (*krasnoles'e*); the second, on the deciduous or black forest (*chernoles'e*).[38] Red and black forest are folk terms, Kaigorodov explains, the former derived from the coppery red cast of pine and spruce bark in Russia's coniferous forests. Within each section the sequence of chapters is determined not by botanical kinship but by the trees' significance in Russian economy—a structure that suggests something important about how Kaigorodov understands the "natural" in natural history—not as a realm separated out from the human, but as something necessary to human life, to be valued for both its utility and beauty.[39] The "Red Forest" section includes chapters on pine (two chapters), spruce, larch, Siberian cedar, and fir; the "Black Forest" section has chapters on birch, oak ("tsar of trees"), linden, aspen, alder, ash, maple, elm, willows, hornbeam, and beech, and an additional sequence of short discussions of "trees and bushes of secondary importance" that are nonetheless well known: these include walnut, mountain ash, bird cherry, wild apple and pear, snowball berry, and buckthorn (2:152–53).

Each section of the book begins with a broad introductory essay, and in the first of these—"The Tree and Its Life"—Kaigorodov takes us from what can be seen with the naked eye into a world visible only through magnification. These passages are interesting because Kaigorodov is always so insistent on what can be learned through simple observation—and yet he prefaces the book with a careful explanation of what *isn't* visible to the naked eye: how water circulates from the root system up into the trunk and out into the tree's leaves. Highly magnified cross-sections demonstrate how water—and then sap—are drawn through wood fibers in springtime. Kaigorodov begins this section with his characteristic teacherly invitation: *Let's take a look.* And just as he had begun the chapter by instructing how we might cut through a bean to see the structure of future leaves and stem, so here he walks us through a process of understanding what is visible to the naked eye only in its ultimate result: leaves transpire, and the small hole we drill in a birch in spring drips sap that tastes wonderfully sweet.

In what follows the focus is on individual tree species, each essay presenting particulars of seed germination, leafing out (often with quite precise seasonal references that inform readers when trees leaf out in relationship to each other), stamen structure, flower parts and their function in the fertility cycle of the tree; how long a given tree can live, with occasional reference to particularly old individual trees; descriptions of bark, branches, and trunk; trees' range and distribution in Russia (reminding readers of the vast number of landscapes even in just the

European part of the empire), either in stands of predominantly one type or in mixed growth forests; the kinds of soil best for a given tree species; their tolerance of drought or moisture, and whether they are sun- or shade-loving. Each essay also contains extensive information about the traditional uses of a given species of tree, with excursions into the lexicon of various forms of woodworking and vignettes of how particular trees are harvested for particular uses. These are effectively essays in traditional forest technology—precisely what constituted Kaigorodov's professional speciality. They are among other things a compendium of the astonishing variety of ways in which Russian peasants made use of their native trees, an illustration of Robin Milner-Gulland's observation that "the traditional Russian village . . . [was] formed almost entirely out of the forest all around it."[40] Kaigorodov talks about the qualities of wood that have determined how it is used by humans, which parts of the tree are used, regional names both for parts of the tree and for the activities that go into its reshaping for human use. Thus he describes the oak slats from which barrels are made, and how it is done in the oak forests of the trans-Volga (2:38); the uses of oak bark in tanning (2:39); harvesting of aspen to make pitchers and other tableware (2:75); the process of procuring and preparing aspen for turning; the use of aspen leaves to feed livestock in northern regions in absence of better grasses; and how aspen makes the best skis of all (2:77). There is in all this a mixture of lexicography and ethnography, a fascination with the ways in which handicrafts and trades have created regional microcultures: "From this brief sketch of the uses of aspen it's apparent what an important role this kind of wood plays in the Russian economy" (2:78). The same could be said about all the species he describes in these sketches.

While the *Chats* often focus on visual, analytical detail, Kaigorodov shifts quite easily into exclamations of delight: "Each linden flower sits on a separate short shoot, and all of these are joined in one common shoot that holds the flowers, the lower part of which is tightly joined with a long, narrow, tongue-shaped, pale-green leaf (the lingual bract), the upper end of which is turned away from the flower-bearing limb." And then we shift from description into sensory recollection: "Linden flowers are quite fragrant. Who hasn't had the occasion to breathe in with delight the honeyed aroma flowing from a linden in blossom, particularly on a warm summer night? The linden is distinguished from all our other woodland trees by the aromatic nature of its flowers, excepting perhaps the bird cherry, whose blossoms likewise have a wonderfully powerful aroma, though they are not nearly as gently fragrant as the linden's blossom" (2:49–50).[41] These essays have fewer offerings of poetry than the school reader he would edit in 1902, but most chapters still begin by quoting a poem or folk song, and there are occasional references within the essays to Russian writers. In the essay on lindens, for example, he quotes a passage from Turgenev's *Hunter's Sketches* after noting the ubiquity of linden alleys in Russia: "From long years past into the present the linden has constituted one of the most beloved trees in park and garden alleys. It may be said without any particular exaggeration that there is in Russia practically no large, old park whose primary adornment isn't an alley of shady linden trees. And it's quite certain that in this respect the linden, above and beyond its beauty, quite deserves such preferential treatment among our other woodland trees, since it surpasses them all in the thickness of its leaf and the intensity of its shade—and what's more, it grows to be a big tree quite quickly" (2:54).[42]

These sketches were written in years that saw increasing public discussion of Russia's forests and deforestation. By the time the essays that made up the *Chats* started appearing in *Family Evenings*, various commissions had been convened to study deforestation and its impacts on hydrology; Markov, Dostoevsky, and Zalomanov had debated the "Forest Question"; and Repin had begun work on his *Procession of the Cross*.[43] We can situate Kaigorodov's *Chats* in this context as well: while they are filled with admiring ethnography of how Russians had turned the woods and their abundance to good use, they also give voice to recurring laments and warnings about Russia's squandering of its forest wealth. The first essay in volume one opens by affirming the "beauty and usefulness" of trees and ends by calling for "love and protection." The second volume echoes the call for "love and care." Individual essays document particular examples of destructive or careless action: the practice of cutting down a whole cedar to get at the nuts, abandoning the tree itself— and thus providing fuel for fires destructive of both forest and wildlife; the loss of vast swaths of linden forest in the process of stripping lindens of bark for summer footwear; the senseless destruction of young lindens by "poor stewardship evident in allowing stock to graze where woods have just been felled, something practiced on both peasant and landowners' forests. The young linden sapling barely has time to show itself where they've cut when it's immediately devoured by livestock; and the process is repeated from one year to the next."[44] A sketch on firewood—"By the Fireplace"—ends by asking his readers to consider the vast expanse of forest (almost five million acres) that is felled each year to warm Russian homes, and what happens when those acres aren't replanted, when there is no sustainable forestry to ensure wood for the future. Two decades later Kaigorodov quotes Tchaikovsky on the horrors of deforestation: "What horrors outdoors. *All, literally all the woods* have been cut down, and now they're cutting what remains. The only thing left is the grove beyond the church: there's nowhere to go walking. . . . Lord, how the disappearance of a forest completely changes the character of a place; how sad it all is! All those pleasant shady corners that still existed last year—bare patches, completely bald!"[45] What Kaigorodov challenges here isn't humans' use of wood: humans, as he puts it in the introductory chapter in *Chats*—have the "right" to make rational use of the gifts of nature; what is unjust and unworthy of humans is the capricious destruction of the "marvelous life of a tree" (1:22). Kaigorodov writes, after all, as a professor of forest technology—someone fascinated by and interested in how humans devise ways to use natural resources. But he seems to have been deeply alarmed at the growing irrationality and greed that drove "capricious" use, and the inability of either individuals or the Russian government to do much about it. In 1882, in the years leading up to passage of the 1888 Forest Law, Kaigorodov submitted a paper to the First Russian Congress of Forest Managers, asking them to "recommend to the government measures whose immediate adoption might curtail however modestly the rapid pace of forest destruction, preventing however partially those dire consequences which such destruction threatens to the well-being of Russia." As Lev Razgon puts it, "The paper was listened to, printed in the *Proceedings*, and—of course—had absolutely no impact on forest owners and the forest industry."[46]

Two passages in particular from the *Chats* give us some sense of Kaigorodov's thinking on forest use and contemporary deforestation; both passages make their points by alluding to Russian history and literature. The first passage, from the second volume's introductory essay, "Black Forest," quotes Sergei Aksakov—one of Russia's great literary naturalists—and Nikolai Nekrasov, whose sentimental verse we considered briefly in chapter 3. The second passage starts with a heroic vision of Peter the Great as the rational transformer of Russia, but ends with a passage worthy of Turgenev's sober view of indifferent nature from the beginning of "Journey into Polesye."

"Black Forest" begins by quoting Aksakov at length:

"More than anything else in the plant world the tree must inspire sympathy. Its enormous size, its slow maturing, its long life, the strength and rectitude of its trunk, the nourishing strength of its roots . . . and finally its sundry usefulness and beauty should, one might think, inspire respect and mercy. . . . But the industrialist's axe and saw know neither, and momentary profit diverts the landowner as well. Never could I see with equanimity either a felled grove or even one large tree as it falls; in that fall there is something inexpressibly sad: at first the light blows of the axe produce only the slightest of quavers on the trunk; the quavering grows stronger with each blow until it becomes a convulsion of each branch, each leaf; as the axe cuts more deeply into the heartwood the sounds grow more muffled, more painful . . . one final blow, the last: the tree shrinks, breaks, creaks, a noise resounds in its crown, and for a few moments it seems to ponder just where to fall, then finally leans to one side, at first slowly, and then with gathering speed and noise, like the noise of a strong wind, it falls to earth! . . . For how many decades it gathered strength and beauty; in so few minutes it perishes, not infrequently from the sheerest caprice of man." (2:4)

Kaigorodov acknowledges, after citing at such length, the justice and beauty of Aksakov's prose, but then goes on to imagine a different kind of voice, someone saying, "Well we can't possibly cry over every tree that falls!" Of course not, responds Kaigorodov—and then returns to the notion of *rights to rational use*: "While we have the right to make rational use of nature's gifts, we have no right to squander them irrationally; and the fact is that we are squandering and destroying our dear Russian forests not only irrationally and without forethought, but—what is much worse—we are everywhere squandering them for the satisfaction of various empty caprices" (2:4–5).

Tears, moreover, won't help. Kaigorodov's essays are often richly emotive, but he repeatedly insists that love must join knowledge in an ethic of care, and that sentiment alone may do much more harm than good. After the passage above he goes on to echo Nikolai Nekrasov's famous verse with its young girl weeping ("Sasha wept as the woods were cut down"), only to insist that "there's no need to cry":

> There's no need to cry when you see a forest, grove, or tree being cut, for tears won't put a felled tree back on its roots, although the author of these lines must admit that he's never understood the strange emotion—call it pleasant satisfaction—which many express at the sight of a tree falling with creaks and groans to the ground. We repeat: there is no need to cry, but to love and conserve woodlands—for that there is great, very great need. For if we continue to regard the destruction of our Russian forests with the same inconstancy as we have thus far, the time is not long distant when our beloved motherland will feel all the gravity of wood scarcity, difficulties which are in fact already palpable in many parts of Russia, which have thoughtlessly squandered their forest riches. (2:5)

The distinction here is, among other things, between easy sentiment and informed love. The distinction between rights to use wisely but not to squander echoes a distinction we encountered in Aleksandr Rudzkii's 1868 essay, between rights to use (*jus utendi*) and abuse (*jus abutendi*); Rudzkii was concerned to establish formal consideration of how either use or abuse bears consequences for the community as a whole.[47] Kaigorodov's *Chats* are of course filled with examples of necessary (and ingenious) forms of use. What seems less clear is how to ensure that use will be "rational"—the Russian is *razumno*—and mindful of long-term need and complex consequences. In the essay on the larch from the first volume of his *Chats* Kaigorodov seems to hold up Peter the Great as a paragon of such rational planning. The passage is worth quoting at length:

Two hours from Petersburg along the Finland rail line, near the halfway point between Petersburg and Vyborg, lies the Raivola station—on Finnish territory—and four versts south of the station lies an extraordinary grove, perhaps the only one of its kind, named Listvyanka (also called Lindulovsk). This grove was planted at the insistence of that brilliant transformer of Russia—Peter the Great. Plantings were first begun under Catherine the First, the major work accomplished in the reign of Empress Anna Ioanovna on the basis of a famous document in the history of Russian forestry: *An Instruction or Edict on the re-establishment and re-planting of forests to meet the needs of the Fleet of her Royal Majesty.*

This larch grove occupies almost 36 hectares [89 acres], and is laid out on the sides of fairly large hills. The planting of larch (Siberian) here was done in straight rows, and in such a way that the distance between trees in a row equals the distance between the rows themselves (planting of trees according to this layout is called planting by quadrants or *one in four*).

As a consequence of being thus planted the distribution of trees . . . is extraordinarily regular, . . . consisting as it were of a mass of intersecting straight alleys. . . . Despite the trees' age the grove is remarkably well preserved; only occasionally are there one or two trees missing, so that the intersecting alleys are extremely regular. If we add to this that the trees in the grove are on average approximately 120 feet tall, so that in looking up at their crowns you "lose your hat," it's not difficult to imagine the awe-inspiring charm of this grove.

What surrounds the grove only intensifies that charm: the hills on three sides are covered with mixed pine-spruce forest, and the bright, tender green of the larch stands out wondrously against a background of dark green; on the fourth side, laving the foot of the hills where the grove stands, a wild mountain spring runs burbling over rocks; its angry mutter echoes beneath the high crowns of centuries-old larch. These stern giants seem to proclaim their displeasure with the restlessness of man, who enters uninvited beneath these green vaults—ready to destroy their ancient, imperturbable calm. . . . They seem as if to sense that the day will come at last, when they too must fall with groans and creaks beneath the blows of an axe. . . . Painful even to contemplate that day. (1:95–97)

What is interesting about the passage is how its tone shifts. Kaigorodov sets out to praise both the towering larch and the mind of the man who envisioned them, Peter the Great: this is not a "native" grove, but one planted against future need, according to an Imperial edict that Kaigorodov lauds. But at some point in the description of the grove and its geometric regularity that tone shifts, and the forest that man has created seems to stand against him. In the final sentences of this virtuoso passage we seem to be revisiting Turgenev's Polesye and the ancient forest that tells man he has no place there. Kaigorodov the professor of forest technology gives way to Kaigorodov the poet and conservationist. The great larches have become animate, seem almost to have persuaded the professor to their own cause—which might be less amenable to the uses of a man even as foresighted as Peter. There is something in this passage of the scale and vision of Shishkin's 1891 canvas *The Countess Mordvinova's Forest*—in which the human representative stands dwarfed by towering mast pines.[48]

Lev Razgon claims that Kaigorodov's appeal to the Congress of Forest Managers fell on deaf ears, and other commentators have noted the phenologist-professor's disinclination to engage in politics. In a brief self-portrait Kaigorodov describes himself this way: "Weak at arguments . . . Absence of administrative capacities . . . Profound antipathy to all kinds of meetings and commissions."[49] Kaigorodov's energies and efforts as someone concerned with conservation turned increasingly to education. When he was appointed in 1900 to a ministerial commission charged with reforming the teaching of science in Russian secondary schools, his contributions to discussions of education went far beyond that institutional framework. Beginning in 1893 Kaigorodov began writing about both pedagogy and curriculum, in a wide range of essays on everything from fishing and photography and their educational worth, to outlines for botanical excursions in St. Petersburg, to a companion reader intended as a model of how schools might create their own locally grounded texts. Kaigorodov's advocacy of what he called the "excursion method" inspired early Soviet reformers, and his recommendations on curricula—framed in the language of holistic study of natural communities and landscapes—are thought-provoking even for twenty-first-century teachers. Kaigorodov's work on environmental education is deserving of study in its own right; our interest here lies primarily in how his lifelong love and study of Russia's forests weave into his concerns with education, and how he articulated the connections between the experience of nature and an ethic of care.

The fundamental impulse behind Kaigorodov's educational writing is deeply Wordsworthian in its emphasis on experiential learning; the pedagogical watchword of his 1900 essay on "Nature in the School of the Future" is *excursions*. Drawn into discussions of just how the study of nature should make a reentry into the school curriculum, Kaigorodov is witheringly critical of what he calls "scholasticism," an approach that carves the natural world into disciplines and subdisciplines, in defiance of the "harmonic totality of nature" in which plants, animals, soil, and climate are inseparably linked. The "communities and collectivities" of Kaigorodov's nature demonstrate "mutual aid, love and altruism" at least as much as they engage in competition and the struggle for existence. Kaigorodov professed to be someone not given to vitriol and debate, but his defenses of holistic nature study spar with both Russian scholastics and popularizers of Darwin. His insistence on the fundamental communitarian or collaborative impulse in natural communities was far from anomalous in Russia, where a broad range of scientists and intellectuals challenged Malthusian readings of Darwin with their emphasis on competition.[50] The intent of Kaigorodov's curricula and methods is to cultivate "feelings present in every human soul," to structure learning in such a way that it acknowledges and develops an impulse that is both physical and spiritual. The heart of that process is leaving the schoolroom behind, going out into the world to observe and experience communities of interdependent life forms, which Kaigorodov groups by landscape—or, to use a more contemporary and overly scientific term—*biome*: "Forest (black and red forests), meadow, field, steppe, garden (park), pond, river, bog, etc. as communities of particular plants and animals, with their varied interdependence on each other, in connection with inorganic nature (soil, shoreline, bottom), and in connection with seasons of the year."[51]

Kaigorodov's curriculum is itself a kind of excursion, a set of directions that guides the reader, teacher, or pupil through a part of the world he asks us to see as a complex whole. Appended to his volume of pedagogical essays is a conspectus of that curriculum, with topics organized by habitat ("the forest as a community"; "the river as a community"), each one accompanied by a detailed outline of subtopics and suggested readings. The habitat explored might also be an urban neighborhood like Kaigorodov's own. The excursions that Kaigorodov described in various journals and newspapers from the early 1880s until just before his death took children and teachers on walks in the outskirts of Petersburg or in the park of the Forest Institute. After 1917 he led excursions for working students and nonstudents as a way of structuring learning during leisure time. What had begun with schoolchildren expanded to include older students, teachers, Red Army soldiers, and workers.[52]

The anthology that Kaigorodov published in 1902 was intended as a companion to school excursions. The need for a reader like *Nature All Around Us*—to replace the "dry as dust textbooks" that fragmented nature's harmony and stupefied schoolchildren—was self-evident for someone who wanted as many classes as possible to *go outdoors*.[53] Given that emphasis, what then of books? Kaigorodov attempts an answer to the question in a brief foreword:

> The natural and uniquely authentic way effectively to cultivate a feeling for nature is to spend as much time as possible in converse with nature. . . . Given this, it's clear that textbooks in the normal sense of the word have no place in nature classes for younger children. One would need to create one's own text for each city, if not school. On the other hand, it's hard to completely dispense with a book. Most appropriate to our task are compilations of sketches and articles about objects and phenomena from the various kingdoms of local nature—anthologies for reading, assembled with children in the lower and middle classes in mind. Commensurate with our aim, such readers should in no way convey the dry-as-dust nature of textbooks. Given that they're intended as aids in the development of a feeling for nature, they themselves should be imbued with that feeling as much as possible (love calls forth love!). Appropriately chosen verse and excerpts from artistic prose are most helpful in this regard.[54]

Russia's poets and literary naturalists share space in *Nature All Around Us* with university professors of zoology, botany, and ornithology—and with Kaigorodov himself. The volume combines natural history, poetry, and fable, illuminated capitals and botanical cross-sections. In "Nature in the School of the Future," Kaigorodov envisioned a pedagogy that would be equal to his vision of nature as a "harmonious totality": "Thus I insist on nature study which leads the student step by step into the harmonious totality of nature, in contrast to contemporary natural history in the *Realschule* and military academies, and nature study in women's gymnasia—which artificially dismember nature, presenting to the pupil disparate elements, perhaps quite elegantly but still artificially systematized. Just what happens with natural history in schools these days (and with nature study as well)? Above all else it puts impenetrable boundaries between worlds: vegetable, animal, mineral (botany, zoology and mineralogy), worlds which are so tightly connected with each other and which interact in a holistic nature."[55]

Kaigorodov defends his *Nature All Around Us* from charges of being "unsystematic" by pointing out that it is organized around the communities of nature that structure his curriculum. The book begins in the forest, in a gathering of verse, natural history sketch, image and fable that itself suggests a community of artists and authors. We progress into the woods on a kind of excursion, both geographic and temporal: we start with Lermontov and head toward Pushkin; moving from the bounty of full summer to "golden autumn" with its pale nature "decked out like a sacrifice." Kaigorodov's own forest writing is woven into the sequence: he includes three sketches from *Chats* and two from a collection called *Blossoms* (*Lepestki*)—one a fable about rational forestry, the other an evocation of falling leaves on an autumn day. Interspersed with these excerpts of prose are poems by Lermontov, Pushkin, and Tiutchev—all canonic exemplars of the Russian poetic tradition—but also by a host of lesser lights: Nikitin, Benediktov, Apukhtin, Mei. There is also an anonymous eight-line verse right before the first prose excerpt (Kaigorodov's general essay on "The Tree" from *Chats about the Russian Forest*), which may well be Kaigorodov's own; there are other examples of unattributed verse in his various collections, and it seems not implausible that the amateur musician and painter was also an occasional versifier.

It is intriguing to read this sequence not simply as an agglomeration but as a coordinated gathering in different modes, corresponding in diversity of tone and content to the inscrutable but magnificent "harmony" of Kaigorodov's natural world. There is in a broad sense movement from summer into fall, and in the prose sequence we move from the general to the more specific: from "the tree" to the pine; from "the Black Forest" to linden flowers. In both Kaigorodov's sketches and in some of the poems there are references to the use, as well as the pleasure, of the forest. *Nature All About Us* also echoes the author's concern with conservation and forestry: "A Forest Fable" is a remarkable if didactic retort to visions of rationally planted monocultures, in which the "Woodland Tsar" (a version of the wood demon *leshii*) objects to a forest laid out on paper and then planted in geometric rows. The "commander of the Green Kingdom" is dismayed at the loss of the "beauty of my forest," a beauty manifest not in regularity but in diversity of form and species, the "enrapturing charm of motley multiplicity" (42). The Woodland Tsar summons his subjects: the ancient oaks, maples, and aspens; thrush, hawfinch, jays, bullfinch, siskins, redpolls, chaffinch—and orders them to "undo humans' gridding of the earth into a cage, as if it were a chessboard." His faithful servants carry out their work of seed distribution (tucked into the fable is a small diagram of various trees' seedpods), and ten years later the "creation of the forester had become unrecognizable!" The good forester gets over his irritation when he sees how "boldly and happily the trees he'd planted grow in community [*v soobshchestve*] with their friends from other tree species, with whom they've grown used to living in freedom, in the forest." A visiting artist starts to praise the forester for his knowledge and skill, but the forester interrupts him, saying he had little to do with it: "It's the work of nature, it's in God's hands. . . . Our best teacher in such matters is Nature itself." What Nature has taught the forester is how to plant healthy forests, and what beauty is—a property not of any human devising, but a quality intrinsic to the diversity and order of the world. Among other things, Kaigorodov revisits in this fable the rational forestry of Peter the Great's larch wood; but where that sketch ended on a somber note, here there is a sense of potential reconciliation between the forester and the "Woodland Tsar"—*if* the forester will allow himself to be taught by nature.[56]

In his very first public lecture, to workers at the Okhtinsky factory, Kaigorodov declared that the popular notion that "science and poetry are opposed and incompatible with each other" was a misconception: "Great scientific discoveries in nature begin with attentive observation of that which lies around us."[57] Kaigorodov's anthology of poetry—for among other things that is what it is—assumes that various kinds of language (metaphor, allegory, botanical description) can coexist and thrive together; this is a version of the diverse ecosystem celebrated in "A Forest Fable"—there is no linguistic monoculture here. Many of these poems involve "attentive observation." They often bring us into a kind of experiential presence, situating us within the lyric persona's immediate apprehension of the woodland. They often suggest intimacy and a recognition of mutuality—the "silvery lily of the valley / nods its head in welcome" (Lermontov)—representing nature as articulate: "the icy stream murmurs a mysterious tale / of the place of peace toward which it runs." Some of the poems are primarily descriptive, while others focus on registering emotional impact: heart's anxiousness grows quiet, the frowning brow grows clear, "I know happiness on earth / and in the skies I see Divinity" (Lermontov). Other poems are sentimental or didactic, including one verse conversation by Benediktov that imagines a tree willingly offering itself for fire and plow, for timbers to build a house or a ship's mast. Some poems Kaigorodov explicitly connects to folk songs, including "The Pine Tree Swayed by the Gate . . . ," which precedes a Benediktov poem: that poem uses the repetition and couplets of traditional folk song to create a percussive juxtaposition of seasonal change with the constancy—and unremitting "sorrow"—of the pine. The next poem (unattributed) imagines the whispering of a churchyard pine as a prayer for the departed, an animist conceit that could come straight out of Russian folk song. Ivan Nikitin's landscape of steppe and wood—"What spaciousness!"— issues in a call to *Understand the living tongue of nature: then you'll say "How wonderful the world!"* It is an injunction that in a sense underlies the whole volume, which leaves no doubt that Russia's poets (both anonymous creators of folk songs and canonic authors of the nineteenth century) have understood and treasured that "tongue." That list of those who understand the "living tongue of nature" well enough to speak it would, of course, need to include Kaigorodov himself:

The Tree

Divine creation
of earth, our mother,
lovely child!
With your verdant vivacity
and wreath of leaves
you shelter us from elements
warm us on a frosty day
feed us in times of famine.

* * *

BY THE END OF THE IMPERIAL ERA Dmitrii Kaigorodov was a beloved and widely hailed writer whose morning strolls and phenological notes inspired legions of his countrymen to similar practices of observation and note taking. He was tutor in natural history to the royal family; he lectured frequently to varied auditoriums in St. Petersburg; he participated in discussions of how to reform science education. Mikhail Tkachenko, in a brief obituary of his teacher, noted that Kaigorodov continued his advocacy of excursion pedagogy in the years following the Bolshevik coup of 1917: "The years of revolution, despite famine and cold, did not halt his work. . . . He continued to direct the training of teachers and lead them on excursions. His circle of students continued to grow: among those on excursions one frequently met not only teachers but students in 1st and 2nd level technical colleges, Red Army soldiers and workers."[58] There is both pathos and a wonderful symmetry in this final image of the professor, lecturing now to Soviet workers rather than to an amateur nature circle at the Imperial munitions factory. In Andrei Bely's great modernist novel of revolution, the privileged son-turned-revolutionary is inscrutable to his father, the bureaucrat Ableukhov: "He used to read Kaigorodov," muses the father. The implied question is clear: *He used to be such a nice boy. What happened to him?*[59]

And what happened to Kaigorodov, whose essays take us away from revolution and toward the woods? The fate of Kaigorodov's work in the Soviet era gives us an intriguing glimpse of both erasure and endurance, and of the ways in which a man who professed disinterest in politics came to inspire a generation of Soviet environmentalists. Telling the story even briefly means thinking about Soviet editions and about reviews and essays that started to appear in the 1970s and '80s. It also means thinking about how, as Alla Bolotova has recently put it, "everyday practices, local interactions, and an abundance of microcosms" made it impossible for the state wholly to control human lives—or the ways in which men and women understood the natural world.[60] On the face of it, Kaigorodov's writings virtually disappeared; but then in the late 1960s an anthology of his sketches was published, and his name resurfaced in late Soviet appreciations of him as a phenologist, essayist, and advocate for the forest. The legacy of his life is embedded in those differing roles, which couldn't really be separated in the man himself. To get a sense of how his legacy endures means considering official institutions but also the models of writing, attention, and education that he championed.

In the years following the Revolution Kaigorodov fell into relative oblivion. Several of his books were reprinted in the 1920s, in inexpensive editions that attempted to retain the visual aesthetic of those published by Suvorin. The phenological network of the Society of Lovers of Nature Study was named for him, but efforts to officially memorialize the "father of Russian phenology" with a museum came to naught. Soviet educational reformers who championed the kind of excursion and habitat-based curriculum that Kaigorodov had envisioned came under increasing fire in the late 1920s, drawn into ideological struggle with a competing reform group headed by Lenin's widow, Nadezhda Krupskaya; the direction they took Soviet education was toward more "practical," technical education.[61] Kaigorodov's son Anatolii was forced into emigration; his daughter was arrested in 1930 and imprisoned.[62] The Stalin era also brought ideological turmoil and repressions to the Forest Institute (renamed the Forest Technical Academy in 1930), where younger colleagues of Kaigorodov suffered both moral and environmental defeat in their battle for sustainable forestry.[63] In the context of pitched battles over socialist construction and sustainable forestry, small wonder that Kaigorodov's works were not reissued: Bobrov suggests that his association with the royal family and the religious references in some of his essays worked against him; nor would his critique of unbridled exploitation, and his skeptical view of overly schematic forestry and monocultures, have won him friends.[64]

The library at the Forest Academy of St. Petersburg maintains several drawers of materials on Kaigorodov, including a lengthy bibliography of articles about him. Kaigorodov's name began to reappear in the Soviet press following the reissue, in 1967, of selected essays under the title *Native Nature*. The volume was published, interestingly enough, by Forest Industry Publishers: shorn of the lovely illustrations and references to God, the volume carries a disclaimer "from the publisher": "Various parts of some of the sketches in this volume (sketches written over 50 years ago) will be perceived as anachronistic in our day. These antiquated points of view are nonetheless of interest, since they make it possible to gauge the colossal changes in the life of our country (in particular the intense development of forest chemistry and other branches of forest industry) which have occurred in the years of Soviet power."[65] Despite the disclaimer—in fact almost contradicting it—the geographer who introduced the volume, Vladimir Zaletaev, affirms Kaigorodov's relevance for contemporary Soviets—"the youthful spirit of his works calls again and again for active struggles to preserve nature, its beauty and values." The run of 150,000 copies sold out immediately. In 1979 Vsevolod Revich, a respected science fiction writer, published a brief appreciation of Kaigorodov in the popular monthly *Nauka i zhizn'*; two years later he wrote about Kaigorodov again, this time for *Bibliograf*, a publication for professional librarians. He celebrates Kaigorodov as the equal of Russia's great writers, hailing him as the "Deputy of the Russian Forest." Two years later Lev Razgon's article—where he quotes the affectionate ditty from the beginning of this chapter—appeared in *Nature*, one of the most well-respected of Soviet science periodicals for a broad readership: along with Razgon's lengthy and comprehensive appreciation of Kaigorodov's work and "soul" (the essay is entitled "A Soul Open to Nature"), the editors reprinted the sketch on starlings from Kaigorodov's *From the Winged Kingdom*. The cover photograph of the issue features a group of happy Soviet schoolchildren bundled against the cold, holding their homemade starling houses.[66]

A scattering of other reviews of *Native Nature* appeared in the 1970s; together with the essays by Revich and Razgon, and several others from the early '90s, it is tempting to see this reappearance of the "Deputy of the Russian Forest" in the context of nascent Soviet environmentalism. Surfacing at various sites in the era of liberalization under Krushchev—among biology students at Moscow University and Communist Youth League activists in the Altai—the Soviet variant of environmental awareness was galvanized both by high-level public outrage at planned industrial development at Lake Baikal, and by the fiction of so-called "Village Writers" with their nostalgic evocation of traditional agrarian Russia.[67] Revich and others celebrate Kaigorodov's extraordinary language, comparing him to the great nineteenth-century literary naturalists; they also insist on the powerful relevance of his ideas for contemporary Soviet life—perhaps even more important now than in his own day. And while they see Kaigorodov as one of the progenitors of Soviet children's literature (Revich), they insist the books weren't written only for children, nor should children be their only readers. There are occasional moments in these essays when ill temper creeps in: the anonymous author of a brief note in *New Forest* (journal of the forest workers' union) points out that Kaigorodov "spent his whole life figuring out how best to harvest and use timber . . . and at the same time the scholar was a naturalist; *but not one of those sentimental 'nature lovers' who thinks woods are only for walking in.*"[68] Calls for republishing his works ("What a present for the reader that would be, re-issued in the Kaigorodov style of the Suvorin editions!"[69]) assume the relevance not only of the essays' information and aesthetic, but of their environmental ethic: "I want to hold on to the image of Dmitrii Nikiforovich as a lover and protector of nature. Rousseau said 'Forests exist before man—he leaves desert places in his wake.' Dmitrii Nikiforovich battled throughout his life with this human propensity, enlivening and inspiring all around him with the flame of love for nature."[70] As Revich put it, "in our day and age no one doubts that nature needs saving. But you'll not save her with the strictest laws, or the most contemporary network of *zapovedniki* [strict conservation areas], although both laws and *zapovedniki* are necessary. Too frequently the boundaries of both laws and *zapovedniki* are violated by the malicious intent of a poacher, or the misunderstanding of a zealous young birdcatcher with a gun on his shoulder. . . . The only way [to save nature] is to awaken in human beings the feeling of responsibility toward all that lives and grows on our planet, an understanding of intimacy with nature, our inseparability from her, the impossibility of existence without her."[71]

Vitalii Bianki's *Calendar of Nature*—one of the most beloved and widely read children's books of the Soviet era—is dedicated to Kaigorodov (who was Bianki's teacher at Petrograd University) and honors the man not just in its dedication, but in the form and spirit of its spritely, loving sketches. Dmitrii Kaigorodov lived through a rancorous and violent period in Russian history and witnessed the inauguration of Soviet power, whose impact on his particular family, as well as on the larger human and biotic communities he so cherished, was to be devastating. And yet his essays transport us into a world almost as idyllic as the miniatures that open them; despite their not-infrequent reference to human misuse of particular tree species, and his caution against "capricious" use of forest abundance, the essays are committed to an ethos of delight and what one wants to call reconciliation—not just of science and poetry, but of urban and rural, elite and peasant, literary and oral cultures. The excursions of his final years seem in fact to reconcile Red Army soldiers with naturalist attentions and love of the woods. Korolenko's memoir of the Civil War presents us with an image of Red Army soldiers' wanton destruction of a walnut tree; Kaigorodov's excursion gives us a very different image of the potential relationship of humans and the natural world. Mikhail Tkachenko suggested that Kaigorodov's first lecture—delivered to those workers at the Okhtinsky factory—demonstrated that "even in such a depressing outskirt of the city as Porokhovye one could find traces of beauty"[72] There is throughout Kaigorodov's work an astounding sense of confidence in nature's own power to bring human beings to their senses, to reawaken the innate feeling for what Kaigorodov would have called nature's *beauty.* Is this optimism or naïveté? The rational forester of "A Forest Fable" sets out to refashion nature on a monocultural grid but quickly sees the error of his ways and the wisdom of the diversity of nature. The narrative resolves not with death, destruction, and division but with a change of heart and a flourishing kingdom. Perhaps it was precisely this mixture of hopefulness, humility, and the openness of hearts and souls to being changed by attention to nature that so captivated generations of Soviet readers, who discovered—in whatever way— both "the Deputy" and the woods he invited them into.

Conclusion

O, wooden music of old untouched forests!
Creation's first converse, cradle of man's own speech.
—Nikolai Zabolotsky, "The Birds" (1933)

THE CAMERA GIVES us an edge of field and forest: we track slowly from left to right, bands of color from the pale cream of buckwheat in blossom to the midnight green of spruce, birch whose milky trunks are obscured by other trees and the summer dusk. We move farther, past a rutted dirt road, and then settle for a long moment to look into the woods themselves: pines whose crowns are far above the cinematic frame, so that all we see is a grove of dark trunks, the beginnings of branches high above the ground. Inside that darkened grove stands a house, separated from us by a palisade of pines. A bank of windows reflects light from somewhere else. The camera pulls back and down so rapidly it makes us dizzy, to a young couple lying amidst a tangle of weeds and overgrown grasses. The man, lying on the ground beside the seated woman, asks her if she wants a boy or a girl. We will get no answer from her: instead, in these last moments of Andrei Tarkovsky's *Mirror*, we watch her look back toward the house and then again toward us. From this couple almost buried in the overgrowth of summer we track in and out of the buckwheat, along the rutted road, at ground level over rotting tree trunks and abandoned remnants of human life: pots, a glass, fence posts, and pieces of canvas. In the final frames of the film an old woman and two children come toward us through the buckwheat. The soaring passages of the *Saint John Passion* come to an abrupt end; the boy stops briefly to let out a whoop, as though he had been playing hide-and-seek and is calling to his companions. He and his sister and the old woman continue on their way, out into the sea of grain. Meanwhile the camera takes us in the other direction, back into the darkness of the forest. The warm luminescence of the field feels increasingly distant, obstructed by jet-black trunks. All is silence, except for three brief whistles, some forest creature greeting the night.[1]

Tarkovsky's *Mirror* situates its viewers in a complex universe of parallel worlds, in which memory takes on a beautiful but also brutal immediacy. Nothing is lost in a world where those who have died erupt suddenly in fields of vision and affection, or anger. Tarkovsky ends his film by tracking along an edge: of field and forest, memory and presence, youth and age. When his camera pauses to acknowledge the house with its shining windows in the woods, we are offered a dream of solidity that is quickly torn away: logs rot, dishpans rust in the well, posts that might have marked a boundary—of property? propriety?—are returning to earth, engulfed by weeds. The almost manic crossing and crisscrossing of the field; the camera's swooping dive from the pinewood to malachite moss and then back into darkness and silence: all of this might serve as a visual allegory of human lives, held by the contrapuntal ascendance of Bach's *Saint John Passion*, but also by the trans-rational sounds, and silence, of the film's end. We end in the forest, in darkness and silence; the enigmatic flickers of light that have given us film stop, and we are left in this place of vertical bars and repetitive whistles to ponder—while we can—what it all means.

Anthony Smith claims that "only an ancestral homeland can provide the emotional as well as physical security required by the citizens of a nation," and that nationalism "always involves an assertion of, or struggle for, control of land"—control that is symbolic and cultural as well as literal.[2] Central to imaginations of Russia as "ancestral homeland," the forest in twentieth-century Russian and Soviet culture offered—as it had in the nineteenth century— emotional security but also emotional and ethical challenge; if we consider however briefly a sampling of both doctrinaire and dissident artists from the twentieth century and beyond, we discover not only solace, but moral rigor and a search for difficult ground. In ways that will be beyond the scope of this brief conclusion, these iterations of the forest often involve revisitations and reconfigurations of tropes and images inherited from the nineteenth century. These artists share Ivan Bunin's sense of standing on the threshold of terrain that is both past and present: cultural memory but also berries on thick moss, the immediacy of physical life.

Images of Russian forest can and do serve as icons of national identity, often in forms that are blatantly nationalistic: Nikita Mikhalkov's *Barber of Siberia*, with its opening credits of endless woodland, and a plot that imagines Russia's vast natural resources as prey to conniving Americans, gives us a facile (if visibly seductive) example.[3] Forest narratives like this can play complex political and even environmental roles, as when Valentin Rasputin's celebration of Siberian village life—including characters who might have walked straight out of Mel'nikov-Pechersky's backwoods—became an icon of opposition to unrestrained Soviet industrialization. Darya, the heroine of that novel, *Farewell to Matyora*, conducts a ritual lament to dead ancestors buried deep in the woods; she, like the "king larch" that resists all efforts to fell it, will stand as an enduring symbol of "Heart-Pine Russia."[4] Leonid Leonov's 1953 novel *The Russian Forest* offered direct challenge, from within "official" Soviet literature, to policies of rampant exploitation of woodland to serve socialist construction. That novel's hero, Vikhrov, champions sustainable yield and a holistic vision of the role of forests in human culture—a direct heir of foresters like Rudzkii, Arnol'd, and Kaigorodov. Through Vikhrov—a professor of forestry—Leonov introduces into the novel a history of Russian forestry that is deeply sympathetic to the kinds of conservationist claims those men had called for.[5]

Quasi-nationalist imaginings of Russia as forest—or forest as Russia—are hardly the exclusive province of official writers or apologists of paternalist order like Mikhalkov. Both Vasily Grossman and Boris Pasternak, in their epics of revolution, civil war, and World War II, evoke images of woodland that are heavily marked by both European and Russian tradition: Pasternak's Zhivago experiences the dense phenomenology of childhood as "dense, indisputable, tangible as a forest," and rediscovers ecstatic connection to life in a rowan tree's embrace.[6] Grossman's *Life and Fate*, completed in 1959 but never published in the Soviet Union, tracks the forest's symbolic and emotional power through various characters' consciousness: it is both a "Northern countryside" that breathes "an old Russia Viktorov had previously only read about," and a landscape out of the Brothers Grimm, in which "a small grey goat was standing in a clearing; the darkness of the forest seemed particularly sinister. Among the dark-brown tree-trunks, the toadstools and the fly-agarics, you could see the wolf's green eyes and his red jaw with its bared teeth."[7] The young Jewish boy David who reads this book with his mother is at first convinced that hers is the "strongest power in the whole world . . . defending him from the darkness of the forest" (206). In the face of Nazi invaders and Soviet collaborators, the mother's power proves insufficient; in one of the most troubling and powerful moments in the novel, we return to Grimm's forest, but now we are in the mind of Hitler himself, walking in "the forest of Gorlitz, on the frontier between Eastern Prussia and Lithuania." Hitler, Grossman tells us, "at first . . . found it soothing to be alone in the forest, but now he began to be frightened. Without his bodyguards and aides, he felt like a little boy in a fairy-tale lost in a dark, enchanted forest. . . . He was like the goat who had wandered into the forest, unaware that the wolf had stolen up on him through a thicket" (657, 659). The links between David and Hitler track the horror of the novel at its most expansive, but also at its most intimate: both have read Grimm's story of a goat who will be "scaped" by the wolf. The forest world of moral nightmare gives way at the novel's end to a very different vision, one that brings us back to the northern countryside of Russia, and the possibilities of rebirth. An unnamed couple leaves a peasant hut and walks off into a landscape of lake, field, and forest, a forest where snow has not yet melted and squirrels are "hard at work in the branches above." "The forest seemed silent. The many layers of branches kept off the light; instead of tinkling and gurgling, it was like a soft cloak swathed round the earth." Grossman's epic account of the violence of twentieth-century ideologies, the ravaged earth of Stalingrad and the compromised lives of the Soviet intelligentsia, ends with silence and a couple emerging from the forest: "Somehow you could sense spring more vividly in this cool forest than on the sunlit plain. And there was a deeper sadness in this silence than in the silence of autumn. In it you could hear both a lament for the dead and the furious joy of life itself" (871).

Grossman holds out in this ending an almost heartbreaking belief that life might return. Other chroniclers of the Soviet century are less sanguine, with bleak visions of human nature—and Russia—that involve revisiting the forest ethnoscape. In Anatolii Kim's 1989 novel *Father Forest* the whole of Russia is a great wood, a dark place where human souls transmigrate into sylvan form, and the curse of the past extends violently into a future marked by rape, abandonment, and aphasia. We feel with Kim as though Mel'nikov-Pechersky's boisterous woodland has been transformed into a landscape worthy of Bosch, in which human relationship is reduced to devouring or disregard.[8] Varlam Shalamov gives us a similarly unforgiving epitaph to woodland dreams: in the forever vanished childhood of "A Child's Drawings" there had been deep woods and a magically helpful wolf, bearing the hero homeward. Now there are guard dogs and sentries with guns, a world from which God has fled, a world in which—as the narrator puts it—"Nature . . . is not impersonal or indifferent; it is in conspiracy with those who sent us here."[9] This particular vignette of Shalamov's imprisonment in far northeastern Siberia begins, fittingly enough, with convicts cutting logs with a circular saw and then splitting them with an ax. Part of the devastating machinery of this brilliant story is its evocation of those saw teeth and their violence, chewing up men, woods, memories of "innocence." Shalamov, in words whose implications are shattering, suggests that "we"—those who come after Stalin and the gulag—are barred forever from those fairy-tale landscapes of pinewood and animal helpers. Part of the work of these brilliant stories is to tease out how nature is an accomplice in the work of destruction; and how, paradoxically, it might shelter memory that will ultimately be turned against those who were the destroyers.

> The logging area kept moving back. Felling the taller trees suitable for building materials in Kolyma takes place along the stream banks where deep ravines force the trees to reach upward from their wind-protected havens toward the sun. In windy spots, in bright light, on marshy mountain slopes stand dwarfs—broken, twisted, tormented from eternally turning after the sun, from

their constant struggle for a piece of thawed ground. The trees on the mountain slopes don't look like trees, but like monsters fit for a sideshow. Felling trees is similar to mining gold in those same streams in that it is just as rushed: the stream, the pan, the launder, the temporary barracks, the hurried predatory leap that leaves the stream and area without forest for three hundred years and without gold—forever. (176–77)

We almost read Shalamov's description here as allegory, thinking to find in his stunted, sun-starved dwarves figures for human beings, "monsters" who will never stand tall. We almost read it as we do Merzliakov's "Among the Spreading Vale," or Nekrasov's "Sasha wept," as a piece of prose that is really more concerned with human than sylvan lives.[10] But then we read that final sentence, its gathering of all creation—humans, trees, nuggets of gold—into one: the "hurried predatory leap" maims them all. Some it destroys for a long time, some it destroys forever.

When Dmitrii Kaigorodov set out to describe for his readers the nature of a linden tree, he turned to Ivan Turgenev.[11] The forest that he and his readers could inhabit both imaginatively and in the most literal sense of the word was an *obshchezhitie*, a common dwelling—a topography of memory, perception, and physical reality, both literal places and shared languages of meaning. Along the edge of forests, as Turgenev puts it in "Forest and Steppe," "imagination lifts and hovers like a bird, and everything stands as if before your eyes, vividly alive." What is vividly alive is both the physical environment (woods, edge, brush, *opushka*) and the past itself, resurrected as we move through land that can flush both woodcock and our own unexpected memories. The human imagination labors to articulate this experience of embodied presence in a complex landscape: forests—the wild ones, whose order is driven not by human reason but by the "forest tsar" or the "forest spirit"—become companions of human language and vision, "cradles," as the poet Nikolai Zabolotsky put it, of human speech.

Turgenev, Korolenko, and Kaigorodov—like Grossman and Shalamov—give us maps of a world whose coordinates are idiosyncratic and personal but can still be followed. We can go to Svetloyar; we can find the place where Nesterov saw cabbages and a meeting place for his Sergius; we can wander through the arboretum of what is now called the Forest Technical Academy. And when we get there we will see those places at least in part through the eyes of men long dead; they will have created within us a set of expectations, even as Mel'nikov-Pechersky led Korolenko to expect something different from what he saw when he got to the tiny woodland lake. *That's it?* Polesye seems less mysterious and forbidding than when Turgenev's hunter confronted it; the arboretum where

Kaigorodov walked is sadly untended and overgrown. But the narrative of change is not solely one of diminishing health: compared with when Korolenko visited, Svetloyar is lushly wooded, and the small arts school in the neighboring village suggests vibrant connections to the past, an unpredictably emerging future. Children have made clay-figure models of Kitezh, illuminated with tiny lightbulbs. On warm summer afternoons you might encounter hare krishnas or devotees of Rudolf Steiner, or Orthodox pilgrims walking slowly around the lake in single file.

The ongoing relevance of these images for contemporary Russia is best illustrated by an image I clipped from a St. Petersburg newspaper in the fall of 2000. Igor' Arkhipov had grafted together two prerevolutionary paintings to comment on proposed forest legislation: in his collage Russia's governing body sits not in a retooled Soviet-era building in the center of Moscow, but in a towering, light-dappled pine forest. It is a brilliant if simple turn of visual rhetoric: Repin's 1903 painting of the constituent assembly has been superimposed on Shishkin's canvas of the Countess Mordvinova's forest. What we get is a world in which towering pines—Kaigorodov's *krasnolesye*, or "red forest"—shelter the assembly, but also stand as silent witnesses of the proceedings. The pines are reminders of a world we all stand within, a world on whose health and sustenance we ourselves depend. They are the context in which the statesmen do their work. They are a precondition of how—and whether—the government will continue to function. Perhaps they are a reproach as well, their own dignity and extraordinary beauty—massive materiality that nonetheless lets through an astonishing amount of light—serving as goads to human humility. The pines remind humans of their proper place: inextricably connected, dependent, with the capacity for dignified action only to the extent that they *remember* the larger world within which they sit.

It is also striking that an artist and journalist for an urban weekly could think of no better way to comment on contemporary politics than by quoting a nineteenth-century poet (Nekrasov) and splicing together two nineteenth-century painters. Among other things, they were counting on their readers "getting it"—assuming that Russian readers at the beginning of the third millennium could count as part of their common cultural vocabulary Nekrasov, Shishkin, and Repin. Arkhipov and Nelli Bogorad, the journalist, pour that old wine into new bottles. The impulse is not conservative but radical: using well-worn images to recall both politicians and populace to dignity of action and moral (and environmental) responsibility. It is as though they are asking Shalamov's stunted trees to *stand up straight*. The metaphorical and allegorical powers of the forest are still with us, but here they are being put to political—and environmental—use: to argue for the trees themselves.

Igor' Arkhipov, untitled. Chas Pik, no. 40, 2000. St. Petersburg. Reproduced with permission of the artist.

The trees and woodlands that inspired the authors and artists I talk about here are still by and large standing, due in no small part to their cultural associations. Tolstoy's Yasnaya Polyana is probably the most famous pilgrimage site for non-Russians, but Lake Svetloyar, Polesye, the arboretum of the Forest Academy, Abramtsevo—are all protected areas, at least in part because of their associations with the authors and artists discussed here. In the ten years I have spent writing this book, I have learned to look at trees differently: it's not just that I have learned the names of species (both in English and Russian), or come to understand something about forest soils and the dynamics of hydrology. The writers and authors of these pages have taught me to see trees and woodlands as resilient communities and companions. The ways in which nineteenth-century writers on forests and the Forest Question have been my companions are probably too numerous to name. Russians' efforts to bring into public awareness an incipient catastrophe of massive proportions has on more than one occasion seemed disturbingly like contemporary efforts to find language and imagery for climate change; I have wondered which aesthetic—Repin's of violent loss, or Nesterov's of divine potential—is more likely to stir the human heart. For several years I found myself pursued by Turgenev's forbidding Polesye voices as I took my morning walk, skirting a boundary between neatly mown lawns and a looming, shadowed woodland; there *is* something both terrifying and hypnotic in that mass of darkness, and I talked to it about death and loss, thinking it might offer an answer, even if it couldn't really hear. Early on in my writing, the Bates College community was wracked by anger at the felling of over ninety trees on campus, an event that—like the destruction of the Orel linden alley—turned out to have been in the works for some time; what replaced the birch, maples, and elms that were cut down was a regular avenue of paper birch, a monoculture that disgruntled faculty and staff quickly attacked as some Massachusetts planner's idea of "Maine." Violence, loss, and the remarkable resilience of our companion trees have shadowed my writing, just as they did Rudzkii's. I started the book in 2001; on September 11 of that year, a month before I would fly to Russia to continue research on Russia's woodlands, two arborists showed up at our front door to plant trees we had ordered in July. Under the eerily empty skies of that September day they planted a plane tree and a redbud. Ten years later both trees give us shelter and shade.

At the very end of this writing process I made a discovery that seemed to offer closure. Oleg Vasil'ev's *Self-Portrait from the Back* captivated me when I first saw it in October of 2001: it seemed uncannily to evoke Turgenev's hunter standing *en face* of Polesye; I loved the way the boundaries of human form seemed to melt into the autumn landscape. There was none of the triumphalism and stark visual distinction of Friedrich's *Wanderer above the Sea*, which it immediately reminded me of. I fell in love with Vasil'ev's image, and let it guide me—but also sort of forgot about it as I worked my way through other texts and images. And then during the summer of 2011 I returned to it, and read some of Vasil'ev's essays, including one in which he talks about where he painted *Self-Portrait from the Back*. It turns out he painted it near Abramtsevo, near the village where Nesterov worked on his Sergius paintings. The woods his figure is entering are Nesterov's, or Sergius's, or Aksakov's. He is marking a way in, a way that will be completely his own, but which has also already been traversed.[12] Standing by the wood, a boy lets out a whoop, as though he has been playing hide-and-seek. Then he follows his grandmother into the field of buckwheat, blossoming and beautiful. We slip back into darkness, sheltered and silenced by the woods around us.

Notes

INTRODUCTION

1. Quoted in L. Afonin and Z. Sidel'nikova, *Pamiatnye mesta Orla* (Orel: Orlovskoe knizh-noe izdatel'stvo, 1962), 5. One of the editors of this small collection of woodcuts and sketches of local history, Leonid Afonin, figures below in my account of the local intelligentsia's resistance to plans to cut down the linden alley in the center of the city. I am grateful to Lucien Weisbrod for his gift to me of this small volume—he is one of the people who has regularly facilitated my journeys back and forth to Orel.

2. Details on the history of the park and its literary associations come from O. Vlasova, *Orlovskii gorodskoi sad* (Tula: Priokskoe knizhnoe izdatel'stvo, 1984). Layout of the park began in October of 1822 by order of Governor Nikolai Ivanovich Shreder; it was formally opened in May of the following year. Vlasova includes Tolstoy, Turgenev, Leskov, Marko Vovchok, Ivan Bunin, and Leonid Andreev in her list of authors who remember the park. Tolstoy visited Orel while working on his novel *Resurrection*, which includes a description of the city's prison; the prison was located in the area now occupied by the amusement park—the opposite side of the park from the linden alley and the parade square. Vlasova, *Orlovskii*, 9, 30. I was also grateful to be able to talk in August 2011 with Elena Ashikhmina, a local historian whose essays on Orel—and collection of historical photographs—have been enormously helpful. See among others her *Orlovskie istorii: Arkhivno-kraevedcheskie zapiski* (Orel: Aleksandr Vorob'ev, 2011).

3. When I first set out to find out more about Afonin, I quickly discovered that he is a deeply beloved figure among Orel's literary and cultural intelligentsia. He was instrumental in establish-ing the Andreev Museum in one of the city's oldest quarters; a wonderfully informal portrait of him hangs in the museum's kitchen. The Bunin library in Orel maintains a bibliography of works both by and about Afonin. See Ol'ga Volochina, *"Ochen' nuzhen Orlu: k 80-letiiu so dnia rozhde-niia L. N. Afonina,"* *Orlovskaia pravda*, June 26, 1998.

4. Those interviews were conducted during two separate trips to Orel during 2001, the first in early June, the second in late October. I interviewed six individuals, all of them with connections

to the university, library, and literary museums. Recordings and transcriptions of the interviews are in my possession. When I cite the interviews I maintain the interviewees' anonymity but provide the date of the interview.

5. BGS interview, October 23, 2001.

6. Vlasova, writing in 1984, divides the park into three areas based on tree age: one group included trees over 150 years old, another was dominated by 60-to-80-year-old trees, and the third area had been replanted after German occupation during World War II. Vlasova, *Orlovskii*, 31.

7. S. I. Fedorov, *Orel* (Moscow: Izdatel'stvo literatury po stroitel'stvu, 1969), 134.

8. One recent fictionalized account (subtitled a "historical humoresque") suggests that the regional party secretary himself didn't think the plan would come to fruition, given the usual lethargic pace at which such things were realized. A. Lysenko, "*O tom, chego ne znaet Vasilii Katanov . . . (Istoricheskaia iumoreska)*," *Kraevedcheskie zapiski* (Orel: Orlovskii kraevedcheskii muzei, 2008), 163–69. I am grateful to Julia Viacheslavovna Zhukova, of the Bunin library in Orel, for bringing this essay to my attention.

9. Blair Ruble provides a brief overview of Soviet city planning in *Money Sings: The Changing Politics of Urban Space in Post-Soviet Yaroslavl* (Cambridge: Cambridge University Press, 1995), 104–7.

10. The distinction between "space" and "place" is central to contemporary thinking in human geography and place-based humanistic discourse: place in the sense I use it here is intimately known, experienced "from the inside" rather than merely viewed at a distance. The expansion of the city square with the Lenin monument at its helm suggests a desire on the part of city planners to impose *their* sense of "place" on a previously existing one—but large Soviet squares are always vulnerable to disintegrating into monotonous and undistinguished *space*, virtually unrelated to preexisting local culture or memory. Contested space in the Stalin era is the subject of Evgeny Dobrenko and Eric Naiman, eds., *The Landscape of Stalinism: The Art and Ideology of Soviet Space* (Seattle: University of Washington Press, 2003).

11. See for example Galya Diment and Yuri Slezkine, eds., *Between Heaven and Hell: The Myth of Siberia in Russian Culture* (New York: St. Martin's, 1993).

12. Thomas Berry, *The Dream of the Earth* (San Francisco: Sierra Club Books, 1988), 194.

13. Barry Lopez, "Landscape and Narrative," in *Crossing Open Ground* (New York: Scribner's, 1989), 61–71. On feeling for nature as a category of cultural analysis see T. Ia. Grinfel'd, ed., *Chuvstvo prirody v russkoi literature* (Syktyvkar: Syktyvkarskii universitet, 1995) and N. V. Kozhukhovskaia, *Evoliutsiia chuvstva prirody v russkoi proze XIX veka* (Syktyvkar: Syktyvkarskii universitet, 1995).

14. R. A. French, "Russians and the Forest," in *Studies in Russian Historical Geography*, vol. 1 (London: Academic Press, 1983), 23.

15. Mikhail Epstein, *Priroda, mir, tainik vselennoi: Sistema peizazhnykh obrazov v russkoi poezii* (Moscow: Vysshaia shkola, 1990), 10. The second citation is from Elena Hellberg-Hirn: "These two types of living space, the southern steppe and the northern forest, created different attitudes to life: the steppe was open for freedom and movement, but also open for invasion; the forest was more secure, but more difficult to live and move around in. Both were endless and sparsely inhabited." Hellberg-Hirn, *Soil and Soul: The Symbolic World of Russianness* (Aldershot, UK: Ashgate, 1998), 27–28. Dmitrii Merezhkovsky, "*Rasskazy Vl. Korolenko*," *Akropol': Izbrannye literaturno-kriticheskie stat'i* (Moscow: Knizhnaia palata, 1991), 74.

16. Robin Milner-Gulland, "Wooden Russia," in *The Russians* (Oxford: Blackwell, 1997), 30.

17. Andrei Platonov, "Among Animals and Plants," in *Soul and Other Stories*, trans. Robert and Elizabeth Chandler and Olga Meerson (New York: New York Review of Books, 2008), 160. The story was completed in 1936.

18. On Mikhalkov and nationalism see Birgit Beumers, *Nikita Mikhalkov: Between Nostalgia and Nationalism* (New York: I. B. Tauris, 2005). Vladimir Megre, *Anastasiia* (Moscow: Dilia,

2003). Megre's books are now available in English translation through the Ringing Cedars Press. "Sasha was crying," a phrase from Nikolai Nekrasov's much-memorized poem "Sasha," shows up in numerous articles on contemporary environmental issues: see for example Nadezhda Azhgikhina, "*Plakala Sasha*," in *Delovoi vtornik*, February 26, 2006 (accessed at http://www.ruj.ru/authors/azhgikhin/08018.html). The article concerns local efforts to preserve a park and recreational space from development. Nekrasov's poem is discussed in chapter 3. The Shishkin/Repin collage appeared in connection with a national campaign to reinstate federal control of the country's forests; the image is reproduced in the conclusion of this book.

19. "*Krainost' lesofil'stva*," published in the *Smes'* section of *Zhurnal ministerstva gosudarstvennykh imushchestv*, 1862, vol. 79, sec. 4, 27–29. A quick Google search suggests that the French have coined *sylvophile* and *sylvanophile* as contemporary, unapologetic versions of our more derogatory "tree hugger."

20. V. O. Kliuchevsky, *A History of Russia*, trans. C. J. Hogarth, vol. 5 (New York: Dutton, 1931), 245.

21. "Nature," in Raymond Williams, *Keywords: A Vocabulary of Culture and Society* (New York: Oxford University Press, 1983), 219–24.

22. Lawrence Buell describes his first book as being about "the extent to which (certain kinds of) literature can be thought to model ecocentric values." Buell, *The Future of Environmental Criticism: Environmental Crisis and Literary Imagination* (Malden, MA: Blackwell, 2005), 22; Glen Love, one of the founding voices of contemporary ecocriticism, has argued that "the most important function of literature today is to redirect human consciousness to a full consideration of its place in a threatened natural world." "Revaluing Nature: Toward an Ecological Criticism," in *Ecocriticism Reader: Landmarks in Literary Ecology*, ed. Cheryll Glotfelty and Harold Fromm (Athens: University of Georgia Press, 1996), 237. Donald Worster explores the emergence of "ecological" understandings of nature from the late eighteenth century in *Nature's Economy: A History of Ecological Ideas* (New York: Cambridge University Press, 1994).

23. Douglas Weiner's landmark histories of environmentalism in the Soviet Union deal only briefly with the prerevolutionary era: in *Models of Nature* Weiner suggests three trends in late Imperial conservationist impulses: "utilitarian, cultural-aesthetic-ethical, and scientific." Weiner, *Models of Nature: Ecology, Conservation, and Cultural Revolution in Soviet Russia* (Pittsburgh: Pittsburgh University Press, 1988), 10. See also his *A Little Corner of Freedom: Russian Nature Protection from Stalin to Gorbachev* (Berkeley and Los Angeles: University of California Press, 1999). Stephen Brain's *Song of the Forest: Russian Forestry and Stalinist Environmentalism, 1905–1953* (Pittsburgh: University of Pittsburgh Press, 2011) appeared as this volume was going to press. Brain's book provides a richly detailed account of the ways in which nineteenth-century forestry—and in particular the ecological insights of Georgii Morozov—endured well into the Soviet era, even as their ethic of sustainable yield and holistic understanding of forest dynamics were repeatedly challenged by the ideologues and bureaucrats of Soviet industrialization.

24. Lawrence Buell, *The Environmental Imagination: Thoreau, Nature Writing, and the Formation of American Culture* (Cambridge, MA: Harvard University Press, 1995), 256.

25. George Steiner, *Martin Heidegger* (Chicago: University of Chicago Press, 1982), 32. Heidegger's place in ecocriticism has been controversial, given his relationship to National Socialism and Nazi "environmentalism." See among others Jonathan Bate, "What Are Poets For?" in *The Song of the Earth* (Cambridge, MA: Harvard University Press, 2000), 268–78.

26. Vladimir Korolenko, "*Les shumit*," in *Sobranie sochinenii v desiati tomakh*, vol. 2 (Moscow: Gosudarstvennoe izdatel'stvo khudozhestvennoi literatury, 1954), 67, 87.

27. David Abram, *The Spell of the Sensuous: Perception and Language in a More-Than-Human World* (New York: Vintage, 1997). As one of the book's reviewers has noted, Abram's tendency to give short shrift to written language contradicts his own marvelous ability to conjure physical reality with the written word. Meg Holden, "A Reply to David Abram," *Environmental Ethics* 24 (Spring 2002): 111–12.

28. Greg Garrard provides an insightful account of how tropes of pastoral and dwelling structure much ecocritical discourse: *Ecocriticism*, chapters 3 and 6. Ursula Heise offers a critical account of "localism" and the emergence of ecocriticism, in "Ecocriticism and the Transnational Turn in American Studies," *American Literary History* 20 (2008): 381–404. For some examples of discourses of home in contemporary American nature writing see *Finding Home: Writing on Nature and Culture from* Orion *Magazine*, ed. Peter Sauer (Boston: Beacon Press, 1992); *At Home on the Earth: Becoming Native to Our Place, A Multicultural Anthology*, ed. David Landis Barnhill (Berkeley and Los Angeles: University of California Press, 1999).

29. Anna Akhmatova, *"Zemlia khotia i ne rodnaia, no pamiatnaia navsegda,"* in *Stikhotvoreniia* (Leningrad: Lenizdat', 1976), 430.

30. "If you really want to understand the tree, you have to encounter it in the forest. If you want to understand the river, you have to explore the watershed. If you want to understand the story, you have to go beyond it, into the ecosystem of stories." Robert Bringhurst, *The Tree of Meaning: Language, Mind and Ecology* (Berkeley, CA: Counterpoint, 2006), 169.

31. Ivan Turgenev, *Polnoe sobranie sochinenii i pisem v dvadtsati vos'mi tomakh*, vol. 4 (Moscow-Leningrad: Izdatel'stvo akademii nauk SSSR, 1963), 386.

32. Ivan Bunin, *Sobranie sochinenii v shesti tomakh*, vol. 1 (Moscow: Khudozhestvennaia literatura, 1987), 263.

33. Kharms's poem ends with a strong and unexpected "togda skorei togda skorei, skorei skazhite nam"—literally, "tell *us* as soon as you see him." Daniil Kharms, *"Iz doma vyshel chelovek."* Here is the whole of the poem:

> *One day a man departed home*
> *with walking stick and sack*
> *for distant parts*
> *for distant parts*
> *he left and didn't look back.*
>
> *He went quite straight and on ahead*
> *and on ahead he gazed*
> *nor slept, nor drank*
> *nor drank, nor slept*
> *Nor slept, nor drank, nor ate.*
>
> *And one fine morning at the dawn*
> *he entered a dark wood*
> *and from that day*
> *and from that day*
> *it seems he's gone for good.*
>
> *But if perhaps some time you chance*
> *to catch a sight of him,*
> *then make all haste*
> *then make all haste*
> *Make haste to let us know.*

Kharms was arrested in 1941 and died of starvation in a Leningrad prison the next year. Kharms's widow was convinced he had narrowly escaped disaster over the poem in 1937. See Neil Cornwell, "The Rudiments of Daniil Kharms: In Further Pursuit of the Red-Haired Man," *The Modern Language Review* 93, no. 1 (January 1998): 134–35.

1. WALKING INTO THE WOODLAND WITH TURGENEV

1. Carl Tseplin, "*O sostoianii khlebopashestva i lesovodstva v Moskovskoi gubernii*," *Zhurnal sel'skago khoziaistva i ovtsevodstva*, no. 7 (1842): 5.

2. "Khor and Kalinych," from which this quote is taken, is the first of Turgenev's *Hunter's Sketches* and first appeared in 1847. Ivan Turgenev, "Khor and Kalinych." *Polnoe sobranie sochinenii i pisem v dvadtsati vos'mi tomakh*, vol. 4 (Moscow-Leningrad: Izdatel'stvo akademii nauk SSSR, 1963), 7. Subsequent references to this edition will be given in the body of the chapter. Volume number is followed by page number; *Pis'ma* designates volumes containing Turgenev's letters.

3. For an account of the story's creation see Turgenev, *Polnoe sobranie*, 7:415–18.

4. *Polnoe sobranie*, 7:416.

5. In subsequent editions Turgenev shortened the note. For the original text, given here, see *Polnoe sobranie*, 4:432.

6. T. Beliaeva, "*Zelenye steny Rossii*," *Nauka i zhizn'*, no. 5 (2004): 20–25. See also M. V. Bobrovskii, *Kozel'skie zaseki (ekologo-istoricheskii ocherk)* (Kaluga: Izdatel'stvo N. Bochkarevoi, 2002). The description of tree species and soils is taken from I. E. Andreevskii, ed., *Entsiklope-dicheskii slovar'*, vol. 47 (St. Petersburg: Brokgauz i Efron, 1890–1904), 457–58. Tolstoy's estate, Yasnaya Polyana, bordered a section of the *zaseki* just southwest of Tula.

7. Bobrovskii suggests that the average width of the *zaseki* was between two and two and a half miles. *Kozel'skie zaseki*, 5–6.

8. Beliaeva points out that a similar sort of felled-tree fortification was used at the battle of Borodino. "*Zelenye steny*," 20. The term *zapoved'* used in relation to the *zaseki* is intriguing, since *zapovednik* is the term used in modern Russia for strict conservation areas.

9. Turgenev, *Polnoe sobranie*, 7:417.

10. Vladimir Dal', *Tolkovyi slovar' zhivago velikoruskago yazyka*, vol. 2 (Moscow: Russkii Yazyk, 1979): 557.

11. Dal' *Tolkovyi slovar'*, 2:557.

12. "We attain to dwelling, so it seems, only by means of building." Martin Heidegger, "Building, Dwelling, Thinking," in *Poetry, Language, Thought*, trans. Albert Hofstadter (New York: Harper & Row, 1971), 145. Jonathan Bate discusses the problematic of "dwelling" for Heidegger and other twentieth-century poets (in particular, Paul Celan and Edward Thomas), along with the Black Forest hut, which Heidegger conceived as the archetypal "dwelling place." Bate, "What Are Poets For?" 268–83. See also "Dwelling" in Robert Pogue Harrison's *Forests: The Shadow of Civilization* (Chicago: University of Chicago Press, 1992), 197–243.

13. On the *leshii* see N. A. Krinichnaia, "*Leshii i pastukh (po materialam severno-russkikh mifo-logicheskikh rasskazov, poverii i obriadov)*," *Obriady i verovaniia narodov Karelii* (Petrozavodsk: Karel'skii filial AN SSSR 1994), 154–81; and Linda Ivanits, *Russian Folk Belief* (Armonk, NY: M. E. Sharpe, 1989), 64–82.

14. *Svoi* and *chuzhoi* have long been regarded as fundamental categories of Russian culture. For a closely observed consideration of the distinction, focusing on a contemporary Russian village, see Margaret Paxton, *Solovyovo: The Story of Memory in a Russian Village* (Blooming-ton: Indiana University Press, 2005), 52–85. For a non-Russian discussion of rituals of passage between the world of the village and the world beyond see Abram, "The Ecology of Magic," in *The Spell of the Sensuous* (New York: Pantheon Books, 1996), 3–29.

15. Krinichnaia's work on traditional Russian culture and the forest has been enormously helpful for this project; she is the lead scholar for a group of folklorists and philologists work-ing in Petrozavodsk, Russia. "*Les v krest'ianskom bytu i verovaniiakh*," *Lesnye navazhdeniia: mifo-logicheskie rasskazy i pover'ia o dukhe-"khoziaine" lesa* (Petrozavodsk: Karel'skii nauchnyi tsentr RAN, 1993), 3.

16. Harrison, *Forests*, 6–7.

17. Joseph Brodsky, *On Grief and Reason* (New York: Farrar, Straus and Giroux, 1996), 228, 225.

18. Krinichnaia points out that the *leshii* often plays the role of soothsayer or prophet: "*Leshii: Totemicheskie istoki i polisemantizm obraza*," especially the final section, "predskazatel' sud'by." *Russkaia mifologiia: Mir obrazov fol'klora* (Moscow: Akademicheskii proekt, 2004), 319–23. The Russian word for bear, *medved'*, refers to honey (*med*) and eating (*ed-*). M. Fasmer, *Etimologicheskii slovar' russkogo yazyka*, vol. 2 (Moscow: Progress, 1986), 589.

19. Modern urbanites can learn to read the landscape or spend a weekend tracking—but if they are hunters, they are likely to have some sense of these things from childhood, learned from the fathers and uncles they have hunted with.

20. On depiction of peasants in nineteenth-century Russian discourse see Cathy Frierson, *Peasant Icons: Representations of Rural People in Late 19th Century Russia* (Oxford: Oxford University Press, 1993); Henrietta Mondry, *Pure, Strong and Sexless: The Peasant Woman's Body and Gleb Uspensky* (Amsterdam: Rodopi, 2006); and Donald Fanger, "The Peasant in Literature," in *The Peasant in Nineteenth-Century Russia*, ed. Wayne Vucinich (Stanford, CA: Stanford University Press, 1968). Frierson and Mondry both note the extent to which these discussions were shaped by understandings of gender.

21. A. S. Pushkin, *Izbrannye sochinenii v dvukh tomakh*, vol. 1 (Moscow: 1978), 275. The editors of the Academy edition of Turgenev note the reminiscence: Turgenev, *Polnoe sobranie*, 7:420.

22. Questions of scale are fundamental for ecology; in this shift from vastness to the minuscule there is also an intriguing echo of Pascal's famous passage in the *Pensées*, "between two abysses." On Turgenev and Pascal see A. I. Batiuto, *Turgenev-Romanist* (Leningrad: Nauka, 1972); and Jane Costlow, *Worlds within Worlds: The Novels of Ivan Turgenev* (Princeton, NJ: Princeton University Press, 1990), 46, 100.

23. The Russian is *prileg*—from *lech'*, to lie down, as in *nochleg*.

24. Robert Louis Jackson, "The Root and the Flower: Dostoevsky and Turgenev, a Comparative Aesthetic," in *Dialogues with Dostoevsky: The Overwhelming Questions* (Stanford, CA: Stanford University Press, 1993), 164–65, 166.

25. Ibid., 185.

26. Thomas Newlin, "At the Bottom of the River: Forms of Ecological Consciousness in Mid-Nineteenth-Century Russian Literature," *Russian Studies in Literature*, special issue, *Russian Nature*, vol. 1, ed. Rachel May (2003), 2:76–77.

27. Mikhail Gershenzon reads this scene of watching as illustrative of a contrast between the "metaphysics of West and East," of Nietzsche and Turgenev: "On the one hand, the will to endless and insatiable growth of will beyond the bounds of momentarily established law; on the other hand, compliant acceptance of law and will, directed solely at elevation of self-control to the level of law." Gershenzon's reading is also focused on the moment of meditation and the lyric voice that bears it; neither peasant figures in his discussion. "*Priroda*," *Mechta i mysl' I. S. Turgeneva* (Moscow: T-vo Knigoizdatel'stvo pisatelei v Moskve, 1919), 64.

28. I do not address here another aspect of the passage—its insistence on the "equanimity" of nature. While this notion underpins much of nineteenth- and even twentieth-century science, it has been challenged by contemporary ecology, which sees the natural world as characterized not by balance and harmony but by disequilibrium and unpredictable outcomes. See Daniel Worster, *Nature's Economy: A History of Ecological Ideas* (New York: Cambridge University Press, 1994) 405–12; and Daniel Botkin, *Discordant Harmonies: A New Ecology for the Twenty-first Century* (New York: Oxford University Press, 1990). Greg Garrard considers the significance of evolving ecological understandings for literary and cultural scholars in *Ecocriticism* (London: Routledge, 2004), 56–58.

29. For a fuller discussion of the novel see Costlow, *Worlds within Worlds*, chap. 4.

30. Leslie O'Bell, "The Pastoral in Turgenev's 'Singers': Classical Themes and Romantic Variations," *Russian Review* 63, no. 2 (April 2004): 280, 286.

31. On the cow's significance as symbol of traditional Russian culture see Arja Rosenholm, "'There Is No Russia without the Cow': The Russian Mind and Memory; the Cow as Symbol," in

Understanding Russian Nature: Representations, Values and Concepts, ed. Arja Rosenholm and Sari Autio-Sarasmo (Helsinki: Aleksanteri Papers, 2005), 69–96.

32. "It's extraordinarily pleasant to lie on your back in the woods and look up! It seems as though you're looking into a bottomless sea, as though it's spread out beneath you, as though the trees aren't rising from the earth, but are descending like the roots of great plants, falling heavily into the glassy-clear waves. . . . You don't move—you are watching: and it's impossible to express in words how joyous, and quiet, and happy you feel. You watch: that deep, clear azure brings a smile to your lips, innocent as the sky itself, as the clouds in the sky, while happy memories seem to wind slowly across your soul in their wake, and it seems more and more as though your gaze is drawn farther and farther into the distance, carrying you with it into that still, glowing abyss, and it's impossible to tear oneself from that height, from that depth." Turgenev, *Polnoe sobranie*, 4:124. The title of this story is often given using a generic geographical term, but like Polesye/*polesye*, "Krasivaia Mecha" designates a specific place, in this case a tributary of the Don located just north of the Orel district. The river's name derives from the Urdmut word for "bluff" or steep bank.

33. Ralph Waldo Emerson, "Nature," excerpted in *The Norton Book of Nature Writing*, ed. Robert Finch and John Elder (New York: W. W. Norton, 1990), 144.

34. Tom Newlin makes a similar point about the passage in "At the Bottom of the River," 80–81.

35. "Turgenev's subtle elaboration of problems, not answers, places him in the company of all those writers who have created what is commonly called the problematic in modern literature." Kenneth Brostrom, "The Heritage of Romantic Depictions of Nature in Turgenev," *American Contributions to the Ninth International Congress of Slavists (Kiev 1983)*, vol. 2: *Literature, Poetics, History*, ed. Paul Debreczeny, 1983, p. 92.

36. The opening chapter of *Fathers and Children* provides a striking example of this.

37. This aspect of forest space is part of what made the paintings of Ivan Shishkin awkwardly unconventional to early viewers: "I asked you to paint a view, not a study of the forest," wrote one of his early patrons. On Shishkin's elaboration of a distinct aesthetics of forest space see Christopher Ely, *This Meager Nature: Landscape and National Identity in Imperial Russia* (DeKalb: Northern Illinois University Press, 2002), 185–88.

38. Anne Whiston Spirn, *The Language of Landscape* (New Haven, CT: Yale University Press, 1998), 32. For Spirn, it is the "fit" of inherent form and attributed meanings that enables deep and sustained cultural resonance.

39. O'Bell, "Pastoral in Turgenev's 'Singers,' " 293.

40. Michael Holquist sees Lermontov's *A Hero of Our Time* as archetypal precursor to Dostoevsky's novels of intellectual and spiritual wandering. Holquist, *Dostoevsky and the Novel* (Princeton, NJ: Princeton University Press, 1977).

2. HEART-PINE RUSSIA

1. N. Boev, "*Kartiny lesnoi zhizni: Epizody iz neokonchennoi povesti*," *Russkii vestnik*, December 1871, 578–79, 591–92. I have been unable to find out anything about just who Boev was—other than that he published short fiction and travel sketches in *Russkii vestnik*, *Otechestvennye zapiski*, and *Zaria* in the late 1860s and early 1870s. The polemical juxtapositions of European feudal castles and Russian contemplative, communal life form part of the Slavophile rhetoric of a writer like Ivan Kireevsky. See his "*O kharaktere prosveshcheniia Evropy i o ego otnoshenii k prosveshcheniiu Rossii (Pis'mo k gr. E. E. Komarovskomu)*" (1852), in I. V. Kireevsky, *Polnoe sobranie sochinenii*, vol. 2 (Moscow: Tipografiia Bakhmeteva, 1861), 275–77. See also Andrzej Walicki, *The Slavophile Controversy* (New York: Clarendon Press, 1975), 137–39.

2. The philosopher Petr Chaadaev used the term "romanticism of retrospective utopia" to describe the Slavophiles; V. I. Kuleshov finds the term particularly apt in distinguishing the

Slavophiles' particular brand of romanticism. Kuleshov, *Slavianofily i russkaia literatura* (Moscow: Khudozhestvennaia literatura, 1976), 78.

3. David Bethea, *The Shape of Apocalypse in Modern Russian Fiction* (Princeton, NJ: Princeton University Press, 1989), 22.

4. Michael Cherniavsky, *Tsar and People: Studies in Russian Myths* (New Haven, CT: Yale University Press, 1961), 116.

5. Lake Svetloyar (Svetlyi Yar) is situated about an hour and a half north of the Volga River near the village of Vladimirskoe in the Nizhegorod *oblast*; it lies between the rivers Vetluga and Kerzhenets.

6. Anthony Smith, "Nation and Ethnoscape," in *Myths and Memories of the Nation* (New York: Oxford University Press: 1999), 150.

7. John Strickland, *Orthodox Patriotism and the Church in Russia, 1888–1914* (Ann Arbor, MI: UMI Dissertation Services, 2001), 121.

8. Vera Chaikovskaia, "*O natsional'nom khudozhestvennom soznanii: Popytka sinteza*," in *Udivit' Parizh: Moskovskie vernisazhi* (Moscow: Znanie, 1999), 179.

9. See for example John Bowlt, "Neo-Primitivism and Russian Painting," *Burlington Magazine* 116, no. 852 (March 1974): 132–40; Bowlt, "Orthodoxy and the Avant-Garde: Sacred Images in the Work of Goncharova, Malevich, and Their Contemporaries," in *Christianity and the Arts in Russia*, ed. William C. Brumfield and Milos M. Velimirovic (New York: Cambridge University Press, 1991); and Oleg Tarasov, "The Projection of Signs: Icon—*Lubok*—the Avant-garde," in *Icon and Devotion: Sacred Spaces in Imperial Russia*, trans. Robin Milner-Gulland (London: Reaktion Books, 2002), 361–82. Dostoevsky's polyphonic recontextualization of saints' lives and popular religious legends provides a narrative example. These are not "invented" traditions; artists and writers tap a preexisting body of image, story, and ritual—although the question of just how widely some rituals were practiced in the 1850s and '60s animates scholarship on Mel'nikov as ethnographer. See Eric Hobsbawm and Terence Ranger, *The Invention of Tradition* (Cambridge: Cambridge University Press, 1983).

10. Roderick Nash, *Wilderness and the American Mind* (New Haven, CT: Yale University Press, 1973); for an influential revisionist consideration of wilderness and American cultural history see William Cronon, "The Trouble with Wilderness; or, Getting Back to the Wrong Nature," in *Uncommon Ground: Rethinking the Human Place in Nature*, ed. William Cronon (New York: W. W. Norton, 1996).

11. Boev refers to Nil Sorskii and Zasodimskii to Stefan of Perm, both important fifteenth-century monastic figures associated with the "trans-Volga elders" and their distinctive traditions of spirituality.

12. The term *indigenous*, which I am tempted to use here, would apply only in the ecological and not in the contemporary legal or anthropological sense, which is embedded in the history of colonialism. Relations between Russian peasants and non-Russian populations inform Zasodimskii's lyric ethnography of Russia's northern European forests, "*Lesnoe tsarstvo*," published in *Slovo*, 1878, nos. 9–11. Zasodimskii describes "Zyrian" or Komi culture. See also Alexander Ogden, "The Woods of Childhood: Forest and Fairy Tale in Pavel Zasodimskii's Nature Writing," *Russian Review* 64 (April 2005): 281–98.

13. Cronon, "Trouble with Wilderness." See also Shepard Krech, *The Ecological Indian: Myth and History* (New York: W. W. Norton, 1999).

14. "Delightful horror" refers to late eighteenth-century definitions of the sublime; see Malcolm Andrews, "'Astonished beyond Expression': Landscape, the Sublime, and the Unpresentable," in *Landscape and Western Art* (New York: Oxford University Press, 1999).

15. *Pustynia* is defined by Dal' in the following ways: with stress falling on the second syllable it means "uninhabited, spacious location, an expanse, the steppes." If stress falls on the first syllable (spelling may be *pustynia* or *pustyn*) the meaning is "isolated dwelling place, cell, hut of a hermit, solitary seeker, who has left behind all vanity." *Tolkovyi slovar'*, vol. 3, 542.

16. Nash, *Wilderness*, 31.

17. The essay initiated a spirited body of response, and what is by now a quite varied set of inquiries into Christian traditions and their connections to the natural world. White's essay, originally published in *Science*, is reprinted in *Dynamo and Virgin Reconsidered: Essays in the Dynamism of Western Culture* (Cambridge, MA: MIT Press, 1968). For an overview of contemporary responses to White see David M. Lodge and Christopher Hamlin, eds., *Religion and the New Ecology: Environmental Responsibility in a World in Flux* (Notre Dame: University of Notre Dame Press, 2006).

18. T. Goricheva, "*Vmesto predisloviia*," in *Khristianstvo i ekologiia: Sbornik statei*, ed. T. Goricheva (St. Petersburg: Izdatel'stvo Russkogo khristianskogo gumanitarnogo instituta, 1997), 7. See chapter 5 for further discussion of Russian Orthodoxy and environmental themes.

19. Boev, "*Kartiny lesnoi zhizni*," 591.

20. Kireevsky, "*O kharaktere prosveshcheniia*," 2:260. See also 275–76. Andrzej Walicki discusses the contrast of castle and monastery as distinctive symbolic spaces within western European and Russian culture, in *Slavophile Controversy*, 137–43. *Sobornost'* refers to the Slavophiles' notion of a spirit of Christian community essential to Russian identity; the word derives from *sobor*—related to notions of gathering, but also the word for a large ecclesial structure.

21. Pp. 594–95. Emphasis mine.

22. The commentary belongs to Dostoevsky, who is citing Fedor Tiutchev's phrase "this meager nature" from the 1855 poem: "These impoverished villages, / This meager nature— / Kindred place of patient suffering, / Places of the Russian people!" Quoted in Christopher Ely, *This Meager Nature: Landscape and National Identity in Imperial Russia* (DeKalb: Northern Illinois University Press, 2002), 193.

23. Andrew Wilton and Tim Barringer, *American Sublime: Landscape Painting in the United States* (Princeton, NJ: Princeton University Press, 2002), 121. On representations of forest clearing, and the artist Thomas Cole's ambivalence about the subject, see Barbara Novak, *Nature and Culture: American Landscape and Painting, 1825–1875* (New York: Oxford University Press, 2007), 135–43. Abbott Gleason has noted, in comparing Russian and American landscape painters, that "the work of Russian landscapists was much less optimistic about the ability of human beings to develop any ascendancy over nature." "*Russkii inok*: The Spiritual Landscape of Mikhail Nesterov," *Ecumene* 2000 7(3): 305.

24. As Chris Ely puts it, "in his somber coat, he himself seems to constitute one small part of the forest world." Ely, *This Meager Nature*, 200.

25. Cf. John Bowlt, "A Russian Luminist School? Arkhip Kuindzhi's Red Sunset on the Dnepr," *Metropolitan Museum Journal* 10 (1975): 121.

26. See for example *Twilight* (1874) and *Stream by a Forest Slope* (1880). On the role of sacred springs within popular Orthodoxy see A. A. Panchenko, *Issledovaniia v oblasti narodnogo pravoslaviia: Derevenskie sviatyni severo-zapada Rossii* (St. Petersburg: Aleteia, 1998).

27. For a comparison of Savrasov and Shishkin's treatments of forest landscapes see Irina Shuvalova, *Ivan Ivanovich Shishkin* (St. Petersburg: Khudozhnik Rossii, 1993), 46–47. She suggests that Savrasov was the only artist who could equal Shishkin in rendering nature and that Savrasov was the more "romantic" of the two, while Shishkin emphasized the forest's natural health, with occasional inclusion of elements of genre painting.

28. Ely focuses on writers working from the 1820s through the 1840s: producing travel memoirs and quasi-ethnographic accounts, these writers depict Russian monasteries from the "tourist's view," focusing on cultural and architectural ensembles rather than picturesque natural scenery. Ely, "The Picturesque and the Holy: Visions of Touristic Space in Russia, 1820–1850," in *Architectures of Russian Identity*, ed. James Cracraft and Daniel Rowland (Ithaca, NY: Cornell University Press, 2003), 82, 83.

29. Ely, *This Meager Nature*, 191.

30. V. F. Sokolova, "*K voprosu o tvorcheskoi istorii romanov P. I. Mel'nikova-Pecherskogo V lesakh i Na gorakh*," *Russkaia literatura* 13, no. 3 (1970): 109.

31. Authors loosely affiliated with so-called "village prose" in the post-Stalinist period included Valentin Rasputin, Alexander Solzhenitsyn, and Vasilii Shukshin, among others. See Kathleen Parthe, *Russian Village Prose: The Radiant Past* (Princeton, NJ: Princeton University Press, 1992). Douglas Weiner addresses the turn toward the rhetoric of homeland in the emergent environmental movement of the 1960s in *A Little Corner of Freedom* (Berkeley, CA: University of California Press, 1999).

32. The novel features, among other things, a beautiful young woman who wins the hearts of both a handsome young man *and* the young man's wealthy father (anticipating the erotic and financial conflicts of *The Brothers Karamazov*); the female healer of the novel articulates a kind of cosmic Christianity that sounds not unlike Zosima's teachings (again in Dostoevsky's novel).

33. Mel'nikov's son described the patriotic atmosphere of his father's youth; quoted in S. V. Sheshunova, "*Mel'nikov*," in *Russkie pisateli 1800–1917: Biograficheskii slovar'*, vol. 3 (Moscow: Bol'shaia rossiiskaia cntsiklopediia, 1994), 578.

34. In August of 1840 Mel'nikov moved apartments and ordered furniture in the Russian style, which he describes in detail in a letter to Andrei Kraevskii; he dreams of "wearing a Russian dress, if only they'll permit it." (Students in Russian universities were required to wear uniforms.) Quoted in Vyacheslav Kaminskii, "*Pavel Ivanovich Mel'nikov (Andrei Pecherskii)*," *Russkii filologicheskii vestnik* nos. 1 and 2 (1908): 6, 7.

35. V. F. Sokolova, *P. I. Mel'nikov (Andrei Pecherskii): Ocherk zhizni i tvorchestva* (Gor'kii: Volgo-Viatskoe knizhnoe izdatel'stvo, 1981), 13; Sheshunova, "*Mel'nikov*," 578.

36. Nadieszda Kizenko, "The Church Schism and Old Belief," in *A Companion to Russian History*, ed. Abbott Gleason (Malden, MA: Wiley-Blackwell, 2009), 145–62. Roy Robson notes that "no one knows how many Old Believers lived in Russia"—Mel'nikov's job was to try to change that. Robson, *Old Believers in Modern Russia* (DeKalb: Northern Illinois University Press, 1995), 19.

37. Sheshunova, "*Mel'nikov*," 579. P. Usov, an early biographer of Mel'nikov, quotes extensively from the latter's official report on Old Belief, in a chapter entitled "Why Paul Became Saul"; Usov points out that much of the report accounts for the strength of Old Belief in terms of the failures of the Russian Orthodox Church in the region—low or nonexistent levels of clergy education; venality, drunkenness, and coarse violence among parish priests who have become a self-enclosed caste. "*Otchego Pavel sdelalsia Savlom*," in *P. I. Mel'nikov: Zhizn' i literaturnaia deiatel'nost'* (St. Petersburg: Izdanie tovarishchestva M. O. Vol'f, 1897), 139–52. Mel'nikov's report has remained an important historical document on Old Belief in the nineteenth century.

38. V. G. Korolenko, "*V pustynnykh mestakh*," in *Sobranie sochinenii v desiati tomakh*, vol. 3 (Moscow: Gosudarstvennoe izdatel'stvo khudozhestvennoi literatury, 1954), 114. For a brief account of differing appropriations of Old Belief in nineteenth-century polemics see Kizenko, "Church Schism," 156–58. Thomas Hoisington suggests that "as a government official, Mel'nikov devoted many years to persecuting the very religious dissenters he ennobled in the two novels." Hoisington also presents a concise bibliography of biographers' and critics' discussion of this aspect of Mel'nikov's work: Hoisington, "Mel'nikov-Pecherskii: Romancer of Provincial and Old Believer Life," *Slavic Review* 33, no. 4 (1974): 679, and note 2.

39. On Mel'nikov's work as a collector of antiquities see Veronica Shapovalov, "Pavel Ivanovich Mel'nikov (Andrei Pechersky)," *Dictionary of Literary Biography*, vol. 238: *Russian Novelists in the Age of Tolstoy and Dostoevsky*, ed. J. Alexander Ogden and Judith E. Kalb (Detroit: Gale Group, 2001), 196–207; Sokolova, *P. I. Mel'nikov*, 89–102. See also the work of Sokolova and Vinogradov cited below.

40. "Under the influence of Dal' he began to write novellas, and at the same time grew interested in ethnography, creating fertile ground for mutual friendship." Kaminskii, "*Pavel Iva-

novich Mel'nikov," 375. Passages from his correspondence with Pogodin are cited extensively in L. Il'inskii, *"P. I. Mel'nikov (Andrei Pecherskii),"* *Russkii filologicheskii vestnik*, nos. 1 and 2 (1912).

41. Publication of *The Brothers Karamazov* began in January 1879.

42. S. Librovich recounts the mass of "author's edits" on the copies Mel'nikov sent to his publisher and suggests they were intended primarily "to convey as precisely as possible all the permutations and nuances of the colorful language of local folk." *Na knizhnom postu: Vospominaniia, zapiski, dokumenty* (Petrograd and Moscow: n.d. [1916?]), 148.

43. The first four installments of *In the Forests* appeared in January, March, May, and July. Boev's story was published in December. In January 1872 the next installment of Mel'nikov's novel appeared.

44. O. O. Milovanova, *"Remizov,"* in *Russkie pisateli: Biobibliograficheskii slovar'*, vol. 2 (Moscow: Prosveshchenie, 1990), 190. "The first one to open my eyes was Mel'nikov-Pecherskii, *In the Forests.* How was I to know about nature for my *Posolon'?* My childhood was all city, factory. And Mel'nikov-Pecherskii overflows with nature descriptions." Natalya Kodrianskaia, *Remizov* (Paris: Natalie Codray, 1959), 140. Remizov begins this passage by saying that "influence" isn't the right word in talking about a literary career; what matters is *who opens your eyes.* On Remizov, see Greta Slobin, *Remizov's Fictions, 1900–1921* (DeKalb: Northern Illinois University Press, 1991).

45. See chapter 5. M. V. Nesterov, *Iz pisem* (Leningrad: Izdatel'stvo Iskusstvo, 1968), 131. A less well known painting of Nesterov's, which announces its connection to Mel'nikov's novel— *Grad Kitezh (V lesakh)* (1917–22)—shares the interest of *Taking the Veil* in women, religion, and a forest setting. See chapter 5.

46. I. Nikonova, *M. V. Nesterov* (Moscow: Iskusstvo, 1979), 20.

47. See Bowlt, "Neo-Primitivism." On Bely's use of Mel'nikov-Pechersky, and his interactions with Mel'nikov's son Andrei (himself an important historian of the trans-Volga region), see Veronica Shapovalov, "From *White Doves* to *The Silver Dove*: Andrej Belyj and P. I. Mel'nikov-Pecerskij," *Slavic and East European Journal* 38, no. 4 (1994): 591–602. Simon Morrison discusses Rimsky's *Legend of the Invisible City of Kitezh and the Maiden Fevroniya* in *Russian Opera and the Symbolist Movement* (Berkeley and Los Angeles: University of California Press, 2002), 118. See also Robson, *Old Believers*, 77–94.

48. D. M. Mirsky, *A History of Russian Literature from Its Beginnings to 1900* (New York: Vintage, 1958), 213–14.

49. Dmitrii Chizhevskii, *History of Nineteenth-Century Russian Literature*, vol. 2, trans. Richard Porter (Nashville, TN: Vanderbilt University Press, 1974), 155–56.

50. Hugh McLean, *Nikolai Leskov: The Man and His Art* (Cambridge, MA: Harvard University Press, 1977), 672.

51. P. I. Mel'nikov (A. Pechersky), *V lesakh* (Moscow: Khudozhestvennaia literatura, 1989) is a well-bound, two-volume edition with commentaries that are more informational than scholarly (the editors do not indicate, for example, Mel'nikov's sources for any of the legends introduced in his text). The print run of this edition (based on a 1977 printing) was an impressive 150,000. The post-Soviet edition reflects the vastly changed world of Russian publishing: Eksmo-Press, a Moscow house, published a single-volume edition on very cheap paper (and with the romance-novel cover described above), with a much more modest print run of 5,000, which sold for sixty-five rubles (about $2) when I bought it in 2000.

52. Hoisington, "Mel'nikov-Pecherskii," 688. Hoisington takes his definition of romance from Harry Levin, *The Gates of Horn* (New York: Oxford University Press, 1963), quoted on 693.

53. Shapovalov, "Pavel Ivanovich Mel'nikov (Andrei Pechersky)," 203.

54. Lotman discusses the novel's position in a tradition of "ethnographic novels": L. M. Lotman, *"Roman iz narodnoi zhizni: etnograficheskii roman,"* in *Istoriia russkogo romana v dvukh tomakh* (Moscow-Leningrad: Izdatel'stvo Akademii Nauk SSSR, 1964), 390–415. The phrase *"byt i mif"* is S. Ia. Serova's, in her commentary to the 1989 *Khudozhestvennaia literatura* edition, vol. 1, 582.

55. P. I. Mel'nikov (A. Pechersky), *V lesakh* (Moscow: Khudozhestvennaia literatura, 1989), 2:269. Subsequent references to this edition will be given in the text.

56. Laurence Coupe, *Myth* (New York: Routledge, 1997), 2, 5.

57. Sheshunova claims that the "structure of the novel lacks any compositional unity." *Slovar' russkikh pisatelei*, 581. Hoisington suggests instead that Mel'nikov's "material . . . acquires a synthetic stylistic quality. The effect is that of a mosaic, of bits and pieces of narrative fitted together to form a unified whole." "*Mel'nikov-Pecherskii*," 692.

58. "The secret assignments which Mel'nikov undertook gave him, as is well known, the reputation among Old Believers of a destroyer. That reputation wouldn't have proved a significant hindrance to first-person ethnographic observation, but it would have completely obviated the possibility of working as a 'field' folklorist." G. Vinogradov, "*Opyt vyiasneniia fol'klornykh istochnikov romana Mel'nikova-Pecherskogo V lesakh*," *Sovetskii fol'klor*, no. 2–3 (1936): 344.

59. V. F. Sokolova, "*Eshche raz o fol'klornykh istochnikakh romana P. I. Mel'nikova-Pecherskogo V lesakh*," in *Poetika i stilistika russkoi literatury: Pamiati akademika Viktora Vladimirovicha Vinogradova* (Leningrad: Nauka, 1971), 180–87.

60. In addition to a Pantheon edition of Afanas'ev's tales in translation for older readers, there are numerous editions of individual tales for young readers, including more than a dozen versions of Baba Yaga tales.

61. Aleksandr Pypin, *Istoriia russkoi etnografii*, vol. 2 (St. Petersburg: Tip. M. M. Stasiulevich, 1891), 115. Pypin sets Afanas'ev's work into the context of German "mythological" schools of folklore; the theory of myth presented in *The Slavs' Poetic Views of Nature* was, according to Pypin, based on the work of Grimm, Shvartz, Max Muller, and others.

62. Vinogradov, "*Opyt vyiasneniia*," 350.

63. Georgii Vinogradov makes a close review of Mel'nikov's use of a variety of sources, with particular attention to Afanas'ev: "*Opyt vyiasneniia*," 347–68. While Sokolova affirms Vinogradov's claim, she notes that the works of Afanas'ev, Snegirev, Dal', and Kireevsky were "not the only source" of his folkloric material, which he "could have and most certainly did observe in life." Sokolova, "*Eshche raz*," 181–82. Kireevsky's collection of folktales was first published in 1848 (Mel'nikov in fact contributed some of its materials). The compilation of "superstitious rituals" belongs to I. Snegirev, *Russkie prostonarodnye prazdniki i suevernye obriady* (Moscow: V universitetskoi tipografii, 1838).

64. *V lesakh*, 1:566. The illustrated weekly *Niva* shows a genre picture in sentimental style of "the eve of *Troitsyn den'*," with peasants hauling birch boughs to decorate the exteriors of their huts. *Niva*, 1888, no. 24:596.

65. "Geo-cosmic" is Vinogradov's phrase. He describes the "cultural background" of the novel in terms of a "battle of two sets of principles: Byzantine-ecclesiastic and pagan-elemental." "*Opyt vyiasneniia*," 348.

66. Eve Levin has written an excellent critical history of the term, which originates in medieval sermons, and then makes its way into a diverse range of scholarly traditions—from late nineteenth-century ethnographers on into Russian émigré scholars of religion, Marxist historians, and feminist revisionist accounts of Russian culture. Levin, "*Dvoeverie and Popular Religion*," in *Seeking God: The Recovery of Religious Identity in Orthodox Russia, Ukraine, and Georgia*, ed. Stephen K. Batalden (DeKalb: Northern Illinois University Press, 1993), 31–52.

67. Women's roles in the novel are central, both as authoritative religious figures and as the embodiments of irrepressible, life-giving energies. They are certainly vulnerable to patriarchal power, but the staunchest defenders of Old Belief in the novel are in fact the matriarchs, whose vigilance gets turned primarily against their daughters and their desire for love.

68. The integration of many strands in a people's religious practice is obviously not unique to Russia. As I write these pages in March of 2008, it is Good Friday, and I'm alternating spells at the computer with the kneading of dough for hot cross buns—a traditional Good Friday food, which my cookbook tells me "dates to the pre-Christian era."

69. A. K. Baiburin, *Kalendar' i trudovaia deiatel'nost' cheloveka (Russkii narodnyi traditsionnyi kalendar')* (Leningrad: Znanie, 1989), 4.

70. V. B. Zaikovskii, "Narodnyi kalendar' vostochnykh slavian," *Etnograficheskoe obozrenie*, no. 4 (1994): 63. See also Margaret Paxton's discussion of traditional and official calendars in the Soviet era in *Solovyovo: The Story of Memory in a Russian Village* (Bloomington, IN: Indiana University Press, 2005), 266–343.

71. V. L. Komarovich discusses three different oral versions (which vary in their account of just *who* was attacking when the city disappeared) in *Kitezhskaia legenda: Opyt izucheniia mestnykh legend* (Moscow-Leningrad: Izdatel'stvo Akademii Nauk SSSR, 1936). Komarovich argues that Mel'nikov used the version published in *Moskvitianin* in 1843. See also Sokolova, "Eshche raz," 186–87.

72. N. V. Sheshunova suggests that Mel'nikov saw the future of Russia as lying with "educated Old Believers." "Mel'nikov," 581. If this is the case then Vasily Borisych seems a good candidate for the "hero" of the novel—he is an artist who combines deep love of the old ways with the ability to make judgments about authenticity and intention.

73. This is the same Riurik with whom the Polesye woods are associated in Turgenev's story. See chapter 1.

74. Mel'nikov's travels in the region brought him into contact with various non-Russian ethnic groups who also live "in the forests." Sokolova points out that the region has had a "mixed population" for centuries, and Mel'nikov actually published on the culture and beliefs of the Mordva people: "Ocherki Mordvy," *Russkii vestnik*, 1867. K. E. Korepova, "Fol'klor narodov povolzh'ia v istoriko-etnograficheskikh rabotakh P. I. Mel'nikova-Pecherskogo," *Fol'klor narodov RSFSR: Mezhvuzovskii nauchnyi sbornik* (Ufa: Bashkirskii gosudarstvennyi universitet, 1976), 166.

75. *Roget's Thesaurus* includes "morass, mere *or* marish . . . bog, mire, quagmire, sump, wash, baygall," among others (New York: Thomas Crowell, 1977), 293.

76. Lomonosov is the author of a famous ode on the northern lights: "Vechernee razmyshlenie o Bozhiem velichestve pri sluchae velikogo severnogo siianiia" [Evening Thoughts on God's Majesty on the Occasion of Great Northern Lights], 1743.

77. The wealth and specificity of languages' adaptation to particular places and needs are, argues anthropologist Hugh Brody, "integral to human skills in all societies." *The Other Side of Eden: Hunters, Farmers, and the Shaping of the World* (New York: North Point Press, 2000), 46–50.

78. "Tolkovyi slovar' V. I. Dal'ia," introductory essay to the 1978 reprint edition of Vladimir Dal', *Tolkovyi slovar' zhivogo velikorusskogo iazyka*, vol. 1. Mel'nikov delivered a lengthy appreciation of Dal' before the annual meeting of the Society of Lovers of Russian Literature in 1872, then published concurrently with installments of *In the Forests*: "Vospominaniia o Vladimire Ivanoviche Dale," *Russkii vestnik*, March and April 1873.

79. On the connection between natural history writing and tropes of the visual see Lynn L. Merrill, *The Romance of Victorian Natural History* (New York: Oxford University Press, 1989). See also "Representing the Environment," in Lawrence Buell, *The Environmental Imagination* (Cambridge, MA: Harvard University Press, 1995). Buell also addresses assumptions about "realism" and environmental writing in "The World, the Text, and the Ecocritic," in *The Future of Environmental Criticism: Environmental Crisis and Literary Imagination* (Malden, MA: Blackwell, 2005). See in particular "Questions of Mimesis: Environment as Invention and Discovery," 30–44.

80. "To a greater degree than science, literature releases imagination's free play, though the play is not entirely free, since the imagination is regulated by encounters with the environment both personal and mediated through the unofficial folk wisdom to which one has been exposed." Buell, *Environmental Imagination*, 94.

81. V. F. Sokolova, "K voprosy o tvorcheskoi istorii romanov P. I. Mel'nikova-Pecherskogo V lesakh *i* Na gorakh." *Russkaia literatura* 13, no. 3 (1970): 110. Vinogradov suggests a source for this "cucumber prayer" in Afanas'ev's collection: Vinogradov, "Opyt vyiasneniia," 357.

82. In Turgenev's "The Singers" the narrator gives us four lines from a song whose words are clearly difficult to pick out "against the endless embellishments and additions." This reproduces the situation of an outsider hearing a song for the first time. Turgenev, *Polnoe sobranie sochinenii i pisem v dvadtsati vos'mi tomakh*, vol. 4 (Moscow-Leningrad: Izdatel'stvo akademii nauk SSSR, 1963), 238.

83. Bel'skii drew on various chronicles and collections of folk songs in addition to Mel'nikov's novel. Richard Taruskin, *"Legend of the Invisible City of Kitezh and the Maiden Fevroniya, The." The New Grove Dictionary of Opera*, ed. Stanley Sadie. Grove Music Online. Oxford Music Online, http://www.oxfordmusiconline.com/subscriber/article/grove/music/O009112. Rimsky himself was deeply committed to the opera and its exploration of Russian religious tradition, viewing it as the culmination of decades of "intellectual and creative searching." G. A. Orlov, *"Tvorcheskaia evoliutsiia Rimskogo-Korskova v 90-e I 900-e gody i* Skazanie o nevidimom grade Kitezhe," *Voprosy muzykoznaniia* (Moscow: Gosudarstvennoe muzykal'noe izdatel'stvo, 1960), 531.

84. Mel'nikov-Pechersky's footnote to this passage explains that "there are at least twelve rounds [*koleno*] of the nightingale's song, and the Kursk nightingale has even more. Each round has its own name" (421). Mel'nikov's terms for the nightingale song passages appear to be his own inventions; I have left them in the original rather than attempting to translate from avian Russian into avian English.

85. Nastya is pregnant by Aleksei at the time of her death. The novel is in fact quite frank—and un-Victorian—about prenuptial sexuality, which it tends to attribute to the erotic intrusions of "Tipsy Yar."

86. Rose Glickman, "The Peasant Woman as Healer," in *Russia's Women: Accommodation, Resistance, Transformation*, ed. Barbara Evans Clements, Barbara Alpern Engel, and Christine Worobec (Berkeley and Los Angeles: University of California Press, 1991), 151.

87. Scholars of various persuasions have identified maternity as key to understandings of Russian culture: *mat' syra zemlia* (Moist Mother Earth), *rodina-mat'* (the motherland), *Bogoroditsa* (God-bearer), *mat'-Rossiia* (Mother Russia) are all instantiations of this symbolic. Georgii Fedotov's study of pre-Christian Russian culture includes "the Cult of Mother Earth" as one of its organizing categories. Fedotov, *The Russian Religious Mind* (New York: Harper, 1960), 11–15. Joanna Hubbs offers evidence from archaeology and psychoanalysis in her feminist reading: Hubbs, *Mother Russia: The Feminine Myth in Russian Culture* (Bloomington: Indiana University Press, 1988). See also Elena Hellberg-Hirn, *Soil and Soul*, and S. D. Domnikov, *Mat-zemlia i tsar'-gorod: Rossiia kak traditsionnoe obshchestvo* (Moscow: Aleteia, 2002).

88. Vinogradov notes that "these images lead once more to Afanas'ev's book." *"Opyt vyiasneniia,"* 354.

89. Boev, *"Kartiny,"* 18–19.

90. Anne Lounsbery, "Dostoevskii's Geography: Centers, Peripheries, and Networks in *Demons," Slavic Review* 66, no. 2 (Summer 2007): 215.

91. David Harvey, *Justice, Nature and the Geography of Difference* (Oxford: Blackwell, 1996), 297.

92. Vinogradov, *"Opyt vyiasneniia,"* 367.

93. Lotman, *"Roman iz narodnoi zhizni,"* 408.

94. Quoted in Sokolova, *"Eshche raz,"* 184.

95. The novel creates a steady refrain of laments about "fallen" Moscow. In Boev's novella, the epicenter of fallen contemporaneity is St. Petersburg—hotbed of radicalism and empty rhetoric.

96. Leonov's memoir is a contribution to *Sergii Radonezhskii*, ed. Vladimir Aleksandrovich Desiatnikov (Moscow: Patriot, 1991).

97. W. J. T. Mitchell, "Holy Landscape," *Critical Inquiry* 26 (Winter 2000): 196.

3. GEOGRAPHIES OF LOSS

1. Alec Paul, "Russian Landscape in Literature: Lermontov and Turgenev," in *Geography and Literature: A Meeting of the Disciplines*, ed. William E. Mallory and Paul Simpson-Housley (Syracuse, NY: Syracuse University Press, 1987), 122.

2. Did the devastating winter have something to do with the poor harvest referred to in "Ovsiannikov the Freeholder"? In that story the upright peasant farmer considers it a "sin to sell grain—a gift from God, and in '40, when there was famine everywhere and terrible inflation, he gave his whole reserve supply to neighboring landowners and peasants." Ivan Turgenev, *Polnoe sobranie sochinenii i pisem v dvadtsati vos'mi tomakh*, vol. 4 (Moscow-Leningrad: Izdatel'stvo akademii nauk SSSR, 1963), 62.

3. Stepan Alekseevich Maslov, 1793–1879, spent over thirty years as managing secretary of the Moscow Society for Agriculture. For a brief biography see "*Stepan Alekseevich Maslov. Nekrolog*," *Russkii arkhiv* 17, no. 6 (1879): 258–64. Maslov also figures in Joseph Bradley's recent account of the Moscow Agricultural Society: *Voluntary Associations in Tsarist Russia: Science, Patriotism, and Civil Society* (Cambridge, MA: Harvard University Press, 2009), 72–74.

4. Karl Tseplin, "*O sostoianii khlebopashestva i lesovodstva v Moskovskoi gubernii*," *Zhurnal sel'skago khoziaistva i ovtsevodstva*, 1842, no. 7:29.

5. An entry in the *Lesnoi zhurnal* from 1843 contains an explanation of "*pravil'noe*" forestry: "Since the time when rule-based management [*pravil'noe khoziaistvo*] has begun to be introduced in woodlands, and more thought given to careful conservation [*sokhranenie*] of them, in order to avert an insufficiency of wood and obtain sustainable yield [*postoiannaia dobycha*], privately owned forests have received the most attention from forest scientists, since such forests more than others have suffered depletion." "*O vygodneishem vozobnovlenii, preimushchestvenno nebol'shikh vladel'cheskikh ili chastnykh lesov*," *Lesnoi zhurnal*, 1843, no. 8:127–28. The term *pravil'noe lesnoe khoziaistvo* is used in the 1888 act; P. I. Zhudra, in his Forest Society address four years earlier, used the term *ratsional'no*—"forests should be protected and rationally managed" (*berech' les i ratsional'no v nem khoziaistvovat'*). Zhudra, *Lesnoi zhurnal*, 1884, no. 1:19. I am very grateful to Stephen Brain for his suggestion that "rule based" (from the root of the word *pravil'noe*, i.e., *pravilo*) would be the best way to deal with this thorny matter of translation.

6. A. S., "*Dilletantizm v lesovodstve*," *Lesnoi zhurnal*, 1850, no. 18:142.

7. Vladimir Dal', "*Dendrometr*," *Tolkovyi slovar'*, vol. 1, 427. On German forestry in the eighteenth century and its development of statistical approaches to forest management see Henry E. Lowood, "The Calculating Forester: Quantification, Cameral Science, and the Emergence of Scientific Forestry Management in Germany," in *The Quantifying Spirit in the 18th Century*, ed. Tore Frangsmyr, J. L. Heilbron, and Robin E. Rider (Berkeley and Los Angeles: University of California Press, 1990), 315–42.

8. G. Koenig, "*O sokhranenii lesov i derev*," with afterword by S. Maslov, *Zhurnal sel'skago khoziaistva i ovtsevodstva*, Moscow, 1841, no. 8:111–12. There is brief biographical information on Koenig in the Brokgaus and Efron encyclopedia, where his first name is given as Gotfab.

9. Speaking in 1884, Zhudra suggests that Murchison made his remark "almost a century ago." P. I. Zhudra, *Lesnoi zhurnal*, 11. Enessa Istomina cites Zhudra in referring to Murchison's visit to Russia "in the beginning of the 19th century." E. Istomina, "*Lesookhranitel'naia politika rossii v XVIII–nachale XX veka*," *Otechestvennaia istoriia*, 1995, no. 4:40. Iakov Veinberg in his 1878 call for increased regulations of forestry on private lands refers to Murchison's audience with Nicholai Pavlovich: "*Vopros ob umen'shenii vod i istochnikakh i rekakh*," *Russkii vestnik*, 1878, no. 2:515. Murchison first visited Russia in 1841; his expeditions to Russia (and his lifelong affection for the country) are discussed in Robert A. Stafford, *Scientist of Empire: Sir Roderick Murchison, Scientific Exploration and Victorian Imperialism* (Cambridge: Cambridge University Press, 1989), 11–16. See also Alexander Vucinich, *Science in Russian Culture: A History to 1860* (Stanford, CA: Stanford University Press, 1965), 344–45.

10. Iakov Veinberg, "*Les i znachenie ego v prirode*," *Russkii vestnik*, 1879, no. 1:22. The commission's report was reviewed by the Transport Ministry (*Glavnoe upravlenie putei soobshcheniia*) and then passed on to the Ministry of State Properties.

11. Veinberg, "*Les i znachenie ego v prirode*," 24, 26.

12. Dorothy Atkinson, "The Library of the Free Economic Society," *Slavic Review* 39, no. 1 (March 1980): 97. See also Bradley, *Voluntary Associations*, chap. 2.

13. When the journal started up publication again in 1871 it was under the auspices of the Petersburg Forest Society, with sections devoted to forest management, reviews of forest law, and articles on the market for wood. The editors' announced intention was to "provide means of communication with those involved and interested in forestry—*lesnichie, lesovladel'tsy, lesopromyshlenniki*." *Lesnoi zhurnal*, 1871, no. 1:2. See also "*Istoricheskaia spravka*," *Lesnoi zhurnal*, cited at http://www.agtu.ru/history_forest.html.

14. "*Istoricheskaia spravka*," p. 1.

15. *Lesnoi zhurnal*, 1843, no. 2 [history of hunting in various countries]; 1847, no. 8: Louis Viardot on hunting in Russia. Viardot was a close friend of Ivan Turgenev.

16. There was a regular column on forestry abroad—"*Inostrannoe lesovodstvo*." On forestry in France: *Lesnoi zhurnal*, 1847, no. 48; in British North America (i.e., Canada), 1848, no. 3; in England, June 1849.

17. See for example *Lesnoi zhurnal*, 1844, no. 3 [forests in the Urals]; 1844, no. 10 [general report on the state of crown forests in 1843]; 1845, no. 6 [forests in the Kharkov region]; 1847, no. 23 [on the Orel region, cited above]. Reports on forestry on estates owned by the Stroganovs were published in 1844, no. 2 and no. 6.

18. *Lesnoi zhurnal*, 1841, no. 3.

19. This is the same essay cited at the beginning of chapter 1. "*O sostoianii khlebopashestva i lesovodstva v Moskovskoi gubernii*," *Zhurnal sel'skago khoziaistva i ovtsevodstva*, 1842, no. 7:5.

20. Maslov, "*Pribavlenie k predydushchei stat'e*," afterword to Koenig, "*O sokhranenii lesov i derev*," 115.

21. Marsh goes on to quote Auguste Jourdier's memoirs of Russia: "Instead of a vast territory with immense forests, which we expect to meet, one sees only scattered groves thinned by the wind or by the axe of the *moujik*." *Man and Nature* (Seattle: University of Washington Press, 2003), 255. *Man and Nature* appeared in Russian translation in 1866: *Chelovek i priroda, ili o vliianii cheloveka na izmenenie fiziko-geograficheskikh uslovii prirody* [cf. David Moon, "The Environmental History of the Russian Steppes: Vasilii Dokuchaev and the Harvest Failure of 1891," *Transactions of the Royal Historical Society* 15 (2005): 149–74. Translation cited in footnote 40.] Nikolai Zobov refers to *Man and Nature* in an 1871 review article that discusses influences of the forest on climate: "*Bibliograficheskoe obozrenie: Klimaticheskoe vliianie lesa*," *Lesnoi zhurnal*, 1871, no. 3:28–40. Marsh's work is referred to on p. 37.

22. The Petrovsko-Razumovskaya Agrarian and Forestry Academy was founded in 1865 and was intended to train agronomists and foresters for new, post-Emancipation realities. It was renamed the Timiriazev Academy in 1923 in honor of the great Russian botanist. Fedor Arnol'd was the director of the academy from 1876 to 1883.

23. S. Luginin, "*Ob okhranenii lesov prinadlezhashchikh chastnym litsam*," *Russkii vestnik*, 1863, no. 7: 229.

24. N. V. Ponomarev, *Sovremennoe sostoianie gosudarstvennogo, obshchestvennogo i chastnogo lesnogo khoziaistva v Rossii* (St. Petersburg: Tipografiia V. Kirshbauma, 1901), 281. A. A. Maksimov gives the figure of 30 percent of land sold; he also gives figures for deforestation by *guberniia* in the period from the Emancipation to 1884. A. A. Maksimov, "*Istoriia razvitiia sel'skokhoziaistvennogo landshafta v lesnoi zone evropeiskoi chasti SSSR*," *Okhrana prirody i zapovednoe delo v SSSR* (Moscow: Izdatel'stvo Akademii nauk, 1962), 120–21. R. A. French cites statistical work done by M. A. Tsvetkov indicating that about 28 percent of Russia's European forests were lost between 1696 and 1914. R. A. French, "Russians and the Forest," in *Studies in Russian Historical Geography*, vol. 1 (London: Academic Press, 1983), 41.

25. Istomina, *"Lesookhranitel'naia politika,"* 43.

26. Ibid., 44. The report was published in 1875.

27. Veinberg, *"Vopros ob umen'shenii vod,"* 526.

28. Istomina, *"Lesookhranitel'naia politika,"* 43.

29. *"Chashki, ploshki, bliuda v Zavozh'e na stankakh tochat,"* V *lesakh*, 1:7. Production and trade in such wooden items is the source of the Patap Maksimych's wealth. On the role of handicrafts in the peasant economy see David Moon, *The Russian Peasantry, 1600–1930: The World the Peasants Made* (London: Longman, 1999), 143–50. Moon points out that handicraft production was of particular importance in the "forest heartland."

30. *"Vedomost' o potrebnostiakh krest'ianina v lesnykh materialakh, na 1844 god, v Il'inskom okruge, v imenii grafini S. V. Stroganovoi, v Permskoi gubernii."* Published in *Lesnoi zhurnal*, 1844, no. 6:365–66.

31. Z. G., *"Opyt sokhranieniia lesa ot naprasnago istrebleniia,"* *Lesnoi zhurnal*, 1849, no. 8:61–63.

32. Aleksandr Rudzkii, *"Ocherki Russkogo lesovodstva,"* *Russkii vestnik*, August 1868, 464. Subsequent references to this essay will be given in the text. Sergei Maslov also notes that Russians may face the same fate as Europeans, who only heat one or two rooms. The author of the 1849 *Lesnoi zhurnal* article on forest protection notes the need for wood to fire "distilleries, sugarbeet and potato-starch processing and other factories dependent on combustion." Z. G., *"Opyt sokhraneniia,"* 61.

33. F. Treimut, *"Vygodno li dlia lesovladel'tsa lesnoi mestnosti vesti pravil'noe lesnoe khoziaistvo?"* in *Trudy imperatorskago vol'nago ekonomicheskago obshchestva*, 1871, vol. 3, 164.

34. Rudzkii, *"Ocherki Russkogo lesovodstva,"* 460. Fedor Arnol'd had worked on systematically mapping Russian state forests from the 1840s. F. Arnol'd, *"O sobiranii materialov dlia lesnoi statistiki Rossii,"* *Lesnoi zhurnal*, 1850, no. 5:37–38; no. 6:45–46. See also Teplyakov, *A History of Russian Forestry and Its Leaders* (Pullman: Washington State University Press, 1998), 6.

35. The pine forests along the shore of the Sura River in the Penza district had been designated as restricted conservation areas under Peter the Great. In 1864 they were reclassified as a model forest, with Rudzkii as director. M. E. Tkachenko, *"Professor Aleksandr Felitsianovich Rudzkii,"* *Lesnoe khoziaistvo*, 1949, no. 3:38. The forest is now a "monument of nature"—one of the categories of protected ecosystems and landscapes in Russia. *"Akhunskii sosnovyi bor,"* accessed online at http://n.inpenza.ru/ahun_sosn_bor.htm. The institution in 1876 of prizes for model forestry was part of state-sponsored efforts to encourage better forest practices. See Istomina, *"Lesookhranitel'naia politika,"* 45.

36. According to Tsvetkov's figures, the Chernigov district went from being approximately 35 percent forested in the late seventeenth century to just under 15 percent forested in 1914. Cited in French, "Russians and the Forest," 40.

37. A. Rudzkii, *"Ocherki sovremennogo evropeiskogo lesovodstva,"* *Zhurnal ministerstva gosudarstvennykh imushchestv*, 1862.

38. Tkachenko, *"Professor Aleksandr Felitsianovich Rudzkii,"* 38.

39. N. Zobov, *"Petr velikii kak pervyi lesovod v Rossii,"* *Lesnoi zhurnal*, 1872, no. 2:1–6. Istomina notes that most European states enforced their rights to woodland for naval use, regardless of whether they were crown lands or privately owned. *"Lesookhranitel'naia politika,"* 36. The point is illustrated by William Cronon's account of forests in the Massachusetts colony: the crown laid claim to all mast trees of a certain diameter, laws which "the colonists violated . . . constantly." Cronon, *Changes in the Land: Indians, Colonists, and the Ecology of New England* (New York: Hill & Wang, 1983), 111. On regulation of woodlands under Peter the Great see also G. I. Red'ko and V. P. Shlapak, *Petr I ob okhrane prirody i ispol'zovanii prirodnykh resursov* (Kiiv: Libid', 1993).

40. Istomina, *"Lesookhranitel'naia politika,"* 37.

41. Ibid., 38, 39.

42. Rudzkii, *"Ocherki Russkogo lesovodstva,"* 466, 467.

43. Ibid.," 452–53. His term is *narodnye bedstviia*.

44. Brian Bonhomme, *Forests, Peasants, Revolutionaries: Forest Conservation and Organization in Soviet Russia, 1917–1929* (Boulder, CO: East European Monographs, 2005), 20.

45. Rudzkii, "*Ocherki Russkogo lesovodstva*," 468. The essay begins by laying out the economics of private forestry, and the numbers are telling: given market conditions post-1861, landowners could make more money by selling their forests and investing elsewhere. While Rudzkii notes that landowners might be swayed by other motives—"as landowners, capitalists, fathers or, finally, citizens"—there seems little evidence that the majority of landowners were so swayed. "From all sides one hears complaints about the immoderate use of landowners' woodlands, and since the Emancipation of the serfs an extraordinary quantity of forests have been taken away. While the exact quantity can't be determined with any satisfaction, nonetheless we cannot deny that it is enormous, and that only the tiniest number of felled areas are returning to woodland, a larger number of them are turned to pastureland, and still larger number stand abandoned" (467).

46. Veinberg, "*Vopros ob umen'shenii vod*," 514. Veinberg introduces parenthetically other examples where the state may legitimately infringe on property rights, including the construction of a factory in the middle of an urban area. Veinberg was invited by the Moscow Society of Naturalists (*Imperatorskoe Moskovskoe obshchestvo ispytatelei prirody*) and the Moscow Society of Friends of Natural History, Anthropology, and Ethnography (*Imperatorskoe Moskovskoe obshchestvo liubitelei estestvoznaniia, antropologii i etnografii*) to review the question "of the influence of forests on hydrology and climate." Ia. Veinberg, "*Les i znachenie ego v prirode*," *Russkii vestnik* 1879, 1:33–34.

47. *Polozhenie o sberezhenii lesov*. From *Polnoe sobranie lesov Rossiiskoi Imperii. Sobranie tret'e. Tom VII*, promulgated 1888, published 1890. The text of the law is available online at Russian Wikisource. My account of the law draws on Istomina, Bonhomme, Ponomarev, Fedor Arnol'd's *Russkii les*, and the entry in the Brokgaus and Efron encyclopedia.

48. Istomina's argument for the law's modest impact rests on her sense that rapid growth in population and industry would have led to greater exploitation of forest resources were it not for the law. "*Lesookhranitel'naia politika*," 47–48.

49. Fedor Arnol'd, *Russkii les*, vol. 1 (St. Petersburg: Izdanie A.F. Marksa, 1893), 14.

50. Ibid., 20.

51. Istomina, "*Lesookhranitel'naia politika*," 47; see also Douglas Weiner's important discussions of the history of conservation and the *zapovednik* system in Russia and the Soviet Union.

52. Arnol'd, *Russkii les*, vol. 1, 5–6. What Arnol'd calls the "northern colossus" seems uncannily like the sublime and forbidding Polesye of the opening paragraphs of Turgenev's 1858 story: the hunter stands on the shores of the Reseta River and surveys an "ancient forest" whose "elemental, untouched power spreads out . . . in front of the viewer," seeming to say "I have nothing to do with you." See chapter 1.

53. Arnol'd, *Russkii les*, vol. 1, 4.

54. Aleksandr Rudzkii, "*Affektirovannye tsennosti lesa*," *Lesnoi zhurnal*, 1879, no. 10:539–55. This essay is now available on the web page of Forest Forum, a branch of Greenpeace Russia. http://forestforum.ru.

55. Rudzkii, "*Ocherki russkogo lesovodstva*," 484.

56. See Joseph Bradley, "Subjects into Citizens: Societies, Civil Society, and Autocracy in Tsarist Russia," *The American Historical Review* 107, no. 4 (October 2002): 1094–1123.

57. Mel'nikov's *In the Forests* was published in *Russkii vestnik* from 1871 through 1874; *Anna Karenina* began publication in the same journal in 1875, with the final installment appearing in 1878. Timiriazev's public lectures (delivered at the Polytechnic Museum in Moscow) were published in *Russkii vestnik* in 1876. Valuev's report was made public in 1875. Istomina, "*Lesookhranitel'naia politika*," 44.

58. F. Treimut, "*Vygodno li dlia lesovladel'tsa lesnoi mestnosti vesti pravil'noe lesnoe khoziaistvo?*" 163.

59. Veinberg, "*Les i znachenie ego v prirode*," 8.

60. Elizabeth Kridl Valkenier, *Ilya Repin and the World of Russian Art* (New York: Columbia University Press, 1990), 93.

61. For the critic Alexandre Benois, this aspect of Repin's work—its fixation on "content" and didacticism at the expense of more purely aesthetic or painterly concerns—was the painter's downfall. *Istoriia russkoi zhivopisi v XIX veke* (Moscow: Respublika, 1999), 274–78.

62. Valkenier, *Ilya Repin*, 93.

63. "*O krestnykh khodakh v g. Orle*," *Orlovskie eparkhal'nye vedomosti*, 1869, no. 2:122–29.

64. "*Za ikonoi*" was published in 1887, *V golodnyi god* appeared in 1892 and 1893. Korolenko's work of this period is discussed in the following chapter.

65. Aleksei Fedorov-Davydov, "*Kartina I. E. Repina 'Krestni khod v Kurskoi gubernii,'*" in *Russkoe i Sovetskoe iskusstvo: Stati'i i ocherki* (Moscow: Iskusstvo, 1975), 555. My account of the chronology of sketches for the painting is drawn from Fedorov-Davydov, who notes that the painting has a "long and complicated history" of creation. See also Valkenier, *Ilya Repin*.

66. I discuss Boev's story in the preceding chapter. Mel'nikov-Pechersky's *In the Forests* also includes a description of a religious procession in a woodland: *V lesakh*, 392–93.

67. Quoted in M. B. Milotvorskaia, "*Tolstoi i Repin*," in *L. N. Tolstoi i izobrazitel'noe iskusstvo*, ed. M. M. Rakovaia (Moscow: Izobrazitel'noe iskusstvo, 1981), 69.

68. Letter to Vladimir Stasov, I. E. Repin and V. V. Stasov, *Perepiska*, vol. 1 (Moscow-Leningrad, 1948), 137.

69. One conservative reviewer of the exhibit was particularly outraged by the whip in Repin's painting. "In an artistic sense the painting is absolutely without significance: . . . The constables are trampling the crowd, charging about in all directions, one of them has brandished a huge whip and is lashing someone with it. You see infuriated features, raised sticks. . . . It's a procession of the cross!" "*Peterburgskie pis'ma*," *Moskovskie vedomosti*, March 18, 1883, 3.

70. Neil Evernden suggests that what a generation of critics attacked as the "pathetic fallacy" is in fact testimony to the connection between human identity and understandings of place. "The Pathetic Fallacy is a fallacy only to the ego clencher. Metaphoric language is an indicator of 'place.'" Evernden goes on to link metaphoric language and anthropomorphism with an animistic sense of the connection of self and an animated "environment." "Beyond Ecology: Self, Place and the Pathetic Fallacy," in *The Ecocriticism Reader: Landmarks in Literary Ecology*, ed. Cheryll Glotfelty and Harold Fromm (Athens: University of Georgia Press, 1996), 101.

71. Nikolai Kostomarov, *Istoricheskoe znachenie iuzhno-russkogo narodnogo pesennogo tvorchestva*, 1905, quoted in Vladimir Boreiko, *Ekologicheskie traditsii, pover'ia, religioznye vozzreniia slavianskikh i drugikh narodov* (Kiev: Kievskii ekologo-kul'turnyi tsentr okhrany dikoi prirody, 1996), 41.

72. For an extensive discussion of Russian poetry and the natural world, organized primarily in terms of landscapes and motifs, see Mikhail Epstein, *Priroda, mir, tainik vselennoi: Sistema peizazhnykh obrazov v russkoi poezii* (Moscow: Vysshaia shkola, 1990).

73. Nikolai Nekrasov, *Stikhotvoreniia*, (Moscow: Nauka, 1987), 102. On folk poetry see A. N. Rozova, ed., *Russkie narodnye pesni* (Leningrad, 1988), 32.

74. "*Katalog XI-i vystavki kartin Tovarishchestva peredvizhnykh khudozhestvennykh vystavok*," in *Tovarishchestvo peredvizhnykh khudozhestvennykh vystavok: 1869–1889. Pis'ma, dokumenty* (Moscow: Iskusstvo, 1987), 254, 263. On oaks' connection in antiquity to the gods see Diana Wells, *Lives of the Trees* (Chapel Hill, NC: Algonquin, 2010), 228–29; they are also regarded in various traditions as "trees of justice": Nathaniel Altman, *Sacred Trees* (San Francisco: Sierra Club, 1994), 170–71. See also Dmitrii Kaigorodov, *Besedy o Russkom lese* (St. Petersburg: Suvorin, 1893), 26, 35.

75. The author of the review cited in note 69 separates the "talented members of the association" (including Shishkin) from those producing "naturalistic smears and tendentious slush." "*Peterburgskie pis'ma,*" 3.

76. The text of the Merzliakov poem can be found in *Russkie narodnye pesni,* ed. V. V. Varganova (Moscow: Pravda, 1988). On Merzliakov see Thomas P. Hodge, *A Double Garland: Poetry and Art-Song in Early-Nineteenth-Century Russia* (Evanston, IL: Northwestern University Press, 2000).

77. For a discussion of Repin's portraits of Tolstoy see Milotvorskaia, "*Tolstoi i Repin,*" 66–90.

78. The estate-museum's website includes an interactive map that identifies which woods and orchards on the estate were planted by Tolstoy and his wife, Sof'ia Andreevna. http://www.yasnayapolyana.ru/museum/manor/index.htm.

79. K. S. Semenov, "*Istoriia lesov iasnoi poliany za sto let i zadacha sokhraneniia i vosstanovleniia ikh*" (Kandidat's degree dissertation, Tula, 1954), 2.

80. *Tolstoy's Letters,* vol. 1, selected, ed., and trans. by R. F. Christian (New York: Scribner's, 1978), 6.

81. Semenov, "*Istoriia lesov,*" 2. Emphasis mine.

82. Semenov worked with "old maps and archival acts" in the 1950s to reconstruct Tolstoy's activities as a forester, and also drew up a plan for conservation and planting at the estate—by then a museum and park/preserve—that would honor Tolstoy's labor and intentions.

83. Nikolai Gusev, *Lev Nikolaevich Tolstoi. Materialy k biografii s 1855 po 1869 god* (Moscow: Izdatel'stvo Akademii Nauk, 1957), 238. The Shatilov estates where Maier had worked until his death in 1860 were later to receive state prizes for their efforts in reforestation. See Istomina, "*Lesookhranitel'naia politika,*" 45. Semenov's account of Tolstoy's plantings formed the basis for his own forest management plan for the estate. Oaks at Yasnaya were seriously compromised in the 1980s by the nearby chemical plant in Shchekino. See Alessandra Stanley, "At Tolstoy's Estate, Bones of Contention," *New York Times,* March 7, 1994.

84. Semenov, "*Istoriia lesov,*" 4. See also "*K istorii proekta lesonasazhdeniia L. N. Tolstogo,*" in *L. N. Tolstoi, Gosudarstvennyi literaturnyi muzei,* ed. N. N. Gusev, vol. 1 (Moscow: Izdatel'stvo gosudarstvennogo literaturnogo muzeia, 1938), 262–65.

85. Ivan Turgenev, *Polnoe sobranie sochinenii, Pis'ma* vol. 3:175. Tolstoy uses the word *literator* as a term of derision for writers consumed with the infighting of writers' circles. For a discussion of Tolstoy's falling out with the literary magnates who greeted his early work, including both Turgenev and Nekrasov, see B. M. Eikhenbaum, *Lev Tolstoi* (Munich: W. Finck, 1968), 261–322.

86. Tolstoy first referred to what would become *Anna Karenina* in 1870 but only began work in earnest in 1873. See C. J. G. Turner, *A Karenina Companion* (Waterloo, Ontario: Wilfred Laurier University Press, 1993).

87. B. M. Eikhenbaum suggests that Tolstoy's "first crisis"—his repudiation of literature and the Petersburg literary circles for the labors associated with his estate—was a "crisis of the epoch," analogous in many ways with the fundamental social shifts occurring in Russian society in the early 1860s. *Lev Tolstoi,* 334.

88. Leo Tolstoy, *Anna Karenina,* trans. Rosemary Edmonds (New York: Penguin, 1978), 183, 688.

89. Veinberg, "*Vopros ob umen'shenii vod,*" 513. The final installment of *Anna Karenina* had been published in *Russkii vestnik* in April of the previous year.

90. Tolstoy, *Anna Karenina,* 689. The reference is to the efforts of Sviazhky and Vronsky at "modern" agriculture. Quoted in Bradley, *Voluntary Associations,* 300, note 100. Thaer's work was translated into Russian by Sergei Maslov.

91. The parallels between Berry and Tolstoy deserve treatment elsewhere. For a beginning, I would suggest Berry's essays in *The Unsettling of America: Culture and Agriculture,* and his many essays focused on the ethics of place and home, along with his critique of industrialized agricul-

ture. Berry's lifelong fidelity to his Kentucky farm parallels in some ways Tolstoy's to Yasnaya Polyana.

92. Dostoevsky, "A Landowner Who Gets Faith in God from a Peasant," *A Writer's Diary*, trans. Kenneth Lantz, vol. 2 (Evanston, IL: Northwestern University Press, 1994), 1074, 1073.

93. Tolstoy, *Anna Karenina*, 307. There have been suggestions that Sergei Valuev, minister of state properties, might well have served as a prototype for Karenin. Whether or not any particular historical figure served as a prototype, the fictional Karenin certainly represents an abstract and rationalized relationship to human problems, in contrast to Levin's much more embodied and place-specific ethic. See Turner, *Karenina Companion*, 150, for information on references to irrigation projects in the wake of the 1873 famine in the Samara district.

94. Leo Tolstoy, "*Perepiska Tolstogo s lesnym ob"ezdchikom A. Luzinovym*," *Literaturnoe nasledstvo*, vol. 37/38 (Moscow: Izdatel'stvo Akademii Nauk SSSR, 1939), 359–60.

95. Tolstoy, "*Perepiska Tolstogo s lesnym*," 359–60. Peasant understandings of rights to access or "usufruct" differed significantly from legal codes that put woodlands off limit: see Boris Mironov's discussion of customary law in late Imperial Russia: *The Social History of Imperial Russia*, vol. 2 (Boulder, CO: Westview Press, 2000), 309–10.

96. Section 3 of *Anna Karenina* includes both descriptions of Levin's physical labor on his estate and the reference to Karenin's bureaucratic work on irrigation policies referred to above.

97. A. Sovetov, "*Peterburgskoe sobranie sel'skikh khoziaiev*," *Entsiklopedicheskii slovar' F. A. Brokgausa i I. A. Efrona*, vol. 45:436.

98. Evgenii Markov (1835–1903) owned and farmed an estate in the Shchigrov district and had a remarkably varied collection of relatives, from Elena Gan and Mme. Blavatskaia to Sergei Witte. His best-known novel is *Chernozemnye polia* (Fields of Black Earth), which S. Vengerov calls a "saccharine idyll." His travel notes of the Crimea were highly regarded; Vengerov suggests they show "fine feeling for nature." Vengerov, "*Evgenii L'vovich Markov*," *Russkii biograficheskii slovar'*, online at http://rulex.ru. See also V. A. Viktorovich, "*Evgenii L'vovich Markov*" in *Russkie pisateli 1800–1917: biograficheskii slovar'*, vol. 3 (Moscow: Bol'shaia Rossiiskaia entsiklopediia, 1994), 526–28.

99. Zalomanov published in various venues in the 1860s and '70s; his father was a "trained estate manager" from the peasantry who graduated from the Agricultural School established in 1822 by the Moscow Agricultural Society—N. P. Zalomanov and his brother had also studied there. Z. D. Iasman, "*Russkie agronomy iz krest'ian v XIX veke*," *Voprosy istorii*, 1985, no. 12:168, 173.

100. Voeikov's essay appeared as the lead article in *Priroda i okhota*, 1878, no. 4:1–23. Veinberg, "*Vopros ob umen'shenii vod*." In the 1890s Vasilii Dokuchaev was charged with major investigations of the relationship between destruction of woodland in steppe regions and subsequent drought conditions. Together with Voeikov, Dokuchaev urged continued research into the exact dynamics of forest cover, climate, and precipitation levels. David Moon, "The Environmental History of the Russian Steppes: Vasilii Dokuchaev and the Harvest Failure of 1891," *Transactions of the Royal Historical Society* 15 (2005): 160.

101. E. L. Markov, "*Istreblenie lesov*," *Golos*, March 18 and 19, 1876. I am much indebted to Chris Ely for first alerting me to Markov's articles, which he scouted out while reading *Golos* as part of his own research in Russian libraries.

102. Dostoevsky was a voracious reader of the contemporary press, with interests that clearly included the fate of Russia's forests as well as contemporary suicides and the radical movement. On Dostoevsky's creative use of journalistic sources see Jacques Catteau, *Dostoevsky and the Process of Literary Creation* (Cambridge: Cambridge University Press, 1989); Irina Paperno, *Suicide as a Cultural Institution in Dostoevsky's Russia* (Ithaca, NY: Cornell University Press, 1997)

103. Dostoevsky, *A Writer's Diary*, 1:519–20.

104. Fyodor Dostoevsky, *The Brothers Karamazov*, trans. Richard Pevear and Larissa Volokhonsky (New York: Vintage, 1991). On birch whips see "Over the Cognac" (132) [book 3, chap. 8]; the narrator isn't quite sure whether the suit involves fishing rights or "wood cutting in the forest"

(10) [book 1, chap. 2]; Dmitrii Karamazov sets off on a wild-goose chase that involves the sale of a woodlot—a goose chase that almost kills him when the *izba* where he is spending the night almost burns down (377) [book 8, chap. 2]. Trifon Borisich is the innkeeper who has "more than half of the peasants in his clutches" (413) [book 8, chap. 6].

105. Dostoevsky, "Dream of a Ridiculous Man," in *A Writer's Diary*, 2:953. Subsequent references to this edition will be given in the text.

106. For a reading of the story attentive to the theme of language, and the way in which it juxtaposes "intuitivism" and rationalism, see Christopher Pike, "Dostoevsky's 'Dream of a Ridiculous Man': Seeing Is Believing," in *The Structural Analysis of Russian Narrative Fiction*, ed. Joe Andrew (Keele, UK: Essays in Poetics, 1982).

107. The question of Dostoevsky's relationship to science has received considerable attention, but that attention seems to have focused primarily on the "materialist" science associated with radical politics. See among others Michael Katz, "Dostoevsky and Natural Science," *Dostoevsky Studies* 9 (1988); and M. Gordin, "Loose and Baggy Spirits: Reading Dostoevskii and Mendeleev," *Slavic Review* 60, no. 4 (Winter 2001): 756–80, in particular note 11.

108. Istomina, "*Lesookhranitel'naia politika*," 47. In an 1873 review of German scientific work on forest hydrology and climate, Rudzkii speaks of the need for "scientific principles" in order to shape practical responses to what is already widely felt and acknowledged, and warmly proclaimed by "many talented authors"—"the impact of forests on the whole life of our people." "*Bibliograficheskoe obozrenie: o vliianii lesov na klimat. Po povodu sochinenii d-ra Ebermaiera*," *Lesnoi zhurnal*, 1873, no. 2:81.

4. JUMPING IN

1. The translator is then confronted with the dilemma of whether to translate Korolenko's title as *In the Wild and Empty Places* or *In the Wild and Holy Places*.

2. V. G. Korolenko, *V pustynnykh mestakh* [In the Wild and Empty Places], *Sobranie sochinenii v desiati tomakh*, vol. 3, 114. Subsequent references to this edition will be made in the text.

3. A. Derman, "V. G. Korolenko," in *Russkaia mysl'*, 1915, vol. 12. Quoted in M. K. Azadovskii, "Poetika *Giblogo mesta* (*Iz istorii sibirskogo peizazha v russkoi literature*)," in Azadovskii, *Stat'i o literature i fol'klore* (Leningrad: Gosudarstvennoe izdatel'stvo khudozhestvennoi literatury, 1960), 516.

4. This is particularly true of someone like John Muir; one thinks, too, of Annie Dillard and *Pilgrim at Tinker Creek*. Richard White provides a critical examination of the link between travel and nature writing in his essay on Peter Matthiessen's *The Birds of Heaven: Travels with Cranes*. White, "The Natures of Nature Writing," *Raritan* 22, no. 2 (Fall 2002): 145–61. On the connection between American environmentalism and religious rhetoric see Thomas R. Dunlap, *Faith in Nature: Environmentalism as Religious Quest* (Seattle: University of Washington Press, 2004).

5. M. G. Petrova, "*Korolenko*," *Russkie pisateli 1800–1917: Biograficheskii slovar'*, vol. 3 (Moscow: Bol'shaia rossiiskaia entsiklopedia, 1994), 78.

6. "At work he was an obvious failure. . . . For me that was without question due to his Don Quixote–like integrity." Korolenko, *Istoriia moego sovremennika*, in *Sobranie sochinenii*, 5:17.

7. Petrova, "*Korolenko*," 78.

8. These lectures appeared in *Russkii vestnik* throughout 1876 and 1877.

9. On Timiriazev see Daniel Todes, *Darwin without Malthus: The Struggle for Existence in Russian Evolutionary Thought* (New York: Oxford University Press, 1989), 156–65; and Alexander Vucinich, *Science in Russian Culture, 1861–1917* (Stanford, CA: Stanford University Press, 1970), 129–33.

10. V. G. Korolenko, *Izbrannye pis'ma v trekh tomakh*, vol. 2 (Moscow: Kooperativnoe izdatel'stvo "Mir," 1932), 320–21.

11. For an account of Korolenko's illegal reading as a student, see Petrova, "*Korolenko*," 78. One of Korolenko's Soviet biographers gives us an example of this kind of ex post facto scolding in his discussion of Korolenko's sketches of factory life, written in the same period as *In the Wild and Empty Places*: "Thus, while he came close to understanding the laws of capitalist production, Korolenko nonetheless proposed at the end of his sketches a purely populist solution to the problem, naïvely pointing to the organization of warehouse *artels* and savings alliances as a way out of the dilemma." A. K. Kotov, *V. G. Korolenko: Ocherk zhizni i literaturnoi deiatel'nosti* (Moscow: Gosudarstvennoe izdatel'stvo khudozhestvennoi literatury, 1957), 37.

12. The speaker was the "statistician and writer Plotnikov." Quoted in S. Prototipov, "*O nizhegorodskom periode zhizni V. G. Korolenko (Ianvar' 1885 g.–Ianvar' 1896 g)*," in *V. G. Korolenko. Zhizn' i tvorchestvo*, ed. A. B. Petrishcheva (Petrograd: Mysl', 1922).

13. On Korolenko's participation in the Multan case see Robert Geraci, "Ethnic Minorities, Anthropology, and Russian National Identity on Trial: The Multan Case, 1892–96," *Russian Review* 59 (October 2000), 544–50. The Karlinsky phrase is from his edition of Chekhov letters, *Anton Chekhov's Life and Thought: Selected Letters and Commentary* (Berkeley and Los Angeles, University of California Press, 1975), 318, note 7. Tolstoy notes in his diary for March 26, 1910, that he has read Korolenko's "*Bytovoe iavlenie*"—an extended, carefully documented protest against the return to capital punishment after the Revolution of 1905—and could not keep from sobbing; the next day he wrote Korolenko a letter of warm praise, expressing hope that the piece would have an impact. L. N. Tolstoy, *Sobranie sochinenii v 22 tomakh*, vol. 22 (Moscow: Khudozhestvennaia literatura, 1985), 373.

14. Dioneo, "*Predislovie*," *Pis'ma k Lunacharskomu* (Paris: Zadruga, 1922), 6. The writer of the introduction contrasts Korolenko's health and strength on returning from Yakutia with other exiles who "had no strength to withstand the icy embrace of the terrible frozen *taiga*, the stupefying atmosphere of a stinking Yakut yurt, a life lived literally in semi-famine, the slow transformation into half beast."

15. Korolenko, *Izbrannye pis'ma*, 2:69.

16. Azadovskii, "Poetika *Giblogo mesta*," 517. It is worth noting that Azadovskii cites a critique of Korolenko for not depicting the "real" natives of Yakutia, a criticism Azadovskii answers by noting that the Chukchi and Tungus live in areas of Yakutia quite different from Korolenko's and that Yakuts are presented in his stories in situations alongside the long-term Russian inhabitants. Azadovskii's final response is that Korolenko was "not an ethnographer" and that his narratives link Russians and Yakuts in a drama that is fundamentally political and economic. "*Yakutiia v tvorchestve Korolenko*," in *Stat'i o literature i fol'klore*, 496–97.

17. White, "Natures of Nature Writing," 150.

18. "[Korolenko] feels and depicts nature as no one since (or before) Turgenev has—a bit less picturesquely, perhaps, than Turgenev, but undoubtedly more *intimately* than even Turgenev." A. Derman, "*V. G. Korolenko*," *Russkaia mysl'*, 1915, no. 12:4.

19. "While Makar's fathers and grandfathers were struggling with the taiga, burning it with fire and cutting with iron, they themselves grew imperceptively savage." Korolenko, *Sobranie sochinenii*, 1:103.

20. Petrova, "*Korolenko*," 81. Korolenko gives an account of the founding of the monastery in the seventeenth century in section 11 of his narrative.

21. The other story of Korolenko's that gets compared to Turgenev is his "Marvelous Girl" (1880), which develops the motifs of Turgenev's "Threshold" (1878) and the image of a young woman standing on the threshold of revolutionary action. N. P. Izergina, "Porog *I. S. Turgeneva i* Chudnaia *V. G. Korolenko* (k probleme esteticheskogo ideala i khudozhestvennogo metoda)," in *V. G. Korolenko i russkaia literatura* (Perm': Permskii gosudarstvennyi universitet, 1987).

22. Rosa Luxemburg, "Life of Korolenko," first published 1919, translation by Frieda Mattick. Accessed online at http://www.marxists.org/archive/luxemburg/1918/06/korolenko.htm.

23. Sergei Protopopov, "*O nizhegorodskom periode zhizni V.G. Korolenko (Invar' 1885 g. – ianvar' 1896 g.*" in *V. G. Korolenko. Zhizn' i tvorchestvo*, ed. A. B. Petrishcheva (Petrograd: Mysl', 1922), 44–45. Korolenko's notebooks have been published separately, and include his drawings: *Zapisnye knizhki (1880–1900)* (Moscow: Khudozhestvennaia literatura, 1935).

24. Korolenko, "*O naznachenii literatury,*" *Sobranie sochinenii*, 8:294–97.

25. The notion that Russia had no past was memorably expressed by Petr Chaadaev in 1829 in his "First Philosophical Letter." *Philosophical Letters and Apology of a Madman*, trans. Mary-Barbara Zeldin (Knoxville: University of Tennessee Press, 1969), 31–51.

26. *V golodnyi god: nabliudeniia i zametki iz dnevnika*, *Sobranie sochinenii v desiati tomakh*, vol. 9, 102. On the famine see Richard G. Robbins Jr., *Famine in Russia: The Imperial Government Responds to a Crisis* (New York: Columbia University Press, 1975).

27. Morris Berman points out that Weber's designation finds a precursor in Schiller, for whom enlightened modernity was accompanied by the "disgodding" of nature. "The history of the West, according to both the sociologist and the poet, is the progressive removal of mind, or spirit, from phenomenal appearances." Berman, *The Reenchantment of the World* (Ithaca, NY: Cornell University Press, 1981), 69.

28. Turgenev, "*Nimfy*" (1878), in *Polnoe sobranie sochinenii*, 13:182–84. "Nymphs" is one of Turgenev's *Poems in Prose*.

29. There is an obvious parallel here with the role of the peasant in "Journey into Polesye" or Kasian in the story from *Hunter's Sketches*—peasants who jolt their gentry companions out of weepy nostalgia and oblivious going-on about the beauties of nature. See chapter 1.

30. The heroes of Russian folk narrative are the *bogatyrs*—but they don't usually do much work. Stepan here seems closer to someone like the Paul Bunyan of American folk mythology. See Daniel Hoffman, *Paul Bunyan: Last of the Frontier Demigods* (New York: Temple University Press, 1952).

31. On the attraction of Old Belief for Russian symbolists see Veronica Shapovalov, cited in chapter 2; and David Bethea, *The Shape of Apocalypse*, 116–17. S. V. Sheshunova notes the radically differing approaches to the Kitezh myth in Korolenko and the generation of Russian symbolists; the latter's fascination she connects to their broader interest in esoteric cults. She is critical of Korolenko for his "materialist world view and focus on social conflicts." "*Grad Kitezh v khudozhestvennoi litera-ture i problema bifurkatsii russkoi kul'tury,*" *Izvestiia RAN, OLIa*, 2005, nos. 7–8.

32. Leonid Ouspensky, *Theology of the Icon* (Crestwood, NY: St. Vladimir's Seminary Press, 1978), 191, 219. On landscape in icons see also Oleg Tarasov, *Icon and Devotion: Sacred Spaces in Imperial Russia*, trans. Robin Milner-Gulland (London: Reaktion Books, 2002), 232–49.

33. There is a kind of "double desecration" at work in the story, since Fyodor Karamazov manages to forget that the woman he is telling the story about was in fact the mother not just of Ivan, but of Alyosha. The desecration is both of the icon and of the sacred image of maternity and filial love.

34. Korolenko's prose here bears consideration for how it engages with traditions of seeing land and earth as feminine. For considerations of gender and the land in the American tradition see Annette Kolodny, *The Lay of the Land: Metaphor as Experience and History in American Life and Letters* (Chapel Hill: University of North Carolina Press, 1975); and Louise Westling, *The Green Breast of the New World: Landscape, Gender, and American Fiction*, Athens: University of Georgia Press, 1996. See also Pam Chester, "The Landscape of Recollection: Tolstoy's *Childhood* and the Feminization of the Countryside," in *Engendering Slavic Literatures*, ed. Pamela Chester and Sibelan Forrester (Bloomington: Indiana University Press, 1996).

35. In addition to his own practice as an amateur artist, Korolenko wrote on visual art. During his years in Nizhnii Novgorod he regularly reviewed exhibits of local artists' work. L. A. Gessen and A. G. Ostrovskii, eds., *Russkie pisateli ob izobrazitel'nom iskusstve* (Leningrad: Khudozhnik RSFSR, 1976), 215–37.

36. Pavel Zasodimskii, "*Lesnoe tsarstvo,*" *Slovo*, 1878, nos. 9–11:80–88.

37. These include essays by Zinaida Gippius and Mikhail Prishvin, poetry by Nikolai Kliuev, Anna Akhmatova, and Maksimilian Voloshin, and paintings by Nikolai Roerich and Mikhail Nesterov. See "*Grad Kitezh*" and "*Skazanie o grade Kitezhe*," in N. L. Brodskii, ed., *Russkaia ustnaia slovesnost': Temy—bibliografiia—programmy dlia sobiraniia proizvedenii ustnoi poezii* (Leningrad: Izdatel'stvo Kolos, 1924), 95–96.

38. The commission was convened in 1837; the quotation comes from an 1863 article in *Russkii vestnik*, cited in full, chapter 3.

39. Brian Bonhomme, *Forests, Peasants, and Revolutionaries: Forest Conservation and Organization in Soviet Russia, 1917–1929* (Boulder, CO: East European Monographs, 2005), 51, 54.

40. See for example Christopher Stone, *Should Trees Have Standing?* (Oxford: Oxford University Press, 2010).

41. Richard White, "Are You an Environmentalist or Do You Work for a Living?": Work and Nature," in *Uncommon Ground: Rethinking the Human Place in Nature*, ed. William Cronon (New York: W. W. Norton, 1996), 172.

42. Cf. Doug Weiner, "Man of Plastic: Gorkii's Visions of Humans in Nature," *Soviet and Post-Soviet Review* 22, no. 1 (1995): 65–88.

43. I give greater attention to the dilemmas of land ownership, poaching, and management in "Who Holds the Axe? Violence and Peasants in Nineteenth-Century Russian Depictions of the Forest," *Slavic Review* 68, no. 1 (Spring 2009).

44. V. G. Korolenko, *Pis'ma 1888–1921* (Petrograd: Vremia, 1922), 30.

45. Korolenko, "*O naznachenii*," 294.

46. Vladimir Solovyov, "*Vrag s vostoka*," *Sobranie sochinenii*, vol. 5 (St. Petersburg: Prosveshchenie, 1911–1913), 459. The essay first appeared in 1891. Solovyov quotes figures from the just-published reports of Vasilii Dokuchaev. For a recent discussion of Solovyov's work and its relationship to environmental questions see Oliver Smith, "Is Humanity King to Creation? The Thought of Vladimir Solov'ev in the Light of Ecological Crisis," *Journal for the Study of Religion, Nature and Culture* 2, no. 4 (2008): 463–82.

47. Solovyov and Korolenko corresponded in the early 1890s, when Solovyov undertook to publish a volume of essays protesting anti-Semitism in the Russian press and in government policies. On its publication in 1891 the book was confiscated by the censorship committee. Korolenko's letters to Solovyov are reprinted in *Izbrannye pis'ma*, 2:14–18.

48. V. G. Korolenko, "*Pis'ma k Lunacharskomu*," in *Zemli! Zemli! Mysli, vospominaniia, kartiny* (Moscow: Sovetskii pisatel', 1991). Bella Korchenova gives an account of how the letters came to be written in "*Zhivaia sovest' russkogo naroda*," *Vestnik online* 19 (330), September 17, 2003. Korolenko's denunciations in the Ukrainian and foreign press of the bloodletting of the "Red Terror" had drawn Lenin's attention; in 1919 he suggested in a letter to Gorky that Korolenko might benefit from some weeks in prison. Lenin suggested that Lunacharsky meet with Korolenko to "explain" to him the party's directives; the two met in Poltava in 1920 and agreed to the correspondence.

49. Korolenko, "*O naznachenii*," 297.

50. V. G. Korolenko, "*Pis'ma k Lunacharskomu*," 172. Subsequent references to this edition will be given in the text.

5. BEYOND THE SHATTERED IMAGE

1. Vladimir Lenyashin, "The 'World of Art' and the World of Culture," *Mir iskusstva: Russia's Age of Elegance* (St. Petersburg: Palace Editions, 2005), 24.

2. Anthony Smith, "Nation and Ethnoscape," in *Myths and Memories of the Nation* (Oxford: Oxford University Press, 1999), 150. See also his "Legends and Landscapes," in *The Ethnic Origins of Nations* (New York: Blackwell, 1987), 174–208.

3. Smith, "Nation and Ethnoscape," 149.

4. Belden Lane's discussion of how perfectly ordinary places come to be regarded as sacred is helpful here: "Mythic Landscapes: The Ordinary as Mask of the Holy," in *Landscapes of the Sacred: Geography and Narrative in American Spirituality* (Baltimore: Johns Hopkins University Press, 2001), 65–72.

5. The inaugural issue of an Orthodox journal "for children and their parents" shows a young boy looking pensive and somewhat troubled, with Nesterov's *The Boy Bartholomew's Vision* behind him. *Otrok: Pravoslavnyi zhurnal dlia detei i ikh roditelei* (2003), no. 1.

6. Thomas Newlin, "At the Bottom of the River: Forms of Ecological Consciousness in Mid-Nineteenth-Century Russian Literature," *Russian Studies in Literature*, special issue, *Russian Nature*, vol. 1, ed. Rachel May (2003), 87.

7. John Chryssavgis, *Beyond the Shattered Image* (Minneapolis: Light and Life Publishing 1999), 119.

8. Autism, Carol Zaleski reminds us, is a "disorder of attention." "Attending to Attention," in *Faithful Imagining: Essays in Honor of Richard R. Niebuhr* (Atlanta: Scholars Press, 1995), 130.

9. Quoted in Christopher Ely, *This Meager Nature: Landscape and National Identity in Imperial Russia* (DeKalb: Northern Illinois University Press, 2002), 219. On Polenova's role in the elaboration of fin de siècle style see Wendy R. Salmond, *Arts and Crafts in Late Imperial Russia: Reviving the Kustar Art Industries, 1870–1917* (Cambridge: Cambridge University Press, 1996), 8–9 and 46–79; and Alison Hilton, *Russian Folk Art* (Bloomington: Indiana University Press, 1995), 227–44.

10. See chapter 3.

11. On reactions to the painting see Nesterov, *Vospominaniia* (Moscow: Sovetskii khudozhnik, 1985), 124–25; and Sergei Durylin, *Nesterov v zhizni i tvorchestve* (Moscow: Molodaia gvardiia, 1976), 138.

12. "The well-known Russian publicist and economist V. P. Bezobrazov has testified that, in the mid-19th century, at every crossroads scattered among the fields and the forests of Vladimir region one would chance on a chapel or a timber post bearing an icon, for 'here there is an incalculable multitude of such posts.' To put icons in the trunks of old trees was a distinctive feature of Russian piety: such images, secretively hidden away from human eyes in the forest depths, seemed naturally to sanctify the wild space." Oleg Tarasov, *Icon and Devotion: Sacred Spaces in Imperial Russia*, trans. Robin Milner-Gulland (London: Reaktion Books, 2002), 46. See also the discussion of folk veneration of natural features, including trees, in A. A. Panchenko, *Issledovaniia v oblasti narodnogo pravoslaviia. Derevenskie sviatyni severo-zapada Rossii* (St. Petersburg: Aleteiia, 1998). Panchenko includes legends about icons that "refuse" to leave their place on trees or by springs (123).

13. Sergei Makovskii, "Nesterov," in *Stranitsy khudozhestvennoi kritiki. Kn. 2-aia.* (St. Petersburg: Panteon, 1909), 80.

14. See chapter 4—the words are Korolenko's in describing primitive icons of landscape.

15. Vasilii Rozanov, "M. V. Nesterov," *Sumerki prosveshcheniia* (Moscow: Pedagogika, 1990), 307–8.

16. Abbot Gleason, "*Russkii inok*: The Spiritual Landscape of Mikhail Nesterov," *Ecumene* 7 (2000) 3: 307.

17. Makovskii, "Nesterov," 80.

18. The text of Epiphanii's *Life* can be found in *Sergii Radonezhskii* (Moscow: Patriot, 1991) and in English in Serge Zenkovsky, *Medieval Russia's Epics, Chronicles, and Tales* (New York: Meridian, 1974), 262–289. The 1892 celebrations occasioned a broad array of published versions of the *Life*, along with accounts of Sergius's significance for Russian literature and culture. See for example Sergei Belokurov, *Prep. Sergii Radonezhskii i Troitse-Sergieva lavra v russkoi literature (Materialy dlia polnoi bibliografii)* (Moscow: Tipografiia Snegirevoi, 1892); "*Zhizn' i podvizhnicheskie trudy Prepodobnago Sergiia Radonezhskago, po drevnomu Slaviano-russkomu prologu i po chet'i-Mineiam Mitropolita Makariia. (Ko dniu 500-letiia ego*

pamiati)," *Strannik*, 1892, no. 9:4–19; "L.," "*Prepodobnyi Sergii Radonezhskii (Po povodu 500-letiia so vremeni ego blazhennoi konchiny, 1392–1892)*," *Khristianskoe chtenie*, 1892, nos. 9–10, 217–255. Margaret Ziolkowski gives an excellent account of the myriad ways in which nineteenth-century artists and intellectuals would have encountered saints' *Lives*. She cautions that "it is not always easy to identify the source of a given writer's knowledge of hagiography." Ziolkowski, *Hagiography*, 26. Visual sources further enrich (and complicate) the matter. To take but one example, Oleg Tarasov looks at one hagiological icon of St. Serafim of Sarov, "one among tens or hundreds of thousands disseminated among the people." Tarasov, *Icon and Devotion*, 75.

19. Nesterov, *Vospominaniia*, 24.

20. Ibid., 36.

21. Ibid., 35.

22. Ibid., 68.

23. Quoted in Durylin, *Nesterov v zhizni*, 61. In 1925 Durylin organized an exhibit of Nesterov's illustration work from the 1880s; Durylin himself describes the majority of these illustrations as "murky, lethargic and gray." On Nesterov's work as an illustrator see also Irina Nikonova, *Mikhail Vasil'evich Nesterov* (Moscow: Iskusstvo, 1984), 17–18.

24. Nesterov, *Vospominaniia*, 88–89.

25. Gleason, "*Russkii inok*," 302.

26. The most famous and influential figure in fin de siècle articulations of the feminine is the philosopher Vladimir Solovyov, whose mystical perceptions of Sophia, or the feminine instantiation of the divine, informed both his own philosophy and a wide array of poets and philosophers. See Judith Deutsch Kornblatt, ed., *Divine Sophia: The Wisdom Writings of Vladimir Solovyov*, trans. Boris Jakim, Judith Deutsch Kornblatt, and Laury Magnus (Ithaca, NY: Cornell University Press, 2009). Tatyana Novikov addresses the significance of Vladimir Solovyov for both Nesterov and the symbolist poet Alexander Blok: "Some Cultural Intersections: A. Blok and M. Nesterov," *Germano-Slavica* 10, no. 2 (1998): 15–27. On androgyny in symbolist culture see Olga Matich, "Androgyny and the Russian Silver Age," *Pacific Coast Philology* 14 (October 1979): 42–50

27. See in particular Alison Hilton, part 4 of *Russian Folk Art*, "Preservation and Revival of Russian Folk Art," and John Bowlt, "Orthodoxy and the Avant-Garde: Sacred Images in the Work of Goncharova, Malevich, and Their Contemporaries," in *Christianity and the Arts in Russia*, ed. William C. Brumfield and Milos M. Velimirovic (New York: Cambridge University Press, 1991).

28. Mikhail Nesterov, *Iz pisem* (Leningrad: Iskusstvo, 1968), 111. Nesterov is describing various projects—both a painting of Old Believer life ("so poetically described in the works of A. Perchersky") and material for his Sergius cycle, which took him to monasteries in the Moscow region.

29. This account is drawn from the memoirs of V. N. Baksheev, cited in Nikonova, *Mikhail Vasil'evich Nesterov*, 20.

30. See for example *Literary Album. In the Forests* by Mel'nikov. *From the Hermitage, Niva*, 1888, no. 30:748. Other early works by Nesterov published in *Niva* include *Pokhod Moskovskogo gosudaria peshkom na bogomol'e v XVII veke* (1888, no. 43:1061) and *Videnie Koz'my Minina* (1888, no. 16:409). Fedorov-Davydov refers to Nesterov's early paintings as "historical genre scenes"; Nesterov himself called the 1888 *Za privotornym zel'em* an "opera picture." Fedorov-Davydov, "Priroda i chelovek," in *Russkii peizazh kontsa XIX – nachala XX veka: ocherki* (Moscow: Iskusstvo, 1974), 76.

31. "I'll have two new paintings in the upcoming Peredvizhnik show: *Taking the Veil* (inspired at one point by the novel of [Mel'nikov] Pechersky, but *not* an illustration of the novel), and *The Annunciation*. Both paintings have a lyrical, quiet character." Nesterov, *Iz pisem*, 131.

32. Mel'nikov's novel, as I note in chapter 2, depicts the elder Marfa as still vulnerable to the emotional turmoil of youth. Nesterov seizes on that quality of intense and fragile beauty in his

young women. Andrei Bely, a symbolist writer of Nesterov's generation who was also influenced by Mel'nikov, turns the Old Believer women into grotesque harpies, with none of Mel'nikov's and Nesterov's delicate, vulnerable virginity. On the Bely-Mel'nikov link see Veronica Shapovalov, "From *White Doves* to *The Silver Dove*: Andrej Belyj and P. I. Mel'nikov-Pecerskij," *Slavic and East European Journal* 38, no. 4 (1994): 591–602.

33. Commentary to the painting at the website of the Nizhnii Novgorod State Art Museum: http://www.museum.nnov.ru/art/collection/excursions/silverage/nesterov.phtml.

34. Nesterov, *Vospominaniia*, 99.

35. Nesterov, *Iz pisem*, 33.

36. Nesterov, *Vospominaniia*, 113–14.

37. "The English were good. Their serious portraits, and also the group of so-called Pre-Raphaelites appealed to me a great deal." Nesterov, *Vospominaniia*, 114.

38. Ibid. Emphasis in the original.

39. William H. Robinson, "Puvis de Chavannes's 'Summer' and the Symbolist Avant-Garde," *Bulletin of the Cleveland Museum of Art* 78, no. 1 (1991): 2. See also Jennifer Shaw, *Dream States: Puvis de Chavannes, Modernism, and the Fantasy of France* (New Haven, CT: Yale University Press, 2002).

40. Nesterov, *Vospominaniia*, 115.

41. Shaw, *Dream States*, 159.

42. Robinson refers to Puvis's "suppressing spatial recession," "Puvis de Chavannes," 20. Shaw, *Dream States*, 151–52.

43. Robinson, "Puvis de Chavannes," 14.

44. Nesterov, *Vospominaniia*, 116.

45. Fedorov-Davydov suggests that "from this complex amalgam" of Bastien-Lepage, Polenova, Abramtsevo, and Sergius himself, Nesterov's painting was born. "*Priroda i chelovek*," 80.

46. Nesterov, *Vospominaniia*, 117.

47. Quotes in original. Nesterov, *Davnie dni*, quoted in Fedorov-Davydov, "*Priroda i chelovek*," 85. The Abramtsevo estate had earlier belonged to the Aksakov family: the father Sergei wrote important memoirs of his childhood that are canonic depictions of Russian nature; his sons Konstantin and Ivan were major ideologues of Slavophilism in the 1840s and '50s. See Rosalind Polly Gray, "Questions of Identity at Abramtsevo," in *Artistic Brotherhoods in the Nineteenth Century*, ed. Laura Morowitz and William Vaughan (Burlington, VT: Ashgate, 2000).

48. John Strickland, "Orthodox Patriotism and the Church in Russia, 1888–1914" (Ph.D. diss., University of California–Davis, 2001), 103.

49. A. M. Liubomudrov, "*Kniga Borisa Zaitseva* Prepodobnyi Sergii Radonezhskii," *Russkaia literatura* (1991) 3:118. The two other speakers were E. E. Golubinskii, a church historian, and Archimandrite Antonii (*hrapovitskii*), rector of the Moscow Theological Academy. Scott Kenworthy provides an extensive account of the planning and execution of the commemorations. "Memory Eternal: The Five-Hundred Year Commemoration of St. Sergius of Radonezh, 25 September 1892," in *The Trinity–Sergius Lavra in Russian History and Culture*, ed. Vladimir Tsurikov (Jordanville, NY: Holy Trinity Seminary Press, 2005), 24–55.

50. Kenworthy, "Memory Eternal," 54.

51. Sergius of Radonezh is celebrated on two days in the Orthodox calendar: September 25 is the saint's fall feast day.

52. Vasilii Kliuchevsky, "*Znachenie Prepodobnogo Sergiia dlia russkogo naroda i gosudarstva*," in *Sergii Radonezhskii* (Moscow: Patriot, 1991), 388. Subsequent references to Kliuchevsky's speech will be given in the text. This volume gathers materials devoted to Sergius, including the canonic *Lives* (in Russian translation) and various historic and literary commentaries; it was published on the eve of the six hundredth anniversary of the saint's death.

53. These are, interestingly enough, exactly the same years in which Frederick Jackson Turner was proclaiming the importance of wilderness for American character—along with a frontier

whose disappearance Turner lamented. See Roderick Nash, *Wilderness and the American Mind* (New Haven, CT: Yale University Press, 1967), 145–47. Mark Bassin contrasts Turner's "frontier hypothesis" with the work of the great historian Sergei Solovyov, noting both men's indebtedness to nineteenth-century geographical determinism. Bassin, "Turner, Solov'ev, and the 'Frontier Hypothesis': The Nationalist Significance of Open Spaces," *Journal of Modern History* 65 (September 1993): 473–511.

54. Nesterov, *Iz pisem*, 68.

55. There is growing evidence that Nesterov continued to produce images of Sergius well into the Soviet period, but those paintings were for obvious reasons not exhibited. Eleonora Khasanova, *"Neizvestnyi Nesterov,"* Bel'skie prostory, 2004, no. 10.

56. Nesterov, *Vospominaniia*, 31. Margaret Ziolkowski gives a brief account of reverence for Tikhon and Serafim of Sarovsk among nineteenth-century intellectuals and artists. Ziolkowski, *Hagiography and Modern Russian Literature*, 13.

57. Nesterov, *Vospominaniia*, 34, 79. Nesterov gives a loving appreciation of Father Fedor, noting that he had a "richly endowed nature, unusual in those days for the clergy. He was interested in everything, but more than anything, after his small wooden church of St. Sergius, he loved art in all its manifestations" (77–78). The description is an interesting contrast with Mel'nikov-Pechersky's depressing account of the low level of culture and ethics among the local clergy in the Nizhnii region. Mel'nikov was certainly a loyal son of Orthodoxy, but he attributed the strength of Old Belief in part to the wretched state of the parish clergy. See P. Usov, *Pavel Ivanovich Mel'nikov, ego zhizn' i literaturnaia deiatel' nost'* (St. Petersburg: Izdanie tovarishchestva M. O. Vol'f, 1897), 142–45.

58. Nesterov, *Iz pisem*, 111.

59. The church on the Abramtsevo estate was built in the early 1880s based on old Russian models. Artists working on the project also painted the iconostasis; Vasnetsov painted the icon of Sergius. See N. V. Masalina, *"Tserkov' v Abramtseve,"* in *Iz istorii russkogo iskusstva vtoroi poloviny XIX-nachala XX veka* (Moscow: Iskusstvo, 1978), 53–54.

60. Tarasov, *Icon and Devotion*, 75.

61. This image from the Sergius cycle represents an episode that has entered popular mythology surrounding Sergius but whose historicity has recently been challenged. See David Miller, "The Cult of Saint Sergius of Radonezh and Its Political Uses," *Slavic Review* 52 (1993): 4.

62. I. A. Iurtaeva discusses Tolstoy's interest in hagiographical texts in the 1880s and his own appropriation and recasting of Epiphanii's *Life* of Sergius in his story. *"K voprosu o traditsiiakh zhitiia v povesti L. N. Tolstogo 'Otets Sergii,'"* in *Literaturnoe proizvedenie i literaturnyi protsess v aspekte istoricheskoi poetiki* (Kemerovo: Kemerovskii gosudarstvennyi universitet, 1988), 123. Nesterov corresponded with Tolstoy in 1906, in connection with a portrait of the writer. When Tolstoy requested that Nesterov send him copies of some of his work, he sent, among others, *The Youth of the Blessed Sergius* and *The Boy Bartholomew's Vision*. Nesterov, *Vospominaniia*, 262–65.

63. *"Zhitie Sergiia Radonezhskogo,"* in *Sergii Radonezhskii* (Moscow: Patriot, 1991), 23, quoting Psalm 119, verse 103.

64. Nesterov, *Iz pisem*, 38.

65. Nesterov described the moment when he saw the girl as a *vision*: "Walking through the village once, I noticed a girl about ten years old, hair cut short, with large, wide-open, astonished blue eyes, sickly. Her mouth looked sorrowful, her breath was feverish. I was struck as if by a vision." *Vospominaniia*, 118.

66. I am grateful to Rev. Lynn Peyton for suggesting this, and for the generous hour she spent with me looking at the painting.

67. As Elena Nesterova puts it, "The painting is about how it becomes possible to follow the course of spirituality; about how and where the path which leads to sainthood begins." *The Itinerants* (St. Petersburg: Aurora, 1996), 92.

68. P. I. Mel'nikov (A. Pechersky), *V lesakh* vol. 1 (Moscow: Khudozhestvennaia literatura, 1989), 296.

69. Elena D. Polenova, Ekaterina V. Sakharova, and Vasilii D. Polenov, *Vasilii Dmitrievich Polenov, Elena Dmitrievna Polenova: Khronika Sem'i Khudozhnikov* (Moskva: Iskusstvo, 1964), 430.

70. She sees this as part of the reason for his disaffection with the early genre work he had done. Nikonova also notes that after the death of his wife, Nesterov turned increasingly to religious reading; he and the artist Vasily Surikov read the fathers of the church together. Nikonova, *Mikhail Vasil'evich Nesterov*, 18.

71. Fedorov-Davydov, *"Priroda i chelovek,"* 87.

72. Fedorov-Davydov refers to *The Hermit* and *The Boy Bartholomew's Vision* as "landscapes of contemplation rather than action." *"Priroda i chelovek,"* 88.

73. Durylin points out that Nesterov was the first in modern Russian art to use the triptych, a form that had been important both in medieval Western art and in Old Russian *diesus* and folding icons. *Nesterov v zhizni*, 160.

74. As with Vinogradov's comment about the "genuine sorrow" at the death of a traditional culture (chapter 2), one wonders just what was going through Durylin's mind as he pondered the sorrow that accompanied the loss of woodlands. He himself had lived through the ravages of Soviet modernization.

75. Boris Zaitsev, *Prepodobnyi Sergii Radonezhskii* (Paris: YMCA Press, 1925), 30–31. See also Liubomudrov, *"Kniga Borisa Zaitseva,"* 117. Liubomudrov suggests that Zaitsev is challenging visions of Orthodox asceticism and humility as being "monstrous deformations of human character." Zaitsev argues for the vitality and "organic qualities" of Orthodox monasticism exemplified in Sergius.

76. Ely, *This Meager Nature*, 218.

77. Cathy Frierson, *Peasant Icons: Representations of Rural People in Late Nineteenth Century Russia* (New York: Oxford University Press, 1993), 191–92.

78. Sergei Durylin records a conversation from 1940 in which Nesterov said he wanted to take his paints to the Tretyakov Gallery, where the painting was hanging, and work some on "Sergius and the bear." *Nesterov v zhizni*, 156.

79. Leonid Ouspensky and Vladimir Lossky, *The Meaning of Icons* (Crestwood, NY: St. Vladimir's Seminary Press, 1982), 128.

80. Jack Haney, *An Introduction to the Russian Folktale* (Armonk, NY: M. E. Sharpe, 1999), 69. See also Jane Costlow, "For the Bear to Come to Your Threshold: Human-Bear Encounters in Late Imperial Russian Writing," in *Other Animals: Beyond the Human in Russian Culture and History*, ed. Jane Costlow and Amy Nelson (Pittsburgh: Pittsburgh University Press, 2010).

81. On the Moscow zoo see P. A. Petriaev, *"Moskovskii zoologicheskii park: kratkii istoricheskii ocherk,"* in *Moskovskii zoopark. Sbornik statei* (Moscow: Moskovskii rabochii, 1949), 9–44.

82. Amy Nelson discusses anticruelty legislation in Russia in " 'The Body of the Beast': Animal Protection and Anti-Cruelty Legislation in Imperial Russia," in Costlow and Nelson, *Other Animals*.

83. Tatiana Goricheva addresses the role of "blessed animals" in Orthodox saints' lives in *"Sviatye zhivotnye,"* *Khristianstvo i ekologiia: Sbornik statei* (St. Petersburg: Russkii khristianskii gumanitarnyi institut, 1997).

84. Quoted in Durylin, *Nesterov v zhizni*, 156

85. Ibid., 152.

86. Novikov, "Some Cultural Intersections," 21

87. Polenova, *Vasilii Dmitrievich Polenov*, 466, 468. Nesterov is not mentioned in Polenova's list of painters participating—he was in Ufa all that fall and would return to Moscow only in late December, with a version of his "bear" painting (*Iz pisem*, 56). While he was perhaps unaware of Polenova's efforts at famine relief, he would surely have been aware of the famine itself, which by

November had become serious enough that the government was calling for the formation of voluntary anti-famine groups. Elizaveta Mamontova responds to Polenova that "life goes on in peace and quiet, but the newspapers destroy the peacefulness. It's horrible how powerless you feel in the face of this enormous disaster [*gromadnoe bedstvie*]" (469). Nesterov was quite aware of how little his own paintings represented contemporary reality; he commented on a canvas of Korovin's, shown at the 1893 Peredvizhnik exhibit, that it depicted "God's world as it really is; it's the exact opposite of my work." Durylin, *Nesterov v zhizni*, 153.

88. Both Vladimir and Apollinarii Vasnetsov saw early versions of the painting. Tretyakov viewed the painting but did not even discuss purchasing it for his collection—a slight that stung Nesterov. Durylin, *Nesterov v zhizni*, 147–57.

89. Fedorov-Davydov, *"Priroda i chelovek,"* 72, 74, 83.

90. Robinson, "Puvis de Chavannes," 11.

91. Nesterov, *Vospominaniia*, 41. The play was written by N. A. Polevoi (1796–1846) and first performed in 1840.

92. Lucy Lippard, "All Over the Place," in *The Lure of the Local: Senses of Place in a Multicentered Society* (New York: New Press, 1997), 7–8.

93. These are Barry Lopez's terms; Barry Lopez, "Landscape and Narrative," in *Crossing Open Ground* (New York: Scribner's, 1989), 64–67.

94. Georgii Fedotov, *The Russian Religious Mind* (New York: Harper & Row, 1946), 374. For a non-Orthodox point of view, see Stephen Cassedy, "Icon and Logos, or Why Russian Philosophy Is Always Theology," in *Flight from Eden: The Origins of Modern Literary Criticism and Theory* (Berkeley and Los Angeles: University of California Press, 1990), 99–120.

95. Durylin's biography of the artist, *Nesterov v zhizni i tvorchestve*, was published in the Lives of Amazing People series, by the publishing house of the Communist Youth League (Moscow: Molodaia gvardia, 1976), 152–53. A brief biography of Durylin is available at http://www.ozon.ru/context/detail/id/356645/.

6. MEASUREMENT, POETRY, AND THE PEDAGOGY OF PLACE

1. N. E. Buligin and G. A. Firsov, "Arboretum of the Forest Technical Academy in St. Petersburg, Russia," *Botanical Gardens Conservation News* 2, no. 6 (June 1996), http://www.bgci.org/worldwide/article/0090/. The arboretum and park are protected both as cultural-historical and environmentally important sites. That status doesn't necessarily bring increased funding, as the author of the brief history of the arboretum on the Forest Technical Academy's home page points out: http://ftacademy.ru/academy/botsad/.

2. "The present collection represents flora of six floristic regions of the world of 54 provinces of the Northern Hemisphere (according to the divisions of A. L. Tachtajan). Only 63 species (5.5%) are native to the environs of St Petersburg. The species from the Eastern Asiatic region (south Russia, Far East, Korea, Japan, China) predominate (348 taxa), followed by the circumboreal species (Europe, Siberia, Canada), Atlantic North America and Rocky Mountain regions. The fewest trees in cultivation are from the Mediterranean and Irano-Turanian regions (174 taxa, mainly garden hybrids)." Buligin and Firsov, "Arboretum."

3. Flooding is a dominant motif both in the city's history and in its mythologies of identity. Pushkin's "Bronze Horseman" (1833) inaugurated a long tradition of writing about watery destruction, including Dostoevsky's *Crime and Punishment*, Bely's *Petersburg*, and Zamyatin's "The Flood."

4. N. Zobov, *"Petr velikii kak pervyi lesovod v Rossii,"* *Lesnoi zhurnal*, 1872, no. 2:1–6.

5. Vladimir Boreiko, *"Kaigorodov Dmitrii Nikiforovich,"* *Slovar' deiatelei okhrany prirody* (Kiev: Kievskii ekologo-kulturnyi tsentr: Tsentr Okhrany Dikoi prirody, 2001), 152. Lev Razgon, *"Dusha otkrytaia prirode,"* *Priroda* 1983, no. 5:71.

6. A. S., *"Dilletantizm v lesovodstve,"* *Lesnoi zhurnal*, 1850, no. 18:142.

7. Biographical information is drawn from a variety of sources, some of which will be indicated below. There is a popular biography that includes an account of the history of the St. Petersburg Forest Institute by R. V. Bobrov, *Dom u zolotogo pruda* (St. Petersburg: Sankt-Peterburgskii nauchno-issledovatel'skii institut lesnogo khoziaistva, 2001); Bobrov worked with the Kaigorodov archives but provides less documentation for some of his sources than one might hope for. See also M. Tkachenko, "*D. N. Kaigorodov,*" in *Pamiati Dmitriia Nikiforovicha Kaigorodova* (Leningrad: Gosudarstvennaia tipografiia imeni Ivana Fedorova, 1925).

8. Dmitrii Kaigorodov, "*Ottsovskii sad,*" *Lepestki: nabroski i rasskazy* (St. Petersburg: Izdanie A. Suvorina, 1905), 77.

9. Kaigorodov served in Radzyn, north of Lublin in eastern Poland. A. F. Ignat'ev and A. N. Martynov, "*Dmitrii Nikiforovich Kaigorodov (k 145-letiu so dnia rozhdeniia),*" *Lesnoi zhurnal*, no. 3 (1991): 131. On Kaigorodov's education see also D. M. Giriaev, "*Fenolog, lesovod, publitsist,*" *Lesnoe khoziaistvo*, no. 12 (1991): 30.

10. "*Okhtinskii uchebno-opytnyi leskhoz.*" This is a history of the forest on the web page of the Forest Academy. http://ftacademy.ru/academu/filial/ohta/. Rudzkii's directorship of the forest, by then organized as the Okhtinskaia dacha, is discussed in V. I. Onegin, "*Sankt-Peterburgskaia lesotekhnicheskaia akademiia (Istoricheskii ocherk),*" *Izvestiia Sankt-Peterburgskoi lesotekhnicheskoi akademii* (St. Petersburg: Lesotekhnicheskaia akademiia, 1993), 11.

11. Aleksandr Krasnolutskii, "*Okhtenskie porokhovye zavody (1715–1917gg),*" *Okhtinskaia entsiklopeidiia: Malaia Okhta* (Moscow–St. Petersburg: Tsentrpoligraf, 2011), 327.

12. Ibid., 331.

13. Ibid., 332.

14. On Mendeleev's participation in smokeless gunpowder experiments at the factory see Michael D. Gordin, "A Modernization of 'Peerless Homogeneity': The Creation of Russian Smokeless Gunpowder," *Technology and Culture* 44, no. 4 (October 2003): 677–702.

15. In 1876 Arnol'd left the institute to take up the position of director of the Petrovsko-Razumovsky Academy in Moscow, and Rudzkii took over as professor of forest taxonomy. "*Arnol'd, Fedor Karlovich,*" *Zhizneopisanie vydaiushchikhsia deiatelei lesnogo khoziaistva Rossii*, at http://www.lesnyk.ru/vek19_8.html. See also chapter 3.

16. Razgon, "*Dusha,*" 61.

17. The factory still stands, on Svetlanovskii Prospekt: in the postwar era the enterprise became one of the engines of the city's transformation into a center of technical manufacturing. See Blair Ruble, *Leningrad: Shaping a Soviet City* (Berkeley and Los Angeles: University of California Press, 1989).

18. Bobrov describes in some detail the process of designing and building the house, which Kaigorodov undertook in consultation with his grown children. *Dom*, 12–21.

19. "*Lesovodstvennaia 'ekskursiia' v* Tolkovyi slovar' velikorusskogo iazyka Vl. Dalia," *Lesnoi zhurnal*, 1882. [Cited in Tkachenko, *Pamiati*]. D. Kaigorodov, *P. I. Chaikovskii i priroda: Biograficheskii ocherk* (St. Petersburg: Tipografiia A. S. Suvorina, 1907). Kaigorodov's translation of the essays of Eliza Brightwen is *Druzhba s prirodoi. Rasskazy Elizy Braitvin v izlozhenii Dm. Kaigorodova so mnogimi risunkami v tekste* [Friendship with Nature: The Stories of Eliza Brightwen as Presented by Dmitrii Kaigorodov] (St. Petersburg: Izdanie A. Suvorina, 1897).

20. A. F. Ignat'ev and A. N. Martynov, "*Dmitrii Nikiforovich Kaigorodov (k 145-letiiu so dnia rozhdeniia),*" *Lesnoi zhurnal*, no. 3 (1991): 132. Mikhail Tkachenko gives tantalizing but brief glimpses of this correspondence, which has not yet been systematically studied.

21. D. M. Giriaev states that Andrei Bolotov kept the first systematic phenological records in Russia; in the late 1830s the Russian Society of Horticulturalists called for observation of "leafing out, blossoming and when flowers have gone by." Giriaev, "*Fenolog,*" 29. On Bolotov see Thomas Newlin, *The Voice in the Garden: Andrei Bolotov and the Anxieties of Russian Pastoral, 1738–1833* (Evanston, IL: Northwestern University Press, 2001).

22. *"Russkoe Obshchestvo Liubitelei Prirodovedeniia,"* Razgon, *"Dusha,"* 64. In his essay on "Nature in the School of the Future" Kaigorodov lamented the use of the terms *estestvennaia istoriia* and *estestvovedenie* in Russian—both strict translations of the German *Naturgeschichte* and *Naturkunde*. In his own essays he tends to use the term *prirodovedenie*, translated here as "nature study." *"Priroda v budushchei shkole,"* in *Na raznye temy, preimushchestvenno pedagogicheskie* (St. Petersburg: Tipografiia Suvorina, 1907), 62.

23. Throughout his career Kaigorodov continued to deliver public lectures in St. Petersburg. The public auditorium of the Pedagogical Museum on Solyanoi pereulok hosted public lectures from 1872 on; speakers included the physiologist Sechenov, the historian Solovyov, the explorer Przheval'skii, and Kaigorodov. Mikhail Tkachenko, *"Polyni perechen' nauchnykh i populiarnykh trudov D. N. Kaigorodova,"* *Pamiati*, 17–37.

24. Tkachenko, *Pamiati*, 6.

25. N. Zobov, *Besedy o prirode. Kniga dlia chteniia v selakh i derevniakh* (St. Petersburg: Izdatel'stvo Gubinskogo, 1894).

26. A. P. Babushkin, *Istoriia russkoi detskoi literatury* (Moscow: Gosudarstvennoe uchebno-pedagogicheskoe izdatel'stvo, 1948), 300.

27. Among those involved in editing and publishing such journals were the feminist and social activist Mariia Tsebrikova; the translator—and brother of the poet—V. N. Maikov; Tatyana Pasek; and Ekaterina Sysoeva.

28. A. G. Dement'ev, *Russkaia periodicheskaia pechat', 1702–1894, spravochnik* (Moscow: Gospolitizdat', 1959), 455–56.

29. In addition to editing books of popular zoology, Vagner published pseudonymously, under the pen name "Kot Murlyka," a series of children's books that are still popular in Russia. Bogdanov's volume of nature sketches, *Iz Russkoi prirody*, is much more "edgy" than Kaigorodov's and includes a Darwinian fable about the cold, cruel world in which a mother mouse regales her children with tales of death and dismemberment. Modest Bogdanov, *Iz zhizni rodnoi prirody: zoologicheskie ocherki i rasskazy M.N. Bogdanova, Professora S-Peterburgskogo universiteta* (St. Petersburg: Tipografiia Iu. N. Erlikh, 1904). Vagner was also an avowed spiritualist. See Michael D. Gordin, "Loose and Baggy Spirits: Reading Dostoevskii and Mendeleev," *Slavic Review* 60, no. 4 (Winter 2001): 756–80.

30. As Jehanne Gheith notes, nineteenth-century periodicals directed at children deserve much more attention than they have tended to get. "Introduction," *An Improper Profession: Women, Gender and Journalism in Late Imperial Russia*, ed. Barbara T. Norton and Jehanne M. Gheith (Durham, NC: Duke University Press, 2000), 9.

31. D. N. Kaigorodov, *"Predislovie,"* *Iz rodnoi prirody: Khrestomatiia dlia chteniia v shkole i sem'e* (St. Petersburg: Izdanie Suvorina, 1902), ii.

32. Tkachenko includes publication details in his bibliography, *Pamiati*, 22. The first half of the *Chats*, on coniferous forests, went into eight subsequent editions; the second half was reprinted three times.

33. Kaigorodov, *"Koe-chto avtobiograficheskoe,"* in Tkachenko, *Pamiati*, 14. In this brief autobiographical statement Kaigorodov also lists the natural history titles available in the library of the Okhtinskii powder factory.

34. The nineteenth-century fascination with "botanizing" led to the development of illustrations to be used in field identification; these illustrations often involve "the isolation of the specimen on a blank page." Gill Saunders, *Picturing Plants: An Analytical History of Botanical Illustration* (Chicago: KWS Publishers, 2009), 125.

35. L. Anisov notes that several of Kaigorodov's works attracted Shishkin's attention, with their "vivid language and most importantly, their love for the forest. And what love it was!" Anisov suggests that the two men had a conversation regarding Kaigorodov's idea of publishing a journal of spring and fall nature in the St. Petersburg region. Anisov, *Shishkin* (Moscow: Terra, 1996), 374.

36. Throughout this discussion I am giving the Russian letters, since my description of the miniatures is keyed to the "look" of those letters. Beyond Russia, the editions of Eliza Brightwen that Kaigorodov translated also use illuminated capitals—but these are more standardized, closer to those of *Family Evenings* than to the Kaigorodov style.

37. The letters illuminated in volume 1 are Ч, С, В, О, У, С, В, И, Р, С, and Л; in volume 2 they are В, Е, Н, П, М, С, and Б. С and В both get repeated. I have been unable to find out just who did the drawings. Each of the capitals is signed, and as I read it the artist may have been A. A. Pisemskii, a landscape artist originally from Kostroma who studied at the Imperial Academy of Art in Petersburg and exhibited in the late 1880s. "*Pisemskii, Aleksei Aleksandrovich*," in A. P. Sobko, *Slovar' russkikh khudozhnikov s drevnieshikh vremen do nashikh dnei*, vol. 2 (St. Petersburg: Tipografiia Stasiulevicha, 1895), 263–67. Four of Kaigorodov's capitals are reproduced in the present chapter. Oak, willow, and elm first appeared in his *Besedy o russkom lese*, vol. 2 (St. Petersburg: Izdanie A. S. Suvorina, 1893), pp. 26, 126, and 116 respectively. Pine appeared in vol. 1 of the same publication, p. 46.

38. D. M. Kaigorodov, *Besedy o russkom lese* (St. Petersburg: Izdanie A. S. Suvorina, 1893). The recommendation to use the book "for forest excursions" is in vol. 1, p. xi (the author's note from the first edition). All further references to this edition will be made in the body of the chapter.

39. Kaigorodov explains the rationale of chapter sequence at the end of the essay on aspen, vol. 2, p. 80.

40. Robin Milner-Gulland, *The Russians* (Oxford: Blackwell, 1997), 30.

41. The rhetorical question "Who hasn't . . . ?" is something he repeats throughout the book; cf. bird cherry, 162.

42. The Turgenev passage is identified only as "from the *Hunter's Sketches*": "Yes! an old linden is a marvelous tree. . . . Even the ruthless axe of the Russian peasant spares it." The passage is found in "My Neighbor Radilov"; see chapter 3.

43. In February of 1878 Iakov Veinberg published "The Question of Lowering Water Levels in Springs and Rivers," in *Russkii vestnik*, and in April of the previous year two different commissions had been convened to consider science of deforestation and hydrological systems. See chapter 3.

44. The discussion of destroying cedars for their nuts is in the chat on the Siberian cedar: 1:115; Kaigorodov quotes an 1877 article from *Our Century* on the practice of stripping lindens of bark (2:60). For the destruction of new growth by grazing livestock see 2:63.

45. Kaigorodov, *P. I. Chaikovskii*, 31. Tchaikovsky's letter is dated 1890.

46. Razgon, "*Dusha*," 64.

47. See chapter 3.

48. The painting is reproduced in Chapter 2.

49. Quoted in Tkachenko, *Pamiati*, 11.

50. "We are appallingly illiterate when it comes to nature . . ., and yet the law of the struggle for existence is known to everyone, even first graders. This accursed law could be elevated to its undeserved pedestal . . . only because of mass ignorance and misunderstanding of the living whole of nature. . . . The struggle for existence . . . gets popularized in all directions—even by poets and artists. But . . . at virtually every step one also finds communities and collectivities [*soobshchestva i sozhitel'stva*] based on mutual aid—mutuality, love and altruism (often of the purest kind)—yet how many know or talk of that!" Kaigorodov, "*Priroda v budushchei shkole*," 67. On Darwin in Russia see Daniel Todes, *Darwin without Malthus: The Struggle for Existence in Russian Evolutionary Thought* (New York: Oxford University Press, 1989).

51. Kaigorodov, "*Priroda v budushchei shkole*," 73.

52. Tkachenko describes how Kaigorodov's "excursionists" gradually broadened to include "not only pedagogues, but 1st and 2nd class students in workers' schools, Red Army soldiers, and workers." Tkachenko, *Pamiati*, 10. S. A. Petrov describes in some detail an excursion that Kaigorodov led in 1921. Petrov, "*Pamiatka o D. N. Kaigorodove. (K chetvertoi godovshchine so dnia ego smerti)*," *Zhivaia priroda*, 1928, no. 7.

53. "We will go outside as much as possible, especially in springtime. . . . In the spring we'll take children outside as frequently as possible—with as much frequency as we can bargain out of the school. . . . Let's grant that (from the point of view of school routine) children may not learn a great deal in so doing (although that's completely unlikely): we'll grant that. But what of the children's *soul*?" Quoted in Tkachenko, *Pamiati*, 9. The excerpt is from a 1902 article published in *Iuzhnyi krai*. The Russian title of Kaigorodov's reader is *Iz rodnoi prirody*. "*Rodnaia*"—*rodnoi* in the genitive case—refers to something dear, familiar, familial—something close at hand. Hence my translation *Nature All Around Us*.

54. Kaigorodov, *Iz rodnoi prirody*, i–ii.

55. Kaigorodov, "*Priroda v budushchei shkole*," 63–64.

56. Kaigorodov, *Iz rodnoi prirody*, 40–47.

57. Citations from the lecture manuscript are given in Bobrov, *Dom*, 56.

58. Tkachenko, *Pamiati*, 10.

59. Andrei Bely, *Petersburg*, trans. Robert Maguire and John Malmstad (Bloomington: Indiana University Press, 1978), 66.

60. Alla Bolotova, "Colonization of Nature in the Soviet Union: State Ideology, Public Discourse, and the Experience of Geologists," *Historical Social Research* 29, no. 3 (2004): 123.

61. Boris Raikov was central to these polemics: see his *Sovremennaia shkola i estestvoznanie* (Petrograd: Nachatki znanii, 1923), where Kaigorodov figures as an innovator in science education and excursions. See also Douglas Weiner, "Struggle over the Soviet Future: Science Education versus Vocationalism during the 1920s," *Russian Review* 65 (January 2006): 72–97.

62. Bobrov, *Dom*, 11.

63. A recent biographical history of Russian forestry provides brief but moving accounts of the fates of M. M. Orlov and G. F. Morozova, both faculty at the Forest Institute: G. I. Red'ko and N. G. Red'ko, *Lesnoe khoziaistvo v zhizneopisanii ego vydaiushchikhsia deiatelei* (Moscow: Moskovskii gosudarstvennyi universitet lesa, 2003).

64. Vladimir Boreiko suggests that Kaigorodov's religious faith would have been problematic. "*Kaigorodov*," 153. The ideological and bureaucratic battles over forestry in the 1930s are recounted in great detail in Stephen Brain's *Song of the Forest: Russian Forestry and Stalinist Environmentalism, 1905–1953* (Pittsburgh: Pittsburgh University Press, 2011).

65. "*Ot izdatel'stva*," Dmitrii Kaigorodov, *Rodnaia priroda (ocherki naturalista)* (Moscow: Lesnaia promyshlennost', 1967). The first essay in the book is "The Tree," and includes a short verse by Kaigorodov included in *Nature All Around Us* of 1907: the first line of the poem—"Divine creation" (*Bozh'e sozdanie*)—is omitted.

66. Vsevolod Revich, "*Deputat russkogo lesa*," *Bibliotekar'*, no. 3 (1981): 42.

67. Douglas Weiner, *A Little Corner of Freedom: Russian Nature Protection from Stalin to Gorbachev* (Berkeley and Los Angeles: University of California Press, 1999), 334–39; Kathleen Parthe, "The Dangerous Narrative of the Russian Village," in *Russia's Dangerous Texts: Politics between the Lines* (New Haven, CT: Yale University Press, 2004), 75–101.

68. "*D. Kaigorodov*," *Lesnaia nov'*, no. 10 (1983): 19. Italics mine.

69. Revich, "*Deputat russkogo lesa*," 43.

70. Ignat'ev and Martynov, "*Dmitrii Nikiforovich Kaigorodov*," 132.

71. Revich, "*Deputat russkogo lesa*," 41–42.

72. Tkachenko, *Pamiati*, 6.

CONCLUSION

1. *The Mirror*, directed by Andrei Tarkovsky (1974, Mosfilm; New York: Kino on Video, 2000), DVD.

2. Anthony Smith, "Nation and Ethnoscape," in *Myths and Memories of the Nation* (New York: Oxford University Press: 1999), 149.

3. *The Barber of Siberia*, directed by Nikita Mikhalkov (1998, Intermedia Film; London: Pathé, 2001), DVD.

4. Valentin Rasputin, *Farewell to Matyora*, trans. Antonina Bouis (Evanston, IL: Northwestern University Press, 1991).

5. "The Russian people have nurtured a number of courageous scientist-defenders of our green heritage. . . . In these walls you will hear the names of Rudzkii and Dokuchaev, Turskii and Morozov, along with others—may their evident achievements, strengthened by your socialist consciousness, inspire you to daring acts of even greater accomplishment!" Leonid Leonov, *Russkii les* (Moscow: Molodaia gvardiia, 1980), 326. The passage comes from a lecture on the history of Russian forestry given by Vikhrov.

6. Boris Pasternak, *Doctor Zhivago*, trans. Max Hayward and Manya Harari (New York: Pantheon, 1958), 86–87, 375.

7. Vasily Grossman, *Life and Fate*, trans. Robert Chandler (New York: New York Review of Books, 1985), 158, 206. All subsequent references to this edition will be given in the text.

8. Anatolii Kim, *Otets-les* (Moscow: Sovetskii pisatcl', 1989).

9. Varlam Shalamov, *Kolyma Tales*, trans. John Glad (New York: W. W. Norton, 1982), 136.

10. See chapter 3.

11. See chapter 6.

12. Oleg Vasil'ev, "*Abramtsevo*," in *Okna pamiati* (Moscow: Novoe literaturnoe obozrenie, 2005), 91, 94. Vasil'ev and his wife rented a summer house (dacha) "between Abramtsevo and Muranova, you could even say between two museums: the Aksakov/Mamontov Museum in Abramtsevo, and the Baratynskii Museum in Muranova." For Vasil'ev the landscape is strongly associated with both Nesterov and Shishkin.

Index

Benois, Alexandre, 154, 239n61
Berry, Thomas, 5
Berry, Wendell, 106, 240–241n91
Bervi-Flerovskii, Vasilii, 119
Bethea, David, 43, 44
Bezobrazov, V. P., 246n12
Bianki, Vitalii, *Calendar of Nature*, 210
Billington, James, 6, 8
birch trees, 62–63, 150
birds and birdsong: Kaigorodov, 181, 185–186,
    187, 189, 194; in Korolenko, 140; in
    Mel'nikov, 60, 61, 66, 72–73, 75; in Nest-
    erov, 180; poaching of, 210; in Turgenev, 13,
    17, 35
"Black Forest" (Kaigorodov), 199–200
Blossoms (Kaigorodov), 205
Bobrov, R. V., 188, 208, 252nn7, 18
Boev, N., as Slavophile, 47, 152, 227n1. *See also*
    "Pictures of Forest Life"
Bogdanov, Modest, 191, 253n29
Bogorad, Nelli, 218
bogs, 67, 69–70; *bolotnitsa* (spirit), 69; destruc-
    tion of, in Orel region, 17
Boiotnikov, Ivan, 21
Bolotov, Andrei, 252n21
Bolotova, Alla, 208
Bolshevik Revolution: and the death penalty,
    143, 243n13; and disruption of culture
    of ecological concern, 10; Nesterov and,
    177–178; and Okhtinsky gunpowder
    factory, 188
Bonhomme, Brian, 90
Boreiko, Vladimir, 186, 255n64
Bosch, Hieronymus, 216
boundaries: circular (*okolitsa*), 25–26; crossing
    of, 11, 12; between forest and village, 25–26,
    27. *See also* edge of the forest
Bowlt, John, 59
Boy Bartholomew's Vision, The (Nesterov),
    147–148, *148*, 150–151, 160, 163, 164,
    166–167, 169–171, 246nn5, 12, 249nn 62,
    65,67, 250nn70, 72
Brain, Stephen, 223n23
Brehm, Adolf, 186, 192
Brezhnev, Leonid, 7
Brightwen, Eliza, 189, 254n36
Bringhurst, Robert, 12
Brodsky, Joseph, 27
Brody, Hugh, 233n77
"Bronze Horseman" (Pushkin), 251n3
Brostrom, Kenneth, 36, 227n35
Brothers Karamazov, The (Dostoevsky), 58,
    74, 111–112, 133, 153, 166, 230n32,
    241–242n104, 244n33

Bruni, N. A., 166
Buell, Lawrence, 10, 223n22
Bunin, Ivan, 4, 13–14, 214
"By the Fireplace" (Kaigorodov), 198

calendar: agrarian/liturgical, 64–65; of seasonal
    change, in Kaigorodov, 188–189, 195
Calendar of Nature (Bianki), 210
Calendars of Nature (Kaigorodov), 185
Catherine II, 89
cedar trees, 198
Chaadaev, Petr, 227–228n2
Chaikovskaia, Vera, 44–45
Chats about the Russian Forest (Kaigorodov),
    185, 190, 192–202, *193–197*, 253n34,
    254n44
Chats on Nature (Zobov), 190
Cherniavsky, Michael, 43, 44
Chernigov district, 89, 237n36
children's literature and periodicals: Bianki's
    Calendar of Nature, 210; family magazines,
    190–191, 253n30; Kaigorodov and, 209,
    210; by Vagner (Kot Murlyka), 253n29
Chizhevskii, Dmitrii, 59
Chukovsky, Kornei, 140
Chryssavgis, John, 149, 176, 181
chuzoi and svoi, 26, 225n14
class: and the Forest Question, 107–108,
    241n95; proletariat, peasants becoming, 109;
    in Repin's *Procession of the Cross*, 94; and Tol-
    stoy's views of property, 107; and Turgenev's
    nature writing, 23
clearings, and human habitation, 26
climate change, 86, 96
compasses, 70
Congress of Forest Managers, 199, 202
Coniferous Wood, The (Shishkin), 48
conservation: Imperial impulses toward, reasons
    for, 223n23; Kaigorodov and, 185, 186, 202,
    205; Koenig and calls for, 82, 84; Koro-
    lenko's position not considered conservation-
    ist, 139–140, 142; Leonov and, 79, 215,
    256n5; nineteenth-century foundation for,
    82, 83–84, 90–91; Peter the Great and, 185,
    237n35; the poetic and, 83; public awareness
    and, 90, 91; as term, 9. *See also* conservation
    areas (*zapovedniki*)
conservation areas (*zapovedniki*): as term,
    225n8; Tolstoy estate as, 103, *104*, 240n82;
    violation of, 210
contemplation: and affective awareness of
    nature, 32; Boev and, 75; Korolenko

and lack of, 122, 132; Markov and, 109; Mel'nikov and, 9; Nesterov and, 148–149, 157, 171–173, 177, 179, 250n72; and Slavophile rhetoric, 47, 227n1; Turgenev and, 23, 34; and Vasil'ev painting, 14

Countess Mordvinova's Forest, Petergof (Shishkin), 51, *54*, 202

critical realism, 173

Cronon, William, 228n10, 237n39

Dal', Vladimir, 24, 58, 71, 83, 189, 228n15, 230–231n40, 233n78

Dante Alighieri, 27, 37

Darwin, Charles, and Darwinism, 119, 203, 253n29, 254n50

deforestation, 9; and agriculture, 86, 88; climate and, 86; and drought, 108, 142; Emancipation of 1861 and, 86–87, 105, 138, 236n22, 238n45; and firewood, 88, 198, 237n32; human role in, awareness of, 86; Kaigorodov and, 198–202; Korolenko and, 136–140; peasants and, 91, 107–108, 109, 137, 241n95; and river flows, impeded, 84, 85; Tchaikovsky on, 198; Turgenev and, 17, 81–82; as unremarked in Mel'nikov's *In the Forests*, 79–80, 136. *See also* Forest Question

Demons (Dostoevsky), 77

dendrometer, 83–84

Derman, A., 118, 243n18

"Dilletantism in Forestry" (A.S.), 83

diversity, monoculture and need for, 205–206, 208, 211

Dokuchaev, Vasilii, 241n100, 256n5

domovoi (village spirit), 26

Dostoevsky, Fyodor: and the Forest Question, 87, 106, 108, 110–114, 198, 241–242nn102, 104,107; ideological landscape of, 77, 78; and Mel'nikov, 55–56, 230n32; and mythologies of the peasant, 29; recontextualization of religious legends, 228n9; on Russian landscape, 48; and theme of desecration, 133, 244n33; and topography of Petersburg, 22; and utopia/dystopia, 77. Works: *The Brothers Karamazov*, 58, 74, 111–112, 133, 153, 166, 230n32, 241–242n104, 244n33; "The Dream of a Ridiculous Man," 112–114, 184–185; "My Paradox," 110, 112, 113; *A Writer's Diary*, 87, 112, 113

"Dream of a Ridiculous Man, The" (Dostoevsky), 112–114, 184–185

drought, 108, 127–128, 142. *See also* famine

Durylin, Sergei, 153, 172, 175–176, 180, 247n23, 250nn73, 78

ecocriticism: and affective awareness of Russian writers, 32; Heidegger and, 10, 223n25; and knowledge of place, 11–12; and trope of home, 11–12

edge of the forest, 13–14; boundary crossings and, 11; Nesterov and, 170; Turgenev and, 12–14; walking into the woods and, 12

education theory, Kaigorodov and, 185–186, 202–205, 207, 208, 254–255n52, 53, 61

Eikhenbaum, B. M., 240n87

Eksmo-Press, 231n51

Ely, Chris, 47, 52–53, 173, 229nn24, 28

Emancipation of 1861 and aftermath: deforestation and, 86–87, 105, 138, 236n22, 238n45; and public opinion, 93

Emerson, Ralph Waldo, 35, 36

"Enemy from the East" (Solovyov), 142

environment, as term, 9

environmental disasters: famine as, 125; of Soviet era, 186, 214

environmentalism: Bolshevik Revolution and legacies of, 10; emergence of, 80; of Korolenko, 142–145; and post-Soviet popular culture, 7; and public consciousness, 114; of Solovyov, 142. *See also* conservation; deforestation; Forest Question

Epiphanii the Wise, *Life* [of Sergius], 152–153, 163–164, 166, 169, 171, 174, *175*, 246–247n18, 249n62

epiphany, 151, 152, 160

ethnoscape, 44, 147, 149–150, 177, 216

Evernden, Neil, 239n70

exile: Korolenko and, 119–122, 243n14; wilderness and, 120

Family Evenings (journal), 190–191, 192, 194, 198, 254n36

famine: Korolenko and, 96, 125, 127–128, 134, 142–144, 143–144; Nesterov and, 176, 250–251n87; Stalin and, 144; Tolstoy and, 127

Farewell to Matyora (Rasputin), 214–215

Father Forest (Kim), 216

Fathers and Sons (Turgenev), 83

Fedorov-Davydov, Aleksei, 96, 97, 171, 177

feeling for nature (*chuvstvo prirody*), 5

Felled Tree, The (Shishkin), 48

the feminine: Isis and nature personified as, 22; land and earth as, 244n34; Nesterov and, 154; Solovyov and, 247n26

figure to ground, relationship of, 158–159, 177–178

flooding, 184, 251n3

"Flower as a Source of Delight, The" (Kaigorodov), 190

folk religion. *See* paganism

Following the Icon (Korolenko), 123, 133–134

the forest and forests: as ally of ultimate justice, 123; antiquity of, 37; black, 194–195, 203; as communal property, 109–110; disappearance into, 14–16, 224n33; as emotional and ethical challenge, 214–218; as emotional security, 214; excessive affection for, 7–8; hostility toward, 8, 26, 42, 80; journeys into, for its own sake, 185; listening to, 10–11, 128–129; as megatext of Russian landscape, 6–7, 222n15; in post-Soviet popular culture, 7, 183; red, 194–195, 203, 218; right to use vs. abuse of, 88–89, 90, 200–201; sound in, 10–11, 123; taiga, 6, 29; as vast and forbidding, 21–22, 42, 48, 238n52; villages made of, 6–7, 196. *See also* Forest Question; forestry; *zaseki* forests

"Forest and Steppe" (Turgenev), 12–13, 217

"Forest Fable, A" (Kaigorodov), 205–206, 211

forest fires, 29, 89, 127–128, 140–141, 198, 243n19

Forest Institute. *See* Forest Technical Academy

Forest Journal, 85–86, 89, 236n13

Forest Law (1888), 90–91, 93, 138, 199, 235n5, 238nn47, 48

Forest Question, 9, 82–84; affective value of forests, 92–93; and class privilege, 107–108, 241n95; and conservation, nineteenth-century foundation for, 82, 83–84, 90–91; governmental commissions and reports on, 85, 87, 198, 254n43; inauguration of, 84–85; journal discussions of, 9, 17, 82–84, 85–87, 93; measurement and the dendrometer and, 83–84; painters and, 94–98, *95, 97–100,* 99–101, *102,* 109, 239n61; and the poetic, 83–84, 115, 186, 206–207; poets inspired by, 98–99; popular science and, 89, 91–93, 108, 115; privately held woodlands, regulation and control of, 86–87, 89–91, 103, 105, 111, 238nn45, 46, 48; protection of forests, 88–91, 107, 114, 138, 185, 199, 235n5, 237nn35, 39, 238nn47, 48; public consciousness and, 87, 90, 91, 93, 114, 198; publicistic writing and, 93–94; reforestation proposal of Tolstoy, 101–105; and rule-based forestry, 82, 91, 235n5; and Russian backwardness, 110–112; and science as fall from grace, 114; and spirituality, 98–99, 109, 113–114, 115, 239n70; two forests of Russia, 92, 238n52; and wood products, dependence on, 87–88, 237nn29, 32. *See also* conservation; deforestation; Forest Question, and literary authors

Forest Question, and literary authors: Dostoevsky, 87, 106, 108, 110–114, 198, 241–242nn102, 104, 107; Markov, 108–110, 112, 114, 198, 241n98; Tolstoy, 101, 103–108, 112, 114

"Forest Sounds, The" (Korolenko), 10–11, 123

Forest Technical Academy (Forest Institute), 183–184, *184,* 188–189, 203, 208, 219, 251nn1–2

"Forest, The" (Kol'tsov), 98–99

forestry: foreign travel and, 89, 188; Korolenko and, 136–137; and measurement vs. mystery, 83–84, 186, 206–207; professionalization of, 85; rule-based, 82, 91, 235n5. *See also* forestry, sustainable

forestry, sustainable: Kaigorodov as advocate of, 185, 198–199, 205–206, 208; late 19th-century center of idea of, 185; and the Soviet era, 208, 223n23; as term, 91

Free Economic Society, 85

freedom, Korolenko and defense of, 143–144, 245n48

French, R. A., 6

Friedrich, Caspar David: *Rückenfiguren,* 14, 21, 48, 121; *Wanderer above the Sea,* 220

Frierson, Cathy, 173

From the Feathered Kingdom (Kaigorodov), 192, 209

Frost, Robert, 27

Garshin, Vsevolod, 191

Gauguin, Paul, 158

Gershenzon, Mikhail, 226n27

Gheith, Jehanne, 253n30

Ghirlandaio, 157, 158

Gifford, Sanford Robinson, 51, *53*

Gleason, Abbot, 154, 229n23

Glickman, Rose, 74–75

Goricheva, Tatyana, 46

Gorky, Maxim, 126, 140, 245n48

Grad Kitezh (Nesterov), 231n45

Grossman, Vasily, *Life and Fate,* 215–216

Haney, Jack, 174

Harrison, Robert Pogue, 26

Harvey, David, 76, 77–78

healing, 74–76

"Heart-Pine Rus'". *See* Rus'; sacred geographies

Hegel, G. W. F., 37

Heidegger, Martin, 10, 24, 223n25, 225n12

Hellberg-Hirn, Elena, 222n15

The Hermit, The (Nesterov), 250n72

History of My Contemporary, The (Korolenko), 123

Hives in the Forest (Shishkin), 48

Hoisington, Thomas, 59–60, 62, 230n38, 232n57

Holquist, Michael, 227n40

Holy Russia, 43–44, 47, 115, 177. *See also* sacred geographies

Holy Russia (Nesterov), 177–178

Holy Spring near Yelabuga (Shishkin), 51–53, *55*

home: desire to return to, 9–10; ecocriticism and trope of, 11–12; Turgenev and, 38

Hunter Mountain, Twilight (Gifford), 51, *53*

Hunter's Sketches (Turgenev): initial publication of, 225n2; and "Journey into Polesye," 19, 20, 27, 34–36, 37; Kaigorodov quoting from, 197–198, 254n42; landscape of, as pastoral, 36; and loss, 81–82, 235n2; as poetic essays, 37

icons: affixed to trees, 150–151, 246n12; desecration of, in Dostoevsky, 133, 244n33; hagiological, 164, *165*; Korolenko and, 132–134, 171; in Nesterov, 149, 151, 152; Nesterov and childhood illness, 163; Orthodox visual culture and, 149; and sacralization of creation, 132–133; of Sergius, 164, *165*; as theological texts, 180

imagination: as a bird, 14, 217; juxtaposed to schematic thinking by Korolenko, 125, 143, 144; literature vs. science and, 233n80; and public opinion, 84, 93, 94; the unconscious and, 10

Imperial Society of Naturalists, 87

In Rus' (Nesterov), 177–178

In the Famine Year (Korolenko), 125, 128, 134, 143

In the Forests (Mel'nikov), 54–57; animism/paganism and, 129, 154, 171; calendrical structure of, 64–65; cities criticized in, 76; deforestation as unapparent in, 79–80, 136; and double faith, 63–65, 232nn66, 68; and folk wisdom, 71–72, 233n80; future of Russia lying with educated Old Believers, 233n72; geo-cosmic scale of, 63, 232n65; getting lost and, 68–70; and healing, 74–76; influence of, 58–59, 72, 231nn44, 45, 234n83; Kitezh legend (Old Believer myth of deliverance) and, 61–64, 65–66, 67, 72, 77, 78; and language, 59, 61, 62, 69–72, 233nn77, 78; and loss of place, 78–79; mosaic character of, 62, 232n57; and nationality, 53–54; nature as setting for, 60–61; Nesterov as influenced by, 154–155, 231n45,

247–248n32; and novelization, 66; paradisal quality of forests, 66–67; and paths into the wood, 68; publication of, 58, 231nn42, 51; research for, 57–58, 62; as romance, 60; and sacred geography, 67; sexuality and, 234n85; and song, 60, 61, 62, 72–74, 234n84; and St. Petersburg, 184; and strangers, 68, 233n74; urban audience of, 60–61; Yarilo legend (pre-Christian myth of creation) and, 61–64, 65, 66–67, 68, 72, 75, 78

In the Wild and Empty Places (Korolenko), 117–118, 122, 125–127, 128–133, 134–141, 242n1

indigenous, as term, 228n12

industrial revolution, 88, 91

Inn, The (Turgenev), 27, 34

intellectual elite, peasant as blank slate and, 29

Istomina, Enessa, 89, 91, 93, 114, 237n39, 238n48

Itinerants (realist painters), 94, 99

Ivanovo, 88

Jackson, Robert Louis, 32

Joan of Arc (Bastien-Lepage), 155–159, *158*, 160, 178

Journal of Agriculture and Livestock, 82, 86

Journal of the Ministry of State Properties, 7–8, 85, 86, 89

"Journey into Polesye" (Turgenev): alternative title for ("Peasants Shooting Bear . . ."), 19, 38; and boundary between forest and village, 25–26, 27; emerald fly-watching passage of, 31–32; and forest as vast and forbidding, 21–22, 42, 238n52; genre of, 23; and *Hunter's Sketches*, 12–13, 19, 27, 36; indirect closure of, 33; landscape of, 20–21, 25, 42; and "man in nature," 22–23, 27; narrator as ethnographer in, 25; narrator as naturist in, 24–25; and nature writing (Russian), 22–23, 38–39; peasants as guides and, 27–31; and place, 22, 23; as poetic essay, 37–38; polesye as term and, 13, 22; and preexisting cultural forms, 44; and religion, 25–26, 42; and rest, 24, 26, 31; restlessness and, 38; and seeing, 23–24, 31; and spirits of the forest (leshii), 26; writing and publication of, 19, 36

Kaigorodov, Dmitrii, 10, 115, 180–181; and animism, 202, 206; background, education, and working life of, 186, 187–189; chats as favorite literary form of, 190; and communities and collectivities of nature, 203, 254n50; and conservation, 185, 186, 202, 205; and deforestation, 198–202; and

Kaigorodov, Dmitrii (*continued*)
ethos of affection and care for the natural world, 185–186, 191, 198, 200, 203, 210; and "excursionist" education theory, 185–186, 202–205, 207, 208, 254–255n52, 53, 61; home of, 189, 252n18; and "icon" of native nature, 181; illustrations and illuminated letters in works of, 192, *193*, 194, *194–197*, 253n34, 254n36–37; legacy of, 183, 185–186, 207–211; and measurement vs. mystery, 186, 206–207; on monoculture and need for diversity, 205–206, 208, 211; as natural historian, 185, 186; and nature and the human, 186, 195–198, 205–206, 210–211; newspaper columns on phenology, 189–190; and poetry, 205, 206–207; and politics, antipathy towards, 202; public lectures of, 189, 190, 253n23; religious references in works of, 208, 255n64; and the royal family, 207, 208; on scholasticism, 203, 208; scope of writings, 189–190; style of, 186, 191–192, 194, 210; as sustainable forestry advocate, 185, 198–199, 205–206, 208; and Turgenev, 197–198, 202, 217, 254n42. Works: "Black Forest," 199–200; *Blossoms*, 205; "By the Fireplace," 198; *Calendars of Nature*, 185; *Chats about the Russian Forest*, 185, 190, 192–202, *193–197*, 253n34, 254n44; "The Flower as a Source of Delight," 190; "A Forest Fable," 205–206, 211; *From the Feathered Kingdom*, 192, 209; *Native Nature*, 208–209; *Nature All Around Us*, 191, 203–206, 255n65; "Nature in the School of the Future," 154n50, 202–203, 204, 253n22; poetry, 205, 207, 255n65; "The Tree and Its Life," 195, 205, 255n65
Kaluga, 17, 19
Karlinsky, Simon, 120
"Kasyan from the Beautiful Lands" (Turgenev), 35–36, 227n32
Kenworthy, Scott, 161
Kharms, Daniil, 1, 14, 224n33
"Khor and Kalinych" (Turgenev), 20, 27, 81, 225n2
Kim, Anatolii, *Father Forest*, 216
Kireevsky, Ivan, 47
Kireevsky, Petr, 62, 232n63
Kitezh City (In the Forests) (Nesterov), 155, *156*
Kitezh legend, 43, 218; invisibility as aspect of, 77; Korolenko and, 117, 131–132, 133, 134–135, 244n31; Mel'nikov and, 61–64, 65–66, 67, 72, 77, 78; Nesterov and, 147, 155, *156*
Kliuchevsky, Vasilii, 8, 26, 160–163, 171, 177, 248n52

Koenig, Gottlob, 82, 83–84, 86
Kol'tsov, Aleksei, 6, 98–99
Korolenko, Vladimir Galaktionovich, 9, 115; and art, 134, 141, 244n35; background and education of, 118–119, 243n11; and capital punishment, 120, 143, 233n13; on change, 144; environmentalism of, 142–145; exile of, 119–122, 243n14; and famine/ drought, 96, 125, 127–128, 134, 142–144, 143–144; and forest as ally of ultimate justice, 123; and forestry, 136–137; and freedom in Soviet Union, 143–144, 245n48; and humor, 125–126, 130; and icons, role of, 132–134, 171; "jumping in" ethic of, 135–136, 144–145, 148; and Kitezh legend, 117, 131–132, 133, 134–135, 244n31; language and, 129, 133, 244n34; *leshii* tales of, 128–129; and literature, role of, 125; and loss, 129–130, 131, 244n29; and Marxism, critique of, 143–144, 245n48; and the masses, view of, 120–121; on Mel'nikov and Old Believers, 58, 118; metaphoric and literal elements, transactions between, 130–131; as modern, 141–142; the mystery and the ineffable and, 129–130; nature and the human and, 118, 121–122, 126–128, 130, 136–141, 142, 144–145; and nature writing, 118, 122; and observation, 185; and Old Believers, 130–131, 133, 134–136; as "one-man civil liberties union," 120, 144–145; and the past, 126; and peasant attitude toward forest, 137–139; as populist, 119, 126, 139, 243n11; on Red Army destruction of the walnut trees, 143–144, 210; Repin's images and, 123, 128, 144; and silence, 129; and Solovyov, 142, 245n47; and sound in the woods, 10–11, 123; and Tolstoy, 120, 243n13; and Turgenev, 122–123, 129, 141, 243nn18, 21, 244n29; walking and traveling of, 12, 123–125; and wilderness, 117–118, 120, 131–132, 140–141. Works: *Following the Icon*, 123, 133–134; "The Forest Sounds," 10–11, 123; *The History of My Contemporary*, 123; *In the Famine Year*, 125, 128, 134, 143; *In the Wild and Empty Places*, 117–118, 122, 125–127, 128–133, 134–141, 242n1; *Letters to Lunacharsky*, 143–144; "Makar's Dream," 122, 243n19; "Marvelous Girl," 243n21; sketches of Lake Svetloyar, *124*, 125
Korovin, Konstantin, 250–251n87
Kostomarov, Nikolai, 98
Krinichnaia, Neonila, 26, 225n15, 226n18
Krupskaya, Nadezhda, 208

Picasso, Pablo, 158
"Pictures of Forest Life" (Boev): author of, as
    Slavophile, 47, 152, 227n1; and Christianiza-
    tion, 47; differentiation of place in, 76–77;
    epicenter of fallen contemporaneity, 234n95;
    and healing, 74; and intellectual life of post-
    Reform Russia, 77; landscape of, 42, 47–48,
    96; and monastic tradition, 41–42, 45, 47,
    75, 228n11; and paganism, 171; and paths
    into the woods, 68; and place, 76–77; publi-
    cation of, 41, 58, 231n43; religious references
    in, 41–42, 45; and retrospective utopias, 43,
    77; and sacred geographies, 43, 44, 46, 47,
    48, 61, 75, 96; urban audience of, 41; and
    wilderness, 46
pilgrimages: American nature writing and, 118;
    Old Believers and, 68; to the past, 161; to
    Sergius's grave, 161–162
Piotrovskaia, Anastasia, 120
Pisemskii, A. A., 254n37
place: art as creating sense of, 12; deforesta-
    tion and loss of, 79–80; and differentiation,
    process of, 76; dislocation and loss of, 77–80;
    distinguished from space, as term, 222n10;
    ecocriticism and knowledge of, 11–12; and
    ecosystem of stories, 12, 224n30; knowledge
    of, and writing, 11–12, 16; loss of, and official
    ideology, 4; memory narratives, and forget-
    ting, 79 80; unconsciousness and sense of, 10
"Plant as a Source of Strength, The" (Timiri-
    azev), 93
Platonov, Andrei, 6–7
Plaything (journal), 190–191
poetry: folk, anthropomorphism in, 98; Forest
    Question as inspiration for, 98–99; of Kai-
    gorodov, 205, 207, 255n65; in Kaigorodov
    essays, 191; and mystery, and the Forest
    Question, 83–84, 115, 186, 206–207; and
    trees, American vs. European poets and, 27.
    See also Bunin, Ivan; Kharms, Daniil; Nekra-
    sov, Nikolai; Pushkin, Alexander
Pogodin, Mikhail, 58
Polenov, Vasilii, 159, 176
Polenova, Elena, 149, 159, 164, 171, 176,
    250–251n87
popular culture: Nesterov and, 148, 246n5;
    post-Soviet, 7, 183, 218; science and the For-
    est Question and, 89, 91–93, 108, 115; The
    Slavs' Poetic Views of Nature and, 62. See also
    Kaigorodov, Dmitrii
populism, 119, 126, 243n11
post-Soviet Russia: environmentalists, Kaig-
    orodov and, 186; Mel'nikov's novel and, 59,
    231n51; popular culture, 7, 183

pre-Christian religion. See paganism
pre-Raphaelites, Nesterov and, 157, 160,
    248n37
private property. See property
Procession of the Cross in an Oak Forest (Repin),
    97, 99
Procession of the Cross in the Kursk District
    (Repin), 94–98, 95, 98, 123, 151, 198,
    239nn61, 69, 70
property: control of private forests, 86–87,
    89–91, 103, 105, 111, 238nn45, 46, 48; for-
    ests as communal, 109–110; ownership of,
    and class privilege, 107–108, 241n95
public opinion: the Forest Question and, 87,
    90, 91, 93, 114, 198; imagination and, 84,
    93, 94; and linden trees of Orel, 2, 4; Reform
    period and, 93; Rudzkii and, 93
publicistics, 93–94, 118
Pushkin, Alexander, 6, 27, 204–205; "Bronze
    Horseman," and flooding, 251n3; estate of,
    13; Kol'tsov memorialization of, 98–99;
    Nesterov illustrating folktales of, 153;
    "Remembrance," 30
Puvis de Chavannes, Pierre, 157–159, 178;
    Summer, 158, 178
Pypin, Aleksandr, 232n61

Raikov, Boris, 255n61
Rasputin, Valentin, 230n31; Farewell to Maty-
    ora, 214–215
Razgon, Lev, 183, 186, 199, 202, 209
reforestation, Tolstoy and, 101–105
Reform period. See Emancipation of 1861 and
    aftermath
religion: "double faith," 63–65, 232nn64,
    66, 68; spirituality and the Forest Question,
    98–99, 109, 113–114, 115, 239n70. See
    also Orthodoxy; paganism; religion and
    nature
religion and nature: Russian Orthodoxy and,
    46–47, 148–150 (see also Nestero, Mikhail);
    trees as monastic protectors, 47; Lynn White
    and Christianity's "hostility" towards nature,
    46, 229n17
"Remembrance" (Pushkin), 30
Remizov, Andrei, 58–59, 231n44
Repin, Ilya, 218; and the Forest Question,
    96–97, 109, 113, 114, 239n61; Korolenko
    and, 123, 128, 144; and post-Soviet popular
    culture, 7; and Tolstoy, 96, 100, 101, 102.
    Works: L. N. Tolstoi Resting in the Forest
    under a Tree, 100, 101; Procession of the Cross
    in an Oak Forest, 97, 99; Procession of the
    Cross in the Kursk District, 94–98, 95, 98,

and ethical ambiguity, 34–36; and the edge of the wood, 12–14; and the Forest Question, 17, 81–82; indirect closure of, 33–36; Kaigorodov and, 197–198, 202, 217, 254n42; Korolenko and, 122–123, 129, 141, 243nn18, 21, 244n29; and loss, 81–82, 129, 235n2; and meekness of spirit (*smirenie*), 33–34; nature and the human and, 6; and nature as workshop vs. temple, 83; Nietzsche contrasted to, 226n27; and observation, 185; and post-Soviet popular culture, 7; and the problematic in literature, 227n35; social relations and the forest, 36–37; song and singing and, 72, 234n82; temporality and, 37–38; theater in Orel named for, 1–2; and Tolstoy, 104–105, 240n85; as walker, 12. Works: *Fathers and Sons*, 83; "Forest and Steppe," 12–13, 217; *The Inn*, 27, 34; "Kasyan from the Beautiful Lands," 35–36, 227n32; "Khor and Kalinych," 20, 27, 81, 225n2; "L'gov," 82; "Loner," 34–35; "My Neighbor Radilov," 81–82, 254n42; *A Nest of Gentry*, 34; "The Nymphs," 129; *On the Eve*, 33; "Ovsiannikov the Freeholder," 235n2; "The Singers," 19, 20, 27, 33, 72, 234n82; "Threshold," 243n21. *See also Hunter's Sketches*; "Journey into Polesye"
Turner, Frederick Jackson, 248–249n53
Turskii, Mitrofan, 256n5
Twilight, Sunset (Shishkin), 48

Ukraine, 118–119, 123, 144
Uspenskii, Nikolai, 191
urbanites, and traditional knowledge, 29, 226n19
Usov, P., 230n37

Vagner, Nikolai, 191, 253n29
Valkenier, Elizabeth, 94
Valuev, Pavel, 93
Valuev, Sergei, 241n93
Vasil'ev, Oleg, 256n12; *Self-Portrait from the Back*, 14–16, *15*, 220
Vasnestov, Apollinarii, 251n88
Vasnetsov, Victor, 152, 163, 164, 177, 251n88
Veinberg, Iakov, 90, 94, 108, 238n46, 254n43
Vengerov, S., 241n98
village, traditional, as made of the forest, 6–7, 196
Vinogradov, Georgii, 62, 232nn63, 65
Vinogradov, Victor, 78
Voeikov, Aleksandr, 108, 241n100
Voice, 87

Volga region: as setting for Korolenko, 118; as setting in Mel'nikov, 57, 68. *See also In the Forests* (Mel'nikov)
Volga River, low water levels in, 85

walking into the woods, and boundaries, 12
War and Peace (Tolstoy), 29
water, and memory, 30–31
Weber, Max, 129, 244n27
Westernizers, and peasants, representation of, 29
White, Lynn, 46, 229n17
White, Richard, 122, 139
wild bees: in Korolenko, 137, 138, 139; in Turgenev, 28, 29
wilderness (American): as blank page, 45; and "delightful horror," 46, 228n14; and the frontier, 248–249n53; and natural church, 51; and religion, 45–46
wilderness (Russian), 42–43; Korolenko and, 117–118, 120, 131–132, 140–141; and moral rebirth, 162–163; Old Believers and flight into, 65; *pustynia*, as term, 46, 228n15; and religion, 46–47; Siberian exiles and, 120; as term, 46; traditional culture gathered from, 45. *See also* nature; nature and the human; religion and nature
Williams, Raymond, 9
Wolf, as term, 126–127
women: archetypal Earth Mother, 61, 63–64, 65, 75, 234n87; healers vs. witches, 74–75; roles of, among Old Believers, 63, 232n67. *See also* (the) feminine
wood products: coal as replacement for, 88; dependence on, 87–88, 196–197, 237nn29, 32; firewood, 88, 109, 198, 237n32; overheating with, 89, 237n32; used in monastery construction, 172; uses of, in Kaigorodov, 196–197, 198–199
Wordsworth, William: "Nutting," 117, 143–144; "The Tables Turned," 183
Worster, Daniel, 17
Writer's Diary, A (Dostoevsky), 87, 112, 113

Yarilo legend, 61–64, 65, 66–67, 68, 72, 75, 78
Yasnaya Polyana (Tolstoy estate), 101, 103–105, *104*, 219
Youth of the Blessed Sergius of Radonezh, The (Nesterov), 164, *167*, 173–177, 249n62, 250n78, 251n88

Zabolotsky, Nikolai, 213, 217
Zaitsev, Boris, 17, 38, 172, 250n75
Zaletaev, Vladimir, 209